WINNIE MANDELA

WINNIE MANDELA

a life

Anné Mariè du Preez Bezdrob

ZEBRA

Published by Zebra Press
an imprint of Struik Publishers
(a division of New Holland Publishing (South Africa) (Pty) Ltd)
PO Box 1144, Cape Town, 8000
New Holland Publishing is a member of Johnnic Communications Ltd

www.zebrapress.co.za

First published 2003
Published in paperback 2004

1 3 5 7 9 10 8 6 4 2

Publication © Zebra Press 2003
Text © Anné Mariè du Preez Bezdrob 2003
Cover photograph © Peter Magubane

PUBLISHING MANAGER: Marlene Fryer
MANAGING EDITOR: Robert Plummer
EDITOR: Marléne Burger
PROOFREADER: Ronel Richter-Herbert
COVER AND TEXT DESIGNER: Natascha Adendorff
TYPESETTER: Monique van den Berg
INDEXER: Robert Plummer
PHOTO RESEARCHER: Carmen Swanepoel

Set in 10.5 pt on 13.5 pt Minion

Reproduction by Hirt & Carter (Cape) (Pty) Ltd
Printed and bound by Kyodo Printing Co (Singapore) Pte Ltd

ISBN 1 86872 926 5

I dedicate this book to my children
and to my grandchildren
to my mother
and to the memory of my father

and to the noble and courageous women who have been my inspiration

Contents

Photographs between pages 144 and 145

Preface

IN HER POEM 'Instead of a Preface', my favourite poet, the Russian Anna Akhmatova, relates an experience during the years of Stalinist terror. She spent months queuing at prisons in Leningrad, where her friends and family were incarcerated. One day, a woman in a queue recognised her, and whispered into Akhmatova's ear:

'Can you describe this?'

Akhmatova said, 'I can,' and the shadow of a smile passed over the face of the woman with the tortured expression and blue lips.

The phenomena of political oppression and racism have mystified me all my life; and after encounters with war in Namibia, Zimbabwe and Bosnia, both as a journalist and a political official with the United Nations, the pursuance of war merged with my other prime field of interest. This has led to an ongoing study of the political history of southern Africa, the former Soviet Union and, most recently, the former Yugoslavia – specifically Bosnia, where I spent two years of the war during the 1990s in the country's besieged capital, Sarajevo. Increasingly, my experiences led to the desire to describe what I have learned.

In my attempts to fathom the psychology of the oppressor, the warmonger and the victim, I have come to understand that there are mere degrees of difference between Stalin, Hitler, Milosevic, Karadzic, Verwoerd and other apartheid leaders. The same applies to the millions of people who blindly follow ideologies and doctrines that range from the immoral to a licence for murder and genocide.

I have also come to know that the human spirit can be temporarily subdued by terror and hardship, but never conquered, irrespective of the duration or form of the oppression. Women, especially, have a unique ability to retain their capacity for nurturing and joy, even during unspeakable horrors and loss.

My life has been marked by extraordinary experiences, and this book is the fusion of various strands, beginning in my childhood, with the invaluable gifts I received from my parents and grandparents. They were living examples of fairness, compassion and moral courage; allowed me the space to develop an individual and enquiring mind; and provided a sterling illustration of the importance of faith.

They laid the groundwork for everything that is meaningful in my life.

My father was bitterly opposed to apartheid, quite extraordinary for an Afrikaner of his generation and class. To him, all people were equal, the only distinction being between good and bad, and this was firmly stamped on the minds of my siblings and me. He defended his principles at considerable cost, but would have agreed with Olive Schreiner: 'It never pays the Man who speaks the truth, but it pays Humanity that it should be spoken.'

My mother provided the first example of women's ability to face difficulties and misfortune with grace, tenacity and humour, and still embrace life with delight. I have immense admiration for her strength of spirit and enduring efforts to overcome setbacks – even tragedy.

My grandparents were the salt of the earth, simple people with little formal education but great wisdom, and they weathered every storm and countless hardships with unflinching faith.

Some years ago, I saw photographs of Winnie Mandela in a magazine, and noticed that as a young woman she had lively, laughing eyes – the soulful, striking eyes many observers commented on. However, in later pictures, her eyes were mute, as if the light in them had been extinguished. That set me wondering what hardships had caused such a woeful metamorphosis. As a former political journalist, I knew a little about her, and I had witnessed the adulation that was showered on her in New York in 1990. Having encountered the unwelcome attention of the authorities and security police with my own opposition to apartheid, I had had a taste – albeit just a fraction – of some of Winnie's experiences. I could relate to her as a woman, as well as identify with the loss of privacy, having your telephone tapped, being watched and followed, not knowing when or where the security police might pounce, worrying what might happen to your small children if some ill fate befell you – and being betrayed by the people you trusted, all the while knowing that you were at the mercy of those who needed no proof of misdeeds and had unbridled power. Add to that two years of full-scale conventional war, comparable on some levels to the situation in South Africa's townships, and my apprenticeship was complete.

From the outset, this book was intended to be more than just the story of a remarkable woman or of South Africa under apartheid. I saw it as a parable for the courage and compassion of women in war, and the effects of ruthless dictatorship: the brutality of unscrupulous leaders struggling for survival, and the enslavement of man, whether in southern Africa or the former Yugoslavia. It makes no difference whether the oppressor is white or black, Cambodian or British, Muslim or atheist – the consequences are the same. What is disputed, stolen and destroyed is not land or mineral rights, but the individual's right to personal freedom and self-determination.

During the war in Bosnia, I got to know many women who were living symbols of opposition to Serb terror. Their resistance was not chronicled in poetry or embodied in political activism; their resistance was life itself. The entire world thought it impossible for Sarajevans – besieged and virtually unarmed – to weather the Serb onslaught and stay alive for more than a few weeks. But for four years, Sarajevo confounded the Serbs and astounded the world. And it was the women who provided crucial support for the vastly outnumbered and outgunned defenders of Sarajevo. They walked for miles and queued for hours for pitiful handouts of food, and carried buckets of water through heavy shelling and gunfire. They buried their children, their husbands and parents, and continued living. As their homes were bombed and burned, they retreated to a back room, or someone else's house, and continued living. They wore their best clothes, put on make-up, and laughed. My friend Gertruda Munitic, an opera singer, kept singing for the people of Sarajevo amidst the deafening roar of exploding bombs. My friend Jasna Karaula, a university lecturer, walked miles and miles in defiance of Serb snipers to deliver life-saving medicines to the sick and wounded. My young friend Anja Kerken, teenage daughter of my neighbours Mima and Seo, did numerous things to make my life more bearable, and walked to within metres of the front line to collect precious firewood for their household. My admiration for these women is total, as it is for the women of South Africa, Liberia and Palestine.

Winnie belongs to this unique fraternity of extraordinary women, most of whom will remain forever nameless. They live, or have lived, in Bosnia, Zimbabwe, Israel, Nazi-occupied Europe, Myanmar, the Congo, the Soviet Union. Many of their names are interchangeable with that of Winnie Mandela – or Anna Akhmatova. Like Winnie, Anna, too, was beautiful, courageous and enigmatic. And, as she pointed out in her poem 'Requiem', she, like Winnie, suffered not in a foreign country or under a foreign power, but among her countrymen. Winnie Mandela, like Anna Akhmatova, was where her people, unfortunately, were.

What the author Joseph Brodsky said of Akhmatova applies equally to Winnie: she never resembled anyone. Though born half a century and half a world apart, both their lives were governed by the controlled terror of a state that tolerated no opposition. Akhmatova's first husband was executed for anti-government activities, many of her friends fled into exile, others – including her son – were imprisoned in Stalin's terrible jails. Her poetry was banned, her dissenting voice silenced. As government changed hands from Stalin to Krushchev, Akhmatova was briefly hailed as a heroine, then again denounced. She kept writing, keeping alive the memory of the millions of victims – as Winnie helped keep alive the struggle against apartheid. These qualities apply equally to the many courageous women I knew in Bosnia, and no doubt to Aung San Suu Kyi in Myanmar, and the millions of nameless women who choose to confront oppression and injustice when it is safer to turn and look the other way.

Elie Wiesel, who survived Hitler's holocaust and dedicated his life to exposing Nazi war criminals, wrote these powerful words:

The opposite of love is not hate, but indifference;
The opposite of life is not death – but indifference to life and death.

ANNÉ MARIÈ DU PREEZ BEZDROB
PARKHURST, JOHANNESBURG
SEPTEMBER 2003

Acknowledgements

FROM THE TIME when I wrote my first poem at the age of ten, I wanted to be a writer. Even then I was fascinated by the mystique of creating a picture from words. It also seemed like a romantic kind of life. Since then, I have learned that being a writer is extremely hard work, and a lonely occupation.

The Dalai Lama said one could measure the importance of something in your life by what you were prepared to sacrifice for it, and if I have committed any excess in the pursuit of my dream, it has been to sacrifice too much rather than too little.

Many people have provided me with inestimable support, friendship and encouragement. It is, unfortunately, impossible to name everyone who has contributed in some way towards this book. One of the many people the world over who touched and enriched my life was Sergio Vieira de Mello, who died in a terrorist attack on the United Nations Headquarters in Baghdad while I was writing these acknowledgements. He was a man of peace and compassion, and the world is the poorer for having lost him. I am indebted to him and the many other people who have in any way shared in my experiences.

Writing this book became a vast journey of discovery. The circumstances and subject matter acted as a catalyst that fused many different components and turned this period into arguably the most enlightening time of my life. The people closest to me played a significant role in this experience, and I am forever indebted to them for their unconditional love and enormous support, and their commitment to and pride in this endeavour, which added an important element of inspiration.

My family is an important haven, both physically and emotionally, and my children and grandchildren are the focus and essence of my life. My son John, my daughter Annéne, and their spouses Trish and Ian, have supported me with endless love, prayers, and physical and financial support. My granddaughters, Mila and Yasmin, are a constant source of comfort and abundant joy. They have added new meaning to my life, and I am eagerly looking forward to my third grandchild, scheduled to arrive in the world at the same time as this book. My mother speeded up the conveyor belt that provides loads of her delicious aniseed rusks and home-made jams, armfuls of fresh vegetables and fragrant roses grown with loving hands.

My late father's legacy – a social conscience and sense of morality – was a shield against significant political and social pressure: in South Africa, in Bosnia, in life. My siblings, as my first companions and fellow travellers, have left indelible imprints on my life, and continue to do so. My late sister Erna was unapologetically her own person, and I admired her eccentric and vivacious spirit and boundless generosity. My sister Deona has been a long-suffering sounding board and source of advice and support, and my brother-in-law Johan pitched in to keep me afloat financially. My brother Johann is always a calm and steady anchor in the sea of women.

I owe a great deal to John and Annéne, my parents, Erna, Deona, Johann, my niece Anlin and my nephew Neil, who all shouldered a share of my family responsibilities while I was travelling the world and pursuing justice for all.

George and Yvonne Lees, co-grandparents to Mila, sponsored me for half a year, and their exceptional generosity both humbled me and made it possible to remain in a room of my own.

I am sincerely grateful to Chris (Chameleon) Mulder, for giving me wings, Armin Bezdrob for support while I was doing my 'apprenticeship', and Max du Preez for his encouragement, research material, information and advice.

My extensive circle of devoted and nurturing friends enthusiastically aided and abetted me, offered moral support, advice, prayers and encouragement. In addition to moral support, I also received crucial financial assistance, without which I could not have continued, from my loyal friends Frankie and Ricky van der Ploeg, René Kitshoff, Dee Cuthbertson, Cedric Thornberry – a fellow author who has played a major role in my life – and my dear friend Maria Wallis, who deserves a special mention. She lent an ear, offered advice, dragged me out of seclusion, and plied me with food for body and soul.

My friends Jean Swanson and Jean Fisher, both writers, provided wall-to-wall moral support, encouragement, inspiration and sound advice; Cape Town Jean via enough Telkom minutes to coat the Great Wall of China, and Namibia Jean with countless e-mails in her inimitable style. Karen Barrett's exquisite gifts and treats from New York lifted my sagging spirit, and Christine McNair massaged, acupunctured and counselled me back into shape.

Julie Thompson in New York, Hermine Spies Coleman in the Midland Meander, and Johan Minnaar in Graaff-Reinet offered the sanctuary of their homes as alternative places to work and write.

Belinda Walton is a singular source of inspiration through her courage, faith and encouragement.

My friends are scattered across the globe and I am eternally grateful for e-mail. From a long list I would like to single out Bill Aikman and Janet in Canada, whose regular and exciting correspondence, encouragement and interest have meant so much to me.

I owe a debt of gratitude to the Reverend Michelle Pilet of St Paul's Anglican Church in Parkhurst, who has patiently and generously offered spiritual guidance and friendship, and to Sally van der Merwe for prayers and support.

Elizabeth Motsitsi, my remarkable domestic assistant, sadly died before completion of the book. She was the embodiment of the compassion and wisdom of African women, and unconditionally provided loyal support and companionship.

Special thanks go to my publisher Zebra Press for sharing and supporting my vision of the book. Marlene Fryer took an interest in me as a person, offering encouragement and assistance well beyond the call of duty, and Robert Plummer kept me going with patience, enthusiasm and heartening feedback.

My editor, Marléne Burger, infused me with her verve and sincere commitment. She treated my precious manuscript with empathy, consideration and care, and her insight and masterful brush strokes significantly enhanced the end product.

I have always found the kindness of strangers exceptionally touching. Many people who didn't know me, and had no need to offer more than cursory assistance, showered me with kindness and support.

Alan Reynolds, Winnie Madikizela-Mandela's spokesman, answered endless questions, provided information and valuable insight, and obliged with patience and good humour.

Liz Lichter of the Parkhurst Library graciously ordered and searched for one book after another, saving me many precious hours.

Helena Prinsloo of the SA Media Centre at the University of the Free State, and Beverley Parsons and Leonie Klootwyk of Beeld and Rapport's Library and Archives, kindly retrieved crucial information.

Sandra Storm and Lebo Tshidi literally kept me in touch with the world.

I sincerely apologise for any omissions, due not to carelessness but to pressure, exhaustion or absent-mindedness.

A number of people provided assistance and information, but wish to remain anonymous. To them, my sincere thanks.

The lives of two exceptional women are directly responsible for this book. Many years ago, Esmé Matshikiza's courage and perseverance first made me aware of the crucial role women play, often without recognition, in the fortune of individuals and countries.

Winnie Madikizela-Mandela's enormous sacrifice has made both the new South Africa and this book possible. Without her tenacious struggle, neither would have seen the light.

The opportunity to write this book was a gift from my Creator. Without faith – my own and that of others – I could never have pulled it off, and I am constantly reminded that all that is wonderful in my life is thanks to His grace and love.

'There are victories whose glory lies only in the fact that they are known to those who win them.'
— Nelson Mandela, Long Walk to Freedom

Prologue

THE WIND CHANGED direction slightly and a sudden gust swirled around the cluster of men on horseback, wrapping them swiftly, unexpectedly, in the sweet, choking odour of death.

The horses, eyes wide with panic, snorted in alarm, tossing their heads urgently from side to side. Two of the stallions staggered onto their hind legs, arching their necks to escape the pungent smell. The other horses started milling around, straining at the reins. With some effort the riders steered them downwind, out of range of the nauseating stench, and rode onto a small outcrop from where they had a view in the direction from which the wind had come.

They stared at the ghastly picture below in shock and disbelief. Shrouded in a dense, tangible silence lay a scene of utter devastation. As far as the eye could see, the ground was littered with the carelessly scattered bodies of hundreds of dead men, women and children, cattle and dogs. Vultures squatted nearby. Thousands of burned elephant tusks added to the putrid smell. The earth seemed to float on a flat cloud of dirty smoke. For miles around them the black, burned countryside was desolate; everything annihilated, laid waste as if devoured by a giant fire-breathing predator.

Nobody uttered a sound as the small group of horsemen under command of Major General Dundas gradually moved closer, glancing in horror at what had been the Pondo Great Place, now nothing but scorched earth and decomposing bodies.

This, then, thought the young Holden Bowker, was the aftermath of that overture of death he had heard for the first time the night before: the Zulu 'war cry', a never-to-be forgotten sound. It made his flesh crawl: 'a shrill, inhuman, whistling roar that passed with lightning speed',[1] suggesting the pace of death as it descended swiftly, mercilessly. It was midnight and they could see nothing, but knew it came from the charging army of Shaka, the Zulu king, as his warriors swept through the cold, coal-black African night.

The small group of white men had gone to the aid of the Xhosa after months of attacks by Shaka's Zulu impi, culminating in the attack on the Pondo Great Place. At the dawn of a new day they found themselves marching alongside several thousand

1

Pondo and Tembu fighters toward 1 500 of Shaka's warriors. The two hostile forces converged on the flaxen winter veld in the pale sun of late winter. It was an ominous sight. Assegais and shields waved like branches in a giant breath of air. Across an open stretch of 150 metres, the Zulu warriors were resplendent in full battledress, their strong ebony bodies still and taut in anticipation of the fight.

The Zulu were outnumbered and there was a brief, bloody battle. The white horsemen formed a flank of the attacking force, but Shaka had been advised not to engage the whites, and the Zulu fighters avoided them, retreating to a hill further away where they regrouped and awaited the pursuing allied Xhosa force. Another bloody clash followed. Brief, brutal. Again the Zulu impi retreated, leaving behind a large number of the cattle they had looted in their raids on the Xhosa. On the battlefield lay three dozen dead fighters, half of them Zulu. The Xhosa decided to let the retreating Zulus go, rounded up the cattle and went off in their own direction.

The small group of white horsemen feared that the Zulus might return, and knew they could not stand against them without the help of the Xhosa army. They turned back to the colony, relieved to be heading for the safety of their homes, trying to forget the images of death and devastation: the dreadful mutilation of small children, limbless women, slaughtered animals, the giant fingerprint of unmitigated and merciless destruction.

After riding for the rest of the day they offsaddled and started a fire, grateful to be on solid ground. They took some meat from their saddlebags, and stood around the fire recounting the journey and the battle while the delicious odour of grilling meat intertwined with wood smoke and curled into the gathering darkness. They were hungry, and waiting for the meal was bittersweet.

Suddenly Holden heard the thin, pathetic cry of a child. He shook his head, convinced that his mind was playing tricks on him after the recurring images of small mangled bodies on the blood-soaked grass. Then he heard it again. He stepped back, out of the circle of conversation and muted laughter, slowly following the sound. It became louder, leading him to a large, flat slab of stone. He started pushing at it and heard the crying again, unmistakably coming from underneath the stone. He squatted, lifted the heavy stone and saw in the half-light that it covered a hole in the ground where, to his astonishment, he saw a small child.

He lifted the child out as gently as he could. It was a small boy of about two, whimpering weakly, limp with fear, barely alive from hunger and exposure. The young Englishman quickly carried him back to the camp. Clearly, the child's mother had hidden him there from the marauding Zulus who swept across the area, praying that he wouldn't be found by wild animals or warriors, and that she might be spared to return and fetch him – or that by some miracle, someone with a kind heart would find him and save his life.

The tiny boy was as terrified as a small animal, and the men tried to comfort and

2

reassure him as best they could. They wrapped him in jackets and a blanket, fed him and put him to sleep close to the fire.

The next morning, Holden tied the small Pondo boy onto his back as he had seen the Xhosa women do. He swung into the saddle wondering whether the child's father was one of the slain warriors lying under the rising sun on the battlefield. Or had he gathered his cattle and set out to start a new life, grieving for a lost wife and a small son, presuming they were dead? With the tiny body snuggling against his back, he galloped off towards the safety of the colony, and his farm.

Behind the disappearing backs of the white man and the black boy* lay the ashes of the Pondo people's hopes and dreams; a black, smouldering scar in the soft green of the countryside.

---

* Bowker entrusted the boy to the care of a black woman on their farm, Tharfield, and promised her a cow to nurture him back to health. He was named Resurrection Jack, and remained part of the Bowker family's weal and woes for seventy years.

Introduction

FROM THE COLOURFUL QUILT of intertwined clans and tribes that make up the Xhosa people, two have become household names due to their links with Nelson Mandela: the Tembu, from which he stems, and the Pondo, which gave the world his former wife, Winnie.

Just as familiar as the Mandela name is that of the mighty Zulu king, Shaka, and the nineteenth-century history of the Pondo and the Tembu is closely interwoven with that of Shaka and his successor, Dingane.

At the end of the 1700s, the area encompassing Natal and southern Mozambique became an extended battlefield as a power struggle raged between the tribal kings of the period. Among the consequences was a phenomenal amalgamation of military force, and Shaka's rise to dominance. His bloody conquests caused major upheaval in all of southern Africa north of the Cape Colony: the Highveld region north of Natal, the Orange Free State and Transvaal, and even as far as present-day Botswana and Zimbabwe. Those who fell victim to Shaka took flight in all directions, causing the greatest chain reaction of catastrophes in African history – known as *mfecane*, 'the crushing'.

In mid-1820, during the winter months in South Africa, Shaka – having consolidated his position as king of the Zulu in a trail of terrifying destruction and bloody atrocities – sent envoys to Ngoza, paramount chief of the Tembu, with an offer to unite their forces. Ngoza contemptuously responded with an insult that could only be interpreted as a declaration of war.

Ngoza and his ally Macingwane, chief of the Qunu, readied themselves for battle against the mighty Zulu. Shaka was confident, and had no reason to doubt that his superb fighting force would be victorious. But midway through the battle, a terrified messenger brought word that the Xhosa were driving back Shaka's invincible army. The threat, however, was short-lived, and Shaka's warriors forced Ngoza's people from their land on the Mzinyathi River. Subsequently, Ngoza was murdered, and many of his people were incorporated into the Pondo tribe under King Faku.

In 1827, Shaka decided to attack Faku's people along the banks of the St John's

River, as well as the Tembu who had settled inland. He began preparing for the campaign in September by sending spies – members of Ngoza's Tembu who had retreated to Zululand, and were familiar with Pondoland – to assess the enemy's position.

In October, Shaka's mother, Nandi, died. Shaka worshipped her, and he was devastated. In the months immediately after Nandi's death, thousands of Zulus died in Shaka's mourning rituals, which brought his nation to the brink of famine and destruction.

By the autumn of 1828, Shaka felt the time was ripe for the Pondoland campaign, and decided that what was originally planned as a purely military expedition would serve as the *iHlambo*, or mourning hunt, for his adored mother. The *iHlambo* required the warriors to spill the blood of their enemy, and Shaka relished the thought of a great 'washing of the spears' in Pondo blood, as befitted Nandi's eminent status. The battered Zulu nation fervently hoped that the campaign would be the last convulsion of their king's savage anguish.

During May, June and July, Shaka's *impi* moved south, killing and plundering as they went. The inland division under Manyundela, one of the king's favourite generals, attacked and virtually destroyed the Tembu. But Manyundela was killed in the battle, and a raging Shaka ordered the execution of hundreds of warriors for not preventing his death.

For the campaign against the Pondo, Shaka selected his senior general, Mdlaka, and a force of some 10 000 warriors. As word of their advance spread, the Pondo fled south. The Zulu *impi* moved as far as the Umtata River, destroying the deserted kraals as they swept through the region. On the return journey, as they crossed the Umzimvubu River and moved out of Faku's country, the Pondo thought the threat had passed, but as they emerged from hiding, the Zulus turned around and attacked and captured Faku's capital, along with 30 000 head of cattle.

It was the aftermath of this campaign that was discovered by Major General Dundas, Civil Commissioner of Albany and Somerset, when he arrived in Pondo-land in August with a small scouting force, the first military expedition involving the British 1820 Settlers in South Africa. Among the men riding with Dundas were four Bowker brothers, one of whom, Holden, recorded the out-come of the battle and the blood-curdling results of Faku's encounter with Shaka's forces.

By the end of July 1828, a defeated and war-weary Faku was moving towards the Cape Colony with the remnants of his people. Ironically, Shaka the conqueror held the vanquished Faku in high esteem. Henry Francis Fynn, the Zulu king's famous English adviser, chronicled Shaka's overtures to Faku:

> Owing to the knowledge I had of Faku, the King of the Pondos, Shaka asked me one morning if I thought, were he to withdraw his army, Faku

would consent to becoming his tributary. I replied in the affirmative and recommended, as an inducement, the return of the girls who had been captured and sent to him by the army, and refraining from destroying more corn. To this he assented. He accordingly sent messengers to Faku with proposals for peace, at the same time returning the females as proof of his *bona fides*; he, moreover, directed his army to withdraw and to stop destroying the corn. Several chiefs of petty tribes in Faku's neighbourhood, with messengers from Faku, returned with the army to thank him for his liberality in thus sparing their lives. They were rewarded with presents of cattle selected from those that had been taken from them.[1]

Faku's wisdom and pragmatic leadership in accepting Shaka's proposals of peace and cooperation were an important reason why the Pondo managed to survive as a cohesive unit.

Shaka was murdered in September 1828 by his brothers Mhlangana and Dingane, and Mbopa, a high councillor and major-domo of his royal kraal. After a violent quarrel with Dingane in March 1829, Nqetho, a chieftain of the Qwabe tribe, rounded up his people and fled south. He clashed with a number of clans and tribes en route to Pondoland, where he encamped near Faku, the paramount chief, who had become a force to be reckoned with. His land had been overrun in waves by Zulu warriors, Zulu refugees, the Ngwaneni and British troops, and finally he was confronted by the Qwabe tribe, but he had built up substantial forces, strong enough to drive the Qwabe back. Nqetho had no choice but to return to Zululand, where Dingane ordered him killed.

In stark contrast to the hostility that governed their associations with other black groups, the Xhosa leaders, including Faku, generally opted for non-aggressive and diplomatic cooperation with the white settlers in the region. When Petrus Lafras Uys inspected the land beyond the Great Fish River, which was the domain of Hintsa, the Xhosa chieftain generously gave him permission to settle in the northern reaches, where the Pondo had settled. When Uys arrived, Faku welcomed him.

The Pondo king's cooperation with the white settlers was not the first example of such collaboration by his people. His ancestry indicated a fairly significant injection of white blood – proof of more than mere business relations between the Pondo and the white settlers.

The east coast of South Africa was the scene of many shipwrecks during the eighteenth century. On the night of 4 August 1782, the East Indiaman *Grosvenor* ran aground when the captain, certain that the ship was still some 300 miles offshore, ignored the urgent warnings of a seaman on watch. The captain's next mistake was to estimate that the shipwrecked survivors would reach Cape Town in no more than two weeks. They set off in high spirits, but the captain's calculations of distance were even worse on land than at sea. After four months, six of the survivors reached a frontier farm hundreds of miles from Cape Town, having suffered severe exposure and hunger. A search party found another dozen, but the rest disappeared without trace.

Rumour persisted that black chieftains had taken some of the missing women as their wives, and, in 1790, an expedition sent to investigate these reports made an astonishing discovery. All the inhabitants of a kraal on the Umgazana River, some four hundred in all, were half-castes – the descendants of three elderly white women who had survived another, unidentified shipwreck as children years before. Some of the inhabitants of the kraal had recognisable English names like Bessie, Betty and Tommy, and others went by adulterations of Geoffrey, Thomas and Michael.

But in time, traces of the blood that had been mixed with those of the black clans all but disappeared. Later expeditions searched for the kraal of half-castes, but it was never found again. By the nineteenth century, very few of the blacks along the coast could trace their descent from shipwrecked whites. Among those who could was Faku.

One of the strongest Pondo clans is the Ngutyana, from whence came Winnie Madikizela-Mandela. From about 1820 to 1850 her great-grandfather, Madikizela, was a powerful warrior chieftain in the Umkomaas area of Natal, but the Ngutyana eventually settled near Izingolweni between Port Edward and the Transkei village of Bizana.

Madikizela earned a reputation as a fierce and merciless leader and seized large tracts of land and a substantial number of warriors and cattle. But even he was no match for Shaka's might and, caught up in the death throes of the *mfecane*, he moved south with his followers and cattle, and settled in Pondoland, where he raided Faku's kingdom. The wise Faku, whose diplomacy with Shaka had safeguarded his people's survival, decided it was better to have Madikizela as a friend than a foe. He bowed the knee to the marauder and offered him his sister as a wife, and the Madikizelas came to be known as 'the nephews of Faku'.[2]

A century after the heyday of Faku, a little girl was born to the Madikizela clan. Her name was Nomzamo, but the world would come to know her as Winnie Mandela.

Despite traditional norms and general compliance with their subordinate role, Xhosa women were held in high esteem, and it was not uncommon for them to be accepted in leadership positions. One such example was Yese, mother of Ngqika, chief of the Rarabe tribe.

Yese is the subject of the first documented history of the enormous power and influence Xhosa women could exercise within their customarily patriarchal society. She also offers another example of an intimate interracial relationship.

Yese was a Tembu, the tribe from which brides were traditionally chosen for Xhosa royals. Said to have been a great beauty when she was young, she became extremely fat as she matured, and as her girth expanded, so did her influence over her son and their people.

Legend has it that Yese appeared to Mlawu, the son and heir of the tribal chief, Rarabe, from a cloud of mist on a mountain, and became his wife. In 1782, when their son, Ngqika, was three years old, both Mlawu and Rarabe were killed in battle against the Tembu. Regency over Rarabe's tribe was entrusted to Yese and Ngqika's uncle, Ndlambe, until the boy came of age.

Yese's power and special status were unique in Xhosa history. Many of the Rarabe saw her as a chief and her position was never questioned, not even when she was seen to be married to a white hunter, Coenraad du Buis, who fled to Ngqika's domain after involvement in an uprising against the British who offered a reward of £200 for his capture, dead of alive. He was given protection by Ngqika for several years and subsequently became a councillor and served as chief adviser to Ngqika. But Ngqika did nothing without first consulting his mother, and treated her with the utmost reverence. Du Buis apparently produced a sizeable clan of half-castes, and it is generally accepted that this is the origin of some of the white blood still evident today in many fair-skinned Xhosas.

Yese broke the mould of Xhosa women as 'the workers, the hewers of wood and drawers of water. They tilled the gardens, built the huts, prepared the food and cared for the children. On journeys, they carried. Nevertheless, any woman of strong mind and determination imposed herself forcefully, and on every level, whether she was a commoner or royal. This is continuously evident, from Ngqika's mother all the way to Winnie Mandela.'[3]

In 1894, nine years after the British established their dominion over Tembuland, they annexed Pondoland, making the Pondo the last of the tribes to come under colonial rule in South Africa. During Faku's reign, all the land bordered by the Umzimkulu and the Umtata Rivers, the Indian Ocean and the Drakensberg mountains, was Pondoland, but during Shaka's reign of terror, the *izidukos* [clans] scattered, and many never returned to the land of their ancestors. Faku, chief of the largest and wealthiest of all the tribes, retreated with his followers into the Umgazi area. In 1842, following the death of Dingane, they were able to resettle part of their ancestral land thanks to an agreement negotiated with the British by the missionary and politician Theophilus Shepstone. In return, Shepstone extorted from the Pondo a paramount chieftainship.

When Nelson Mandela was practising as a lawyer, he found a copy of the treaty recorded in a *Government Gazette*:

We hereby for ourselves, our heirs and successors and for and on behalf of our respective tribes acknowledge and profess that from and after the execution hereof Theophilus Shepstone, Esquire, is and hereafter shall be, the Paramount and Exclusive Chief and Ruler of ourselves and the tribes belonging to us, as also of the country or territory now occupied or here-after to be occupied by us or any of us or any part or portion thereof.

And we acknowledge Theophilus Shepstone, Esquire, as such Supreme Chief or Ruler, as effectively and to all intents and purpose, as firmly as if he had been or had become such Paramount Chief or Ruler by succession according to our laws or usage.

The treaty also gave Shepstone 'the full and complete control of Port St John's, [the trade line to the Cape], with power and authority to do and perform every act and matter necessary to the proper supervision and management of matters of such Port, short of fiscal alienation to one mile on each side of the river nor extend up its course beyond the influence of the tide'.

Faku signed the treaty on 5 June 1854, and the heads of six other clans – the Nikwe, Mbulu, Xesibe, Boto, Twana and the Ngutyana of Madikizela – signed identical agreements.

During Faku's lifetime, the British effectively demanded only a *de jure* presence in the region, but his descendants were plagued by problems inherent to the treaty that ultimately led to dispossession of their land.

The Tembu, who had dared to defy – and beat – Shaka, were incorporated into the Pondo, and Faku, in turn, held in some esteem by Shaka, bowed the knee to Madikizela.

This august chess game of shifting power, intrigue and alliances forms the backdrop for the majestic history of the Pondo tribe and the Ngutyana clan – and that of the most famous woman in South Africa's recent history, Winnie Madikizela-Mandela.

She hailed from an imposing line of authentic and indisputable leaders. During a life beset with tragedy and trial, she ceaselessly demonstrated the well-chronicled characteristics of her ancestors, who were fearless and autocratic, with a natural penchant to command, and typified their dauntless courage, stubborn pride and instinctive aptitude for survival against all odds.

Winnie Madikizela was to the manner born.

PART I

Winnie Madikizela

'Without courage, all other virtues become meaningless.'
– Winston Churchill

1

A country girl

SATURDAY 26 SEPTEMBER 1934 broke exactly the same way as the day before, and the day before that. It was no different from any other day in early spring. The large Madikizela homestead at Idutywa in the Bizana district of the Transkei lay bathed in deep, pre-dawn silence. Gradually, out of the blanching darkness, came the sounds that announced a new day: the twittering and chattering of birds, cocks crowing at dawn; as the light spread, the cool earth warmed up rapidly under Africa's forbidding sun.

When Nomathansanqa Gertrude Madikizela went into labour, there still was nothing to indicate that the day might mark something special.

The new baby's first cry should have elicited happy exclamations and congratulations. Instead, initial reaction to the birth of Gertrude's fifth child was mute disappointment. It was a girl. Yet again, a girl. They had all been hoping for a boy. The tiny baby's paternal grandmother made no attempt to hide her displeasure as she told the weary mother: 'You are wasting our time.' The little girl's father, Kokani Columbus Madikizela, was equally unenthusiastic, whether from a lifetime habit of respectfully agreeing with his mother, or genuine disappointment. 'I'm tired of girls,' he said. 'I want a boy.' Gertrude, too, had been praying for another son. Her eldest child was a boy, but Pondo custom dictated that a mother's possessions were inherited by her youngest son. If Gertrude's position in the family – indeed her life – was to be at all meaningful, her contribution passed on to her descendants, she needed to bear a second boy.

Little could the Madikizelas have known that the tiny girl to whom they had given such a miserly welcome would become an icon of twentieth-century South Africa, and leave an imprint larger and more important than any other woman – or Madikizela male – on the country's history.

Columbus Madikizela did not register the baby, because it was not compulsory to record black births. Three months later, Columbus, Gertrude, the grandparents and extended family gathered at the Methodist Church in Idutywa, and in the small corrugated iron building the new baby was christened Nomzamo Zaniewe Winifred. Columbus admired the Germans for their discipline and industrial achievements, and demonstrated his reverence for both the industrious Aryans and the missionaries who had led him to Christianity by calling his daughter Winifred, the ancient Germanic name meaning 'friend of peace'. Though rarely used, her first name, Nomzamo, would prove prophetic – it means 'she who will endure trials'. When she went to school, she became known as Winnie.

Winnie Madikizela's birthplace was an idyllic spot in a country that was heading towards great turmoil. The Pondoland of her childhood was a luxuriant patchwork in shades of green: vast plains of savannah, cultivated blocks of maize and other crops, and clumps of trees. As far as the eye could see, one hill after another rolled toward the horizon under a jolt-blue sky. The abundance of rivers and streams meant that Pondoland was green in all seasons. There were no roads or power pylons and the only signs of human presence were traditional clay huts, round and white with thatched roofs, strewn across the landscape like scattered pebbles. Every settlement had a cluster of huts of various sizes, depending on the status and prosperity of the family, each one used for a specific purpose – sleeping, cooking, storage, socialising.

The world of the Pondo was prosperous, peaceful and orderly, steeped in the dictates of countless generations. But it was changing. Colonisation was followed by an invasion of missionaries from Europe, traders and farmers, and the demand for labour, land and even the cattle owned by the blacks was threatening a traditional way of life. When the settlers encountered hostility that resulted in skirmishes with the Xhosa, soldiers with superior weaponry were sent to the Transkei to protect them, leading to almost a century of acrimony and bloody warfare. The Xhosa were finally subdued and then systematically impoverished as the discovery of diamonds and gold towards the end of the nineteenth century, and the fledgling industries that mushroomed on the Witwatersrand, gave rise to new demands for cheap labour.

Economic and industrial progress in southern Africa carried a price tag of inevitable upheaval for the indigenous population, seemingly unobserved, and certainly unrecorded, by whites. Land was taken from communities who were forced to obey restrictions and pay taxes, which they neither understood nor could afford. To earn the money they needed, they were obliged to find jobs in the mining and industrial sectors, which in turn doomed them to a life as migrant labourers. Their tried and trusted way of life was receding into oblivion, and the future would bring little but disrupted communities, growing poverty and racial disharmony.

The Madikizela home was within a few hours of Durban, a modern city and popular tourist destination famous for its wide sandy beaches fringing the warm waves of the Indian Ocean. Less visited but equally picturesque was the neighbouring Wild Coast. Port St John's, subject of a treaty signed by Winnie's great-grandfather and Theophilus Shepstone, had been developed as a coastal resort, but – both under colonial rule and apartheid – was reserved for whites only. Even though it was so close, hardly anyone from Bizana had ever been to the coast. For them, the vast blue water of the Indian Ocean and the endless stretch of white sand outlining its edge was the fabric of legend: distant, unreal.

In the 1930s, the district of Bizana was seen as remote, as were most settlements in the hills of Pondoland. But the footprints of the flourishing white population were spreading all across South Africa. The small towns and fertile farms that dotted the countryside were in white hands, and the land the Xhosa had cherished as their own for generations was administered by white officials enforcing their laws with total disregard for ancient traditions and customs.

The life of the rural Pondo was spartan. Winnie's early childhood was no different than that of any other peasant girl, but the Madikizelas were more privileged than most. Though not affluent, the family was influential and lived comfortably. Her grandfather, Chief Mazingi, had been a prosperous trader and farmer with large expanses of land and twenty-nine wives, and his numerous residences and families were spread between eMbongweni and Idutywa. His land produced a good harvest of maize, and provided grazing for his large herds of sheep and cattle.

Chief Mazingi was a man of vision, with the courage to challenge his own revered traditions and customs. Having realised that illiteracy had rendered his people defenceless against exploitation and subjugation by the white colonists, he was determined that his own children would break the restrictive mould of ignorance. Chief Mazingi was impressed by the Methodist missionaries, who offered education and assistance in a multitude of endeavours. He embraced their God, then employed a teacher and established a school, decreeing that the new generation of Madikizelas would abandon their traditional way of life. His children had no choice but to exchange their familiar and carefree existence for the arduous task of learning to read and write, and acquire the perplexing skills of the white people.

Chief Mazingi flouted tradition even further by appointing his senior wife, Seyina, as his business manager. She was a strong, spirited and intelligent woman with a large body and a booming laugh, which became her trademark. She was also the mother of three daughters and six sons, the eldest of whom was Winnie's father, Columbus.

The chief was a shrewd businessman, who realised that cooperation with the whites could be turned to his advantage. He gave a large piece of his land to traders in the area, and in return took ownership of a trading post, which Seyina was allowed to continue running when he died. She was the first woman in Pondoland to achieve such status and independence, and was tremendously proud of her singular position. However, when new traders refused to honour the agreement and took the store from her, her pride and joy turned to deep bitterness and hostility towards whites.

Remote and undeveloped as Pondoland was, the mission schools that sprang up like mushrooms offered new opportunities, and the Madikizela family remained among the forerunners of change in the community. Columbus and two of his brothers became teachers, while another qualified as an agriculturist. One of Seyina's sons joined her in the business, and the youngest, Xolane, succumbed to the lure of gold and city life and went to work on the mines. Shortly afterwards he contracted phthisis, a form of tuberculosis, and died.

Unlike her husband, Seyina resisted conversion to the Christian faith for as long as possible, but eventually she gave in, exchanging her *isidwebe* [cowhide skirt] for a dress of German print such as was commonly worn by Christian women. But although she attended church, she maintained the traditional rituals that she believed were fundamental to the prosperity and spiritual well-being of her family.

Her son Columbus was a perfect example of the new breed of blacks, embracing both the traditions of his people and the innovations of the whites. He was a christianised schoolteacher in a business suit whose salary was paid by the government. But he was also a proud Pondo leader who was fully aware of the injustices forced upon his people by the white settlers. He taught his pupils the facts as they were recorded in the textbooks: of explorers, settlers and governors representing foreign interests, but he also ensured that they were well versed in the effects of this history on their own people. In time, from her seat in his classroom, his daughter Winnie would soak up both his independent thinking on the politics of South Africa and his resentment against the injustices of colonial rule.

As the son of a tribal chief, Columbus was a man of some influence in the community, even though he had rejected his legacy as head of his tribe in favour of teaching in a mission school. He regularly represented eastern Pondoland at meetings of the territorial council, or Bunga, and since he was fluent in both English and Xhosa, served as interpreter when the tribal court sat at Komkhulu. The fiercely traditional Seyina was intensely disappointed when he turned his back on his birthright, but never confronted him openly and was relieved that he had not totally forsaken his traditional role and responsibilities.

His dual roles as headmaster and Bunga councillor meant that Columbus was a respected member of the community. He differed visibly from his peers. The Pondo tribesmen wore colourful blankets, but because Columbus had to wear a suit to work, this became his customary mode of dress. Gertrude kept his suits well pressed, while his shirts were neatly darned, with starched white collars. In a community where agriculture was a way of life, it added to his stature that Columbus, like his father, was a successful farmer. The one thing he was not, however, was a jovial family man.

Columbus loved his children, and they never doubted this, but in his dealings with them he maintained the aloof, stern approach of a schoolteacher. Even at home his children always rose when he entered a room, and almost never spoke to him if their mother wasn't present. But although there were no playful antics or open displays of affection, he devoted a great deal of time to his children.

Winnie's mother, Gertrude Mzaidume, was the first domestic science teacher in the Bizana district, and by all accounts a fashion-conscious beauty in her youth. Fair skinned with blue eyes and straight hair, her lineage was thought to include a liaison between a Pondo woman and a white trader. Gertrude was a strict mother, applying rigid discipline with as much commitment as she enforced the high standards of cleanliness she had learned from her mother. She was an ardent Christian and practising Methodist, and insisted that her children pray at least twice a day, usually in a corner of the garden where high grass had formed a protective shelter. Witch doctors were still a dominant feature of Pondo society, but Gertrude constantly impressed upon her children that Christian principles, not traditional custom, should form the basis of their lives. As a teenager, Winnie would briefly rebel against the almost fanatical religious practices forced on her by her mother, and which she didn't understand.

Both Columbus and Gertrude had broken the mould, shunning tradition and adopting a Western way of life. Winnie grew up in an unusual environment, exposed to both the legacy of generations of traditional leaders and the dynamic pioneering example of her parents. Heir to the fiercely proud and stubbornly individual character traits of her ancestors, she was bright and intelligent, with intuitive insight and an acute awareness of her surroundings – and her place in them – from an early age. Her family and childhood were not perfect, but she had a secure and happy upbringing.

In black communities, it is customary for those of means to feed the children of poorer families, and Columbus often took in the needy, with the result that there were sometimes as many as twenty other children around the table in the Madikizela home. The littlest ones ate from large enamel dishes, up to ten of them sharing a dish, and as they grew older they got their own plates. There was always fresh meat, milk and produce from his lands, which Columbus could provide for his large household only thanks to his agricultural enterprise. Black teachers earned far less than their white counterparts, and on his salary from the Cape Education Department alone, their comfortable lifestyle would have been impossible.

Lunch was typically boiled meat with vegetables, but supper was Winnie's favourite meal. It was known as *umphokoqo*, a porridge of sour milk and maize meal, cooked to the consistency of coarse granules. Even more than the food, however, Winnie found the gathering of families around the huge log fires magical. Flames leaped and danced against the backdrop of the dark, starry sky, and the smoke from burning wood mingled with that from pipes puffed by the old men and women. When it grew quiet, the elders held the children spellbound with tales of wonder, old and young locked in a cocoon of contentment and tranquillity.

Winnie was the fifth of nine children. When she was born she had a brother, who was the eldest, and three sisters. As she grew, Gertrude found Winnie the most wilful and trying of all her children, and Winnie felt from an early age that she fell short of her mother's expectations, not least because she was not a boy. Some of her earliest memories were of her mother praying to God every day for a son. As a little girl, Winnie neither knew nor could understand the intricate Pondo tribal custom that fuelled her mother's obsession and longing for another son. She also thought of herself as the ugly duckling of the family, partly because she didn't have the same fair complexion as her mother, but also because the minister's wife had once mistaken her for a boy, an innocent enough error, but one that assumed huge proportions in Winnie's mind. She resolved to satisfy her mother's desire for a son by acting like a boy, and she enthusiastically dedicated all her energy to her cause.

Winnie was tall and strong and had no difficulty being accepted as a playmate by boys her own age. They taught her to set snares and fight with sticks, and in no time she could beat most of them in the regular stick fights. They divided into groups, climbed trees and lay in wait for the unsuspecting 'enemy', then jumped down to launch fierce surprise attacks. When she tired of playing with the boys, Winnie made clay toys and animals that she baked in the crude kiln built by the bigger boys. The kiln was also used for roasting the odd chicken that strayed across their path, or for *dassies* [rock-rabbits] and springhares that the boys caught in their traps.

But rather than impressing and charming her mother, Winnie's attempts at being a boy only aggravated the situation. Gertrude often scolded her for running around with the boys, especially if she took her sister, Nonalithi, along. Winnie was desperately disappointed, but salve for her wounds came from both her father and Seyina, her Makhulu [grandmother]. Despite their disappointment at her birth, Winnie soon became the favourite of both Columbus and his mother. However, being Makhulu's favourite did not mean that Winnie was spoilt, and she worked as hard as all her siblings at household chores. Makhulu showed her affection by telling her granddaughter many wonderful stories of legendary heroes and great victories in battle, monsters and evil spirits in the forests, and of the Bushmen, the skilful hunters and prolific painters who were all but eradicated in the early 1900s. Winnie listened in awe as Makhulu told her that their people had been living in that part of Africa for centuries before Jan van Riebeeck established the Dutch East India Company's settlement at the Cape in 1652 – even before the Portuguese seafarers first landed on African soil in search of a sea route to India.

Makhulu enjoyed entertaining the children with her stories of how white men with blue eyes, long beards and straight hair came to Pondoland, warning the little ones that with their Bibles and their money, the strangers had come to steal their people's cattle and destroy their customs. Her obvious resentment of the whites made a strong impression on the children.

Makhulu's affection for Columbus and his children did not extend to Gertrude. Gertrude was a modern woman who even dressed differently from the other christianised women in the village, all of whom had settled for the uniform German print dresses and headscarves. Like their mother, Gertrude and her sister wore elegant dresses and crocheted hats. Makhulu's resentment was further fuelled by the fact that Gertrude was a Christian, and she held her daughter-in-law responsible for the fact that her son was barred from taking more wives. Moreover, Gertrude was a schoolteacher, and when Columbus had announced that he wanted to marry her, his mother undiplomatically told him he was mad to wed someone who not only wasn't a *muntu* [black], but more of a man than a woman. 'Marry a wife,' she advised, 'not a fellow teacher.'

Her counsel was to no avail, and Makhulu never hid her displeasure over her eldest son's choice of wife. Winnie and her siblings were always aware of the tension between their mother and grandmother, since Gertrude openly scorned Seyina's traditional tribal values and clung adamantly to her own modern beliefs. Seyina had a very different outlook on life, dwelling on a past steeped in pagan values that even Gertrude's grandparents had rejected, and which were a constant assault on her Christian conscience. Underlying their different views, however, was the real source of the tension between the two women: vying for Columbus's affection.

Seyina had long since decided that the best way of dealing with her son's 'affliction' was by keeping him close to her, while at the same time making it clear that she did not respect Gertrude's position as his wife. Winnie often accompanied her mother to her special sanctuary, where she prayed to God for her family's physical and spiritual welfare. From these prayers the little girl gathered that Makhulu's beliefs were sinful, and that her grandmother would not be granted access to the heaven of her mother's God. In time, she also realised that her mother never asked God to make Makhulu a better Christian, as she did for the rest of the family. And it was clear that Gertrude was concerned about Columbus, for she always asked God not only to make him a good Christian, but to save him from Makhulu's evil influence. Since that particular prayer reaped no result, Winnie came to the conclusion that God was not paying attention to her mother's earnest pleas.

Makhulu, praying to the spirits of the forefathers in the cattle kraal, ironically asked for much the same as Gertrude: strength for her sons, and not to be angered by the errant ways they had embraced. But her prayers also included complaints against her sons, or requests for advice and assistance in disciplining a wayward daughter-in-law – more often than not, Gertrude.

More than anything else, Makhulu could never forgive Columbus for the constant reminder that Gertrude had brought white blood into her family. Columbus was in a difficult position. He was a Christian and an active member of the church, but he dared not openly defy his mother. In deference to her, and to Winnie's puzzlement, he sometimes joined in the cruel jibes about Gertrude's white blood, reminding his children that she was a *mlungu* [white].

To Gertrude's chagrin, there were many special occasions when the ancestors would be called upon and the finest beast in their herd slaughtered as an offering. Whereas she could studiously ignore Makhulu's private prayer sessions, these rituals almost always involved her family. Winnie found the rites fascinating, and as an adult could recall every detail: Makhulu's chanting of the required dictum, appealing for protection, prosperity and peace, followed by the slaughter of the carefully selected beast. After the solemn ceremony the meat would be cooked and meted out to the villagers in order of seniority: the men first, then the women, and lastly the children who, their grandmother said, had their entire lives ahead and would continue to eat, while the adults were already dying.

Having eaten their fill, the adults would congregate in small groups, the men off to one side drinking beer and talking, the children listening wide-eyed and mostly uncomprehending, but totally content.

Winnie grew up in the three utterly distinct homes of her mother and her two grandmothers, and the stark differences in the personalities of the powerful women who ruled over their respective domains influenced her in specific ways and moulded her character. Her maternal grandmother, Granny, was the total opposite of Makhulu, and Winnie was both intrigued and delighted by Granny's eccentric ways. Granny was a staunch Christian, and like Columbus and Gertrude, very active in the Methodist Church. She cooked food that was favoured by whites and sewed her own fashionable dresses, which she wore with great elegance.

Granny, the fountainhead of Gertrude's obsession with cleanliness, applied rigid hygiene rules to both her person and her home. Everything in the house was clean and orderly, a practice inherited by Gertrude and perpetuated by Winnie, who developed an almost compulsive obsession with neatness and cleanliness. Of her many routines, Granny's 'toilette' fascinated Winnie the most. It took hours each day, starting with a bath. When Winnie stayed with Granny, it was her responsibility to fetch water from the river for the bath. After drying herself vigorously, Granny would massage her skin with a preparation she made from hot paraffin mixed with melted candle wax. Then she would comb out her hair and ask Winnie to braid it in dozens of small plaits. At night, Granny would take off her dress, carefully stretch it out on the bedframe under her mattress, and leave it overnight so that all the creases would be pressed out. In the morning, the dress was as good as new, and ready for wear.

Gertrude's home consisted of seven rondavels and a brick building in which Columbus slept. Makhulu, in turn, reigned supreme in her kraal of twenty huts, set in a large garden with trees and sandy pecking ground for the chickens. Some distance away was the cattle kraal and Columbus's plantation. At Makhulu's kraal the atmosphere was always festive, with cooking, eating and drinking, and the constant coming and going of aunts and uncles and dozens of cousins. Gertrude rarely visited her mother-in-law, but Makhulu glided into what she considered to be her son's house whenever she pleased, paying hardly any attention to Gertrude and making it clear that when she had matters of importance to discuss with Columbus, she preferred Gertrude's sitting room. This might well have been because Gertrude's home was so well organised, tidy and comfortable. Gertrude was forever putting things in their place, and when she wasn't teaching she was cleaning her house. The children were assigned a multitude of chores to help maintain her high standards, starting at daybreak when they had to clean the yard, picking up everything including twigs, and sprinkle water on the open ground around the huts to subdue the dust and keep it from blowing into the house and settling on the highly polished Victorian furniture. All her life, Winnie retained stark memories of Gertrude's uncompromising demands for order. In later years she would recall that her mother was so strict that when she sent the children to collect wood or water, she would spit in front of the fire and tell them they had to be back in the house before the spittle dried. Those not quick enough to do Gertrude's bidding were either smacked or sent to bed without supper.

Winnie loved Makhulu. The atmosphere in her house was more relaxed than that of either Gertrude's or Granny's, and she especially liked listening to Makhulu's stories and learning the many traditional skills Makhulu was eager to teach, such as how to weave grass mats and make clay pots. The children also learned to ride horses, milk cows and cook maize meal porridge, including Winnie's favourite dish, *umphokoqo*. Makhulu also taught the children how to brew beer, something Gertrude would no doubt have frowned upon. 'Makhulu taught me things that my mother had taken care to see I'd never learn. She took me into the ways of our ancestors, she put the skins and beads that had been hers when she was a young girl on me and taught me to sing and dance.'[1]

Winnie didn't know that there were people of different colour until Makhulu drew her attention to the fact with her stories of their appetite for money, and for the land and cattle of the Pondo. Winnie was left with the impression that a bad person and a white person were one and the same thing for Makhulu, who had embarked on a silent boycott of the commodities introduced by the whites, cautioning that they were a trap to separate black people from their money. There was no furniture in her huts but grass mats and small stools made from rough wattle, and nothing on the floors but cow dung, which was kept shining clean.

She made one exception: a blanket to wear around her shoulders in winter.

Columbus and Gertrude saw to it that their children were kept on the straight and narrow. They went to church regularly, with all the children in tow and dressed in their Sunday best. Afterwards, they would visit neighbours and anyone in need of assistance. Winnie found the church services unintelligible and boring, but Sunday school less so, in all probability because it held the appeal of prizes for the best pupils – a challenge she could relate to.

Notwithstanding the fact that her young life was complicated by conflicting ways and perplexing family relationships, Winnie was generally carefree and happy. The Madikizela children had strict routines, and both before and after school they had to perform certain chores, but there was plenty of time to play as well. Like all the children in the district they ran barefoot until they reached their teens, and even after Winnie realised that her attempts to be a surrogate son had failed to win her mother's esteem, she preferred the company and games of the boys. She wore shorts, rode cows and horses bareback, fought with sticks and played with the boys. The other girls fussed over their dolls and competed to see whose mother could produce the best dolls' clothes, but this didn't interest Winnie in the least. The highlight of the year was Christmas, and Columbus spared no effort to make it a special occasion, buying new clothes for everyone and toys for the children. On Christmas Day, presents were exchanged in an atmosphere of great excitement, and an ox was slaughtered to add to the festivity.

As in all families, there were fights and arguments between the siblings, and Winnie, because she was tougher than the other girls, frequently emerged victorious – which often resulted in an unpleasant encounter with Gertrude, who firmly believed that to spare the rod was to spoil the child. Winnie was by no means always the guilty party in these altercations, but she was most often on the receiving end of Gertrude's stick. When the sisters quarrelled, Gertrude inevitably assumed that the boisterous Winnie was the culprit, and usually restored order by giving her a few stinging slaps. The others soon cottoned on and complained loudly to Gertrude when they were at the losing end, knowing that she would almost certainly punish Winnie.

Once, after being provoked by her younger sister, Princess, Winnie made a knuckleduster by knocking a nail through a baking powder tin. As the dispute continued, she triumphantly brought her secret weapon into the fray. Unfortunately for Winnie, her strategy was flawed: she aimed for her sister's upper arm, but Princess dodged, and the nail struck her on the cheek, penetrating the skin and causing the wound to bleed profusely, as facial injuries do. She was crying, rubbing the blood and tears all over her face. Winnie was horrified – and dreaded the consequences. It looked far worse than it was, but Princess still had to be taken to Dr Thompson in Bizana for stitches. Back home, Gertrude gave Winnie a beating that she never forgot.

Winnie would never have accused her mother of loving her less than her brother and sisters, but she knew Gertrude was unfair, and sometimes, after undeserved punishment, she would sob with frustration and heartache. Occasionally, her father would set aside his characteristic aloofness to intervene and console her. He never touched his children in affection or in anger, but showing compassion for Winnie's distress laid the foundation of the close relationship they later developed. Winnie also basked in the attention of her uncle, Lamginya, who had declared her his favourite niece. He was a bus driver, and there was great excitement when he piled all the children into his bus and took them for a ride. Unlike their parents, he openly showed affection for the children, played with them and cuddled them.

When Winnie was six, she was enrolled at her father's school. She loved it from the start, was a good and eager pupil and excelled at her studies. Her father was pleased with her academic progress, and she flourished under his encouragement and support. Three years later, the Education Department transferred Columbus to eMbongweni. This meant that the family had to move, and Columbus sold the farm. Their new home was not far from the Great Place at Komkhulu, and all the pupils at the new school, along with all the residents of the village, were Madikizelas, members of the extended family created by Chief Mazingi, his twenty-nine wives and dozens of children. According to tradition, sons settled with their wives at the family home, and when a kraal became too large, a new one would be formed. The Madikizelas inhabited six of the twenty-six settlements in the Bizana district, and until she went to boarding school at the age of twelve, Winnie had no idea that there were people with surnames other than her own.

Life was different in eMbongweni. Without the farm as back-up, the family's standard of living deteriorated, their home was reduced to three rondavels, the number of cattle diminished and there were no longer farm labourers to help with the work. Columbus ploughed the land himself, helped by the children. The fact that Winnie was only nine years old made no difference. She was strong enough to work and had less homework than the older children, so she was up at dawn to help her father in the fields, and after breakfast they set off for school together. In the afternoons she led the oxen for Columbus as he ploughed, and helped him hoe. It was hard work for a little girl, but she never complained because she was developing a new relationship with her father, a closeness and comfortable collaboration that compensated for the lack of intimacy with her mother. She cherished the serenity and reassurance of their time together. 'We hardly spoke, but his gentle presence gave me support. It was as if God walked with me.'[2]

Columbus spared no effort to provide his family with a decent standard of living. He harvested honey from beehives he had set up in the forest, which Gertrude boiled and bottled, and they raised chicks and sold eggs. This provided another level of excitement – and education – for Winnie and her siblings. She and her sister Nonalithi took it in turn to monitor the temperature in the incubation room, and when it rose above a certain level they would run and fetch Columbus to adjust the settings.

Columbus was an intelligent man with a wide range of interests. Passionate about his people's history, he took great care to ensure that all his pupils learned about their heritage from the Pondo perspective. Sometimes he gathered all the children in the shade of a large tree, and told them of the events that had shaped the country and its people. He told them how fearless Xhosa warriors armed only with spears had fought against the guns and bullets of the white settlers to defend their land in the nine Xhosa wars – which their textbooks called the 'Kaffir Wars' – and explained that the black leaders who were portrayed as primitive savages in the history books had, in fact, been cunning strategists and courageous fighters. At times he would be so overcome with emotion while describing the prejudice and unfairness, he would have to leave the room to regain his composure. Winnie never forgot those lessons.

Columbus owned an impressive library of books ranging from *Aesop's Fables* and other fiction to encyclopaedias and reference works, and Winnie read them all. She loved reading and was always top of her class. At school she was quiet and submissive, and some classmates thought she was shy, but in her free time she was still a tomboy, full of fun and always laughing, fighting the boys at the drop of a hat. Her older sister, Nancy, was her shadow, and blindly followed Winnie into mischief. Winnie was indisputably the leader, increasingly showing her strong will and laying down the law, but she was also a compassionate child, quick to show concern and kindness. When some of her classmates had to stop going to school because their parents couldn't afford the fees, Winnie was extremely upset. Columbus and Gertrude had constantly taught their children the importance of education if they wanted to get anywhere in life. Winnie badgered Columbus until he paid the outstanding fees from his own small salary, and the children could return to class. Another time, when Winnie found out that a girl she knew was staying away from school because she had nothing to wear, she gave the child one of her own dresses. Columbus rewarded her selflessness by buying her a new dress – and another for the needy girl.

Winnie also benefited from her father's position as a tribal councillor. Columbus kept his family and other residents of eMbongweni in touch with the outside world through his frequent visits to Umtata for sessions of the Bunga. They also received regular updates on the progress of World War II whenever he went to Umtata or into Bizana on horseback. The children listened wide-eyed to tales of the terror wrought by the Nazis, the enormous battles in Europe and the bombings, though they could not imagine what any of this was like. Even in their remote corner of the country, they experienced the effects of the war. Many of the young men had joined the army, only to find that they were not allowed to carry guns. Nevertheless, they proudly showed off their smart uniforms when they came home on leave before sailing for Egypt. Some would not return – killed, ironically, while on active service, but unarmed. As the war dragged on, there were shortages of foodstuffs that everyone had always taken for granted, such as sugar, of which there sometimes was none for weeks on end. Even soap became scarce, a real calamity in Winnie's home where cleanliness was paramount. Gertrude immediately put the children to work collecting a herb from the hillsides, which she used to make a traditional soap called *inqubebe*.

Because there was no public transport, the children rarely visited Bizana. When they did go, it was on foot, with the entire family walking for a day and a night. It was an exhausting journey, and the children had to force themselves to keep going till they arrived, bone tired, at Granny's home at Ndunge, a kilometre outside Bizana. Ironically these visits, the highlight of their lives, were also the only times the children felt deprived, as they feasted their eyes on the unbelievable array of goods in the general dealers' stores: soft, colourful blankets, large rolls of cloth, sweets, clothes and dozens of other things that their parents could not afford to buy. Fortunately, as soon as they were back at home, these luxuries were forgotten.

Life was good for the Madikizelas. They were not wealthy, but they had enough of everything, and they were part of a close-knit community and a supportive and caring family. The children were secure in the knowledge that their parents, although strict, had their best interests at heart; Winnie was happy at school and enjoyed the untroubled life of a rural child. But her contentment was about to be shattered by a string of tragic events that started when her eldest sister, Vuyelwa, came home from boarding school with tuberculosis. With Vuyelwa's illness, Gertrude's prayers became more frequent and more intense. She begged God to make Vuyelwa well, but her daughter's condition steadily deteriorated, and with no treatment available for the disease and little information on how to deal with it, her chances of survival were slim.

Gertrude's desperate prayers were to no avail, and Vuyelwa died one Sunday after the family returned from church. Her passing severely shook Winnie's belief in her mother's God, who, it appeared, had paid no heed to Gertrude's desperate and frequent prayers.

Unbeknown to all of them, Gertrude – who never recovered from the shock of her daughter's death – was also ill. She had probably contracted tuberculosis during the long months of nursing Vuyelwa, and another pregnancy also took its toll, though it produced the youngest son Gertrude had longed for. As her health deteriorated, Winnie and Nancy took it in turns to stay home from school and nurse their mother, watching helplessly as she withered away.

Finally, during her illness, Gertrude reached out to Winnie, often calling her to sit beside the bed with the baby. Her eyes were sunken, dim and exhausted, and it seemed to Winnie that her mother was watching her and the baby in her arms as if she were already in another world. Sometimes, Gertrude would stretch out her hand to stroke the baby, but even that exhausted her. She told Winnie to lead a good, decent and honest life, and Winnie listened intently, memorising every precious word. Young as she was, she understood that this time with Gertrude was a treasure to be cherished. It didn't matter that she didn't understand all of Gertrude's instructions, she was simply happy to be finally forging a bond with her mother.

Gertrude's illness turned Columbus into a walking ghost. He sat with her for hours, then locked himself up with a pile of exercise books and worked until late at night. He retreated into his anguish, barely speaking to the children, and they thought he was avoiding them.

Vivid and painful images of Gertrude's dying did nothing to restore Winnie's faith. 'As I watched her lips move and her tear-drenched face, I hated that God who didn't respond to her and who instead came for her when she was breastfeeding a three-month baby boy – my brother Thanduxolo.'[3]

Still a child herself, Winnie had to prepare the wailing baby's bottles and try to comfort him, spending hours at night rocking and cuddling him, and trying to lull him to sleep with sugared water.

When Gertrude's last moments drew near, the elders gathered round her bed, and Winnie and Nancy sought refuge in another rondavel, clinging to one another in fear. Just before dawn, a bone-piercing shriek cut through their sleep, and their older sister Irene burst through the door, sobbing.

In keeping with tribal custom, relatives came from near and far, the outer walls of the Madikizela home were painted with black ochre and the windows smeared with white. Black funeral dresses were made for the children on their mother's sewing machine, and their heads were shaved. Bewildered and weeping much of the time, they could do nothing but watch the preparations for their mother's funeral. The whole district turned out for the occasion, and Winnie had never seen so many people. The church was too small and the service had to be held outdoors. All the children sat beside the coffin, which was draped in black. On it lay Gertrude's church uniform, folded as neatly as if she had done it herself.

The girls were crying bitterly, and Winnie thought their sorrow would never end. After the service the coffin was carried to the Madikizela family cemetery at the far end of Makhulu's garden, where all the graves were marked with simple white crosses. Winnie, shivering with dread, clung to Nancy, unable to watch as the casket containing her mother's body was lowered into the ground.

Two oxen and a number of sheep were slaughtered to feed the mourners. In a strangely hushed atmosphere, the family elders sat near the cattle kraal, heads bowed, while the women huddled and whispered on the grass.

Relatives came to assist Columbus with the care of the children and to help with the baby. They meant well, but had no idea how to run Gertrude's well-ordered home, and soon the household was chaotic. Columbus, stricken by his loss, didn't notice for a while, but as soon as he recovered from the initial grief and realised what a state his home and family were in, he immediately took action. It was almost unheard of for a Pondo father to bring up his own children, but he informed the family that this was his intention, and sent all the well-meaning relatives back to their own homes. The children took responsibility for tasks their mother had trained them to perform, and gradually Gertrude's orderly household was restored.

But their lives were changed forever. Nancy went to live with an aunt, Irene, and her brother Christopher returned to boarding school. Winnie remained at home with her younger siblings, the baby and her father. Columbus's sister had come to live with them to take care of the household, but Winnie still had to care for the baby.

If there was one positive consequence of the tragedy, it was that Columbus inevitably grew closer to his children. Winnie washed his clothes in the river and continued to help him with the farming. Acknowledging her support, he would bring her the *Farmer's Weekly* to read when there were articles relevant to their activities. When he had to go to Umtata for meetings of the Bunga, she missed him terribly. The other children would never entirely lose their awe of their father, but Winnie confided in him and turned to him for advice on everything. Columbus depended on her a great deal as well. With her older sisters away at school, Winnie assumed many of her mother's duties. The baby cried constantly and she tried her best to comfort him, fed him his bottle, rocked him to sleep and even took him and her youngest sister, Princess, along when she did her chores in the fields, carrying one on her back and the other in her arms.

Her days filled with adult responsibilities and chores, Winnie had little time to grieve for her mother. But at night, Gertrude's death haunted her in dreams and nightmares.

2

For whites only

THE NEWS THAT World War II had ended was brought to eMbongweni by a truck driver, who told the Madikizelas that there were big celebrations in the streets and town hall at Bizana. The children begged Columbus for permission to go and join in the merriment, and when he agreed they clambered onto the back of the truck, laughing and chattering with excitement.

But eMbongweni was sheltered from the realities of life in South Africa. To their shock and disappointment, they found the town hall doors barred, and were told the celebrations were for whites only. For Winnie, being shut out was like a physical blow to her stomach, but the children could do nothing except peer through the windows at the celebrations within. White children and their parents, wearing their Sunday best, were eating and drinking, celebrating to the music of a band. Uneasy about the black children looking longingly through the windows, some of the whites threw fruit and sweets onto the ground outside, and the children scurried to pick the treats up from the dirt.

It was Winnie's first experience of black–white relationships in South Africa. Deep in her mind she heard the echo of her father's words about the injustices towards blacks, and afterwards she began to notice that his neatly pressed suits and darned shirts were shabby in comparison with the clothes worn by white officials who came to the school. Reminded of the losses suffered by her people in the Xhosa wars and fired by youthful indignation, she made a resolution to start where her ancestors had left off, and get back her land.

Columbus's passionate lessons about Xhosa history stirred anger among his pupils and a determination to work for change – emotions that were the forerunner of their political consciousness. During music lessons, he taught the children rousing patriotic songs. One was about the founding of the African National Congress (ANC) in Bloemfontein in 1912, and Winnie remembered the words for years after she had left school.

Columbus also taught them other songs about the history of the Xhosa people, songs that had been written by traditional composers, and at home Winnie listened to the songs her brothers had learned from the elders about the contract workers who went to work on the mines, and their sadness at having to leave their homes and families behind.

Whites who mistook the dignity and respect of tribal blacks for docility and subservience could not have been more wrong. Increasingly, black parents were realising that their children had to be educated if they were to have a future in the changing world. This often required back-breaking sacrifices by black families, because education was neither compulsory nor free, as it was for whites. Nevertheless, many black parents were prepared to endure whatever hardship was required to pay for their children's education.

Winnie was fortunate that in her family an education was taken for granted, and the highlight of her existence continued to be the hours she spent at school. She took to heart her father's repeated admonitions on how important it was to have a proper education and, moreover, to speak fluent English. But when she was in Standard 6, the highest class at her father's school, her education was interrupted when Columbus told her he had been instructed by the department to close down the senior class because the school was overcrowded. With immediate effect, Standard 6 would become the responsibility of secondary schools, and Columbus's school would only offer classes up to Standard 5 in future. Winnie and all the other senior pupils would have to leave at once.

Winnie was distraught. It was March, close to the end of the first term, and all the secondary schools in Bizana and neighbouring Ndunge were full. Columbus decided Winnie could work on the lands until the start of the next school year. She was heartbroken, but would not have dreamed of questioning her father. Every day for the next nine months she walked the long distance to a little stream to fetch a drum of water for cooking and washing, returning with the container balanced on her head, a difficult feat learned at an early age by all young black girls in rural areas. Winnie also herded cattle and sheep, milked the cows, tended crops and helped with the heavy work of preparing the fields for planting. There was no division of labour on grounds of gender – in fact, black women traditionally performed the lion's share of manual labour, and still do, in rural areas. Winnie toiled industriously, waiting patiently for the year to pass until she could return to school and complete her education.

Luckily for her, Bantu Education – which was inferior in every way to that of the whites' – was not introduced until the early 1950s, and she thus received as sound an education as any white child at the time. The standards were high and all schools followed the same syllabus, with an emphasis on academic subjects such as Latin, English, chemistry, physics and mathematics. With the introduction of Bantu Education, standards for black children dropped dramatically, with fewer subjects being taught and with a more parochial focus. Pupils no longer learned about the outside world, and over time fewer blacks were taught to speak proper English.

Amid the demands of daily life, the trauma of Gertrude's death began to ebb, and her family gradually came to grips with the changes her loss had brought. Columbus struggled to feed and educate his nine children on a less than adequate salary, and worked hard to supplement his income from his farming enterprises. Between teaching and caring for his family, he had time for little else. But in their closed community it was inevitable that he, an attractive and educated man of influence and means, a man with status – and a widower to boot – would be noticed by the eligible women.

A new teacher, Miss Jane Zithutha, joined his school, and soon began to single Winnie out, spoiling her and giving her sweets. Then she started giving Winnie letters for Columbus. When Winnie told Makhulu, her grandmother nodded knowingly, deep in thought. Miss Zithutha rented a room about a kilometre from Winnie's home, and one day, without warning, Columbus asked Winnie to go and live with her, because she was lonely and uneasy about living alone. When Makhulu heard this, she again nodded knowingly.

But Miss Zithutha would not become Mrs Madikizela. Nature at its most terrifying would prevent that. One day, while a fierce storm was brewing, Makhulu told Winnie to fetch the cattle from the field. The clouds were darkening fast, and in the distance there was thunder and lightning. As Winnie approached the kraal, there was a resounding explosion and a blinding flash. She heard Miss Zithutha scream as the tree in front of her hut crashed and fell on the structure. Within seconds the hut was enveloped in an orange blaze. Columbus was running and shouting, trying to get water to put out the fire, but it was too late, and Miss Zithutha was dead.

With their lives having barely settled back into a pattern after the untimely deaths of Vuyelwa and Gertrude, the Madikizelas were once again plunged into tragedy, with conflict soon to follow. Despite embracing aspects of the Western way of life, centuries of tradition could not be discarded without cost, and the family did not escape intrigue and upheaval as modern influence clashed with tribal custom.

Winnie's brother Christopher, having completed his studies for a teacher's diploma, was teaching in the district. One day he arrived home unexpectedly, bringing with him what appeared to be a person, completely wrapped in a blanket. It was early in the morning, and he asked a startled Winnie to check whether his bedroom was clean and the bed made up. She did as he requested, neither protesting nor asking any questions. Then he asked her to stand guard in front of their father's room, and slipped the blanketed bundle into his own room. Winnie was asked to prepare food and to bring water for washing to the room, after which Christopher locked the door and left. Eerily, for the rest of the day no one said anything about the person locked in the room. Winnie suspected it was a woman, but couldn't ask anyone. That evening, Christopher came home with one of their uncles, and they disappeared into Columbus's room, where they talked for hours.

The next day, Christopher took the woman, still wrapped in the blanket, to another hut. Everyone pretended not to look, but Winnie caught a glimpse of a slender, fair hand. During the day a group of women went into the hut and hung a curtain, behind which the woman remained hidden for a week. During this time her relatives arrived, and had long meetings with the Madikizela elders. At the end of the week Winnie's uncle returned with representatives from the kraal of Chief Lumayi, and it finally emerged that it was his daughter in the hut. More shocking was the news that she and Christopher were already married, despite the strict convention that children did not marry without their parents' blessing.

Winnie was too young to be told why there had been no wedding, with the compulsory family tradition of a church ceremony and the bride in a white dress and veil. But there appeared little else to do except celebrate the strange marriage. An ox was slaughtered, and the young, very beautiful bride emerged from behind the curtain in a long green printed robe and elegant traditional headdress. She was fair skinned, as Gertrude had been, but Columbus appeared not entirely happy with the situation, and Christopher and his bride soon left and set up their own home. Winnie surmised that her father was probably upset because they had eloped and married without consulting him. Xhosa custom dictated that marriages be arranged by the tribal elders, and it was uncommon for young people to make their own decisions and arrangements. Some years later, when she was confronted with a similar situation, Winnie would be reminded of the dramatic circumstances surrounding her brother's marriage.

The family's bad fortune continued. An aunt fell ill, and although they nursed her lovingly, she died. Then Winnie's sister Irene took ill and was sent home from boarding school. She seemed possessed of strange spirits, wailing constantly and babbling unintelligibly while her body went into spasms. To prevent her from harming herself, her distressed family had to tie her to the bed.

Columbus, not knowing how to deal with his daughter's affliction, went to fetch the *inyanga* [witch doctor] Flathela, who was known to see and talk to witches, and could exorcise evil spirits. Flathela said Irene's problem was linked to the entire family. He put *muti* [protective charms] around the house, burned strange objects in Irene's room and ordered everyone to shave their heads. Placing the family in a semicircle formation, he made incisions on their cheeks and rubbed a black substance into the cuts. He pressed on Irene's head with the palm of his hand and spoke in a strange language. From the tone of his voice, he seemed to be pleading and scolding in turn. Then he beat Irene, who cried in a voice that was not her own until she collapsed and lay still, fast asleep. Flathela said he had exorcised the witches – and when Irene awoke, she was well.

Irene's affliction led to an unexpected reversal of Winnie's fortune. Columbus arranged for her to take her sister's place at the school in Ndunge, which was also where Granny lived, and during the school terms she stayed with her maternal grandparents.

In September, almost six months after her education had come to an abrupt halt, Winnie was back in the classroom, facing new challenges. She had fallen behind the other children, and was shocked to learn that her class was about to write revision tests in preparation for the year-end examinations. But she was not too disappointed by her results. There were 200 Standard 6 pupils at Ndunge, divided into three classes, and Winnie was placed fifty-eighth in her group of seventy-two. For the rest of the year she worked even more diligently, and two months later was one of only twenty-two pupils in her group to pass the final examinations. Winnie was overjoyed, as was Columbus, who knew better than most what odds she had overcome, and he slaughtered a sheep in her honour – something he had never done for any of his daughters before. Ever conscious of her mother's rejection, Winnie was deeply grateful for her father's recognition.

Now it was time for her to go to boarding school at Emfundisweni in Flagstaff, a hundred miles from home. Winnie packed two steel trunks that she would take with her, one containing her clothes, the other a considerable amount of food, which Makhulu said was a waste of money, but Columbus seemed deaf to her criticism.

It was the start of a new and exciting period in Winnie's life. For the first time she would have to wear shoes, and her father took her to Bizana to buy them, along with the black and white uniform she would wear at school. As she tried her shoes on for the first time, Winnie embarked on a lifelong fascination with clothes, even though wearing the new footwear was unexpectedly painful. Her feet, toughened by years of going barefoot in the veld, rebelled against confinement. For quite some time she experienced acute discomfort, discarding the shoes whenever she could to spare her aching feet. As a reward for her good marks, Columbus also bought her an overcoat. At home, the children wrapped themselves in blankets to keep warm.

The coat was far too large for her, but like most of the children she knew, she was used to wearing clothes that didn't fit properly. Limited resources forced parents to pass clothes down from one child to the next, and when they did buy something new, it was usually a few sizes too big to allow the child to grow into the garment and make it last as long as possible. Winnie treasured her coat and wore it for the next few winters, studiously ignoring other children's sniggers at her oversized apparel.

Inevitably, venturing into the outside world meant exposure to the racial discrimination that was the reality of life in South Africa. It was impossible to ignore and touched every facet of black people's lives. All the shops in Bizana, even those catering exclusively to the black population, were owned and run by whites, and customers from the outlying areas might walk for a day or more to reach them. Some of the Pondo tribesmen rode into Bizana on horseback, proud and erect; while others made the long journey on foot, walking for a day or more, their wives often toting a baby nestled snugly on their backs, other children in tow. They arrived tired, hungry and covered in dust, but there was nowhere in Bizana for them to refresh themselves, nowhere they could sit down and have a meal, not even an outdoors area where the exhausted travellers could rest their feet. White arrogance made no allowances for the dignity, wisdom and practical experience of people from other cultures. It took many decades before whites even began to grasp that some of the blacks they treated with such disdain were people of stature in their own communities, where they were respected, even revered. The tribesmen were dignified people, and when they went to town the men tended to their business, met in small groups in the street to exchange news and share views; while their wives talked and gossiped with one another before setting out, once more, on the long journey home.

After shopping for her new clothes, Winnie and her father went to buy food at one of the stores. It was crowded with Pondo tribesmen wrapped in colourful traditional blankets. As Winnie waited for Columbus to be served, she noticed a tribesman buying a loaf of bread, some sugar and a cold drink, which he took to share with his wife, who was trying in vain to soothe her wailing baby. Clearly exhausted, the woman sat down on the floor in a corner of the store and put the baby to her breast. The man squatted on his haunches next to her and broke off pieces of bread for them to eat. Without warning, the white youth who was serving Columbus started shouting and charged at the man and his wife in the corner. He yelled at them to get out, that he wouldn't have *kaffirs* making a mess in his shop, and kicked at them and their food.

Winnie was appalled. She fully expected the shop owners, apparently the boy's parents, to intervene, but they just laughed. The buzz of conversation died abruptly, and no one uttered a word. Winnie looked expectantly at her father, who always spoke out strongly against any wrongdoing. Surely he would say something?

But Columbus, too, was silent. He had taught all his children to respect others and to have pride in their race, and Winnie could see that he was deeply disturbed at the humiliation meted out to his kinsman, so she could not understand why he said nothing. Only in later years, once she understood the complex dynamics of the relationship between the races, did she realise that had her father spoken, he might have made the situation worse.

The incident left an indelible impression on Winnie and made her aware, for the first time, that her father was fallible. In time, she would recognise that one of apartheid's by-products was that from an early age, black children saw their parents and families humiliated without making any attempt to protest or defend themselves. For children from families who taught them respect and compassion for fellow human beings, this was confusing. They could not understand why their parents were so often treated so shabbily by whites, and parents were at a loss to explain that they had done nothing to deserve such treatment, meted out on no other basis but the colour of their skin. It was an injustice that created an entire nation of people who expected to be victimised and brutalised, and in the long term cowered and did almost anything to avoid situations that might lead to humiliation and punishment, accepting servility as the norm. The pent-up frustration of generations would reach breaking point in Soweto in 1976 – but that was a long way off, and twelve-year-old Winnie Madikizela could not even begin to imagine her role in the future South Africa.

In January, with beating heart, she boarded a bus in the company of other children on their way to Flagstaff. She spent three years at Emfundisweni, where the only diversion from her studies was a flirtation with the idea of having a boyfriend. All the girls in her class wrote notes to the boys they liked, but there was no physical contact, and the relationships were confined to furtive glances exchanged in church.

Bit by bit, Winnie's character was taking shape. Outwardly, she was still an unsophisticated country girl, but her parents had laid a solid ground for her development: Gertrude, with her strict religious morality and uncompromising discipline; Columbus, by sharing his passion for acquiring knowledge and skills, through his pride in his people, and by his example of compassion and assistance for those in their community who were in need.

Not surprisingly, she passed her junior certificate (Standard 8) with distinction, and when she went home for the holidays Columbus surprised her with news of his ambitious plans for her. It had been clear to him for some time that Winnie possessed both the ability and motivation for further study, and he was pondering the best route for her to follow. Initially, he wanted her to go to Fort Hare University, but a nephew who had studied there warned against it. He said there were too few female students, with the result that the young men were always pursuing them, and it was not the right place for Winnie. So, mindful of her natural compassion for others, Columbus decided on the Hofmeyr School of Social Work in Johannesburg, the only institution that trained black social workers. But Winnie had two more years of school to complete, and she would have to do even better than before in order to be accepted as a student.

Those years would be spent further afield at Shawbury, a Methodist mission school at Qumbu. Like many of the other pupils, Winnie would become politicised there. The teachers were all Fort Hare graduates and members of the Non-European Unity Movement (NEUM), and Winnie was strongly influenced by their philosophy. She had also read about the ANC in *Zonk* magazine.

Not surprisingly, her favourite teacher was a lot like Columbus, and taught his pupils about the struggle for equality in much the same way that Columbus had taught history. The two men shared a high regard for the Germans, and Winnie's teacher venerated Bismarck. He would make his way down the long corridor to the senior classroom bellowing: 'The unification of Germany, Bismarck believed, could not be attained through parliamentary speeches and debates, but by means of b-l-o-o-d and iron.'[1] He always reached the classroom as he got to 'b-l-o-o-d', and entered to gales of laughter from the pupils.

The struggle in South Africa, he taught, was no different. Winnie left Shawbury convinced that her people would win their freedom only by means of blood and iron. While she hated the name Winifred, she thought the diminutive, Winnie, would serve as a constant reminder of her people's oppression, and spur her to action for change.

Shawbury also saw the start of Winnie's development into the striking woman who would capture the heart of more than one of South Africa's most prominent men. Sometimes, however, her blossoming beauty drew unwelcome attention. The first time this happened was on a school outing to Tsolo. The bus stopped at Flagstaff, and the pupils were stretching their legs when one of Winnie's friends pointed out that a dwarf was staring at her. He approached her and asked if she knew how pretty she was. Winnie was dumbstruck and had no idea how to react, but when he gave her a 10-shilling note and said it was the first instalment for her lobola [bride price], she was near panic. Before he left, he told her she would be his wife as soon as she was fully grown. Afterwards, her friends told her the man was called Khotso, that he was wealthy and something of a legend in the district, and already had many wives. Winnie was mortified but her friends laughed, and then helped her spend the money.

The next such encounter was far more serious, and affected her schoolwork so badly that she slipped from the top of her class to thirteenth place, something that had never happened before. Her distress was exacerbated when Columbus issued a reprimand for her poor performance, and threatened that his plans for her would have to be abandoned if she didn't pull up her socks. She ached to tell him the root of her problem, but was too ashamed. The trouble was that she looked older than her fifteen years, and was sometimes even mistaken for a teacher. The assistant principal had noticed the tall, slender young woman, and began making advances to her. As head prefect, it was Winnie's job to fetch the keys to the bookcases from him, and one day he pressed a tightly rolled cash note into her hand. She felt so humiliated that she burst into tears. When he continued giving her money, she decided to confide in her fellow head prefect, Ezra Malizo Ndamase, who was also supposed to be her boyfriend, though this meant little more than working together on some school projects and sharing their duties as prefects. When Winnie told Ezra what had happened, she started crying, and a bewildered Ezra was too embarrassed to comfort her. He never said a word about the matter, and Winnie regretted having told him.

The assistant principal taught three subjects to Winnie's class, and she found it impossible to concentrate on any of them. Disappointed by Ezra's reaction, she did not want to tell any of her other classmates, and dared not confide in her father or the matron, Mrs Mtshali. The matron was something of a martinet who regularly inspected the girls, and if she found anything untoward, would make the offender lie naked on the floor and beat her with a whip. Winnie was forced to help her strip the girls and found the duty mortifying, thinking it a shameful way to treat a girl. She had no doubt that if she told Mrs Mtshali about the money she would be accused of encouraging the teacher, and be beaten, naked, on the floor as well. The disgrace would be harder to bear than the pain, so she kept the awful secret to herself.

Generally, though, life at Shawbury was stimulating and challenging. Winnie was popular with her peers, partly because she was always willing to help them where she could. One of her school friends, Nomawethu Mbere, would later recall how Winnie, having abandoned her youthful rebellion against religion, took the lead in organising their church attendance on Sundays. Nomawethu looked up to Winnie, whom she saw as reserved, even introvert, but with obvious leadership qualities and a remarkable talent for disciplining other pupils. Winnie was two classes ahead of Nomawethu but regularly helped the younger girls with their assignments, so much so that one teacher admonished Nomawethu for being too far ahead in the curriculum, thanks to Winnie's coaching.

Shawbury was one of a number of mission schools in the Transkei run by various religious denominations. When the National Party government introduced its Bantu Education programme, most of these schools closed down rather than apply the lower standards. But many of the young blacks of Winnie's generation emerged from the mission schools well equipped to make their mark in both South African society and the liberation struggle.

Had there been any scholarships for blacks, Winnie would undoubtedly have been an excellent candidate for one, but Columbus had to pay all her tuition fees from his sparse income. It was a huge financial burden, but he was determined that she would get a decent education. His daughter Nancy noticed that he was struggling, and made a personal sacrifice on Winnie's behalf. The two sisters had always been close, and after their mother's death the bond between them deepened even more. Nancy shared their father's confidence in Winnie, and she left school and began to take casual jobs that brought in a small amount of money. Most of it went to Winnie for pocket money, and as soon as she was able, Winnie repaid Nancy's generosity by sending her the fare to Johannesburg and arranging for her to train as a nurse at the Bridgeman Memorial Hospital.

After the National Party came to power in 1948, South Africa found itself increasingly in the stranglehold of Afrikaner nationalism. Laws drafted with the sole intent of segregating black and white were rushed through parliament, provoking an inevitable backlash from an outraged black community. The early 1950s were momentous years in South African politics, and Winnie was at Shawbury in 1951 and 1952. It was not her marriage to Nelson Mandela that made Winnie an activist, but the germination of seeds planted many years earlier by her father and teachers.

At Shawbury, she made her first acquaintance with political debate. Some of the teachers belonged to the Society of Young Africa, the so-called Conventionists, a theoretical, academic organisation that held no appeal for ordinary people, but was greatly admired by the senior pupils, who had no contact with any other political movement.

Their political awareness shifted into higher gear in 1952, when a young lawyer named Nelson Mandela – who was rapidly emerging as a leader in the liberation struggle – orchestrated what became known as the Defiance Campaign. Winnie and her friends knew all about this legend in the making, and about other ANC leaders whom they idolised, sang songs and talked about for hours. The campaign was to be a non-violent protest against the 'Europeans Only' signs in public areas such as post offices and railway stations, and against the newly introduced pass laws and urban curfews for blacks. Anyone taking part was inviting arrest, and many chose imprisonment over bail or an admission of guilt fine.

At Shawbury, the pupils gushed with pride and excitement when they read in *Zonk* and *Drum*, popular magazines among blacks, that 8 500 people were prepared to flout the discriminatory laws. Of those, 8 000 were arrested. Some of the Shawbury pupils decided that they, too, wanted to defy authority by boycotting their classes, citing inadequate facilities and unsatisfactory hostel conditions.

Winnie found herself in a predicament. Her final examinations were looming, and mindful of the sacrifices Columbus and Nancy had made on her behalf, she knew her first obligation was to complete her education. As head prefect she was also expected to help maintain discipline, and although her sympathies lay with her fellow pupils, she showed a wisdom and maturity way beyond her years, and decided she would not take part in the boycott.

The Shawbury 'uprising' made news throughout the country, with newspapers carrying front-page pictures of protesting girls in school uniforms. The fact that schoolchildren had become involved in the protests sparked an outcry from whites, and caused outrage and consternation among the authorities, who were already uneasy about the Defiance Campaign. The Education Department acted ruthlessly and expelled a large number of pupils. Only those due to write the matriculation exams, and who were not among the agitators, were allowed to remain at school. The rest were told to reapply for admission in the new year.

Winnie left Shawbury with a first-class pass, and when she arrived home for the holidays learned the happy news that after six years as a widower, Columbus had decided to marry again. Winnie's new stepmother was an unmarried school-mistress, Hilda Nophikela, who was warm and kind and welcomed into the family by all the Madikizela children. A special bond developed between Winnie and Hilda, but Makhulu was far from impressed. She refused to go and meet her son's bride-to-be, insisting that Hilda should come to her – clearly intending to slight the newcomer. She told the children bitingly that Hilda was interested only in Columbus's money, and would take what was rightfully their inheritance. Hilda refused to be drawn into the conflict and went to Makhulu's house as ordered, wearing her veil. It was tradition to slaughter a beast in honour of the meeting, but Makhulu shocked the family by halting the ceremony, declaring that this union did not warrant the ritual slaughter of an animal.

For the first time, Winnie and her siblings realised that their strong-willed grandmother's troubled relationship with their mother had little or nothing to do with Gertrude, and everything to do with Makhulu's prejudices and preconceptions.

Fortunately, the unpleasantness was soon pushed into the background as Winnie and her family became caught up in planning for her further studies in Johannesburg. She adored and trusted her father, accepting without question that he had made the right choices for her, and was confident that she was ready to step into the adult world.

She was, in fact, already a quite remarkable young woman. Columbus had sown the seeds of political awareness and concern for others, but it was the female members of her family that had shaped her other traits. From Makhulu she inherited an imperious dignity, and from Granny, her strict adherence to hygiene and love of beautiful clothes. Gertrude had moulded the basis of her faith, tenacity and strength of character, and her Aunt Phyllis, a teacher who had studied at Fort Hare, would play an important role in her future.

Her mother's sister was the first secretary of the Young Women's Christian Association (YWCA), and while Winnie saw little of her during childhood, they would form a strong bond once Winnie went to Johannesburg. She even lived with Aunt Phyllis on the East Rand for a time.

By the age of eighteen, Winnie had been exposed to controversy, conflict and tragedy, and already understood the need to be both tough and caring. As an adult, those qualities would expand into grace, empathy, charisma and great courage.

3

The magical city of gold

THE FIRST APARTHEID GOVERNMENT'S Bantu Education system was designed to trap South Africa's black population in subservience, and to institutionalise impoverished minds and stunt metaphysical growth. It restricted their teaching syllabus, placing the emphasis on subjects that would qualify pupils for unskilled labour: agriculture, gardening, woodwork, domestic service.

Academic subjects were systematically whittled out of the curriculum, and for decades after the introduction of the Bantu Education Act in 1953, black school leavers were equipped to be little more than carriers of water and hewers of wood. The government's intent was spelled out clearly by Dr Hendrik Verwoerd, minister in charge of Bantu Education at the time and later prime minister: 'There is no place for the Bantu in the European [i.e. white South African] community above the level of certain forms of labour. Racial relations cannot improve if the result of Native [i.e. black] education is the creation of frustrated people who, as a result of the education they receive, have expectations in life which circumstances in South Africa do not allow to be fulfilled immediately.'

Winnie was fortunate enough to escape this fate, matriculating two years before the introduction of Bantu Education. As the law that would condemn millions of blacks to a wholly inferior education was being debated in parliament, she was embarking on the journey that would qualify her as a social worker.

For the first time in her life she would travel beyond the small, dusty towns of the Transkei, armed with a knowledge of the outside world acquired from her father and his books, her love of reading newspapers, and her teachers. Going to Johannesburg, South Africa's biggest city, was a breathtaking adventure, and during the December holidays there was a steady flow of relatives visiting with advice. Winnie had to sit, eyes respectfully downcast, listening patiently, as the older women – most of whom had never ventured out of Bizana – warned her of the dangers in eGoli – the City of Gold. They urged her to beware of strangers, and to be especially wary of *tsotsis* [gangsters], who were a danger to unsuspecting young girls. Nancy made faces and giggled behind her hand while Winnie tried her best to keep a straight face, although in reality she was growing more impatient by the day to shake off the dust of the familiar and venture into the unknown. Makhulu grumbled that Winnie had enough of an education and had no need to go to Johannesburg. Why could she not stay at home like other girls?

The tribal elders cautioned Winnie not to forget Pondoland, and to live according to the proud traditions of her people. When they were alone, Columbus assured Winnie that there was nothing to be concerned about. He had organised everything and showed her the letters from the college and the Helping Hand Hostel, where he had arranged for her to live. The hostel was in Hans Street, Jeppe, close to the city centre and far from the overcrowded black townships where crime was rife.

Winnie had never been on a train or at a railway station, however, and Columbus was concerned about her safety on the overnight journey to Johannesburg – afraid that men with less than honourable intentions might accost her. Fortunately, two of their tribesmen, Moses and Jeremiah, migrant labourers on the gold mines, were travelling to Johannesburg on the same train, and Columbus asked them to take care of Winnie.

On the day of their departure, Winnie followed her two escorts to the crowded third-class carriages reserved for blacks. They pushed and shoved until they found an empty space on one of the hard, wooden seats. Winnie squeezed in next to the window and arranged her cooked mealies, fruit and cold tea – refreshments for the journey. Meals were served in the comfortable first- and second-class carriages that had separate compartments for between two and six people, but these were ominously marked 'Europeans Only'. Black passengers in the dirty and uncomfortable third-class coaches had to provide their own food, or go without.

On the platform, Columbus maintained his stoic dignity while he said his farewells, but Nancy was openly weeping. Winnie shed no tears while waving to her father and sister as the train jerked and began to move slowly away from the station. She had inherited her father's self-restraint, and she was excited. As the train gathered speed she sat quietly, wondering what lay ahead. Faster and faster, the train rushed past all that was familiar, heading for a strange place that was nothing but a legend.

There wasn't much time for reverie, however. Moses and Jeremiah began to tell her about life in the city and the black townships, the hardship of the miners who lived in hostel compounds, the lack of privacy and family life, the puny wages. Winnie was perturbed by what she heard. At home she had seen how the migrant labour system disrupted families, leaving wives to take care of homes and children on their own, often eking out a living from the land without any financial support, while husbands and fathers struggled to survive on the mines. She considered writing to her father and asking him to discourage men from going off to work on the mines, but realised they had little choice. There was widespread poverty in the Transkei, and for many men there was no other way of paying the compulsory taxes.

As night fell, the passengers tried to make themselves as comfortable as possible on the hard benches, and the carriage grew quiet as they drifted off to sleep. At daybreak, Winnie was surprised to see that the countryside through which the train was passing was flat and uniformly brown, except for the occasional splash of green. With images of the rolling emerald hills of Pondoland still fresh in her mind's eye, she was disappointed by the anticlimax of the Transvaal landscape. Even the sky was different – not the bright, brilliant blue she was used to, but a muted blue-grey. In a moment of panic Winnie thought she would never be able to stay in this ugly place. Little could she know that, in time, she would love it even more than the Transkei.

As the train crawled slowly towards the city, Moses and Jeremiah pointed out large, yellow sandy hills in the distance – Johannesburg's landmark mine dumps. After the gold was extracted from the crushed rock, the remaining slag was poured around the mines, forming man-made mountains. On the outskirts of the city, the dumps towered high above the train like the walls of a fortress, golden and formidable. Behind them lay the uneven skyline, etched against a backdrop of muffled sunlight and pale blue sky.

Moses and Jeremiah said goodbye and left Winnie on the platform, a bewildered country girl with her luggage balanced on her head, surrounded by a noisy, jostling crowd. Soon, two white women found her and introduced themselves as Mrs Phillips and Mrs Frieda Hough. Mrs Phillips was the wife of Professor Ray Phillips, head of the Jan Hofmeyr School of Social Work, while Mr Hough was a lecturer and the fieldwork director at the school. Mrs Phillips reassured Winnie that although Johannesburg might seem frightening at first, she would soon settle down once she met the other students. Winnie, whose only previous experience of whites had been hostility and condescension, was pleasantly surprised by the warmth of the two American women. Mrs Phillips and her husband were Congregational Church missionaries, while Mrs Hough, a social worker herself, was the daughter of missionaries. She had married an Afrikaner, Michiel Hough, one of a small number of whites who did not support apartheid and who later became a professor and head of the sociology department at Fort Hare. The Hofmeyr School was the only one of its kind in South Africa, and had been established in 1943 to train social workers to support the black South African troops in North Africa during World War II. After the war the school was turned into a college for training black social workers, but Winnie was the first student from a rural area.

The two women drove their charge to the Helping Hand Hostel. It was a weekday, and although still early morning the streets were alive with people, traffic and noise. For Winnie, it was love at first sight. In an instant she knew that this was where she belonged, among the fashionably dressed throngs, the cars and the imposing buildings.

The hostel had been set up by the Congregationalist American Board to offer safe and alternative accommodation to domestic workers, who often lived in tiny rooms in the backyard of their employers' homes. In time, teachers and nurses also came to live there, and a section was reserved for students such as Winnie, who would stay in the hostel for the next four years. The authorities waged a constant battle to move the facility out of the white residential area into one of the black townships, but this would only happen some years later.

After Mrs Phillips and Mrs Hough had settled her into her new home, some of the other students took Winnie into the city to show her around. She was mesmerised by the elegant shop window displays, especially the beautiful clothes and shoes. But she also realised that just beyond the glamorous façade, the ugly face of poverty cast a dark shadow over the city. For the first time in her life she saw beggars on the streets, some blind or crippled, huddled in hopeless bundles on the sidewalks, dressed in rags, hands outstretched for coins from passers-by. All the beggars were black.

Despite the marked contrast to her life in Bizana, Winnie adapted quickly to her new surroundings. Hostel life suited her, being used to an extended family and years at boarding school. She soon made friends and began to copy the examples they set.

Many of the girls used cosmetics, creams and fragrant toiletries, sleeping in nightdresses and slipping into dressing gowns in the morning. Winnie slept in her petticoat and dressed as soon as she arose. The other girls routinely dressed, undressed and showered in front of one another, but at first Winnie's decorous upbringing prevented her from doing the same. Gradually her roommate, Sarah Ludwick, who was slightly older, introduced her to modern underwear and sanitary products, comfortable pyjamas and sheer nightgowns, high-heeled shoes and elegant dresses.

The hostel was comfortable, companionable and centrally situated, and Winnie realised she was privileged compared with the vast majority of black women in Johannesburg. Rural women worked hard and lacked many comforts, but they were relatively protected, shielded by tradition and convention from the demands and challenges of cities divided by apartheid. Live-in domestic workers were separated from their families, while factory workers endured harsh conditions. From conversations with the working women living in the hostel, Winnie learned that black women in the city all had two things in common: long hours and pitiful salaries. As weeks turned into months, Winnie began to understand more fully her father's commitment to teaching his pupils about the injustices inflicted on black South Africans. She wrote long letters to Columbus, questioning the fairness of a system that allowed whites to live in comfortable homes set in elegant suburbs, while blacks were crowded into neglected townships, denied the right to live and work where they pleased, or enjoy the many benefits reserved for whites alone. When Columbus replied, it was to remind her to focus on her studies, and that politics was not for girls.

But Winnie found it impossible to ignore the rising tide of black politics. Most of the students at the Hofmeyr School were members of the ANC, and they often discussed among themselves the struggle against racial discrimination. The ANC was actively organising, and there was growing support for a black trade union movement, though it would be thirty years before one was recognised. Torn between a desire to become actively involved in the political movement and the need to fulfil her father's expectations, Winnie concentrated on her studies, using whatever spare time she had to read and learn about political developments. Her father had paid her tuition fees for the first six months in advance, but if she performed well enough she might be considered for a scholarship, which would greatly ease the financial burden on Columbus. Nancy, too, was working hard to help pay for Winnie's education, stripping the bark from wattle trees in her father's plantation and selling it to a white man from a tannery in Durban. Trade in the bark, used in shoemaking, was illegal, but the little money Nancy made provided Winnie with much-needed money for books, stationery and personal items. Nancy also sent Winnie her first pretty dresses after Winnie wrote and told her that her clothes were totally unsuitable for city life. She sent some pictures torn from magazines to illustrate what was fashionable, and Nancy immediately bought material from the local store. She asked their cousin, Nomazotsho Malimba, who was a dressmaker, to make clothes for Winnie like those in the pictures.

When she was awarded the Martha Washington bursary, things changed for the better, and Winnie threw herself with abandon into activities offered by the college. She proved especially good at netball, shot put, javelin and softball, and earned a host of nicknames: 'Steady but Sure', 'Commando Round' and 'Pied Piper', referring in turn to her round face and long nose; and 'The Amazon Queen' and 'Lady Tarzan' because she solved many problems using her physical strength. She also joined the Gamma Sigma Club and met students from the University of the Witwatersrand, St Peter's Seminary and the Wilberforce College.

Winnie's closest friends were Marcia Pumla Finca and Harriet Khongisa, while Ellen Kuzwayo, an older student, assumed the role of chaperone, protecting the younger girls from unwelcome male attention. Ellen would later become a well-known social worker, political activist and writer, but as students the four were inseparable. Together they took cookery lessons at the sprawling old Wemmer complex, run by the Johannesburg city council, where blacks traded traditional herbs, clothing, foodstuffs and traditional drinks. Winnie also learned to dance, joined a choir and attended Non-European Unity Movement meetings at a hall in Doornfontein. She realised just how much she had grown when Professor Phillips invited her to a dinner for a group of American professors who were visiting South Africa, and wanted to meet 'the rural student' they had heard was adapting successfully to city life and doing well in her studies. She talked to the American academics and answered their many questions in perfect English, and after dinner they expressed their disappointment to Professor Phillips that 'the rural student' had not been present. They were more than a little surprised to learn that the unsophisticated tribal girl they had been expecting was, in fact, the eloquent young woman they had met. This was Winnie's first exposure to Western prejudices about Africa, and she was both proud to have been taken for a city girl and shocked to realise that people from abroad assumed everyone from the rural areas to be raw and unrefined.

Though she still thought of herself as a country girl, Winnie certainly did not believe that this automatically made her backward or in any way inferior, and her intelligence, enthusiasm and the compassion she brought to field projects soon gained her recognition as the school's star pupil.

Practical experience was a key component of the social work course, and Winnie's first assignment was at the Salvation Army home for delinquent girls, Mthutuzeni. Where Winnie came from there was no such thing as a delinquent girl. Some were more challenging than others, yes, but none had real problems with their parents or would have dared to run away from home to make their own way. But the girls at Mthutuzeni all came from broken homes or were orphans. They suffered from depression, were argumentative, and some were totally uncontrollable and confused, with no sense of their place in the world. Winnie found that she could get through to some of them, not by applying the theory of social work she had been taught, but by getting them involved in sport, and her first practical course ended successfully.

Winnie was easy-going, and her warmth and sunny nature helped her to make friends easily. Many of the friendships she formed during her early years in Johannesburg would remain intact for decades. The other students often teased her for not having a boyfriend, but photographers soon discovered her beauty. They often visited the hostel in search of pretty models for 'glamour shots' in the popular magazines aimed at black readers. She became a firm favourite and was frequently asked to pose for the cameras. She saw her participation as a bit of fun, but one of those who photographed her was Peter Magubane, who would become an acclaimed lensman and a lifelong friend.

Winnie had been in Johannesburg for some months before she first went to Soweto. The sprawling township's name was a contraction of South-Western Townships, of which there were twenty-six, with a combined population of more than a million people. She and some friends made the twenty-five-kilometre trip in a bus, and Winnie's introduction to the vast and unattractive place that she would grow to love and call home, was a shock. The Helping Hand Hostel was in Jeppe, a clean, safe suburb, with electricity and street lights that came on after dark. Late-afternoon Soweto, and the area around as far as the eye could see, lay under a grey cloud of smoke from thousands of fires. There was no electricity in most of the township, and people cooked on open fires, or on coal or paraffin stoves. There was a pervading odour of kerosene in the air, and the dirt roads were riddled with potholes. It was growing dark, and the blackness spread unhindered, cloaking row upon row of identical matchbox houses. Some sections of Soweto were less squalid than others, but the majority of residents lacked not only comfort, but also the basic amenities. Some of the tiny houses sat proudly in minute gardens with neatly tended flower and vegetable beds, and inside they were clean and surprisingly cosy, the odd piece of good furniture polished to a soft gleam. When Winnie's work took her into the townships later, she was filled with respect and admiration for the courageous efforts of the residents to create homes from such inhospitable surroundings.

Gradually, Winnie was beginning to understand what lay at the heart of black political aspirations, but apart from attending a few meetings of the Trotskyist Unity Movement with her brother, she avoided getting actively involved. Nelson Mandela was the patron of Hofmeyr College, and the school's motto was 'Know Thyself'. The students, including Winnie, came to associate this concept with his name. The hostel residents introduced Winnie to the ANC's slogans and literature, as well as the idea of a trade union movement. Invariably, the names of Nelson Mandela, Oliver Tambo and Duma Nokwe were mentioned, along with that of the ANC president, Chief Albert Luthuli.

Johannesburg was exciting beyond Winnie's wildest expectations. The political undercurrent created an atmosphere of breathless anticipation, as though the world was poised to undergo great change. The ANC was the star player in this unfolding drama, holding protest meetings and endless debates about the aims and success of a policy of peaceful protest. Many of the organisation's followers disagreed with the passive approach, which the government flatly ignored, and demanded action. Winnie discovered daily newspapers and became an avid reader – as were her fellow students and residents – of the *Rand Daily Mail*, seen as a 'liberal' white newspaper. Another favourite was the black newspaper *Golden City Post*, which was soon to be banned.

In 1955, excitement mounted with preparations for the Congress of the People. Meetings were held across the country, delegates were appointed, and the people's grievances and demands recorded. The National Action Council invited all interested organisations to submit suggestions for inclusion in a freedom charter with the following message: 'We call upon the people of South Africa, black and white – let us speak together of freedom! Let the voices of all the people be heard. And let the demands of all the people for the things that will make us free be recorded. Let the demands be gathered together in a great charter of freedom.'

The congress took place on 25 and 26 June 1955. It was a massive gathering at Kliptown, outside Johannesburg, and people from all levels of society were represented by the 3 000 delegates. The overwhelming majority were black, but there were more than 300 Indian representatives, 200 coloureds and 100 whites. It was a vibrant, colourful event. Women wore Congress skirts, blouses and scarves, the men Congress armbands and hats. No one took any notice of the dozens of policemen and Security Branch members taking notes and jotting down names. The Charter was read section by section, and adopted by acclamation. On the afternoon of the second day, as the final vote of approval was to be taken, dozens of policemen suddenly swooped, pushing people off the stage and confiscating every document and piece of paper they could lay their hands on. They even confiscated the signs advertising 'SOUP WITH MEAT' and 'SOUP WITHOUT MEAT'. A police officer announced that they suspected treason, and that no one was to leave without permission. While the police interviewed each delegate in turn, the rest loudly and jubilantly sang 'Nkosi Sikelel' iAfrika'.

Despite the government's orders that the congress be broken up, it was a landmark event in the political struggle and sent out a clear call for change. It was also the first and last gathering of its kind for forty years. Increasingly stringent legislation prohibited a repeat of such cooperation until the early 1990s, but the Freedom Charter survived as the blueprint for a future, democratic South Africa, and immortalised the maxim: 'South Africa belongs to all who live in it, black and white.' It was a moderate, non-inflammatory document, but the government nonetheless declared it a criminal offence to publish copies. For the ANC, the Freedom Charter was the equivalent of the American Declaration of Independence, and throughout the liberation struggle the organisation remained loyal to its objectives.

In their final year at Hofmeyr College, students had to do practical fieldwork. Winnie was sent to the Ncora Rural Welfare Centre at Tsolo in the Transkei, run by a Mr Zici, himself a graduate of the college. The centre served a large, poverty-stricken community south of Pondoland, as well as Tsolo – the area from which Nelson Mandela came. It was also the seat of Chief Kaiser Matanzima's royal kraal. Before going to Tsolo, Winnie went home on holiday. At the end of her break, Professor Hough and his wife unexpectedly arrived at the Madikizela home. They had made the long journey from Johannesburg, and then to Tsolo, to ensure that Hofmeyr College's star pupil was well settled. The conspicuous arrival of the white couple in a smart car caused quite a commotion in the community, especially when it emerged that they had come to fetch Winnie, but she took it in her stride. Columbus's love and confidence had equipped her to grow into a self-assured young woman of whom her father was immensely proud.

She enjoyed the assignment at Tsolo, felt at home in the rural environment, and was excited about the centre's involvement in farming and in organising communal markets where people brought their produce for barter. She also attended tribal meetings – an exceptional honour, because women were traditionally excluded from such meetings, but Winnie was admitted because she was a social worker. The meetings were held at Qamata, the Great Place of KD Matanzima, in a large hall that could accommodate 1 000 people at a time, and was always full.

She met both Kaiser Matanzima and his brother George, a generous man whom she found friendly and hospitable. From his successful legal practice he dispensed free advice to needy people, and often made his car – the only one in the area – available for the use of others. His generosity extended to money matters, and he had earned a reputation for donating substantial amounts to worthy causes.

Winnie encountered heart-wrenching poverty at Tsolo. She had grown up among poor peasants, but had never seen such hardship. There was widespread malnutrition and large numbers of small children died as a result. Frustratingly, she could do little to alleviate the suffering, which reinforced her belief that dramatic social change was needed in South Africa.

Towards the end of her term in Tsolo, Winnie was doing paperwork in her office at the Welfare Centre when an elderly woman, who was visiting from Bizana, came by to see her. After the usual greetings, the old woman asked Winnie whether she was pleased about the marriage.

'What marriage?' Winnie asked, puzzled.

The old woman laughed slyly. 'They are arranging for you to marry Chief Ququali's son, the one who is at Lovedale College.'

Winnie was crushed. No one had mentioned any such plan when she was at home before going to Tsolo, nor since. She knew the chief belonged to the same royal house as Mandela and the Matanzimas, but no matter how beneficial marriage into so prominent a clan would be, Winnie knew that her father would not have made such a decision without telling her. She had never even met the young man in question, so how had the chief decided she would be a suitable future daughter-in-law? Almost certainly, in line with tradition, the tribal elders had arranged this marriage, in which case Columbus would have no choice but to respect their decision. But Winnie saw herself as an emancipated woman and could not conceive of having such an archaic custom imposed on her. Her mind was filled with the prospect of returning to Johannesburg and starting a career as a social worker. She had not studied for three years to be trapped in an unwanted and loveless marriage to a stranger. Quite possibly she would be one of several wives, stranded and isolated in the rural Transkei for the rest of her life. She knew only too well that rural wives were expected to be servile and accept all the restrictions imposed on them, and refused even to consider such a life for herself.

Winnie realised that it would serve no purpose to appeal to Columbus, and that if she stayed in Tsolo she would be abducted and forced into the marriage. The chief's Tembu tribesmen, on horseback and wearing the white blankets such an act prescribed, would wait for the right moment, kidnap her and keep her locked up until the chief's son was brought from college, and they would be forced to get married. Columbus would have no choice but to accept the situation and the accompanying lobola. Winnie remembered the drama when her brother brought his wife to their home wrapped in a blanket, albeit with her cooperation. She had witnessed such ceremonies and seen the beseeching eyes of young brides forced into marriage as they emerged from captivity.

Winnie knew she had only one option. She packed her bags, explained her predicament to Mr Zici and hastily left for Johannesburg. No matter what the consequences were, she would not risk being carried off to a degrading life by Chief Qaquali's men.

The old woman's unthinking question had given Winnie her one chance to escape, but what she did was unthinkable for a young Pondo woman and a serious affront to the tradition of unquestioning obedience to her parents and elders. She knew her flight would cause both difficulties and embarrassment for her father, and wished she could have spared him.

As soon as Winnie got back to Johannesburg she wrote to Columbus and begged his forgiveness for running away, but told him she could never enter into an arranged marriage. She was also able to tell him that she had been awarded her diploma in social work with distinction, and had won a prize as the best student. Winnie was one of the last graduates of the Jan Hofmeyr School of Social Work, which was closed down by the government in terms of the Bantu Education Act soon afterwards. Later generations of black social workers were trained at what became known as 'bush colleges' in the various homelands.

The years had sped by and Winnie was on the threshold of a career as a fully fledged social worker, but first she had to find a post. Shortly after the final results were announced, Professor Phillips summoned her to his office and told her, with a broad smile, that she had been awarded a much sought-after scholarship and could further her education by studying sociology at a university in America. Winnie was elated. Not only did this news exceed her wildest dreams, but she had no need to worry about whether she would find a suitable position. She was going to America! She immediately rushed to the post office to send a telegram with the news to her father and Hilda.

Her student days over, Winnie moved into one of the hostel's ten-bed dormitories, reserved for working women. She paid 11 shillings a week for her accommodation, excluding meals but including the use of communal recreation rooms and the kitchen, where they were allowed to prepare their own food. Adelaide Tsukudu, a staff nurse at Baragwanath Hospital, slept in the bed next to hers. She was a Tswana from a farm in the Vereeniging district, about ninety kilometres south of Johannesburg, and she and Winnie became close friends, their futures destined to be entwined in ways they could never have imagined at the time.

Adelaide was already in love with Oliver Tambo, whom she would later marry, and Winnie went with her to many ANC meetings at Trades Hall. Winnie found the meetings exciting on both a political level and because they allowed her to meet the workers, the very people she would deal with as a social worker. It was at Trades Hall that she first heard of SACTU, the South African Congress of Trade Unions.

Adelaide and her other friends were as excited as Winnie herself about the prospect of her trip to America, and they spent many happy hours fantasising over what life would be like in the USA. Typically, Winnie scoured the library for books and information on the far-off land that would be her home for the next few years.

But, one day, the postman brought an official envelope, addressed to her, from Baragwanath Hospital. The hospital was on the outskirts of Soweto, the only one in the area for blacks and the largest in the southern hemisphere. As a student, Winnie had often gone to Bara, as it was known, and had even lectured there, but she was utterly astonished to find that the letter contained the offer of a post as the hospital's first black medical social worker. Adelaide found her sitting on a bench in the hostel entrance hall, staring incredulously at the letter. Without a word, Winnie handed her the sheet of paper. Adelaide, always high-spirited and demonstrative, shrieked and threw her arms around Winnie in delight.

Winnie was overwhelmed. She had already set her sights on further study in America, but what she really wanted was to be a social worker, and now she had the chance to do so, and in Johannesburg, which she loved. She would have to make an agonising choice, and after weighing all the pros and cons, consulted Professor Phillips. He listened to her carefully, but pointed out that ultimately only she could decide what was best for her. She wished she could have discussed her predicament with Professor Hough as well, but he was furthering his studies in Boston and would not return to South Africa until 1957.

When Winnie wrote to her father for advice, he also counselled that she would have to make her own choice, but as Winnie read his letter she thought she could discern, between the lines, that her father believed their people needed her. She knew her decision would have a profound influence on her life, and in the end was absolutely certain that she had to accept the post at Baragwanath Hospital.

When she told Professor Phillips of her decision, and her regret at not being able to accept the American scholarship, he assured her that she would probably be able to use it at a later date. Some years later, when the occasion did arise for her to study abroad, she again decided against it.

Her fateful decision to stay in South Africa set her on the path of a meeting with Nelson Mandela – and a life of political activism, persecution and imprisonment.

4

Mandela wants to marry me

THE NEW GENERATION of educated urban blacks quite naturally formed the black elite of the fifties. This burgeoning group of young professionals – lawyers, teachers, doctors, nurses and social workers – was changing the face of South Africa. They moved in a relatively small circle, and many were friends, colleagues or even members of the same extended families.

When Winnie presented herself at Baragwanath Hospital in 1956 to take up the newly created position of medical social worker, she was a carefree, cheerful and self-confident young woman. Stories and photographs appeared in the newspapers, savouring the achievement of the girl from Pondoland who turned out to be both beautiful and gifted. Winnie sent the newspaper cuttings to Columbus and Hilda.

She launched her career with determination and enthusiasm, and without the slightest premonition that her dreams and ambitions would be dashed by her own principles and choices. Before long she was flooded with cases and totally absorbed in her work: tracing patients' relatives, sorting out problems related to accident claims and work-related injuries, and arranging funerals. In addition to being patient and compassionate, Winnie was cheerful and dedicated, and became a firm favourite with patients and staff alike. While doing fieldwork in her final year at college, Winnie had come to believe that there could be no worse poverty than she encountered in Tsolo, but what she found in the townships of Johannesburg was all the more shocking when contrasted against the abundance in the City of Gold. Acutely aware of the appalling conditions under which most people were forced to live and angered that this was the result of inequalities built into the system, she needed every grain of tenacity not to be demoralised.

One of her duties was to visit new mothers at home after they had given birth at Bara. The conditions were often heart-rending. People lived in makeshift shacks thrown together from nothing but discarded corrugated iron and board, with stones holding down the roof and rags and newspapers stuffed into openings to keep out the elements. Malnutrition was common, not only because many families could not afford adequate food, but also because young, uneducated mothers were often ignorant about proper feeding. Research she carried out in Alexandra township to establish the infant mortality rate indicated an alarming ten deaths in every 1 000. As a result of relationships between young urban women and migrant workers – who most often had wives at home – thousands of township babies were illegitimate. Without any means of support, many of the desperate mothers abandoned their newborn infants, often leaving them at Bara.

The first time Winnie had to deal with an abandoned baby, she asked one of her friends, Matthew Nkoane, who was a senior reporter with the *Golden City Post*, to help her trace the mother by publishing the details of the case. It worked, and after reuniting mother and child, Winnie helped her to cope with the initial difficulties. After that, she and Matthew collaborated on more cases, tracing not only runaway mothers but also the relatives of elderly patients who had been left at the hospital. The *Golden City Post* also helped raise funds for the burial of patients who died at the hospital, but whose bodies remained unclaimed. Matthew later joined the breakaway Pan Africanist Congress (PAC), but despite their political differences he and Winnie remained friends for many years.

One of the young doctors at Bara was Nthatho Motlana, who had studied for a BSc degree at Fort Hare before attending the medical school at the University of the Witwatersrand and going on to specialise in paediatrics. Like most of his peers at Fort Hare, he had joined the ANC Youth League and later became its secretary. During the Defiance Campaign he was arrested with Nelson Mandela and thousands of others, given a nine-month suspended sentence and then banned for five years. Motlana later became a leading political figure in Soweto. As chairman of the Committee of Ten, the sprawling township's unofficial representative body, he was arguably the most prominent man in Soweto in the 1970s. He and his wife Sally became friends with both Winnie and Nelson Mandela, whom he had met at Fort Hare, and when Mandela was imprisoned he appointed Motlana one of the guardians of his children.

It was inevitable that Winnie's path would cross Motlana's at Bara, and like the rest of the staff, he was impressed by her. They got on well, and in later years he would say he found working with her both stimulating and encouraging because she was always cheerful and laughed easily – valuable attributes when working under great strain and in difficult circumstances. Winnie had profound concern for the welfare of others, and would assist them even at the expense of her own comfort and safety. Motlana recalled that she always had an acute social conscience, and thought nothing of spending part of her own small salary to help others. She was only a young woman, but frequently spent her free time scouring the townships for the destitute and elderly who had no one to care for them. She often phoned Motlana in the middle of the night and asked him to treat someone who needed medical attention.

For Winnie there was no such thing as an insurmountable obstacle, and when she was convinced that she was right she would not budge under any circumstances. Her colleagues at Bara admired the fact that she was prepared to stand up for her patients against those in authority, both inside and outside the system. Once, Dr Motlana diagnosed pellagra in a patient, and ordered him to take sick leave for three weeks. But the man's employer refused to release him for the prescribed period, and the patient turned to Winnie, as his social worker, for help. Undaunted, the young woman wrote a scathing letter to the white employer justifying the doctor's orders, and the patient got his sick leave.

Throughout her years at college and during her first year of work, Winnie had remained romantically uninvolved. But in 1957 she met Barney Sampson, a gallant, fun-loving man, and soon they were regularly seen in one another's company around town. Barney was working as a clerk and studying part time while living in a rented room in the backyard of a house in a white suburb. He was always well dressed, and he and Winnie, who had developed a taste for beautiful clothes, made a handsome couple. Barney was full of good humour and they laughed a lot, and Winnie enjoyed the company of her attentive and elegant companion. But her family did not approve. Sampson was obviously not a traditional black name, and they questioned Barney's origins. Winnie was not at all bothered by his lineage, but she was concerned that he was almost completely apolitical, showing no interest in the need for change – something that was of major importance to her. She also didn't like his submissive manner towards whites.

Winnie had decided to stay at the Helping Hand Hostel in Jeppe, although it meant commuting daily to the hospital, which was a fair distance away. She was happy at the hostel, and enjoyed the company of the many young women of different cultures and backgrounds. Their diverse experiences gave her valuable insight into the myriad social problems challenging the black population, and especially those faced by women working in an urban environment. Life was often particularly hard for them, and Winnie learned a great deal about coping with the difficulties of daily life. She listened with real interest when they discussed the gross injustices of influx control measures, which dictated where blacks were allowed to live and work; their employment conditions; the struggle for a living wage; and the bus boycotts when fares were raised beyond the means of workers living on or below the breadline, and thousands walked to work rather than pay the higher fares. Young white women spent their time talking about relationships, marriage, their careers and entertainment, but at the hostel in Jeppe conversation centred on apartheid and the National Party government, which was widely detested.

There was an old piano in the hall, and students who could play thumped away at it on evenings when they sang freedom songs, adding the names of their political leaders, including Nelson Mandela and Oliver Tambo. Winnie had heard a great deal about Tambo, not only because he was a prominent political figure, but also because he was courting her friend Adelaide. When they were in bed at night, Adelaide would talk and muse about the clever lawyer she was soon to marry, and who was in partnership with Mandela. Winnie first met Oliver when he arrived early to fetch Adelaide for a date, and she ran downstairs to tell him her friend would not be long.

When Adelaide joined them, she told Oliver that, like him, Winnie was from Bizana. He had been educated at the Holy Cross Anglican Mission not far from the Madikizela home, and in keeping with tribal custom they were members of the same broad extended family. Oliver was delighted to meet a 'niece' from home, and Winnie was equally thrilled to learn that Adelaide, whom she already regarded as a sister, would be formally related to her through marriage to Oliver.

What Winnie could not know was that the introduction to Tambo would lead to a meeting with Mandela, or that quite soon she would be courted by not one, but two prominent members of the royal Tembu line.

Baragwanath Hospital's reputation had spread throughout southern Africa, and it drew both patients and physicians from all over the subcontinent. Newly qualified doctors, white as well as black, were eager to serve as interns because the large number and diversity of cases offered invaluable experience. One day, the staff was told that a group of distinguished visitors from the Transkei would visit the hospital. The VIPs turned out to be Chief Kaiser Matanzima and a group of his councillors. When they came to Winnie's office to talk about her work, she reminded Matanzima that they had met at Ncora. He appeared not to remember her, but as they talked he invited her to run the welfare centre at Tsolo. Winnie agreed to consider the offer, but made it clear that she enjoyed working at Bara. Matanzima was insistent, proposing that they discuss the matter over dinner, and arranged that one of his advisers would pick her up after work.

When Winnie told Adelaide why she wouldn't be going back to the hostel with her that evening, Adelaide immediately speculated that Matanzima had his eye on her. Winnie dismissed the suggestion, insisting that the meeting would be purely professional. She was fetched in a battered green Oldsmobile and taken to house 8115, a corner property in Orlando West. Matanzima had a candlelight dinner waiting, and she began to think that perhaps Adelaide had been right, after all. Winnie didn't know it, but the house and car belonged to Mandela, and since he and Matanzima had grown up together, it was only natural that Mandela would place both his home and his car at Kaiser's disposal during his visit.

As she dined with Matanzima that night, Winnie had not the slightest inkling that within the year she would be the mistress of that very house, and the wife of Nelson Mandela.

After returning to the Transkei, a clearly smitten Matanzima wrote Winnie an endless stream of letters, but she continued to make light of his attentions – until she heard that his councillors were preparing to approach Columbus for her hand. She realised that her innocent but naive responses had been misinterpreted, and was determined to stop a second attempt to force her into an unwanted marriage. She had no wish to become a rural wife, and stopped writing to Matanzima immediately. But she was about to be swept off her feet from another, totally unexpected quarter.

One afternoon, Nelson Mandela gave his friend Diliza Mji, a medical student, a lift from Orlando to the University of the Witwatersrand. While passing Baragwanath, he noticed a young woman waiting at the bus stop, and was immediately struck by her beauty. He briefly considered turning around and driving past her again, just to see her more clearly, but he didn't. But he couldn't forget her lovely face.

Soon afterwards, Winnie went to the Johannesburg regional court to support a colleague who had been assaulted by the police, and who happened to be represented by Mandela. When the tall, handsome lawyer walked into court, Winnie heard spectators whisper his name, and she thought he cut an awesome figure.

Around the same time, Winnie was given a lift back to the hostel one evening by Oliver and Adelaide. They stopped along the way to buy food for Adelaide, who was hungry, but Oliver found he had forgotten to bring any money. Then he noticed his friend Nelson in the shop, and told Adelaide to let him pay, which Mandela did. When he and Adelaide came out of the shop, Oliver introduced Winnie, remarking that Mandela must surely have seen her picture in *World* or *Drum*, since she was always 'dancing about' their pages. Mandela was dumbstruck. It was the beautiful young woman he had seen at the bus stop. In later years he would say that he had no idea whether such a thing as love at first sight existed, but that he knew, the moment he met Winnie, that he wanted her for his wife.

His marriage to his first wife, Evelyn, had fallen apart, and Mandela's friends had long speculated about who might capture the heart of the dashing and debonair lawyer and rising political star. He was thirty-eight, tall and well built, dressed stylishly and exuded confidence. Furthermore, he was a successful attorney and already a hero among black South Africans. Mandela had been seen in the company of Ruth Mompati, his secretary, and Lillian Ngoyi, president of the ANC Women's League, but the love of his life would not be one of the sophisticated political activists he already knew, but rather a young and unspoiled country girl.

The day after their brief meeting, Nelson telephoned Winnie and invited her to lunch on Sunday, as he had something to discuss with her. She was terrified. Not only was Mandela considerably older, but also the patron of her alma mater, where the students had simply taken it for granted that anyone whose name appeared on the official letterhead was far too important a personage for them to know. She was so flustered that she couldn't work for the rest of the day, and spent all of Sunday morning trying on one dress after another, then tossing them aside as too frilly and too girlish. In the end she borrowed a more sophisticated outfit from a friend, even though she felt uncomfortable in clothes not her own.

In keeping with custom, Mandela did not call for Winnie himself, but sent a friend, Joe Matthews, who had been a fellow student at Fort Hare and was a Youth League activist. He was also the son of Professor ZK Matthews, one of South Africa's first black professors, and both father and son were among the Treason triallists. Joe drove a very nervous Winnie to Mandela's office. Even though it was Sunday, he was working, since for him every day was a working day. Winnie found him surrounded by piles of legal files, and felt acutely ill at ease and tongue-tied in Mandela's company. But he soon captivated the shy young woman with his charisma, and in no time at all they were laughing and talking together. Winnie was surprised and impressed by his optimistic view of the Treason Trial and the fact that he refused to be cowed by the severity of the situation. After a while they walked to Azad's, an Indian restaurant, where Mandela ordered curry and they talked about Pondoland and their shared origins. He told her he was a member of the royal Tembu line, and spoke about his nephews, Kaiser and George Matanzima, who were from the lesser or right-hand house. The mention of Kaiser's name came as a shock to Winnie, and she wondered briefly whether she should mention that he had courted her. But Mandela carried on talking about other things, and the opportunity passed.

He told her about his childhood, that his father had died when he was twelve, after which he, George and Kaiser were brought up by King Sabata. He had met Tambo at Fort Hare, and Winnie was surprised to learn that Oliver had seriously considered entering the Anglican ministry, but had accepted a post teaching mathematics at St Peter's School in Johannesburg instead, then decided to become a lawyer. Mandela had been steered towards the legal profession by another ANC stalwart, Walter Sisulu, who had been forced to leave school in Standard 4 to help support his family, working underground as a miner, as a kitchen cleaner and in a bakery, while studying part time. As one of the original members of the Youth League, Sisulu had progressed through the ranks of the ANC, was its secretary general and one of its most highly regarded members. The two were good friends, and it was thanks to Walter's urging that Mandela had decided to study law at the University of the Witwatersrand. He then articled with a white lawyer, and in 1952, Winnie's last year at school and with the Defiance Campaign under way, Mandela and Tambo set up their law partnership. They were the first black lawyers with offices in the heart of Johannesburg, and that was possible only because they rented rooms in a building owned by an Indian. The government was in the process of moving all people of colour out of so-called white areas, but several properties were still legally owned by Indians. There were continued attempts to force Mandela and Tambo out of the city and into the black townships, miles away from the courts and their clients who were in jail, but they resisted and managed to stay put, although they had no idea for how long. Winnie was fascinated.

When the waiter brought the plates of steaming curry, Winnie tucked in. She was used to bland and mostly boiled food and had never eaten curry before, and was totally unprepared for the taste shock. She could hardly swallow the spicy dish, and to add insult to injury, her eyes were watering and her nose started running. She was mortified, and tried her best not to be seen as a country bumpkin. Mandela was gaily telling her that he could happily eat curry three times a day, so Winnie struggled on with the unfamiliar flavours, and with a great effort managed to eat most of her food.

Mandela couldn't keep his eyes off his lovely companion. Even though she was clearly suffering some discomfort, he found her utterly enchanting. They were constantly interrupted by people consulting Mandela, and Winnie felt quite excluded. After lunch he suggested they should go for a drive, and told her that he had actually contacted her to ask if she could help raise funds for the legal costs of the Treason triallists. Not once had he asked Winnie about her political views or affiliations, but he seemed to take it for granted that they were similar to his own. Like most black South Africans, she had been following the course of the trial since the previous year, when the police had arrested and charged some of the ANC's top leaders, including the president, Chief Albert Luthuli. Mandela and Tambo were also among the 156 accused, but were out on bail, charged with high treason. A fund had been established to cover their legal costs and to support the families of those who lost their jobs after being arrested. Despite generous financial support from abroad, a great deal more money was needed, said Mandela, and he thought she might have some ideas about how funds could be raised. Winnie had never been involved in anything of the kind and had no idea how she could help, but she would not dream of refusing.

Returning to the car along a rocky path after a walk in the veld, a strap on one of Winnie's sandals snapped, and she had to walk barefoot for the rest of the way. Nelson held her hand to support her, but she read nothing more into it than a kindly, almost fatherly, gesture. But, as they reached the car, he told her it had been a lovely day – and kissed her. Winnie was stunned. This famous man, the hero of thousands, whose name was known throughout the country, had spent an entire day with her, told her about his life and dreams, and kissed her! She had no idea what to think.

The next day he telephoned to say he would pick her up after work, and arrived dressed for his workout at the gym where he trained as a boxer – and that became their regular pattern. If legal affairs delayed him, he would send someone else to fetch Winnie, spend whatever time he could with her between meetings and other commitments, then drop her off at the hostel.

Even at that early stage, Winnie would observe ruefully in later years, life with him was really life without him, and he never pretended that she would have any special claim on his time. Theirs was never a frivolous romance, said Winnie, because they never had enough time for one.

She was tremendously flattered by Mandela's attention, but found it hard to believe that this great man was really interested in her. Scared that she might make a fool of herself, she told no one she was seeing him, not even Adelaide. She was alone and confused, and had no idea that she was about to find herself at the centre of a battle for her affections between two of the most prominent black men in the country.

When she stopped writing to Matanzima, he hurried back to Johannesburg to find out why. He telephoned her at the hospital and informed her, with no room for argument, that someone would fetch her from work so that they could meet. She was duly driven to the same house in Orlando West where she and Kaiser had dined, but when she entered, to her total amazement, found herself face to face with both Matanzima and Mandela! She still had no idea that the house belonged to Mandela. Both men greeted her warmly but looked puzzled, neither having been told that Winnie knew the other. They asked her to wait in the dining room while they concluded a meeting in the lounge, where several older men were engaged in serious discussion. The longer Winnie waited, the more anxious she became about the predicament in which she found herself. She respected both men, addressing each as 'chief'. What would they say to her? What would she say to them? Suddenly she was overcome by panic. She slipped out of the house and went back to her office at the hospital, leaving the two men to settle the matter.

The discovery that they shared a mutual interest in Winnie led to an unpleasant confrontation between Mandela and Matanzima. But as the older and more senior man in tribal rank, Mandela prevailed. Kaiser abandoned his pursuit of Winnie, though not without bitterness, and Mandela turned the full force of his attention on her in a way that left no doubt as to his intentions.

In the months that followed, they spent time together whenever they could. She went to see him at the Drill Hall, where the preparatory examination for the Treason Trial was in progress, and visited him at his office, met his children Thembi, Makgatho and Makaziwe, and attended ANC meetings and political discussions. Mandela was both courting her and steering her deeper into politics. He offered her the use of his office when she needed a quiet place to study, and they were together almost every day, talking and laughing and exploring each other's feelings, but less time was spent on romantic banter than on serious political matters. Mandela made it clear to Winnie from the outset that he was fully committed to the liberation struggle, and would be satisfied with nothing less than the scrapping of all apartheid laws and an end to the oppression of blacks. He insisted that this was not a struggle for blacks only, but for everyone who supported a just and democratic society. He was equally comfortable with people of all races, and many of his closest confidants were members of other racial groups. He firmly believed that not race, but racism, was the problem, and he was adamant that the struggle had to achieve economic equality as well as racial integration. Winnie was appalled when he told her of the many injustices that confronted him daily in his legal practice, and how many thousands of blacks had been turned into criminals as a result of the petty apartheid laws, often for something as minor as not carrying a pass. Winnie also learned everything important about the Treason Trial and the defence tactics of the accused.

She had still told no one of her budding relationship with Nelson, and Adelaide continued to believe Winnie might marry Kaiser Matanzima. When she finally discovered the truth, Adelaide was astounded. It was Oliver who inadvertently spilled the beans when she went to fetch him at his office one day. There was a long queue of clients, and she asked if Oliver still had to see all of them. He laughed and said, 'No, those are all Nelson's clients. He will have to deal with them when he can tear himself away from Winnie.'

Adelaide could not believe that Winnie had managed to keep secret something so momentous as a romantic liaison with Nelson Mandela. As soon as she got back to the hostel she told their other friends, and when Winnie arrived she was greeted by squeals of delight and good-natured teasing, and inundated with questions. She tried in vain to explain that there was no more to it than just 'going out together'.

For Mandela, certain that Winnie was the woman he wanted to marry, it became important to include her in every facet of his life. He wanted to introduce her to his political colleagues, and arranged for her to attend a session at the Drill Hall. When the hearing adjourned, he introduced her to Chief Luthuli, Walter Sisulu, Professor ZK Matthews, Moses Kotane, Ismail Meer and Dr Monty Naicker. They all found her charming, but in an aside, one of the group warned Nelson: 'Such intimidating and seductive beauty does not go with a revolutionary.' Nelson laughed, but Winnie was visibly annoyed by the remark. 'You have no sense of humour,' he chided.

On weekends, Nelson took Winnie with him when he visited friends and sympathisers in the white suburbs, especially the Bernsteins, where they often met and relaxed, sipping wine and talking politics. There was no consciousness of colour at these gatherings; they were just a group of like-minded people spending some time together. Winnie was the odd one out, twenty-two years old, innocent and naive, and not yet active in politics. But she was happier than she had ever imagined she could be, and while not all his friends fully approved of Nelson's choice of companion, the animated, well-dressed and strikingly beautiful woman with soulful eyes nevertheless left a vivid impression. She made a concerted effort to embrace Mandela's political friends as her own: she visited Ismail and Fatima Meer in Durban, venerated Lillian Ngoyi and Helen Joseph, and regarded Tambo as a father figure. In many respects she still had the trusting heart of a child, and her dependence on Mandela and his older friends indicated a deep need for the guidance and support of parents.

She was awed by Mandela's position and demeanour as a hereditary chief, as well as the ease with which he moved among affluent whites, and accompanied him to both political consultations in the white suburbs and meetings in the townships.

On 10 March 1957, Mandela asked Winnie to marry him. He proposed, rather unconventionally, after a picnic on a white-owned farm along Evaton Road, south-west of Johannesburg. He stopped the car at the side of the road and told her that he knew a seamstress who would make her wedding gown, and that Winnie should go and see her. Ray Harmel's husband Michael was among the Treason triallists, and in addition to being an activist, Ray was a superb dressmaker. Unusual as the proposal was, Mandela had spoken without any arrogance, and Winnie, madly in love with him, wasn't offended. She felt they had a special understanding that made further discussion unnecessary.

For Mandela, who did not believe in polygamy, this would be his second marriage, and his choice of wife was important. Winnie was young, but he had instantly recognised her inner strength, the courage and determination that would make her the perfect mate. His only reservation was whether he had the right to expect her to share a difficult and uncertain life with him. He pointed out all the disadvantages: depending on the outcome of the Treason Trial he could go to prison, perhaps for a long time; he was constantly hounded by the police, and no doubt as his wife, she would be too; and, most importantly, he had dedicated his life to the struggle, and everything else, including personal feelings, would take second place. Like a calling to the ministry, it was a commitment for life, Mandela warned.

Winnie was attracted to both Mandela the man and to his dream of justice and change, and the prospect of being able to make a real difference thrilled her. It was what she had dreamed of since, as a child, she listened with anger and sadness to her father's accounts of the injustice visited on generations of blacks in South Africa.

Although she had not yet verbalised or clearly defined her own political philosophy, Winnie identified completely with Mandela's ideals and vision for

South Africa's future. When she decided to marry him, his hopes and plans became hers as well. She committed herself to the ANC and the struggle for freedom with a fervour that would endure through almost three decades of persecution. Mandela explained his idea of organising support in both the rural and urban areas, and had drafted plans for ANC volunteers to always be available to inform and motivate the people, right down to grassroots level. Along with Sisulu, Tambo and others, he was spearheading the struggle. It was a path fraught with danger and he kept nothing from Winnie, because he wanted her to have no illusions about her future with him.

But their courtship was not all gloom and politics. They were a striking couple, both tall and always elegantly dressed, and so obviously in love that they infused everyone around them with their *joie de vivre*. They both loved jazz, and many a Sunday evening found them at Uncle Joe's Café in Fordsburg, listening to musicians such as Dollar Brand, Kippie Moeketsi and Dudu Pukane. They were completely engrossed in one another, openly holding hands and sharing affectionate touches, and Mandela could seldom take his eyes off her.

As the Treason Trial dragged on, the state withdrew the charges against most of the accused, until only thirty – including Mandela – remained. As proceedings entered the second year, the law practice of Mandela and Tambo began to fall apart, since they were almost never there. Both men had run into grave financial difficulties, but when the charges against Tambo were dropped, he tried to repair the damage as best he could. Mandela couldn't even pay the balance of £50 he owed on a plot of land he had purchased in Umtata, and lost it. He explained the situation to Winnie and warned her that they would more than likely have to live on her small salary alone.

His divorce from Evelyn was finalised in 1957, and though both he and Winnie realised that if he was found guilty he might well be sentenced to death, they decided to go ahead with their wedding plans.

Mandela's bail conditions did not allow him to leave the Johannesburg magisterial district, and he was unable to travel to Pondoland to ask Columbus for his daughter's hand in marriage, as custom demanded. So Winnie had to do it. Early one Friday morning, she set off for Bizana. Her family had not expected her, but were pleased to see her. Throughout Saturday she tried to pluck up the courage to approach her father. That evening, while helping Hilda make tea for Columbus in the kitchen, she confided in her stepmother, showing her a photograph of Nelson. 'Ma,' said Winnie, 'this man wants to marry me. I've come to get your approval, because I also want to marry him. His name is Nelson Mandela.'

Hilda was taken aback when she heard the name, and immediately asked whether it was *the* Mandela, the ANC leader. Winnie confirmed that it was, indeed, and Hilda called her daughter to take the tea to Columbus, then sat down to talk to Winnie. The man had been charged with treason, she pointed out. What kind of life would Winnie have with a man who might be sent to prison, a man totally dedicated to politics? No doubt that was why his first marriage had failed. Winnie merely gazed at the photograph, and from the dreamy expression on her face Hilda realised that all her protests were in vain. She agreed to talk to Columbus.

Shocked, sad and proud all at the same time, Columbus, too, tried to draw Winnie's attention to the pitfalls of a union with Mandela. He had three children to support, faced the possibility of a long jail term, was dedicated to his cause, and had chosen a difficult road to follow. Winnie was both young and inexperienced, but she had already been made two good marriage offers, and others would come along. But he knew his daughter, and he had no doubt that if Winnie had already made up her mind, he could not stand in her way. Finally, he simply said, 'God be with you,' and told her that Mandela should send his people to negotiate lobola.

Excitement rose to fever pitch at the Madikizela kraal when Mandela's representatives arrived from the royal kraal for the negotiations. The bridegroom usually paid lobola to the bride's father in the form of cattle, the number determined by the wealth and status of her family and some hard bargaining. It took several days before agreement was reached, and soon afterwards an impressive retinue of royal Tembu representatives drove a herd of cattle into Columbus's kraal. He slaughtered an ox, and the deal was sealed with ritual celebrations, much eating and the drinking of beer.

A bride was never told how many head of cattle she was worth, and Winnie never did find out how many beasts Mandela had pledged in exchange for her hand.

Nelson and Winnie celebrated their engagement in Johannesburg on 25 May 1958. She was living with her Aunt Phyllis, and the party was held at her house. Mandela was one of the most prominent blacks in the country, and the event was well publicised. The *Golden City Post* carried a special announcement that the attorney Nelson Mandela and social worker Miss Winnie Madikizela were to announce their engagement at a party at the home of Mr and Mrs P Mzaidume in Orlando West, and that the wedding was planned for 14 June.

Aunt Phyllis spared no effort to make the evening memorable for her niece. Winnie wore an elegant light-green gown that Nelson had bought for her, and was radiantly beautiful. The champagne flowed as he slipped the engagement ring onto her finger amid loud applause and cheers. The next day, news of the engagement was carried in the social columns of the Johannesburg *World*.

After the engagement, Mandela suggested that Winnie should move in with his aunt, so that she could get to know his family. His mother had not quite come to terms with his divorce from Evelyn and worried about the children, who had been traumatised by the separation and might well find their father's impending marriage difficult. To spare their feelings she kept herself aloof from the wedding arrangements, but after the ceremony Winnie would live with her, and Mandela thought a spell with his aunt would make the transition easier. Winnie initially resisted the idea, but eventually relented and moved in.

Winnie Madikizela had taken the first steps to becoming Winnie Mandela.

PART II

Winnie Mandela

'It is better to be killed standing than to live on your knees.'
– Mexican saying

5

Madiba and Zami

PREPARATIONS FOR WINNIE'S wedding turned not only the Madikizela house-hold, but the entire village on its head. The whole district was abuzz with excitement, and the tribal elders reminded Columbus that the wedding had to befit the status of the bridegroom, who was not only a member of the royal house of the Tembu, but a respected political figure revered by millions of black South Africans.

Columbus and Hilda put their heads together. Guests would be coming from Johannesburg and other parts of the country, travelling long distances to attend the festivities. As a courtesy to them, it was decided that traditional festivities at the Madikizela home would follow the church ceremony, as well as a Western-style reception in Bizana. But there was a problem. The only venue in Bizana that was big and grand enough for the kind of reception they envisaged was the town hall, and they knew that it was reserved for use by whites. Columbus, however, went ahead and applied to hire the hall, and to his astonishment the request was granted.

This was the first wedding that Columbus would host. Those of Winnie's siblings who were already married had chosen to make their own arrangements, but Winnie had asked for his blessing, and he and Hilda would give her the wedding of her dreams. Columbus was no longer just a poor schoolteacher, but had become a wealthy businessman who owned several shops and a fleet of buses, and he could afford to spare no effort to make the wedding memorable.

Throughout her life Winnie was a trailblazer, and her marriage was no exception. Since Mandela was a lawyer, close attention was paid to the legal formalities of the union, and at the time Winnie was one of the few black women to have an ante-nuptial contract. It gave her the right to conduct business transactions without having to first seek her husband's permission, and ensured that she remained in control of her own possessions. She would be spared her mother's anguish over having to produce at least two sons in order to comply with the hereditary custom of the Pondo.

Traditionally, black marriages were in community of property, which effectively reduced the woman's status to that of a minor, unable to make even the smallest legal decision without her husband's signed permission, and gave men total power over the disposal of any assets. A strong woman like Winnie was not about to surrender her newfound independence, no matter how much she loved Mandela.

As the wedding day approached, excitement rose to fever pitch all over Pondoland. The most distant Madikizela relatives wanted to be a part of the preparations, even if this involved nothing more than discussing which cattle would be slaughtered to feed the expected crowd. While the men pondered this important decision, the women brewed large vats of traditional beer, a low-alcohol beverage made from maize or sorghum, with the consistency of gruel. They also stamped maize kernels for porridge (called grits in the southern US and polenta in Europe), and planned and prepared other dishes that would be cooked in three-legged black iron pots. Columbus asked Winnie's Aunt Phyllis, who had some experience in catering for large crowds, to help, and she took charge of the food preparation.

In terms of his banning order, Mandela had to apply for special permission to attend his own wedding. He was granted four days, after which he had to report back to police in Johannesburg. While in the Transkei he had to stay in Bizana and restrict his activities to the wedding ceremony. He and Winnie made the long drive to Bizana with the bridal party, which included his sister Leaby, Georgina Lekgoate and Helen Ngobese. The most important piece of luggage was Winnie's wedding gown, made, as Mandela had suggested, by his close friend Michael Harmel's wife, Ray.

The trip was a nightmare for Winnie. An unexpected attack of pre-wedding jitters gave her diarrhoea, and much to her embarrassment Mandela had to stop the car at regular intervals so that she could run for the cover of bushes beside the road. When they reached eMbongweni after dark, the entire household and a host of relatives were waiting, and Hilda led a shrill chorus of ululating to welcome them. As dictated by custom, the bride and groom were immediately separated and would not meet again until they stood before the altar. Mandela and his party were escorted to the home of a family member, Simon Madikizela, while sisters and aunts helped an exhausted Winnie to bed. When she had not recovered by the next day, Makhulu diagnosed her as having been bewitched. She jealously guarded over Winnie, and although Mandela discreetly sent his friend Dr Mbekeni to treat the ailing bride, it was the care and counsel of her wise old grandmother that had the necessary calming effect.

Winnie's wedding day began with a warm bath in a large iron tub. Aunt Phyllis helped her to dress in the exquisite gown of luxuriant satin and frothy lace. Her hair was swept up in soft curls and adorned with a wreath of flowers and a short, gossamer veil. She was radiantly beautiful and transparently happy. As she stepped through the door of her childhood home clutching a bouquet of roses and lilies, relatives waiting outside greeted her with a dance of joy. Makhulu led the way with ululations and exuberant high leaps that belied her age. The Madikizela kraal was teeming with the horses of tribesmen who had come from near and far, and when all the guests were gathered they boarded Columbus's buses for the trip to the Methodist church in Bizana. The father of the bride, in a new black suit with a carnation in the lapel, went ahead and waited for the bride at the church door. She arrived in a car festooned with ribbons in the ANC colours.

Winnie and Nelson's wedding was a unique fusion of religious and traditional tribal customs. The church was filled to capacity when the groom slipped a gold band onto the bride's finger and the minister pronounced them man and wife. Their eyes locked, and their faces shone with a happiness that clearly came from deep within.

They stepped out of their aura of oneness into the celebrations, ushered in by the choir with a Xhosa hymn, followed by a praise singer who recited traditional rites and lauded both the families. The guests followed the wedding party to the burial ground at the ancestral home of the Madikizelas, where they paid their respects – the first of many traditional rituals that would mark their first hours as a married couple.

Nelson, the newest member of the Madikizela family, presented the older women with headscarves, and each, in turn, danced up to the groom to receive the gift, ululating recognition and appreciation. This was followed by a demonstration of the bride's virginal purity as her retinue walked round and round the Madikizela kraal, the young women in front, the older ones behind. Then Winnie's kinsmen sang 'Baya Khala Abazali' ['Your family is crying'] to express the sadness of parting with her. The bride was expected to wail and cry at this point, but Winnie was incapable of feigning sorrow on this happiest of days, and was smiling broadly. Irene nudged her and hissed that she should at least pretend to weep, but no matter how hard she tried, Winnie could not stop smiling. Nelson's sister saved the moment by declaring that the bride could not possibly cry, since she had just married a prince. There was unanimous agreement.

With the Madikizelas having taken leave of Winnie, Nelson had to formally introduce her to the Madiba clan. An urgent whisper from Irene reminded Winnie that she had to keep her eyes downcast, as it would be seen as an insult if she looked her new in-laws in the eye. But with the best will in the world, Winnie could not disguise her joy. It was obvious to everyone that Nelson adored her, and there wasn't a serious face or moment of gloom on their wedding day. The Madikizela men caught the groom's party off guard and playfully 'kidnapped' Duma Nokwe, and demanded the traditional ransom. Columbus paid a goat for his release, and Duma promised to deliver the full ransom of an ox at a later date.

The celebrations moved to Bizana in the late afternoon, where proceedings opened with the usual speeches. Columbus spoke of his love for Winnie, voiced admiration for his son-in-law's commitment to the struggle, and warned both of them that only the deepest devotion would allow their marriage to withstand the threats they faced from all sides and enable them to weather the challenges they would face. Because of the terms of his banning order, Mandela couldn't make the traditional bridegroom's speech, and his sister Constance had to speak on his behalf.

Then the couple cut the wedding cake. Thirteen tiers were served to the guests, but the fourteenth layer was left untouched and carefully wrapped so that Winnie could take it to Nelson's ancestral home for the final wedding rite. According to tradition, part of the cake had to be cut at the bridegroom's homestead in front of the family elders, but because Nelson's four-day period of grace was drawing to a close and he had to get back to Johannesburg, the ceremony had to be postponed. Winnie kept the wrapped cake for many years, intending to honour the tradition when Nelson was released from prison, but he never did manage to take Winnie to his home to do so.

Apart from this departure from custom, the only sadness for Winnie on her wedding day was the absence of her dear friend Adelaide Tambo. She was due to give birth at any time, and had been unable to make the long journey to eMbongweni. Oliver, however, as Nelson's partner and a Madikizela relative, did attend the wedding.

After the formal reception, guests made their way to Columbus and Hilda's home for more merry-making. In an atmosphere of unbridled joy, they settled down to a meal of the many dishes prepared in the weeks before the wedding, including meat and maize porridge, and many of them stayed for a whole week of celebration. But Winnie and Nelson had to leave, and on the eve of their departure Columbus took them to the hut where he had stored their traditional wedding gifts: grass mats, clay pots and an array of small live animals. Mandela graciously declined the gifts, but took two chickens as a gesture of recognition for the generosity of the givers. On their drive back to Johannesburg, the chickens escaped from the car when they stopped for lunch, and the newlyweds ran around screaming and clucking, trying to capture them. They eventually gave up and fell to the ground, laughing, leaving the chickens to fend for themselves.

When they reached Orlando the sun had not yet set, and according to tradition the time was not right for them to start their married life. So they drove to Lillian Ngoyi's house, and waited until darkness fell. Only then did they drive to house No. 8115 where, not too long before, Winnie had faced two ardent suitors vying for her hand. Nelson's mother, friends and other relatives were waiting for them, and another celebration followed.

Nelson and Winnie Mandela embarked on their married life determined not to allow the uncertainty of what the future held to cloud whatever time they would have together, and to start a family immediately. Nelson's love for Winnie had given him new hope and heart for the difficulties that lay ahead, and in later years he would say he felt as if their marriage gave him a second chance at life. There was neither time nor money for a honeymoon, so Winnie settled in house 8115 without delay. Mandela had been renting the property from the Johannesburg municipality for several years, barred from buying property except in certain areas designated by the apartheid laws. He had a ninety-nine-year lease on the tiny corner house, which had an indoor bathroom, electricity and running hot water – rare luxuries in the sprawling township.

As before, the Treason Trial dominated their lives. Nelson had already formed his lifelong habit of rising early, around 4 am, before going for a run around the township. He found the tranquillity of the empty streets, the crisp air and the breaking day rejuvenating. Once the sun was up, the brief respite from smoke and kerosene fumes was dispelled as fires and small stoves were lit to hastily cook a pot of porridge and brew a cup of tea before the streets burst into life and thousands of people rushed to work in buses and taxis that wove their impatient way into the city.

Winnie made Nelson a breakfast of orange juice and toast, a small bowl of porridge and sometimes a raw egg before he took a bus to the trial in Pretoria. Winnie went back to work at Baragwanath Hospital, and her mother-in-law took care of the house. When time allowed, Nelson would call at his law office before going to the trial each morning, and when court adjourned in the afternoons he would spend long hours at the office in an effort to keep the practice afloat and earn an income. Political work and meetings with other ANC officials usually took up the rest of the evening, and he often arrived home after midnight. He was rarely there over weekends. Winnie soon found out that the life of a struggle leader's wife was a lonely one. Often enough, though, their house was filled with people and laughter, political discussion and debate, and she found the constant stream of visitors stimulating. After living in a hostel for so many years she enjoyed having her own home, even though not everything in it was to her liking. But she exercised patience, making discreet changes slowly. She didn't touch Nelson's study, which he had partitioned off from the lounge and furnished with a couch, three cane chairs, a bookshelf and a display cabinet. On the wall was a picture of Lenin, addressing a huge crowd. It was Nelson's kingdom.

A few weeks after their wedding, a group of Nelson's tribesmen arrived to ceremoniously admit Winnie into the Madiba tribe, and she was given the name Nobandla, which he adopted as a term of endearment. She affectionately called him Madiba. To the world outside they were Nelson and Winnie Mandela, but away from the public glare they were Madiba and Zami, short for Nomzamo.

One night a loud banging on the door rudely awakened everyone in the house. Winnie was frightened and bewildered, and had no idea what was going on. It was 1.30 in the morning, but Nelson quickly told her not to worry, that it was just a regular police raid. He hastily pulled on some clothes and rushed to the front door. Winnie sat in bed with the blankets pulled up under her chin, her heart pounding as faceless men shone torches at all the windows and yelled for them to open the door. She had known that the house and Mandela's office were raided frequently, but not that everything about these incursions was intentionally designed to unsettle the victims as much as possible. She watched in horror as policemen rummaged through their personal possessions, threw books off shelves, emptied drawers of clothing onto the floor, even read their personal letters, all the while making insulting remarks about *kaffirs*.

They found nothing incriminating, just turned the house upside down, and left. In time, Winnie would come to realise that they *never* expected to find anything incriminating, and that the raids formed part of the psychological warfare waged against opponents of the apartheid system. After she and Nelson had tidied up, she made coffee and they went back to bed. He warned her that she would have to get used to these midnight invasions of their privacy, which were a regular feature of his life. Winnie dreaded the prospect, but no raid was ever again as traumatic as the first.

The first year of marriage was a challenging time financially. For more than two years, Nelson and Oliver Tambo had spent most of their time attending the Treason Trial and preparing their defence, and their legal practice was in dire straits. They generated hardly any income from it, and were struggling to pay the office rental and provide for their families. Both men had to rely heavily on their wives to make ends meet, and Mandela's burden was about to increase. In July, Winnie found that she was pregnant.

Nelson had adopted a lifestyle that demanded more than his diminished income allowed. He had a permit to keep alcohol at home (blacks were not allowed to store hard liquor, even in their homes, without such a permit), and although he himself was a teetotaller, there was always a variety of beverages for guests. He also liked buying exotic foods and experimenting in the kitchen. Winnie was learning that there were many things about her famous and charming husband that she had not known before their wedding, such as his taste for good living and his offbeat sense of humour. He had a knack for relating the most outrageous stories with a deadpan face, which she found exasperating at first. She was driven close to tears of embarrassment when he told people he had promised to marry her only after she agreed to refer all accident claims covered by the Workmen's Compensation Act to him. But his friends knew when he was joking and they loved to listen to his anecdotes, especially those with a political sting in the tail.

Winnie was often angry with Nelson over what she considered to be his careless spending, and told him he was an economic disaster. He seldom had any money in his pocket, and when he did he would buy something they didn't really need. He often brought home boxes of fruit and vegetables as part of his quest for a healthy lifestyle, which included regular exercise and eating well.

Mandela also had a rebellious streak, and at times this drove him to wilfully challenge the law. His former wife, Evelyn, was not happy about the poor education her sons were getting in Johannesburg. She discussed her concerns with Kaiser Matanzima, and he suggested that the boys be sent to school in the Transkei, where he would watch over them. Evelyn asked Matanzima to take this proposal to Mandela, who immediately agreed that the rural conditions and superior education of a mission school would be to his sons' advantage. He took them shopping for school clothes and then drove them to the Transkei himself, without permission from the authorities, and in clear contravention of his banning order and bail conditions. He explained to Winnie that he would honour the restrictions on his movements up to a point, but was not prepared to police himself. She was understandably anxious about his decision. It was a long, tiring trip, and he had to travel through the night in order to appear in court the next day and avoid being caught out. Any number of things could go wrong, and Winnie spent a sleepless night, worrying about her husband until he was safely home again.

Whenever possible, Winnie attended the trial, both to support Nelson and because of her own political interests. Her exotic beauty, dignity and obvious strength swept through the depressing courtroom like a fresh breeze. When Nelson and Winnie were together, they turned heads. They were glamorous, basked in the glow of their love, and despite the potentially disastrous consequences of the trial, they appeared invincible. Winnie was becoming increasingly involved in the work and operations of the ANC, and it seemed to Mandela's friends that he was grooming her to play a significant role in the movement. And they had to admit, however grudgingly, that she was more than capable of doing so.

The political atmosphere in South Africa took a turn for the worse when Dr Hendrik Frensch Verwoerd became prime minister in 1958. Like tyrants such as Hitler and Stalin, he was not born in the country he would rule with a right-wing rod. His Dutch parents emigrated to South Africa when Verwoerd was a baby, and during the 1920s, while studying in Germany, he was influenced by the doctrine of the emerging National Socialist (Nazi) Party.

ANC leader Chief Albert Luthuli described Verwoerd as apartheid's 'most ardent and relentless apostle',[1] and his policies would incite blacks to protest on an unprecedented scale. They demanded a minimum wage of £1 a day and the eradication of the Group Areas Act, the unjust permit system, the increase in poll tax and – above all – the proposed extension of the hated pass laws. Previously, passes applied only to men. But moves were afoot to make it mandatory for black women, too, to carry at all times an identify document called a reference book, which contained the bearer's personal particulars and a photograph. The pass was used to control the movement, employment and residence of blacks. The system divided communities and tore apart families, often forcing husbands and wives to live in different areas. Every black person over the age of sixteen had to carry their reference books at all times, and produce them on demand to any police officer, day or night. Failure to do so resulted in summary detention, and was an offence that carried a £10 fine or one-month prison sentence. Offering an excuse that a pass had been lost or simply forgotten at home made no difference, and some 500 000 blacks went to jail each year for pass offences, earning South Africa the dubious distinction of having one of the highest prison populations in the world.

Whites were not required to carry similar identity documents, but ironically they did not escape the consequences of the draconian laws. Ruthless police officers thought nothing of leaving small white children stranded and crying on their way from school or the neighbourhood shop if the black nanny who was walking them home could not produce her pass; and white employers spent a disproportionate amount of time tracking workers who had disappeared without a trace, and bailing them out of prison. Blacks viewed the pass laws with such contempt that they no longer had any regard for the stigma of going to jail. In fact, repeat pass law offenders were seen by many as political heroes.

Black women had staged numerous protests against the pass laws, of which the largest was a march by 20 000 of them on the Union Buildings in Pretoria in August 1956. Luthuli believed that the active participation of women in the struggle would force political change in his lifetime; and in his autobiography *Long Walk to Freedom*, Mandela said the women's anti-pass protests had set an unequalled standard for anti-government protests. In October 1958, Lillian Ngoyi organised another mass protest in Johannesburg, and Winnie, already an active member of the ANC Women's League, decided to take part. Nelson had encouraged and supported her membership of the Orlando West branch of the league, but he was taken aback when she told him of her decision. By and large, she had been shielded from the reality of life as it was experienced by most black South Africans, and he warned her that this single act of defiance could change her life dramatically. He was particularly concerned that she might lose her job at Bara, a state-run hospital, especially since they were relying almost entirely on Winnie's salary at the time. She was also in the early stages of her first pregnancy, and Nelson feared the effect that possible imprisonment might have on her.

But although she shared his concerns, Winnie had made her decision. On the day of the march, Nelson made breakfast for his battle-ready wife and drove her to the home of his old friend Walter Sisulu, whose wife Albertina was one of the protest leaders. Then he took the two women to Phefeni station in Orlando, from where they would take a train into the city.

Many years later, Mandela said that as she waved to him from the train window, he felt as though Winnie was setting off on a long and perilous journey, the end of which neither of them could know. His presentiment of doom proved justified. At that point, despite being Nelson's wife, Winnie was not regarded as a threat by the government. She had no record of political activism and was a model employee. But the anti-pass demonstration would place her squarely in their sights.

Hundreds of women from townships around Johannesburg marched on the Central Pass Office that day. There were professional women and office workers in smart suits, factory workers in overalls, rural residents wrapped in tribal blankets. Some were young and educated, others old, bent and illiterate. They represented all the major ethnic groups and every social sphere. Many had babies strapped to their backs. They sang and chanted anti-pass slogans, and some of them blocked the entrance to the pass office, turning away both clerks arriving for work and people who had come to collect or apply for the iniquitous documents. The pass office was brought to a standstill, but within a few hours dozens of armed policemen arrested all the protestors and ordered them into waiting police vans. They sang and chanted all the way to Marshall Square, Johannesburg's police headquarters. More than 1 000 women were arrested, and Mandela and Tambo were called to arrange their bail. Nelson rushed to Marshall Square, where Winnie greeted him with a bright and reassuring smile. But her induction into the rigours of political activism had only just begun.

From the police cells, the women were moved to the Fort, the prison in Braamfontein, which was totally unprepared for the sudden influx of so many awaiting-trial prisoners. There were not enough blankets, sleeping mats, toilets or food for the women, who milled around in the main hall and on a second-floor balcony while waiting to be processed. They were lined up in groups, ordered to undress, and told to squat so that warders could conduct vaginal searches for contraband. Then the women were told to dress again and shown to the cells – filthy, stinking and lice-riddled. Each woman was given a single blanket, caked with dirt and reeking of urine, and the cells were so overcrowded that there was hardly enough space for them to lie down. The ANC leadership, including Mandela, wanted to arrange bail for the women, but Lillian Ngoyi, the national president of the Women's League, and Helen Joseph, secretary of the South African Women's Federation, which was affiliated with the Women's League, argued that in order for the protest to be effective, the women should forego bail, refuse to pay any fines and serve whatever sentence the courts handed down. But not all the women were prepared to spend a month or more in prison, and a compromise was reached: they would stay in jail for two weeks, after which the ANC would pay their fines.

Meanwhile, the protests would continue. The widely reported arrests did not deter other women, and during further demonstrations another 1 000 were arrested. As the number of prisoners increased, conditions at the Fort deteriorated even further. A terrible stench from the sanitary buckets hung over the overcrowded cells, there were endless queues for showers, and Winnie was revolted by conditions that assailed her senses day and night.

As a result of the appalling conditions and the shock of her situation, she started haemorrhaging. Terrified that she was having a miscarriage, Winnie sank to her knees and buried her head in her hands. Albertina Sisulu, a trained midwife, realised that something was terribly wrong, and pushed the women surrounding Winnie out of the way so that there was enough room for her to lie down. Albertina took off her own jacket and wrapped it around Winnie to keep her warm, and gave strict instructions that she was not to move. The simple, basic care paid off, and Winnie's baby was saved.

The women subsequently appeared in court and were convicted. The ANC, with the help of family members and well-wishers, raised the amount needed to pay their fines, and the women were free to go home. Unpleasant as her first spell in prison had been, Winnie was still in defiant mood, and she refused to apply for a reference book for years. In fact, she only capitulated after Nelson was sent to prison and she was told she would not be allowed to visit him without one.

While at the Fort, Winnie had befriended two young Afrikaans wardresses. They were curious about the protest, and sympathetic when Winnie explained it to them. When she was released, Winnie invited them to visit her and Nelson at their home. They took the train to Orlando and had lunch with the Mandelas. Afterwards, Winnie took them on a tour of the township. At the end of the pleasant outing, the visitors thanked their hosts and said they would like to visit again. Unfortunately, two young white women on a train to a black township drew the attention of the security police. The outing was reported to their superiors, they were dismissed, and the Mandelas never heard from them again.

The triumph of Winnie's elevated status as a jailed ANC protestor was overshadowed by the shocking, though not entirely unexpected, news that she had been sacked. Although this was exactly what Nelson had warned might happen, it was still a heavy blow. She loved her work and had been happy at Bara. Moreover, they needed her salary. There were critical reports in some newspapers, which noted that Winnie, the bright graduate of the Jan Hofmeyr College, had sacrificed the chance to study in America on a scholarship in order to serve black South Africans, only to be dismissed for advocating women's rights. The authorities took no notice, Winnie's father sent her some money to tide them over, and a while later she managed to get a job at the Johannesburg Child Welfare Society.

In early 1959, near the end of her pregnancy, Nelson had to go out of town to attend an executive meeting of the ANC. He assured Winnie that he would be back well ahead of the scheduled birth. But the baby had a different agenda, and Nelson arrived home a day after their first daughter was born. When he first laid eyes on her, he proudly announced that she was a true Tembu princess. The next day he arrived at the hospital with a beautiful layette for the baby, and a few days after that with a selection of pretty nightgowns for her mother.

When Winnie and the baby went home, both her mother-in-law and Walter Sisulu's mother were waiting to offer her traditional counsel on how to care for the infant. Winnie was horrified when Nelson's mother informed her they had arranged for an *inyanga* [tribal healer] to give the baby a traditional herbal bath, and she refused to take part in what she considered an unsanitary and outdated custom. She also stubbornly refused to drink the herbal tea the elderly women had prepared for her, but she acceded to custom when it came to naming the baby. It was the prerogative of a Tembu chief to name all babies born into the Madiba clan and the Mandela family, and Chief Ndingi named the little girl Zenani, which meant 'what have you brought to the world'. The Madikizela family prophetically named her Nomadabi Nosizwe [battlefield of the nation], and Winnie shortened her name to Zeni. She was a beautiful and happy child, and her devoted parents showered her with love.

As soon as she could, Winnie again began helping Nelson with his work for the ANC. He, in turn, took great pains to explain his political philosophy to her. The expected outcome of the Treason Trial left little room for optimism, and he seemed anxious to share as much as he could with Winnie in whatever time they had left together. At a practical level, he realised that Winnie needed to learn to drive, and offered to teach her himself. Inevitably, as when any husband tries to teach his wife to drive, the lessons led to marital strife and often ended in shouting matches, until Nelson admitted defeat and asked his friend Joe Matthews to instruct Winnie instead.

As for any other young woman, marriage and motherhood demanded compromises from Winnie, but she was determined to remain true to herself. Much as she loved and admired her Madiba, as she called him, she would not hide in his shadow, or become known as nothing more than just his wife. So, when Zenani was five months old, Winnie left her in her grandmother's care, and went back to work.

6

A declaration of war

ANY DESIRE OR intention that Nelson and Winnie Mandela might have had to lead a normal life would have been thwarted by government policies that provided compelling grounds for them to continue their political crusade.

In 1959, parliament passed the Promotion of Bantu Self-Government Act, creating eight ethnic homelands called Bantustans. The legislation formed the basis of the state's *groot apartheid* [grand apartheid]. Blacks were outraged by the obvious injustice of a policy that set aside 13 per cent of the land in South Africa for more than 70 per cent of its people. Although roughly two-thirds of black South Africans lived in so-called white areas, the new law determined that they could only claim citizenship of their traditional homelands. The aim was clearly to drive blacks out of, or as far away as possible from, areas inhabited by whites, and to fragment them into separate tribes in order to divide them and prevent them from functioning as one cohesive group.

The policy of divide and rule dated back to 1950, when the Population Registration Act classified people according to race. 'White' was a single category, but people of mixed blood were subdivided into groups such as Cape Coloured, Malay and Griqua, while in addition to Chinese and Indian there was a separate category for 'other Asian'. By breaking down the identity of blacks along tribal lines, the government's intention was clearly to present the whites as the single biggest ethnic group, since, taken as a whole, the blacks were unquestionably in the majority and posed the most serious political threat.

A slew of supporting legislation followed the 1950 law, including the Prohibition of Mixed Marriages Act, the Group Areas Act, the Native Labour Act and the Reservation of Separate Amenities Act. The Extension of University Education Act was unashamedly discriminatory, as it barred 'non-whites' from universities that had until then been open to all. At every level of society, the government was putting into effect measures to honour promises that would prevent blacks and other non-whites from being integrated into the wider community. However, the Bantustan system did not lead to true self-government or independence in the homelands, nor was it ever intended to do so, since the Bantustan 'governments' were hand-picked by and financially dependent on the South African authorities. Verwoerd promised that the Bantustans would engender so much goodwill among blacks that, unlike white urban areas, they would never be used as the springboards for rebellion. He couldn't have been more wrong.

The escalating strife in Africa did not go unnoticed internationally. The United Nations declared 1960 'Africa Year', in support and celebration of the principle of independence after the continent's long exposure to colonialism. In order to strengthen the protest against apartheid, Chief Albert Luthuli, president of the ANC, called for an international boycott of South African products.

The 1960s would hold numerous hardships for the Mandela family, both personally and politically, but as the decade began, Winnie had no inkling that the international spotlight would fall as much on her as on Nelson. In cities across South Africa, there was growing interaction between the white intelligentsia and educated blacks, Indians and coloureds. The National Party could not allow a multiracial society to take root, as this would seriously challenge its policy of segregation, and those who practised free association were labelled communists.

Nelson and Winnie had become close friends with Paul and Adelaide Joseph. Paul was a senior member of the Indian Congress, had been active in the Defiance Campaign and was one of the defendants in the Treason Trial. Adelaide and Winnie were both members of the Women's Federation, and had attended a course in public speaking arranged by Hilda Bernstein and Helen Joseph, a white woman of British descent who was to become one of Winnie's closest friends. But Winnie didn't feel the need for formal instruction on how to get her message across, and suggested that she, and other activists, should simply speak from the heart when expressing their views on the injustices they opposed. She was right. When she made her first public speech after joining the Women's Federation, she made such an impact that her audience composed a song in her honour there and then. Her candid, shoot-from-the-hip delivery became one of her trademarks, and her public addresses reflected an innate insight and natural empathy that could not be learned.

Nelson's professional life was under tremendous strain, and by the end of 1960 his law practice had all but ceased to exist. More and more of their friends went into exile, and their vibrant social network was in tatters. Winnie bravely soldiered on, meeting the many challenges of being a young mother, wife and working woman, supporting her husband morally, politically and financially. She was often alone. Mandela regularly spent the night in Pretoria after consultations with his legal team, and when he did come home, Winnie had to share him with the ANC. Many a meal was interrupted by telephone calls, and he often had to meet with other ANC leaders or arrange bail for members.

Sometimes they would see one another only for a brief period in the morning, when he dashed into the house to take a bath and change his clothes before joining his co-accused in the Treason Trial. Winnie later said she couldn't recall a time when they had a truly normal family life. As Nelson had warned her before they got married, the struggle always came first, but this did not prevent him from being a loving husband and father, even though his wife and children always had to share him with the nation.

At times, though, he could be infuriating, such as when he returned from court with a group of people and blithely told Winnie he had invited them to taste her wonderful cooking – at a time of the month when there might be only a single chop left in the fridge! He had no sense of the practical demands of domestic life and never even had a bank account, but Winnie never resented his commitment to the struggle, and in between all her other duties, found time to further her own involvement.

She greatly admired Lillian Ngoyi, prominent in the ANC and another accused in the Treason Trial, and learned much from other prominent ANC women such as Albertina Sisulu, Florence Matomela, Frances Baard, Kate Molale and Ruth Mompati. She also developed good relationships with Hilda Bernstein – the only member of the Communist Party of South Africa (CPSA) to serve on the Johannesburg City Council for three years during the 1940s – and Ruth First, an academic, editor of several radical newspapers and author of several books. She and her husband Joe Slovo, an advocate, played leading roles in the liberation struggle. Ruth was killed by a letter bomb in Mozambique in August 1982.

But more than any other woman, it was Helen Joseph who influenced Winnie, despite the thirty-year difference in their ages. Winnie regarded Helen as a mother figure, and was grateful for the advice and support the older woman offered. Helen had become politically active during World War II, and had founded a number of civil rights organisations that made her a target of the police Special Branch. She and Lillian Ngoyi were the only two women accused in the Treason Trial.

By 1959, serious tensions within the ANC reached crisis proportions. As president of the Youth League, Nelson knew that some of the members were becoming increasingly disgruntled, challenging the ANC's moderate policies, which they condemned as ineffective. A major bone of contention was a proposed alliance with the CPSA and white liberals, and Mandela spent many a night reasoning with the dissidents until the early hours of the morning in a bid to close an ever-widening rift.

When he was released in February 1990 after more than twenty-seven years in prison, it was generally accepted that Mandela had developed his reconciliatory vision during the long years behind bars. In fact, as early as 1959, when he fell into bed too exhausted and exasperated to sleep, he would tell Winnie that the dissidents seemed incapable of grasping that black racism in retaliation for white racism would never result in a country that was free and fair for all, but would tear South Africa apart. For him, the challenge was always to find a way for people of all races to live together in harmony. He worried about opportunists who saw the struggle as a vehicle for adventure, and didn't understand the tremendous patience, effort and hard work that were needed to normalise an entire society.

In November 1958, a militant group with strong Africanist leanings broke away from the ANC, and in April 1959 formed the Pan Africanist Congress. Their leader, Robert Sobukwe, was a university lecturer, and a strong and charismatic leader. He saw the PAC as the ANC's rival for black support, but the organisation never managed to muster enough of a popular following to take the lead in the liberation struggle.

The restrictive pass laws continued to evoke opposition, and the ANC planned to launch a national protest on 31 March 1960. The Mandela home in Orlando West became the campaign headquarters, and Winnie threw her full weight into the preparations. Then the PAC announced that it, too, would organise anti-pass protests, but ten days earlier, on 21 March.

Winnie didn't go to work that day, staying home so that she could monitor radio reports of the PAC campaign. But except for news that Robert Sobukwe had been arrested, there was no reference to the PAC campaign, which had drawn fairly large support in Cape Town but little response anywhere else. That afternoon, one of Winnie's colleagues in the Women's League, Beatrice, burst into the house and told Winnie hysterically that the police were shooting people in Sharpeville. Beatrice lived in Vereeniging, ninety kilometres south of Johannesburg, and Winnie realised at once that she would not have driven that distance unless something was seriously awry. But Beatrice was so distraught that it took a while for her to tell Winnie what had happened.

That morning, Beatrice had heard that people were gathering in Sharpeville, the black township a few kilometres outside Vereeniging, and had decided to see for herself what was going on. By the time she arrived, some 5 000 people had congregated outside the police station, but, Beatrice said, they were doing nothing except mill around and talk, and someone told her they were waiting for an announcement about the pass laws. At noon, said Beatrice, a large contingent of police arrived in armoured cars, and from time to time helicopters swooped low over the crowd, which paid little attention to this activity. Suddenly, Beatrice heard gunfire, and within seconds people were screaming in terror and running in all directions, while shots rang out and dead and wounded people fell to the ground. Beatrice rushed to her car and drove to Soweto as fast as she could.

News of the massacre spread like wildfire through Soweto, but details only emerged in the days that followed: sixty-nine people dead, including ten children and eight women, most of them shot in the back, and another 176 wounded. In the wake of the Sharpeville shootings, riots broke out in the Cape Town townships of Langa and Nyanga. In Langa, where thousands of blacks took to the streets, the police killed fourteen people and wounded dozens more. Condemnation from both inside and outside South Africa was swift. The police had shot and killed blacks before, but not on this scale. The United Nations Security Council passed a resolution by nine votes to none (with Britain and France abstaining) that condemned the South African government for its actions, and called for the introduction of measures that would promote racial harmony and equality.

The ANC leaders anticipated that the government would use the crisis as an excuse to clamp down on black political activity, and decided to send a senior representative abroad to ensure that the organisation's voice would still be heard. Their choice fell on Oliver Tambo, and six days after Sharpeville he left in haste for Botswana, from where he would make his way to London via Kenya, Tanzania and Ghana.

The ANC's reading of the situation proved correct. The government declared a state of emergency, banned a host of political organisations, including the ANC and PAC, and rounded up 2 000 activists. Among them were Nelson Mandela and Chief Albert Luthuli, who was awarded the Nobel Peace Prize while he was in prison.

In the early hours of 30 March, a familiar banging on the door heralded a police raid on the Mandela home. Half a dozen armed security policemen turned the house upside down, confiscating practically every document in the house. Nelson had been compiling a family history and legends about his ancestors, and even those notes were taken. He never saw them again. The police had no warrant but they arrested him and refused him permission to call his lawyer. When Winnie asked where he was being taken, they would not tell her.

After less than two years of marriage, Winnie was alone, her husband in jail, and any semblance of normal life was gone forever.

Before Tambo left the country, he asked a friend, Hymie Davidoff, to close down the practice of Mandela and Tambo. Davidoff sought permission from the authorities for Mandela to assist him over weekends, and, astonishingly, they agreed. Every Friday afternoon he was driven to Johannesburg from Pretoria by a Sergeant Kruger, and back again on Monday morning, having slept in the police cells at Marshall Square. Kruger was a decent man who treated Mandela well and shared with him the snacks he bought to eat during their weekly drives. Mandela was surprised that Kruger left him alone in the car while he went into a store, and at first thought how easy it would be to escape and be swallowed up by the crowds of people on the pavements. But an unspoken code of honour developed between the two men and Mandela never broke it, not even when Kruger relaxed his guard to the extent of allowing his prisoner to go to the café on the ground floor of the office building on his own. Kruger also allowed Winnie to spend time with Mandela at the office on these working weekends.

She visited her husband in Pretoria several times, taking Zenani with her. She was just over a year old, starting to walk and talk, and some of the prison warders allowed her father to hold and cuddle her. At the end of each visit, Winnie had to brace herself to wrench an unwilling, and clearly puzzled, Zeni from her father and go home without him.

With the ANC now banned, Winnie's positions had ceased to exist, but the organisation simply went underground and there was still a great deal of work to be done. Indeed, officials who had escaped detention took on the additional responsibilities of those in prison, and were busier than ever. Among those arrested was Joe Matthews, who had been asked by Nelson to give Winnie driving lessons. In his absence she decided to teach herself, practising in the driveway of her home. During one such session, she demolished most of the garage door but, undeterred, decided the next step was to drive in traffic. She thought it prudent to have someone accompany her, and Mandela's secretary, Ruth Mompati, was her first choice. They were good friends, and Ruth was pleased when Winnie offered to drive her to work one morning.

Within minutes of lurching into the heavy peak hour traffic, however, Ruth realised that Winnie had absolutely no idea what she was doing. Ruth clung to her seat in terror as other drivers hooted furiously and Winnie dodged one car after another. Against all odds, they reached Ruth's office safely, but she told Winnie she would never set foot in a car with her again. Somehow, Winnie persuaded her to change her mind, and Ruth acted as navigator for the learner driver until she was ready to take her driving test. But she needed a licensed driver to accompany her to the test grounds, and since her friends were either at work or in jail, she asked a pump attendant at the filling station where she had become a regular customer to go with her. Nelson was both surprised and pleased when he learned that she had passed the test at her first attempt, though he was less happy, when he finally arrived home, about the state of the garage door. Three years later, the car that had survived Winnie's driving lessons was destroyed when someone planted a bomb in it. The perpetrator was never identified.

The government crackdown had left little doubt that Oliver Tambo would have to remain in exile for an indeterminate time, and the ANC had to find a way for his wife, Adelaide, and their two small children to join him. Winnie was closely involved in planning their escape, but found it distressing and emotionally draining. Adelaide was one of her dearest friends, and she dreaded losing her. It took three months of careful planning before Adelaide, on foot and disguised as a peasant woman, crossed the border into Swaziland with her daughter Thembi and son Dali, just eighteen months old. She had no travel documents and had to wait for almost a month before Ghana's president, Kwame Nkrumah, sent an aircraft to fetch her.

They had to land in the Belgian Congo (later renamed Zaire) to refuel, and Adelaide unwittingly became embroiled in what was about to erupt into a full-scale civil war. Following independence from Belgium at the end of June 1960, the rich mining province of Katanga had seceded from the Congo, and Belgian troops had been flown in to restore order and protect hundreds of Belgian nationals. Heavy fighting broke out, and in July, 4 000 troops from Ethiopia, Ghana, Guinea, Morocco and Tunisia were airlifted into the strife-torn area under the banner of the United Nations to support the Congolese forces.

In the midst of this escalating crisis, the aircraft carrying Adelaide Tambo and her children landed in Katanga. Crew and passengers were immediately arrested, and Adelaide spent an anxious night in a Congolese prison. The next day, high-level negotiations secured her release and she was able to continue her journey to Ghana. Finally, three months after leaving South Africa, she joined her husband in London, and while Oliver went about setting up the external wing of the ANC, she found a job as a nursing sister and made a home for her family. It would be many years before she and Winnie saw one another again, but they remained close friends, and Adelaide was one of Winnie's staunchest supporters.

Mandela was still in detention when he was called to give evidence at the Treason Trial in August 1960. The entire country was riveted by what he had to say, and even Winnie, who had a good idea of how he would present his case, was captivated. Many political analysts believe that the way he set out the ANC's policies and actions during his evidence in chief and cross-examination established his reputation and leadership qualities, not only in South Africa, but around the world. At the end of August, the five-month-old state of emergency was lifted, and Mandela was released.

Winnie revelled in the joy of having her Madiba home again. The Treason Trial continued, but she cherished the evenings, when he came home. For a while their lives were almost normal, but time was running out for Soweto's uncrowned royal family. One Sunday morning, Adelaide Joseph witnessed at first hand the adulation of the ordinary people for Mandela. Driving through the township, Nelson's car was recognised immediately by men, women and children, who waved and shouted in greeting, calling out 'Mandela! Mandela!' as he passed. Adelaide said later that it was then that she knew, without a doubt, that he was the man South Africa needed, and she was always struck by the fact that neither Nelson nor Winnie ever forgot 'the people down at the bottom'. During Mandela's long years in prison, Winnie made it her business to visit the families of other political detainees and arrange financial aid for them because, she said, they were not the Mandelas or Sisulus, but the ordinary, 'forgotten' people.

In stark contrast to Verwoerd's predictions about the Bantustans, resistance to apartheid was intensifying. In Pondoland, both the Mandela and Madikizela families felt the impact. In parts of the region, people suspected of collaborating with the government were assaulted, some even killed. In Tembuland, resistance that had first become apparent in 1955 was growing fiercer. Winnie was especially concerned about the situation in Pondoland, where a serious uprising was brewing. The media essentially ignored the growing tensions, but visiting relatives and friends brought first-hand accounts of the unrest, and the news spread via the 'bush telegraph'.

In Bizana and other troubled areas, many people vehemently opposed the establishment of a Bantu Authority to replace the traditional Bunga. Pondo tribesmen were deeply suspicious of the Bantu Authority, which intensified when the government amended the Land Trust Act and allowed the Bantu Authority to decide on the distribution, zoning and fencing of land. Grazing lands were divided arbitrarily, and in some cases fences were erected across graves in family cemeteries. This was sacrilege to the Pondo and caused widespread outrage. Another highly emotive issue was the culling of cattle, which, the Bantu Authority claimed, was essential to promote conservation. But the Pondo found it difficult to understand why the number of cattle they could own had to be limited, while no such restrictions were placed on white farmers. There was also widespread unhappiness over the forced resettlement of large numbers of people to areas that were already overcrowded, and where soil erosion was a serious problem. It seemed to fly in the face of the supposed concern about conservation. People had farmed on the same land for generations, and became convinced that the Bantu Authority wanted to force them off the land to work as cheap labour on white farms and in the mines. In an attempt to halt the resistance, the Bantu Authority offered financial compensation to tribal chiefs to enforce the legislation. Some chiefs agreed, and this, in turn, gave rise to even greater opposition. A number of Pondo tribesmen formed a body called Intaba, which means mountain, to organise opposition to the Bantu Authority.

Intaba's first step was to persuade the compliant chiefs and headmen to reject the scheme. Those who refused or hesitated were given a chilling ultimatum: resist the Bantu Authority, or face death. Twenty chiefs who refused to support Intaba were killed and their kraals burned.

The ANC supported the tribal hierarchy and issued a statement denouncing chiefs who supported the Bantustan policy. The government was well aware that the cooperation of the tribal leaders was crucial to the success of their policies, since rural people were generally inclined to follow the lead taken by their chiefs. At the same time, support at grassroots level would be an important psychological victory for apartheid over the ANC, and might even lead to a wedge being driven between the organisation and the tribal leaders. Chiefs were told that the ANC planned to usurp their power, but that if they supported the government, their authority would be assured.

Many chiefs could not resist the promises and monetary rewards offered by the government, and the majority of them eventually declared support for the Bantu Authority. The chiefs arranged to be protected by armed guards, and throughout Pondoland the atmosphere was one of anarchy. When ordinary tribesmen turned on their chiefs, burned down their huts and assaulted or killed them and their supporters, the government retaliated by detaining hundreds of people. Many were imprisoned for up to ten years, and twenty were sentenced to life imprisonment.

Mandela was mortified when his kinsman and close childhood friend, Chief Kaiser Matanzima, joined the ranks of the government supporters, sending a raiding party to Rwantsana where, under police protection, they set fire to dozens of huts. From the moment she first heard about the revolt, Winnie was deeply concerned about her family, but not for a moment did she think Columbus would side with the Bantu Authority. It therefore came as a terrible shock when she received news to the contrary.

Jeremiah, the young migrant worker who had been one of her travel companions when she went to Johannesburg in 1953, always called on Winnie when he returned from Bizana, bringing news and messages from home. During the Pondoland unrest, he came to tell her that tribesmen had met at Ngquza Hills to consider action against Chief Botha Sigcau, and armed resistance against the government. The authorities sent a heavily armed police contingent to break up the meeting. According to Jeremiah, the tribesmen had surrendered and offered a white flag, but the police opened fire on them anyway with machine guns, shooting many in the back as they fled. At least thirty men were killed, though official statements claimed that only six had died in what was described as 'tribal unrest'. The rest fled into the forests, some with bullet wounds, and regrouped.

Ultimately, after many bloody clashes, Intaba prevailed, and again warned chiefs against cooperating with the government. A group within Intaba, called the Horsemen, carried out the revenge attacks, and chiefs who ignored the warnings were sent a final message – the Horsemen are coming – before Intaba acted against them. Those who escaped fled to hastily erected refugee camps in Bizana and Umzimkulu.

Jeremiah's news was bad enough, but then he told Winnie the worst: Columbus had been involved. Intaba had wanted to use his buses to travel to the meeting, but he refused, citing his job with the Education Department as the reason he could not help them. They saw his reluctance as support for the government, and branded him a collaborator. Intaba hijacked the buses and forced the drivers to take them to the meeting, and now Winnie's family feared that Intaba would kill Columbus.

Winnie listened to Jeremiah with a sinking heart. She accepted that her father had been placed in an impossible situation due to his job as a teacher, but she was worried about his safety. Columbus knew he was a marked man, however, and took precautions to protect his family. One night, while he was working in his study, the Intaba Horsemen came. Columbus, Hilda and other family members managed to escape and hide in the garden until they left, but Makhulu, old and frail, could not. She was asleep when the attackers, angered at not being able to find Columbus, beat and stabbed her before setting her hut alight. Amazingly, she survived, but she was paralysed from the waist down and died fairly soon after the attack.

Winnie was inconsolable when she heard that her beloved grandmother had become a victim of the violence. The unrest in Pondoland continued, and nearly 5 000 people were arrested. Intaba called a boycott of white shops, and Pondo and Tembu tribesmen travelled to Johannesburg to inform the ANC about the situation in the Transkei. They told Mandela that the chiefs were seen as acting out of self-interest and greed, and that supporters of Matanzima and Sigcau were waging terror against those who opposed the Bantu Authority. They feared that Matanzima would depose Sabata Dalindyebo, the paramount chief of the Tembu, and take control of the Transkei.

Mandela was stricken by the news that members of his own clan were at war with one another. While he and other ANC leaders met with the tribal representatives, Winnie was in the kitchen, preparing food for the visitors. Enoch Mbhele, a man she knew from home and who had worked for Columbus as a bus driver, brought a pile of plates from the lounge, greeted her cheerfully and sat down, chatting about nothing in particular. Suddenly, he switched gear and told her, matter-of-factly: 'Your father is a lucky bastard, but we shall get him yet.' Then he added, menacingly: 'He won't be so lucky next time.'

Winnie went numb. Mbhele must have realised that she was in an impossible situation, torn between her father and her husband, but when she pleaded with him to consider her feelings, he simply laughed. She retreated to her bedroom and sobbed bitterly over the predicament she was in. She adored her father, but she had just fed men, under her own roof, who were plotting to kill him. And she didn't feel as though she could discuss her anguish with Madiba. As she had feared, it wasn't long before the rumour was spread that she had harboured her own father's enemies in her house.

After more than a year of conflict, a handful of white traders – utterly dependent on the custom of the Pondo people for their livelihood – brought an end to the strife by complaining to the government that the boycott was ruining them. The government agreed to make certain concessions, and the Land Trust scheme was not enforced in Pondoland.

But for Winnie and her family, the Pondo revolt would have far-reaching consequences. After the Intaba attack on his home, Columbus resigned as a teacher, threw his support behind Kaiser Matanzima and accepted a position as a minister in his cabinet. Her father now stood in direct opposition to everything that Winnie and Nelson believed in, and his decision tore the Madikizela family apart. Winnie's brothers had joined Intaba, and she felt that Columbus had betrayed everything he had taught his children about the need to strive for justice and respect. Columbus was instrumental in drafting the constitution for the self-governing homeland of Transkei. Matanzima rewarded him with the portfolio of agriculture and forestry, an important position in an area so dependent on farming.

Winnie always believed that Matanzima had misled her father into thinking that by serving as a homeland leader, he would be contributing to the liberation of his people. Years later, Columbus acknowledged as much.

7

In the eye of the storm

WHEN WE APPEAR to be repeating our parents' mistakes, the theory holds, we are paradoxically trying to rectify what we missed in our own childhood. Winnie dreamed of having a big, close and happy family, and before Zenani was a year old, she was pregnant again. But, as had been the case when she was in the Fort, she started haemorrhaging, and this time, even though Nelson rushed her to his friend, Dr Mohamed Abdullah, the miscarriage could not be prevented.

While Nelson was in prison after the Sharpeville massacre, Winnie found that she was pregnant once more. She was pleased, but this pregnancy, too, was beset with problems. She suffered so badly from acute nausea that she consulted Dr Motlana. He gave her an injection of Sparene, which was often used and believed to be a harmless drug in such circumstances. But in Winnie's case, it gave the young doctor what he later said was one of the most terrifying experiences of his career. She collapsed and he could not detect a pulse. He called two of his colleagues to help him carry her to his car so that he could rush her to hospital. When the first doctor entered his room, he feared the worst, like Motlana, and exclaimed: 'What have you done? You have killed Mrs Mandela!' Fortunately, their other colleague had more experience of the drug and knew that a small percentage of people were allergic to it. Winnie was one of them. She recovered completely, but the incident haunted Motlana for many years.

When the Treason Trial adjourned in December, Nelson received word that his son Makgatho was ill at school in the Transkei. Once again violating his banning order, he drove through the night to go to the boy, and on reaching Qamata found that Makgatho was in need of medical care. Nelson wrapped him in a blanket and drove straight back to Johannesburg.

In the meanwhile, Winnie had gone into labour.

For her second delivery she didn't go to Baragwanath Hospital, but to the Bridgeman Memorial Hospital where her sister Nancy had done her training. She was in labour for many agonising hours before their second daughter was delivered by forceps on 23 December 1960. Afterwards, Winnie developed puerperal fever and was placed in an oxygen tent. When Nelson arrived home in the early hours of the morning with his sick son, he heard that he had a second daughter and a desperately ill wife. Inevitably, the police had been unable to resist raiding the house while the occupants were away, and it was in chaos. He simply left the mess and rushed to Dr Abdullah with Makgatho, then left him at home with Leaby and went to the hospital to see Winnie. She was still running a high temperature and was almost delirious. Nelson was furious, convinced that her condition had been caused by hospital neglect, and ignoring the objections of the medical staff, he bundled her and the tiny baby into his car and took them home, calling Dr Motlana to examine his wife. She made a full recovery, and the little girl was called Zindziswa, after the daughter of Samuel Mqhayi, the celebrated Xhosa poet, who had been a source of inspiration to Mandela while he was at school at Healdtown. According to legend, the poet's wife had given birth to a daughter while he was away on a long trip. He had not known that she was pregnant, and when he returned home, assuming that another man had fathered the child, had stormed into the house with an *assegai* [spear] to stab the mother and child to death. But when he saw that the baby looked exactly like him, he retreated and said, '*u Zindzile*,' which means, 'You are well established.' He then named his daughter Zindziswa, and many years later the Mandelas did the same, but abbreviated her name to Zindzi.

As soon as she could, Winnie went back to work at the Welfare Society. Apart from the fact that she now had two babies to care for, there was little change in their routine. After being in court each day, Nelson either stayed in Pretoria for several hours to consult with his lawyers, or rushed back to Johannesburg to do what little legal work he could from the quiet of Ahmed Kathrada's flat at No.13, Kholvad House. When he was at home the telephone would ring incessantly, or he would be called away, and he marvelled at Winnie's patience with the frenetic lifestyle he had imposed on her. Busy as she was, Winnie took on the job of finding suitable schools for Nelson's sons. He wanted them settled in a safe place if he should be imprisoned, so it was decided to enrol them at Anglican boarding schools in Swaziland – Thembi at St Michael's and Makgatho at St Christopher's.

Winnie's day began early, when she drove to Kliptown to leave Zeni in the care of friends. Then she rushed to Fordsburg, where Paul and Adelaide Joseph lived. Adelaide had offered to take care of Zindzi along with her own small children, and Winnie, in turn, supplied the Josephs with medication and advice on how best to take care of their handicapped son. Having settled her children, Winnie would go about her social work, and when possible drive to Pretoria to drop in on the Treason Trial.

Just before the end of the trial, the judge adjourned proceedings for a week. This coincided with the expiry of Mandela's banning order, and he was able to slip away to the All-In African Conference in Pietermaritzburg on 25 March. He was the keynote speaker at the conference, which was attended by 1 400 delegates from across the country.

After five years, Justice Rumpff finally delivered the verdict in the Treason Trial on 29 March. As Winnie took her seat in the courtroom she appeared composed, smiling reassuringly at Nelson and the other accused, but inwardly she was in a storm of apprehension and uncertainty. Like many observers, she was convinced the defendants would not be sentenced to death, although this was the usual penalty for treason. The international community had expressed vocal opposition to the way the South African government was dealing with its political problems, but the state had done everything possible to prove that the accused were guilty, producing thousands of documents in support of the charges. Winnie was terrified. She had already had a taste of what life was like with Nelson behind bars, and that had been for only a few months. What would she do if he had to spend years in prison? How would she cope, alone with two small children? What if he *did* get the death penalty?

With her heart in her throat, she listened to the judge evaluating the testimony of 150 witnesses. Each word seemed to drop heavily like a clod of dark, damp soil, and she steeled herself to hear the worst. When Rumpff reached the crucial part of his deliberations, she dared not hope that she had understood him correctly: 'On all the evidence presented to this court and on our finding of fact, it is impossible for this court to come to the conclusion that the African National Congress had acquired or adopted a policy to overthrow the state by violence, that is, in the sense that the masses had to be prepared or conditioned to commit direct acts of violence against the state.' With growing incredulity and elation, Winnie heard the judge say that the prosecution had failed to prove that the ANC was a communist organisation, or that the Freedom Charter envisioned a communist state. After speaking for forty minutes, Justice Rumpff told the men in the dock to stand for his verdict. The court was as silent as a church. Then, incredibly, the judge said the words no one had dared to hope they would hear: '*The accused are accordingly found not guilty and are discharged.*'

There was an explosion of sound as cheers erupted. The accused embraced each other and waved to their family and friends in the courtroom. There were floods of tears as they moved outside, and Winnie rushed into Nelson's arms. They hugged one another with uninhibited joy. A large crowd of well-wishers lustily sang 'Nkosi Sikelel' iAfrika'. Surrounded by the jubilant crowd, Mandela told Winnie to go home, as he had to meet with his advisers.

Ecstatic and relieved as she was, Winnie's heart was heavy. She had known for some time that in the unlikely event that he was found not guilty, it would be not the beginning, but the end of her life with Madiba. She had told no one, but she knew he was not coming home. What she didn't know, was for how long.

Shortly before the end of the trial the ANC's National Executive had met secretly to discuss the future, and decided that if Mandela were not convicted, he would go underground. They knew only too well that the National Party would step up its repressive measures, and that the government wanted to rid itself of the ANC leadership. If the accused were acquitted, the authorities would do everything possible to crush the ANC's support. Nelson had told Winnie of the executive's decision, and one day, while washing a shirt, she had found a receipt in the pocket showing he had paid the rental on the house for six months in advance. He had also had the car serviced, and she knew he was doing whatever he could to make her life easier while he was away, either in prison or in hiding. He told her he did not relish the thought of living as an outlaw, but that it was something he would have to do. She had tried to prepare herself for the worst, but had not expected that he would have to disappear immediately, without spending even a day or two at home. In her autobiography, *Part of My Soul Went With Him*, Winnie said there had been no opportunity to discuss the implications of his life underground, and in *Higher Than Hope*, Fatima Meer said it had not even occurred to him that he should discuss the decision with his family before agreeing. He simply took their full support for granted.

Just before the last day of the trial, Mandela came to the house with Walter Sisulu, Duma Nokwe and Joe Modise, and asked Winnie to pack a suitcase of clothes and toiletries for him. After the verdict she drove back to Johannesburg, deep in thought and struggling with her conflicting emotions. A jubilant crowd was waiting at the house to celebrate their leader's freedom, and she bravely joined them, keeping to herself the terrible secret that he would not make an appearance himself.

In later years, Mandela often said he could not have coped underground without Winnie's support. But when he left, it was extremely difficult for her. She was a young, country woman with a thin veneer of big-city sophistication, alone in the terrifying world of 1960s South African politics.

Mandela set off for Port Elizabeth to discuss the structure of the underground operation with Govan Mbeki and Raymond Mhlaba, and met members of the media to talk about the campaign for a national convention. From there he went to Cape Town for more meetings, and then to Durban to discuss the form of action planned by the ANC to protest against the establishment of the Republic of South Africa on 31 May. A referendum among white voters in October had voted in favour of a republic, but at the Pietermaritzburg conference the ANC had called for a national convention to draft a new constitution without a colour bar. Knowing that the government would not consider such a request, the ANC also called for countrywide demonstrations and a three-day stayaway to protest against the establishment of a republic.

As soon as the police discovered that Mandela was not around to be served with a new banning order, they issued a warrant for his arrest. He became, in his own words, a creature of the night. By day, he stayed out of sight in one of his many hideouts – empty flats, other people's homes, wherever he would be invisible. During this period, under trying and often tense conditions, he wrote prolifically, planning and plotting in solitude. But he missed Winnie and the children terribly. When darkness fell, he would meet with various groups and recruit members for the ANC. He travelled only when it was essential, sticking mainly to Johannesburg and the surrounding area. He managed to elude the police in a game of cat and mouse that captured the imagination of the South African newspapers, which dubbed him the 'Black Pimpernel', after Baroness Orczy's fictional hero of the French Revolution, the Scarlet Pimpernel, who, in similar daring fashion, had remained one step ahead of his pursuers. Wild rumours abounded about Mandela's whereabouts, but in reality his life was anything but a romantic adventure. He was constantly on the move, spending a few weeks with a family in Market Street, Johannesburg, two months with Wolfie Kodesh in his bachelor flat in Berea, masquerading as the gardener and living in the servants' quarters at a doctor's house in Norwood, and hiding in a safe house in Cyrildene. He even spent two weeks on a sugar plantation in Natal. But he never considered giving himself up, even though he was deprived of everything he held dear – Winnie, their children, his work as a lawyer.

Nelson's life in the shadows was a frightening experience for Winnie. She knew he would be arrested if he came home, and she tried hard to fight depression and despondency. When her spirits were at their lowest, she received a visit from someone who would become a pillar of support to her. He was an Anglican priest, the Reverend Leo Rakale, and as a result of his devoted ministry, Winnie joined the Anglican Church. With religion having played such a major role in her childhood, she found her faith anew, and it sustained her in the difficult years ahead. She shared the Anglican faith with her close friend Helen Joseph, who, like Winnie, was banned, and for sixteen years suffered continuous harassment, personal attacks – including one where her gate was rigged with explosives – and frequently received death threats.

Winnie saw Nelson regularly while he was underground. It was a very dramatic period in her life, and she would wait for 'the sacred knock' at her window in the dead of night, never knowing when she would see him. During the first few months he could sneak home for an hour or so, but the police soon started watching the house on a twenty-four-hour basis, and it became riskier for Winnie to see her husband. Sometimes, someone would arrive at the house and order her to follow him in her car. They would drive a certain distance from the house, switch cars, change direction. Winnie usually had no idea where she was. Wolfie Kodesh noticed that while Mandela was living with him, tears came to his eyes whenever he spoke about Winnie and the children. Wolfie arranged several visits for them, but many attempts had to be aborted for fear of detection. Because the Mandelas were so loved and respected, many of their friends were willing to take the risks involved in arranging for them to spend a little time together. Even in the police force there were loyal supporters, including a black sergeant who would regularly tip off Winnie as to the police's plans, and tell her, for example, to make sure that Madiba was not in Alexandra on a specific night, because there was going to be a raid. Nelson and Winnie's meetings were mostly arranged by whites who were not suspected of any covert activities. Often, Winnie didn't even know them, but would suddenly find herself in a strange house, the residents having arranged to go out while she and Nelson met. But their friends in Soweto were also involved. One evening, Dr Motlana's wife, Sally, received a telephone call warning her to expect a visitor. When the doorbell rang, she almost fainted when she recognised Mandela. He asked her to fetch Winnie, and she rushed over and told Winnie to make herself as beautiful as she could, because an important person wanted to see her. Sally left the two of them alone, and as she walked away she heard them laughing happily.

Mandela was underground for seventeen months, and often popped up in the most unexpected places. Once, while Winnie was driving in the city, she stopped at a red traffic light and glanced casually to the left. To her shock, she realised that the chauffeur in the car next to hers was her husband. He had pulled his cap well down, but it was unmistakably Nelson. He showed no sign of recognition, and fearing that someone might be following her, Winnie quickly looked straight ahead and drove off as soon as the light turned green.

Difficult as it was for Winnie not to know where and how he was, she only had to open the *Rand Daily Mail* every morning to find out where he had been. Some journalists had begun reporting on his activities and alleged whereabouts regularly, and readers followed his movements as they might a fictional serial. Mandela played along, and later admitted that he kept the legend of the Black Pimpernel alive by calling certain reporters from public telephones, either ridiculing the incompetence of the police or passing on information about the ANC's plans. The security police were convinced that sooner or later Mandela would go home to see his children, and watched Winnie like a hawk. But Nelson knew better than to fall into that trap.

Among those frequently involved in arranging secret meetings for Nelson and Winnie were attorney Harold Wolpe and his wife, Ann-Marie. They had known Winnie since Mandela started courting her, and Harold greatly admired Nelson's leadership style. In October 1961, the ANC found sanctuary for Mandela at Lilliesleaf Farm in Rivonia, a rustic suburb north of Johannesburg. The property was ostensibly the home of Arthur Goldreich, who moved in with his family. On the surface, it was no different from any other farm in the prosperous area, but in reality, it was the headquarters of Umkhonto we Sizwe, or MK [Spear of the Nation], the ANC's military wing. After fifty years of non-violent protest, the ANC had decided to launch a controlled campaign of sabotage against symbolic installations. It was due to start on 16 December with twenty-three acts of sabotage against carefully selected targets. The campaign was to be spearheaded by Joe Slovo, assisted by Goldreich and Wolpe, whose experience and expertise as the 'extremely dangerous' men the security police labelled them, were inadequate and seriously flawed.

Winnie and the children often visited Mandela at Lilliesleaf, an ideal setting for their family reunions. During their stolen moments together, the girls ran around and played with their father. Nelson carried Zeni through the orchard, or took her rowing on the stream. Ironically, at Lilliesleaf they had the privacy Winnie had always longed for. She cooked meals they could enjoy as a family, without interruption. It was like living in the eye of a storm, and because it was the only place where they were together as a family, Zeni came to think of the farm as home. For years after Mandela was imprisoned she insisted that her father was living in the big house in Rivonia, and kept asking Winnie when they were going home to him.

Mandela was not insensitive to Winnie's difficulties, and he did what he could to make life easier for her. When he heard that she was having problems with their old car, he sprang into action. One day someone approached her at work with a message to drive to a particular intersection in the city. When she got there, a tall man in a chauffeur's white coat and peaked cap opened the door, and ordered her to move across to the passenger seat. It was Mandela, in one of his many disguises, which were so effective that even Winnie did not instantly recognise him. He drove to a car dealership, and in broad daylight traded in the old car and bought another one. Then he drove Winnie back to Sauer Street, one of Johannesburg's busiest thoroughfares, and at a stop sign got out of the car and disappeared into the throng of commuters.

But Mandela's friends were very concerned about the lack of security measures, especially at Lilliesleaf. To the farm workers and all but the top ANC leadership, Mandela was known as David Motsamayi, a houseboy or male servant. The fact that Winnie was a frequent visitor who might be recognised by any number of people was enough to cause Paul and Adelaide Joseph to warn that they were being reckless. But the ANC in general was naive and inexperienced when it came to clandestine operations. Fatima Meer recorded that shortly after Mandela came to her home one morning, a close friend of theirs telephoned and nonchalantly asked whether Nelson had arrived. Fatima was shocked and feigned ignorance, saying there was no such person at her house. But the caller insisted that he had dropped Nelson there a few hours earlier. Fatima again said, firmly, that there was no one by that name in her house, and ended the call. When she told Mandela, he was irate. Both of them were astonished at the idiocy of the caller, as it was assumed that every known activist's telephone was being tapped. Mandela briefly considered finding somewhere else to hide, but in the end decided to stay with the Meers for a few days. An experienced underground operative would have left at once.

Joe Slovo said his admiration for Mandela grew while he was a fugitive, and that as South Africa's most wanted man he took serious risks, still insisting on leading from the front. Winnie was little more than a helpless onlooker, and could do nothing except wait and see what happened next.

In December the media reported that Chief Albert Luthuli had been granted a visa to travel to Oslo to accept the Nobel Peace Prize. The fact that a man who had been portrayed as a dangerous communist agitator should receive the highest accolade from the international community was a slap in the face of the South African government, and an important psychological triumph for the ANC, though it did them little good inside the country. Soon afterwards Luthuli was banished to Natal, and later died under suspicious circumstances, leaving the ANC with his maxim: 'Let your courage rise with danger.'

The ANC was ready to raise the stakes, and Mandela, commander-in-chief of a fledgling revolutionary fighting force, prepared to start the sabotage campaign. White South Africans had celebrated 16 December as a religious holiday – Dingane's Day – since a Boer commando defeated the Zulu king at Blood River in 1838, and it was on this day in 1961 that the ANC planned to detonate its first home-made bombs at power plants and government offices in Johannesburg, Port Elizabeth and Durban. At the same time, leaflets setting out the MK manifesto would be distributed throughout South Africa, announcing the existence of Umkhonto we Sizwe. The government response was an even harsher crackdown than any in the past, and the capture of MK operatives became the primary police objective. These were dangerous times, and Winnie had to cut back on her visits to Lilliesleaf. Zeni and Zindzi were too young to understand what was happening, but Makgatho, aged eleven, had been entrusted with the knowledge that his father was on the run, and instructed never to reveal the true identity of 'David Motsamayi' to anyone. But keeping so big a secret could not be easy for a small boy, and one day, when Makgatho was playing with Arthur Goldreich's son Nicholas, also aged eleven, they found a copy of *Drum* magazine, which Winnie had brought. Inside was a picture of Mandela taken before he went underground, and Makgatho exclaimed: 'That's my father!' Nicholas did not believe him, and Makgatho, determined to prove he was telling the truth, blurted out that his father's real name was not David, but Nelson Mandela. To settle the squabble, Nicholas ran to his mother and told her what had happened. Hazel Goldreich was alarmed and told Mandela, but because plans were already under way for Mandela to be smuggled out of the country to visit various African states, and London, they decided to do nothing.

The night before his departure on 10 January 1962, Nelson and Winnie met secretly at the home of white friends in Johannesburg's northern suburbs. While he was abroad, Winnie read the daily newspapers closely, the only way she could follow his progress. He met with President Julius Nyerere of Tanzania, Emperor Haile Selassie of Ethiopia, and the presidents of Sudan, Tunisia, Mali, Guinea, Liberia and Algeria.

In London, he spent time with the Tambos and an old friend from Orlando, composer Todd Matshikiza, writer of the hit musical *King Kong*. Matshikiza's wife Esmé was awed by Mandela's vision of the future, which she thought was nothing less than divinely inspired. She suggested he should stay in London to avoid capture, but he was adamant that a leader should be with his people.

While he was away, Nelson kept in touch with Winnie through letters that were delivered by hand, so that she never knew how the underground mail network operated. The police had begun harassing her as soon as they learned that he had sneaked out of the country, following her constantly and searching the house, looking for any shred of information that would indicate when he planned to return. Winnie told a reporter from the Johannesburg *Sunday Times* that the police searched or visited her house almost every day during the first three weeks of June, often arriving just as she and the children were about to go to bed.

Sometimes they were pleasant and businesslike, but at others they were rude and aggressive, which frightened the children. It didn't help that newspapers reported that Nelson was back in South Africa while he was actually still in Addis Ababa. On 20 June, the police arrived at the house at 10 pm, and were furious that Winnie wasn't home. Her sister, who was living with her, demanded to see a search warrant, but they pushed past her and ransacked the house. Agitated neighbours gathered outside, and a group of youths showed their resentment by setting fire to the police motorcycles. The fuel tanks exploded just as Winnie arrived home, and the police stormed out, firearms drawn, shouting accusations at Winnie for the damage caused.

In their determination to apprehend Mandela, security was stepped up at all border posts, but not only did Mandela elude his hunters, he managed to slip a precious cargo past them as well – the national dress of each country he had visited, as a gift for Winnie. The day after his return, she and the children went to Lilliesleaf Farm for a brief visit, but it was a nerve-wracking trip. The police were manning roadblocks all around Johannesburg, so it was decided that Winnie would travel in a Red Cross ambulance, with Zeni and Zindzi beside her, and pretend to be a woman in the final stages of labour. It was a convincing performance, complete with a doctor in attendance and stethoscope at the ready, and it worked.

Nelson had been both invigorated and inspired by his travels, and shared the experience with Winnie in detail. But they both knew time was running out. The South African government had called in the help of the British secret service to find the elusive Mandela, and Winnie left Lilliesleaf that day with a strong premonition of doom. When they parted, her eyes were filled with tears, a memory he carried with him for many lonely years. It was seventeen months since he had gone underground, and this would be their last private moment for almost three decades.

Winnie left Lilliesleaf with her wardrobe of authentic African clothes, and the next day Nelson went to Durban for a meeting with Chief Luthuli and MB Yengwa. He spent his last day of freedom for more than twenty-seven years with a number of friends, including Ismail and Fatima Meer, JN Singh, Dr Monty Naicker and Yengwa, at the home of photo-journalist GR Naidoo. They ate and drank merrily, discussed politics and laughed a lot, not least over the fact that the police were hunting for Mandela everywhere, yet here he was, openly partying with friends. Some of those closest to Mandela at the time thought he had grown so careless that he seemed almost to be inviting arrest. Dennis Goldberg pointed out that the stress of living a secret life sometimes became so great that people subconsciouly made deliberate mistakes in order to put an end to the subterfuge. Perhaps it was inevitable, then, that on Sunday 5 August, while travelling back to Johannesburg, Mandela was apprehended by armed police in three vehicles. It was just two hours since Mandela, in his customary role as chauffeur, had left the home of the Meers with his 'employer', Cecil Williams. The police had the registration number of the car, and any protest was futile.

Just hours before newspaper headlines around the world shrieked that the Black Pimpernel had been captured, one of Nelson's friends went to Winnie's office at the Child Welfare Society. He looked terrible, his face pale and unshaven, his hair tousled. She knew immediately that something was wrong, and fearing that Nelson might have been shot trying to avoid capture at a police roadblock, all she could ask was: 'Is he all right?' The man replied, 'No, we think he'll be appearing in the Johannesburg court tomorrow.'

She was stunned. In that moment, Winnie felt the full impact of a political dream's collapse. Nelson was lost, not only to her and his children, but to the struggle, to the cause of their people – at the height of his career.

She could never remember how she got home that day, but she knew that her life would never be the same again. In later years, she said that when he was captured, part of her soul went with him.

Winnie had married Nelson Mandela on 14 June 1958, and he had gone underground in April 1961. By the time he was arrested, they had been married a few months longer than four years, but between the Treason Trial, the five months he had spent in prison during the state of emergency and his life on the run, they had shared a home life for just more than two years.

Some people within the ANC suspected GR Naidoo of tipping off the police, but there was never any proof that anyone betrayed Mandela, and he himself dismissed all speculation of a traitor. Walter Sisulu, Duma Nokwe, Joe Slovo, Ahmed Kathrada, even Winnie herself, discounted rumours of betrayal from within the ANC as mischief-making by the government, designed to cause a rift in the organisation.

8

Traitors for friends

ON 7 AUGUST 1962, Nelson Mandela was charged with inciting black workers to strike and leaving the country without valid travel documents.

In the spectators' gallery at the Johannesburg magistrate's court, Winnie was clearly distressed. She knew that he would go to prison, and that whatever hope of a return to normality she might have fostered during the seventeen months he was a fugitive had been smashed. Difficult months, possibly years, lay ahead, and somehow she would have to manage on her own, with two small children to raise. After years of expecting it to happen, the sword of Damocles had finally dropped.

As Mandela left the courtroom, he smiled at her brightly, reassuringly. She knew he was trying to put on a brave face, and when she was allowed to visit him a few days later, she, too, tried to hide her fears, and took extra care with her appearance. Either because she wasn't yet thinking straight after the shock of his arrest, or in defiance of the dire situation in which he found himself, she took him a gift of new, expensive pyjamas and a silk dressing gown. The clothing was wholly unsuitable for prison, and Nelson knew he could never wear the garments, but he expressed his gratitude because he knew she had wanted to show her love. They talked about family matters and how she would support herself and the children. Mandela named friends who would help her, and told her about clients who still owed him legal fees. The most painful decision was what to tell the children, and Mandela insisted that it be the truth, and asked her to explain that he would probably be gone for a long time.

He did his best to comfort her, pointing out that they were not the first family to face such a predicament. He gently reminded her that he would need her support more than ever, and that their cause was just, but that it demanded personal sacrifice. The officer on duty turned a blind eye and allowed them to embrace, and they clung to one another, even though they had no idea that it would be more than a quarter of a century before they would hold one another again. The kindly officer allowed Nelson to accompany Winnie part of the way to the main gate, and he watched her until she disappeared around a corner, alone, but with her head held high.

Although Mandela's arrest was a shock, he, Winnie and the ANC leaders had all known that it was inevitable. In September, Winnie wrote to Adelaide Tambo in London that it had nevertheless come as a grievous blow 'at the wrong time', and reminded her how important it was for Oliver and the ANC's external wing to muster as much support for Nelson as possible. Winnie understood the political climate well enough to realise that Nelson might be in jail for some years, and Bram Fischer, who was both Nelson's attorney and friend, along with other supporters, urged her to leave the country and study abroad. But, like Mandela, she refused, believing that her place was with her people, and making it clear that she would not desert the man she loved. She was well aware, though, that there were certain people within the ANC – to say nothing of the security police – who would welcome her departure.

Shortly after Nelson's arrest, Winnie was summoned to the Transkei for a meeting with the tribal elders at his home. She thought they wanted to discuss the situation with her, but was appalled to learn that they actually wanted her to consult a witch doctor and take part in rituals they believed would save Mandela from imprisonment. Winnie's upbringing and her mother's staunch resistance to tribal worship drove her to refuse. Later, she regretted not going along with the plan, which would have made no difference to the outcome, but would have appeased those close to Mandela. She realised too late, she said, how deeply she had offended family members to whom traditional rituals meant a great deal, and had perhaps been too scared that, by participating, she might fuel the fires of bigots who proclaimed that blacks were uncivilised and thus unfit to run the country.

The first time Winnie was invited to stand in for Mandela at a political event was at the Indian Youth Congress's annual conference. Wearing a yellow sari and a garland of yellow carnations, she used her opening speech to repudiate rumours that an ANC comrade had betrayed Mandela. On his behalf, she stated emphatically that the organisation would not waste time conducting an internal witch-hunt, since the government clearly hoped its propaganda would lead to dissent in the ranks and a weakening of opposition to its policies. The press reported more on her beauty and eloquence than the substance of her speech, but the 250 delegates elected Mandela their honorary president. Afterwards, Winnie went to the Fort to see Mandela, who was not only delighted to see her looking wonderful, but elated when she told him how well she had been received.

Nelson had often warned Winnie to beware of opportunists and informers, and she was about to experience at first-hand the danger of taking people at face value. At the Fort, Mandela had run into an old acquaintance, Moosa Dinath, a successful businessman and Transvaal Indian Congress member, who had been imprisoned for fraud. Mandela had mentioned to Winnie that Dinath, whom he had earlier introduced to her, was at the Fort, but what he didn't tell her was that he found it strange that a prisoner convicted for a non-political offence was allowed to spend a great deal of time with him, or that he had become aware that Dinath was allowed to spend whole nights outside the prison, with the acquiescence of the chief warder, Colonel Minnaar.

Dinath had married a white woman in the Mozambican capital of Lourenço Marques (now Maputo), but she still went by her maiden name of Maude Katzenellenbogen. In due course, Maude introduced herself to Winnie and invited her to her home, a rundown house within walking distance of the Fort. They were roughly the same age, both had young children and a husband behind bars, and became good friends. Maude gave Winnie a welcome cheque for £4, as well as groceries and clothes for the children at a time when she was in need of assistance. She also told Winnie there was no need for her to take food to Nelson, as she lived so close to the prison that she would happily do so.

So when Winnie got a message that Dinath wanted to see her, she had no reason to be suspicious, though she was surprised when she was taken to an office rather than the visitors' area. Dinath immediately assured her that nothing had happened to Mandela, as she feared. A senior officer, who was his friend, was present as proof that he approved of the proposal he was about to make, Dinath said. He would allow Mandela to 'escape' from the Fort, in exchange for a cash payment of £600 – but the plan would have to be carried out as soon as possible, in case the authorities decided to transfer Mandela to another facility. Would Winnie be able to raise the money?

Winnie was both surprised and apprehensive, and realised that Dinath expected her to ask the ANC for the money. She said she thought this could be done, and Dinath explained that as soon as the money was paid, he would provide Mandela with a saw to cut through the bars of his cell. He would also be given a firearm, and allowed to leave the prison without being stopped. The plan was foolproof, said Dinath, but the full amount had to be paid in advance.

Winnie's blood ran cold. Neither Moosa nor the warder seemed to think she would find it odd that Nelson was to be given a saw, when the door of his cell was to be unlocked in any event. Instinctively, she realised that this was a trap, and that far from allowing Mandela to walk out of the Fort, the authorities planned to kill him, and would defend their action by citing an armed escape. She was also confused. She viewed Dinath as a friend, and Mandela had said nothing to make her believe otherwise, but she hid her feelings and indicated that she was willing to go along with the plan. After a sleepless night she reported the conversation to Walter Sisulu, who agreed that it was most likely a trap, and told her he would deal with the matter. But he advised Winnie not to go back to the Fort. She obeyed, and heard no more of the plan, assuming that Dinath had been manipulated or terrorised by the authorities into making the offer. No one in the

ANC ever told her whether this was the case or not, and her friendship with Maude continued. In years to come, Winnie would be betrayed time and again by people she trusted, and her gullibility would cause her great sorrow and disappointment.

The weekend before his trial began on 15 October, Mandela was suddenly transferred to Pretoria. His lawyers objected in vain, and the ANC, which was organising 'Free Mandela' protests, realised that the government was hoping the last-minute change of venue would prevent courthouse demonstrations. Walter Sisulu had also been charged with incitement, but he and Mandela would be tried separately, one in Pretoria, the other in Johannesburg. It made little difference to the ANC supporters, though, who turned out in large numbers at both trials.

Winnie made a striking entrance into the Pretoria courtroom, clad from head to foot in the distinctive national costume of the royal Tembu line: a beaded headdress and ankle-length skirt. Mandela, too, caused great excitement when he entered the dock wearing a lion skin, the traditional garb of a chief, which had been a gift from his paramount chief. As he raised a clenched fist and cried 'Amandla!' [power], everyone in the public gallery, including the media, rose to their feet. The authorities were infuriated by this naked display of African pride, and afterwards tried to confiscate Mandela's karos [animal skin], but backed off when he threatened them with legal action. Determined to make someone pay for the impact of this defiance, the Minister of Justice served Winnie with notice that she would be barred from the courtroom if she continued to wear tribal dress. Since she had no intention of being locked out of her husband's trial, Winnie complied, but every day she wore an outfit in the colours of the ANC – black for the people, green for the land, and yellow for the gold riches of the country – or one of the colourful outfits Nelson had brought her from the African states he had visited. Hundreds of other black women, however, continued to wear their own traditional outfits to court in solidarity with Winnie.

Members of Madiba's clan led a strong show of support, and outside the court a praise singer lauded the Tembu people's opposition to injustice and narrated Mandela's genealogy. When supporters outside sang 'Nkosi Sikelel' iAfrika' and 'Chuchaliza Mandela' [Advance Mandela], the police warned them that they were violating an order that banned meetings in support of the ANC and Mandela, and gave them five minutes to disperse. But ANC officials quietened the crowd and persuaded those who could not gain entry to the packed courtroom to wait quietly and patiently outside.

Mandela conducted his own defence, neither calling any witnesses nor contesting the charges, though he placed on record that he did not consider himself guilty of any crime. It was with a heavy heart that Winnie heard her husband tell the court: 'It has not been easy for me during the past period to separate myself from my wife and children, to say goodbye to the good old days when, at the end of a strenuous day at the office, I could look forward to joining my family at the dinner table, and instead take up the life of a man hunted continually by the police, living separated from those who are closest to me, in my own country facing continually the hazards of detection and arrest. But there comes a time, as it came in my life, when a man is denied the right to live a normal life, when he can only live the life of an outlaw, because the government has so decreed to use the law to impose a state of outlawry on him. I was driven to this situation and I do not regret having taken the decisions that I did.'

The prosecutor, PJ Bosch, laid out the state's case: Mandela had spoken illegally at the conference in Pietermaritzburg; organised protests against South Africa becoming a republic; incited workers to go on strike, with the result that tens of thousands of people had not gone to work from 29 to 31 May; and he had left the country illegally and travelled to foreign states.

Prior to the verdict being handed down, Nelson was allowed two visits a week. Winnie, despite the distance and difficulties involved in taking time off work to go to Pretoria, made the trip as often as possible, taking him food, books and clean clothes. But she was not allowed to take the children to see him.

On 6 November, the day before Mandela was to be sentenced, the United Nations voted for the first time to impose sanctions against South Africa as punishment for its continued apartheid policies. In Washington and Moscow, the Cuban missile crisis threatened to plunge the world into nuclear war, but in Pretoria, police armed with tear gas were concerned only with cordoning off the area in front of the court and limiting the number of people allowed inside. Winnie sat with Mandela's aunt and other relatives from the Transkei, and showed nothing of her trepidation as she heard her husband sentenced to a total of five years in prison, with hard labour and no possibility of parole: three years for incitement to strike, two for leaving the country without travel documents.

It was the harshest penalty handed down by any South African court to date for political offences, but as always in the face of the treatment meted out to them by the authorities, neither Winnie nor Nelson showed any public emotion – they would not give the government the satisfaction of knowing how deep their anguish was. Her head held high, Winnie joined the crowd in singing 'Nkosi Sikelel' iAfrika', and in a statement to New Age she said: 'What has happened should take none of us by surprise, for we are faced with a vicious oppressor. I will continue the fight as I have in all ways done in the past. I shall certainly live under great strain in the coming years, but this type of living has become part and parcel of my life. The greatest honour a people can pay to a man behind bars is to keep the freedom flame burning, to continue the fight.'

She honoured her word. From that moment on, she dedicated her life to keeping the cause – and Mandela's name – alive.

Surprisingly, Walter Sisulu was given an even heavier six-year sentence. While he was on bail pending appeal, the ANC decided that Sisulu would take Mandela's place, go underground and lead the struggle.

On the day he was sentenced, Nelson gave Winnie a letter he had written, filled with loving reassurance and encouragement. She would describe it as the most wonderful message any wife could ever hope to receive. He urged her to be brave, and reminded her that in his absence she would occupy an important position in the community. He also warned her that she would have to face many problems without his support, and that there were people who would try to trick her and cause her downfall. Winnie cherished the letter and read it anew whenever her spirits flagged. When the security police confiscated it during one of the raids on her home, she was shattered by the loss. Despite repeated appeals the letter never was returned to her, but the words were ingrained on her mind, and in the years ahead she constantly drew on their comfort and inspiration. And she frequently recalled her husband's warnings.

The police would spare no effort to undermine Nelson Mandela and the ANC, and they identified Winnie as a useful tool after seeing how easily she had been lured into the elaborate ring of informers and false friends they set up to ensnare her, starting with Dinath and Maude. Shortly after Nelson's arrest in August, the police 'dirty tricks' brigade had started a rumour that Winnie was having second thoughts about tying herself to a man so much older than her, and had made a secret pact with the communists to sell him out. The next rumour, started by a police informer and quickly spread by township gossips, was that she had married Mandela only for his name, and wanted to divorce him. Winnie was outraged by the malicious lies, but took comfort in the fact that those who knew her would attach no importance to such absurdities.

Among the people who had entered Winnie's circle was Mary Benson, a British writer who had acted as a secretary for both Albert Luthuli and the Treason Trial Fund, and would later become one of Mandela's biographers. As a result of her close ties with the ANC, Benson was facing deportation, and wanted to do what she could to help the movement while she was still in South Africa. This included providing money for Winnie to buy a Gestetner copying machine on which she could reproduce information leaflets. When Winnie told Maude Katzenellenbogen of Benson's generosity, Maude convinced her to install the machine at her house, arguing that the police would surely confiscate it if Winnie kept it at her own home. It was a valid point, and Winnie had no reason to distrust Maude, so she accepted the offer. Maude also suggested that Winnie use her address for mail from ANC contacts outside the country. Various pseudonyms were used for this correspondence, since anything addressed to either Winnie or Nelson the security police were bound to intercept. Later, at one of the lowest ebbs of her life, Winnie would discover that the police had details about all the leaflets she had produced, and the names of all the people to whom her mail had been addressed.

Journalist Gordon Winter was a fully fledged state agent who insinuated himself into Winnie's life. They had met in 1961 at a multiracial party hosted by the *Rand Daily Mail*, and Winter had worked hard, ever since, to convince Winnie that he was a white liberal who fully supported the struggle and sympathised entirely with black people. His cover as an agent of the dreaded Bureau of State Security (BOSS) was strengthened when he helped a few activists escape from South Africa, and was deported to his native England after being found guilty of 'revolutionary activities'. This helped to establish his bona fides with the ANC in exile, and Winnie never had any reason to regard him as anything but a sympathetic friend. In that role, he obtained vital information from her, including the names of some ANC comrades and addresses to which her mail was sent. Many years later, when he was unmasked as a spy, Winter would admit that even though he was betraying her, he liked and respected Winnie, and admired her spirit.

Mandela spent his first few months in prison in virtual isolation. He was allowed no visitors or any letters for four months, and Winnie focused all her longing on April 1963, when she would be able to see him for the first time. But on 28 December 1962, she was served with a banning order that restricted her to the magisterial district of Johannesburg, prohibited her from entering any educational premises, and barred her from attending or addressing any meetings or gatherings where more than two people were present. In addition to the physical limitations on her movements, the banning order silenced her voice, as the media were no longer allowed to quote anything she said.

When news of the banning order reached Mandela in prison, he was shocked, even though he had expected the authorities to take some form of reprisal against his wife. Perhaps even more than Winnie herself, he immediately realised the full implications of the ban. He relied on Winnie to handle all their affairs, including some related to the children of his first marriage, which could be seriously impeded by the restrictions on her movements. In addition, the police would now have ample legitimate excuse to victimise her, and knowing how stubborn she could be, he feared for her safety. Concern over Winnie and the children caused Mandela to have disturbing nightmares for some time, and in due course his worst fears materialised.

Winnie's top priority was the care and welfare of Zeni and Zindzi, as well as Mandela's three older children, Makaziwe, Thembi and Makgatho. They had already suffered greatly as the result of their father's imprisonment, and Makgatho, in particular, was struggling to come to terms with his absence. Evelyn's children had a good relationship with their stepmother, and before her banning order it was Winnie who fetched the children from their school in Manzini, Swaziland, for the holidays. After she was banned, Nelson's friend, Brian Somana, would pick them up.

As time passed, life became a lot harder for the boys. They changed schools and could go home only once a year. When they spent school holidays in Swaziland, Makgatho was puzzled that they could not stay with the principal, Father Hooper, in his large, empty house, but had to live with his maid, whom they called Ma Mashwana. With five people in her own family, her small two-roomed house was overcrowded, but the Mashwanas became a surrogate family for the Mandela boys during the long school year. Later, Walter Sisulu's son Zwelakhe joined them, and the boys built their own separate hut. Their lives were further complicated by the fact that they didn't have passports. But they learned from their friends how to cross the international boundary undetected, and would take either a train or a bus to the border, walk into South Africa at night and then be taken to Johannesburg from Piet Retief by an Indian taxi driver.

Winnie's many responsibilities weighed heavily on her, and she was grateful that she could carry on working. But the banning order complicated her life in numerous ways. In order to cope, she developed two personalities – in company, she hid her problems behind a brave face and brilliant smile, but in private she grew increasingly anxious and lonely. Winnie had never really been alone in her life, surrounded first by her own family, then by friends and fellow students, and, most recently, the throngs of people that gravitated to her after her marriage to Nelson. At times she feared the loneliness would drive her mad, and she tried to counter it by helping those in need and working so hard that she was totally exhausted when she fell into bed at night. With most of Mandela's close associates in exile, in prison or in hiding, people in trouble often appealed to Winnie for assistance. One of them was Ruth Mompati, and at last Winnie could return the favour of Ruth's help when she was learning to drive.

After Mandela's arrest, Ruth was instructed to remove all the files from his office before the police seized them. Naturally, the police had then started looking for Ruth, and she went to Winnie for help. While he was on the run, Nelson had once stayed in a house directly opposite a police station, bargaining on the fact that the police would hardly think he would be hiding right under their noses. Now, applying Mandela's logic, Winnie took Ruth into her own home, even though it was under surveillance. When Winnie left for work in the morning, she would lock the door behind her, as though no one else was home. Meanwhile, inside, Ruth was finalising what she could and referring pending cases to other lawyers. One day, a number of men arrived with a furniture truck. They said they were from Levine's Furnishers and had come to repossess household goods on which the instalments were overdue. Mandela had bought the furniture on a hire purchase agreement, and somehow had neglected to make provision for continued regular payments after his arrest. Winnie had received no final demand or notice of repossession, but every piece of furniture was removed. Even the linoleum on the kitchen floor was taken, and when Winnie arrived home, all that was left were books, bedding, clothing and her kitchen utensils. She fought back her tears, swallowed her pride and borrowed a small paraffin stove from a neighbour to make supper for the children. Afterwards, she spread blankets on the floor, where she, Ruth, Zeni and Zindzi huddled together.

But Winnie didn't sleep. She wracked her brain all night to come up with a solution to this latest problem. In the morning she went to see Godfrey Pitje, a lawyer who had been an articled clerk with Nelson, and who owed him a number of favours. He agreed to lend her enough money to buy some basic items of furniture, and though it took a long time, she repaid him out of her small salary every month.

Shortly afterwards, Ruth went into exile in London, where she worked for the ANC for many years before being transferred to Lusaka. Winnie lost yet another friend, but she did not begrudge Ruth the opportunity to escape to safety, and she had left just in time. The police began raiding the house regularly, and would certainly have arrested Ruth. The yelling and bright lights shining through the windows that heralded every raid terrified the children, and it became increasingly difficult for Winnie to comfort them while strange men rifled through their possessions and made ominous remarks. But frightening and unsavoury as these early raids were, they were just the beginning of years of harassment and victimisation.

9

The Rivonia Trial

WITHOUT WARNING, Mandela was moved to Robben Island at the end of May 1963. No explanation was given to him and Winnie was not even informed of his transfer until she arrived to visit him at Pretoria Central Prison. Even then, she was told only that he had been moved, and it took a number of enquiries to find out where.

Ironically, even though he was a convicted prisoner, Nelson was in a far better situation than Winnie, who was entirely at the mercy of the security police. He had been absorbed into a system that was regulated by strict rules and regulations that dictated how prisoners were to be treated, and, in addition, he knew the law and was a well-known political figure. Mandela used these factors to his advantage, and he had barely set foot on Robben Island before making it abundantly clear that he would tolerate no transgression of the rules. He sternly told a warder who had tried to assault him that if he so much as laid a hand on him, the matter would be taken to the highest court in the land, and that when Mandela was finished with him, the warder would be as poor as a church mouse. No prison official ever laid another hand on him.

Winnie, however, was just beginning to understand how vulnerable and exposed to abuse she was. In May she was arrested for attending a gathering, but when the case was heard, she was acquitted. She had written to Mary Benson that the police had resorted to fabricating evidence against her.

In June, she was given permission to visit Nelson on the island – for thirty minutes, after a journey of 1 400 kilometres from Johannesburg and a ferry ride across ten kilometres of choppy sea from Cape Town harbour. She found conditions on the island abhorrent. The 'visitors' room' was a rickety shelter built right on the shore, with double wire mesh separating prisoner and visitor. There was nowhere to sit, and she and Nelson had to stand for the entire half-hour. The worst was that all she could see of him through the distorting mesh was an outline, and they had to raise their voices to hear one another, with white warders standing by and listening to the entire conversation. They were allowed to speak only English or Afrikaans – Xhosa and other indigenous languages were forbidden, because the warders could not understand them. And they were warned in advance that if they touched on any topic except family matters, the visit would be terminated immediately. Winnie was severely depressed when she left the island, her sole consolation that she had been able to establish for herself that Nelson was well, and that he had been glad to see her.

Barely a month after his abrupt relocation to Robben Island, Mandela found himself being whisked back to Pretoria, again with no explanation. The government issued a terse press statement claiming the move was for his own protection, because PAC prisoners on the island had threatened to assault him, but it wasn't long before the truth came out.

Since December 1961, the ANC had carried out sporadic acts of sabotage against symbols of apartheid, including Bantu Administration offices, both to hurt the government and in the hope that the instability would deter foreign investors. On 1 May 1963, the new Minister of Justice, BJ Vorster, introduced the iniquitous ninety-day law that allowed security police to detain people in solitary confinement for successive periods of ninety days at a time. In practice, this could – and did – mean that political activists were held for an indeterminate period, 'until this side of eternity', as Vorster said, without being charged or brought to court, and with no access to family members or legal representatives. Over the next two decades, thousands of people would simply disappear without trace and be interrogated mercilessly by the security police until they offered 'satisfactory' information. Veteran parliamentarian and human rights champion Helen Suzman described the process as 'torture by mindbreaking'. Among those held in detention without trial was Albertina Sisulu, the first woman to feel the wrath of the ninety-day law. The scope for abuse was self-evident, and the first death of a detainee was that of Looksmart Solwandle Ngudle, allegedly found hanged in his cell on 5 September 1963.

Amid all the signs of a renewed crackdown, the ANC was planning its most ambitious opposition yet. Operation Mayibuye would encompass sabotage and insurrection, authorised at the highest level within the movement – but rigorous questioning of detainees had given the security police enough information to plunge the ANC into crisis.

On 11 July, a seemingly innocuous dry cleaner's delivery van drove up to Lilliesleaf Farm. A young security guard tried to stop the vehicle, but was overwhelmed by heavily armed police who jumped from the vehicle. In one fell swoop, they arrested Walter Sisulu, Govan Mbeki, Ahmed Kathrada and Arthur Goldreich. Joe Slovo and Bram Fischer, who sometimes went to the farm several times a day, were not there at the time, but in the days following the raid, many other key members of the ANC were picked up. Those arrested at Lilliesleaf had been betrayed by one of their own, Bruno Mtolo, and since he had been privy to Mandela's movements prior to his arrest in 1962, many people later came to believe that he had also

116

betrayed Mandela. The penalty for treachery was often death, and, later, the brutal township necklace, a tyre doused with petrol, set alight around a person's neck, would become the most frequently used weapon of retribution against 'sell-outs'.

Four prominent ANC detainees – Goldreich, Harold Wolpe, Abdullah Jassat and Mosie Moolla – provided a triumphant respite from the general gloom within the organisation by staging one of the most audacious escapes in South African legal history. Held under close guard at Marshall Square police headquarters in Johannesburg, and with the government trumpeting the arrests as a major coup, Goldreich noticed that one of the young policemen guarding them seemed worried and depressed. He struck up a conversation with Johannes Greeff, who was only eighteen, and learned that he was desperately in need of money to pay for repairs to a friend's car, which he had damaged in an accident. Goldreich seized his chance, and magnanimously offered to arrange for young Greeff to get the money. Greeff helped him make a telephone call, ostensibly to arrange the funds, but in reality Goldreich used the call to alert his contact that they were planning an escape. By the simple action of allowing Goldreich to use the telephone, Greeff had already crossed the line, and the prisoners were quick but careful to exploit this unexpected opportunity. They bided their time, establishing a friendly relationship with Greeff while prosecutors toiled into the night to prepare the case that would convict them, and when the moment was right, offered Greeff a large sum of money to help them escape. He concurred.

Ann-Marie Wolpe, Harold's wife, had organised many of Winnie and Nelson's clandestine trysts when he was on the run, and she was given the task of arranging the getaway once the escapees got outside. She arranged that a car be parked some distance from Marshall Square to take them to a safe house in Johannesburg until they could leave the country. On the night in question, everything went according to plan, but it took the four men longer than expected to make their way to the getaway car, and the driver became more and more nervous until, convinced that the plan had failed, he drove off without them. When the four fugitives arrived at the designated spot and found no transport waiting, they had to improvise, and decided to split up. Two Indians and two white men together on the streets of Johannesburg in the dead of night would almost certainly attract the wrong attention, so they took off in opposite directions.

Astonishingly, just minutes after Goldreich and Wolpe started walking, a motorist stopped and offered them a lift. Furthermore, and by sheer coincidence, he turned out to be someone they knew and trusted! He drove them to their destination and promised solemnly to say nothing to anyone about their encounter. Moolla and Jassat experienced similar good fortune when they bumped into a friend, a waiter who was on his way home from work. He gave them temporary sanctuary until they could move to a safe house.

The next day, Ann-Marie Wolpe was arrested and questioned relentlessly, but she had genuinely not known the addresses of the safe houses that were to be used, and after twenty-four hours the police released her, none the wiser about where the four escaped men were hiding.

The newspapers printed every detail they could come up with and relied heavily on speculation about the whereabouts of the wanted men. Their photographs appeared in almost every newspaper, which added to the danger that they would be found, but for ANC supporters, victory was sweet. The police were smarting from the humiliating blow the four had struck, and searched everywhere. Special vigilance was applied along all the country's borders, which the authorities knew the men would try to cross at some point.

But the fugitives bided their time, Goldreich and Wolpe moving from one house to another until they finally took refuge in a tiny cottage. Terrified of attracting attention, they scarcely moved, and were too afraid to even strike a match in case someone saw or heard anything and discovered their presence. Finally, they were hidden in the boot of a friend's car and sneaked over the border into Swaziland, where they disguised themselves as priests. Wolpe called himself the Reverend Eric Shipton, and they pretended to be on a visit to missions in southern Africa. This made it possible for them to charter an aircraft, and in due course the two 'churchmen' made it all the way to England.

Johannes Greeff never got his money. He was arrested and agreed to help his colleagues set a trap for the man who was to deliver it. But Goldreich's friends had expected this to happen, and simply never went to the rendezvous. Greeff was convicted of helping the four men escape, and went to prison.

Winnie was alarmed when she heard that Mandela was back in Pretoria to stand trial along with the leaders arrested at Lilliesleaf. All she could think about was that this turn of events would undoubtedly lead to his five-year sentence being extended.

On 9 October 1963, the accused were taken to the historic Palace of Justice on Pretoria's Church Square for the opening day of *The State v the National High Command and others*, later known as *State v Nelson Mandela and others*, which would for evermore be called the Rivonia Trial. Near the Palace of Justice – restored to its former glory and used again as a court of law for the first time in forty years from mid-2003 – is a statue of Paul Kruger, president of the Transvaal Republic, who fought against British imperialism and oppression of his people in the closing years of the nineteenth century. The inscription on the statue, taken from one of Kruger's speeches, reads: 'In confidence we lay our cause before the whole world. Whether we win or whether we die, freedom will rise in Africa like the sun from the morning clouds.' Though the politics of Boer and black were worlds apart in the 1960s, the ANC could not have put their hopes and aspirations more clearly than the man with whose descendants they were now at war.

Mandela's physical appearance shocked his family and friends. He had lost some twelve kilograms. Because he was a convicted prisoner he could not wear his own clothes to court like the other accused, and was forced to wear the prison uniform: khaki shorts and open sandals. It was humiliating and he loathed it. He bore little resemblance to the confident and well-dressed man who had so impressed the world with his eloquence during the Treason Trial, and even after his arrest in August 1962.

Winnie's banning order was still in place, and she was refused permission to travel beyond Johannesburg to be in court on the first day of the trial – and to add to her distress, the police launched a raid on her home as well. The family members of other accused were also targeted, both Albertina Sisulu and Caroline Motsoaledi having been detained under the ninety-day law. Sisulu's young son Max had also been arrested. Imprisoning and victimising the wives and children of those involved in the struggle was a very effective way for the state to apply pressure on them; many were strong enough to handle almost anything the authorities did, but the harassment of their loved ones caused great despondency, and in some cases was successfully used to turn otherwise loyal ANC supporters into police informers.

Winnie appealed to the Minister of Justice for permission to attend Mandela's trial. He agreed, but warned that she could be barred at any time if her attendance or behaviour caused any kind of disturbance. Not for the first time, she was struck by the irony that the same government which insisted that black people had no place in 'white' society, and encouraged them to preserve their own culture (within their designated homelands, of course), forbade her from wearing traditional Xhosa dress to court. But the government knew full well that traditional dress was more than a fashion statement, and that it evoked a level of pride they had no wish to confront in an already volatile situation.

The case against Mandela was largely based on documents that had been seized during the raid on Lilliesleaf Farm. He had often asked his comrades to destroy any papers containing possibly incriminating information, but enough of them had survived to provide the prosecution with evidence of his involvement in sabotage and MK's activities. Surprisingly, the Rivonia triallists were not charged with high treason, as expected, but with sabotage and conspiracy, which meant the case could proceed without a lengthy preparatory examination. Treason charges also placed a far heavier burden of proof on the state. However, the maximum penalty was the same for both treason and conspiracy – death by hanging.

The ten accused were fortunate that instead of being in the dock with them, Bram Fischer and Joe Slovo could be members of the defence team. Fischer, who was later sentenced to life imprisonment himself, came from a prominent Free State family with deep roots in Afrikaner politics. His father was judge president of the Free State, a fact that caused the government great embarrassment. He was a brilliant advocate and immediately pointed out crucial flaws in the allegations, which implicated Mandela in acts of sabotage carried out while he was in prison. The judge rejected the indictment, thus acquitting the accused on a legal technicality.

Pandemonium erupted in the courtroom, but the jubilation was short-lived. The triallists were immediately rearrested and held while the prosecution amended the indictment. It was a scenario that would play itself out repeatedly in other cases against the government's opponents over the next few years. In the second round of the Rivonia Trial, which began on 3 December, the accused were charged with conspiracy to overthrow the government by means of revolution, and nearly 200 acts of sabotage.

As with the earlier Treason Trial, Winnie's emotions fluctuated between hope and despair. She and relatives of the other accused pooled their resources to buy food for the prisoners each day, and she lived for the moments when she could catch Nelson's eye and see him smile, or for the snatches of conversation they could exchange. She also took heart from the enormous international support for Mandela, especially when the United Nations General Assembly voted unanimously for the immediate release of the Rivonia triallists and all political prisoners in South Africa.

But the prosecutor, Percy Yutar, was resolutely building a case that would warrant seeking the death penalty, and it was obvious to all the accused, and their loved ones, that they were literally on trial for their lives.

The mood in court was overwhelmingly grim, but once in a while, there were moments of amusement, too. Ahmed Kathrada became known as the court jester, responding to Yutar's blistering cross-examination in an inimitable way. On one occasion, Yutar asked Kathrada if he knew 'one Suliman Salojee'. Kathrada replied that he knew *two* Suliman Salojees.

'And who are they?' Yutar asked.

'Suliman Salojee and Suliman Salojee,' said Kathrada.

In their consulting room below the court, the accused often communicated by way of notes, which they read and then quickly burned. One of the Special Branch officers guarding them was a Lieutenant Swanepoel, a beefy man with a ruddy face, who was convinced that the accused were constantly hatching new plots. One day, while he was watching them from the door, Govan Mbeki scribbled a note in a melodramatic way, and handed it to Mandela. Madiba read it, nodded ever so slightly and passed the note to Kathrada, who glanced at it before pointedly taking out a box of matches, as though to burn the note. Swanepoel burst into the room, grabbed the piece of paper and muttered that it was dangerous to burn things indoors. When he had left, obviously pleased to have intercepted what he clearly thought would be a major piece of incriminating evidence, the accused all burst out laughing. What Mbeki had written was: 'ISN'T SWANEPOEL A FINE-LOOKING CHAP?' Swanepoel was not amused.

During the eleven months of the trial, Winnie had little cause for amusement. It was generally believed that in the face of mounting international condemnation, the government would not dare impose the death penalty, but there were no assurances, and Winnie was deeply distressed at the thought that Nelson might pay with his life for the cause. She was under enormous pressure, having to work, take care of the children and provide as much support as she could for Nelson. She was up at dawn each day to dress and feed her daughters before dropping them off on her way to the office, where she started work long before anyone else in order to make up for the hours she spent at the trial. Whenever possible, she raced to Pretoria, then had to rush back to Johannesburg again in time to fetch the children and be home by 6 pm, as her banning order required.

On Monday 20 April 1964, the defence began presenting its case. No one, least of all the accused themselves, expected the verdict on 11 June to be anything but 'guilty'. The question, however, was what sentence would be handed down. Would they be condemned to death, or would their lives be spared? And if they were to live, how long would they spend in prison?

That night, Mandela, Sisulu and Mbeki discussed the final strategy with their lawyers. No matter what the sentence, they would not appeal. If they were given the death penalty, they knew there would be mass protests, and an appeal would not only rob the expected demonstrations of their drama and momentum, but might lessen the impact of international demands for the ANC leaders to be released. On the other hand, if the death sentence was not handed down, the judges might decide on appeal that the court had erred, and impose the death penalty themselves, leaving the prisoners with absolutely no room to manoeuvre.

It was a calculated gamble, but they were adamant that they would not appeal, regardless of the sentence. Court procedure dictated that the judge would ask Mandela, as Accused No. 1, if he could offer any reason why the death penalty should not be imposed. Mandela would reply that he was secure in the knowledge that his death would be an inspiration to the cause to which he had devoted his life.

Nelson Mandela prepared himself to die.

His young wife prayed desperately that he might live.

Two days before Nelson and Winnie's sixth wedding anniversary, on Friday 12 June, the accused entered the court to learn their fate. Mandela waved to Winnie and his mother, the two most important women in his life, sitting together and united in love and fear, knowing that whatever the outcome of the day's events, he would not be going home. The defence offered two pleas in mitigation of sentence, one by well-known advocate Harold Hanson, and the other by internationally renowned author Alan Paton, who was also national president of the Liberal Party, a devout

Christian and an outspoken opponent of violence. Hanson said although the methods used by the ANC were illegal, their aims were not, and he reminded the judge that his people, the Afrikaners, had also resorted to violence in order to attain freedom. Paton made the point that while he was an advocate of peace, the men before court had been faced with only one of two alternatives: to bow their heads and submit, or to resist by force. If they were not granted clemency, he said, the future of South Africa would be bleak. The men in the dock were the last credible ANC leaders alive, and, as such, the men with whom the government would one day have to negotiate.

Sadly, Paton did not live long enough to see his prophecy fulfilled.

Judge Quartus de Wet, judge president of the Transvaal, looked ill and nervous as he deliberated his decision. Then came the crucial point, when he asked Accused No. 1 if there was any reason why the death penalty should not be imposed.

In an address that lasted four hours, Mandela painstakingly explained the injustice of apartheid, the painful contrasts between the lives of white and black South Africans, and the aspirations of the ANC. The silence in the courtroom was absolute as he looked directly at the judge and delivered one of his most powerful and famous statements: 'During my lifetime I have dedicated myself to this struggle of the African people. I have fought against white domination, and I have fought against black domination. I have cherished the ideal of a democratic and free society in which all persons live together in harmony and with equal opportunities. It is an ideal which I hope to live for and to achieve. But if needs be, it is an ideal for which I am prepared to die.'

Though awe-inspiring, his chilling words signalled to Winnie that he was ready to sacrifice his life for his beliefs. In that instant, she knew instinctively that he was already lost to her and their children. She clung to what she knew was true: that it was a just cause and demanded total dedication. But with every fibre of her being, she hoped and prayed that she would not have to face the future as the widow of a martyr.

Despite a deathly quiet in the courtroom, the judge's voice was almost inaudible when he uttered the fateful words: 'The sentence in the case of all the accused will be one of life imprisonment.'

He had spoken so softly that most of the spectators had not heard him at all, and Dennis Goldberg's wife, Esmé, called to him and asked what the sentence was. 'Life!' he called back with a grin. 'Life! To live!'

Mandela turned around and beamed at the gallery, searching for Winnie's face in the crowd, but there was chaos, and he couldn't see her. People were shouting and the police were pushing and shoving at the crowd. Then the prisoners were ushered out of the courtroom to the cells below.

There was no doubt that the continued protests and international pressure saved the ANC's leaders from the gallows. But life imprisonment meant literally that – in South Africa, political prisoners did not qualify for parole or early release.

For Winnie, the agony was over, but the ordeal had just begun. Nelson's life had been spared, but it was stolen from her forever, and she faced a long, bleak future alone.

The *New York Times* commented: 'To most of the world [the Rivonia men] are heroes and freedom fighters, the George Washingtons and Ben Franklins of South Africa.'

A report in *The Times* of London said, prophetically: 'The picture that emerges is of men goaded beyond endurance … The verdict of history will be that the ultimate guilty party is the government in power – and that already is the verdict of world opinion.'

No one who was at or near the Palace of Justice that day could forget the sound of 'Nkosi Sikelel' iAfrika' echoing through the heart of Pretoria, the seat and symbol of government oppression. It sent shivers down Winnie's spine. Mandela had always found the anthem beautiful and moving, but now it took on new meaning as a hymn of farewell to the ANC leaders, and a reminder that they were blanketed with the devotion of their people.

In a retrospective of that day published in the London *Observer* on 20 March 1983, former *Rand Daily Mail* editor Allister Sparks wrote: 'I fully expected to see a shaken Mrs Mandela emerge from the courthouse. But no. She appeared on the steps and she flashed a smile that dazzled. The effect was regal and almost triumphant, performed in the heart of the Afrikaner capital in her moment of anguish, and the crowds of Africans thronging Church Square, with Paul Kruger's statue in the middle, loved it. They cheered, perhaps the only time black people have ever summoned the courage to cheer in that place.'

In the midst of the crowd, Winnie's thoughts turned to her daughters. Zeni was five, Zindzi a year younger, and as they waved goodbye to their father, she was acutely aware that they would be grown women before they saw him again. Her heart ached as never before, but suddenly, someone grabbed her shoulder, and she turned to face a security policeman who barked at her: 'Remember your permit! You must be back in Johannesburg on time!' She was dumbstruck. How could anyone think about anything except the human tragedy playing out in front of them? Not even a drop of empathy with a woman who had just lost her husband, nothing but the cruel need to remind her that they still had the upper hand, that they controlled her life. Momentarily, Winnie lost control, and kicked the huge policeman, hard. He showed no sign of noticing, possibly putting the blow down to the jostling of the crowd.

As Nelson and the other ANC leaders were driven away in a fortress on wheels, Winnie kissed the palm of her hand and waved it at the vehicle. Zeni and Zindzi solemnly followed her example, blowing kisses at their father, even though he could no longer see them. And then the prisoners were gone, and hundreds of cars made their way back to Johannesburg as if in a giant funeral procession.

To add to her woes, Winnie was again in trouble with the tribal elders. They had wanted her to take *muti* from a witch doctor into court in her shoe, to protect Madiba from the white man's retribution. Torn between wanting to show respect for her elders and her own beliefs, she had seriously considered accepting the small vial of brown, oily liquid that looked as though it contained hair, but in the end she could not bring herself to do it. She knew that it could not possibly affect the outcome of the trial, but after Nelson was sentenced the elders accused her of selling him out to the white man, of not wanting him to be free.

But tribal displeasure was just one of the tribulations that beset Winnie's life from the moment Nelson went to jail. Never again would she have peace of mind or know tranquillity.

Mandela's life, by contrast, would settle into a familiar and predictable pattern, albeit a harsh one. And he would be safe, shielded by regulations that were closely monitored by organisations such as Amnesty International and the Red Cross. It would be a life of deprivation, to be sure, but there would be compensations: solitude that was conducive to studying, writing and planning, and, in time, a slow trickle of victories against the system. He would also be part of a unique fraternity, bound to one another by a common goal, shared distress and colourful symbolism. Every night, before the lights were turned out, Pretoria Central Prison would resound to the swelling chorus of black prisoners singing freedom songs. Seconds before the lights were dimmed, the singing would stop, plunging the entire jail into silence. Then, from cells throughout the building, men would shout 'Amandla!' and others would thunder the response, 'Ngawethu!' It was a rousing war cry from hundreds of throats, reminding all the political prisoners that however long it took, power would be theirs, one day.

Winnie saw Nelson once more before he was taken back to Robben Island. She was heartbroken, but, as always, he managed to restore her spirit and imbue her with fresh courage. And, as before, he warned her to beware of the difficulties that lay ahead: malicious rumours, police traps, the potholes of being a young woman without a husband. He expected, said Mandela, that Winnie would live up to his expectations.

He and his comrades were confident that growing international pressure would ensure that they served no more than ten years in prison. Their lawyers agreed, and one police officer even went so far as to predict that world outrage over his life imprisonment would force the government to release Mandela within five years. The prisoners and the pundits were all very wrong.

The government was making calculations of its own, and arrived at the conclusion that in just a few years, a Mandela out of sight would also be out of mind, the ANC a spent cause, abandoned by foreign supporters. For a while, it seemed they might be right. In 1964, the London *Times* mentioned Mandela fifty-eight times, a year later only twice, and in 1966 not at all. The *New York Times* referred to him twenty-four times in 1964 and not at all in 1965 or 1966 – and a single reference in 1967 was to Winnie, not Nelson. After that, the international media all but ignored both Mandela and the ANC. Western governments had effectively written off the organisation, and in South Africa there was barely a trace of Mandela's name in the media. Moreover, resistance inside South Africa seemed to have been crushed. The ANC was going through one of its darkest periods, and Nelson Mandela was sliding into oblivion.

Winnie, however, had pledged to keep his name alive, and she was not about to abandon him or the struggle for liberation.

She began applying for permission to visit Nelson as soon as he was transferred to Robben Island. As a 'D' category prisoner he was entitled to only one visitor and one letter every six months, but for Winnie and Albertina Sisulu, both 'banned' persons, special leave had to be granted by the Minister of Justice to travel to Cape Town at all. The first letter she wrote to Nelson was almost totally blacked out by the prison censor, and little more than the salutation and closing were legible by the time it reached him. The same applied to the letters he sent her.

Two months after he returned to the island, she was granted permission to visit. Barred from associating with other passengers on the ferry, she had to make the voyage from the Cape Town docks below deck, and suffered an attack of claustrophobia. As she walked towards the prison buildings, she noted that the armed guards in the watchtowers faced outwards, towards the sea, and realised that escape from this rocky island would be impossible. She walked down the gravel path to the visitors' waiting room, and, when her name was called, made her way down the narrow passage, past the thick, uneven glass of the small windows through which the distorted faces of the prisoners on the other side looked like frightful apparitions in an impenetrable void. She was deep in thought, wondering how many times she would tread the same disconsolate path over the course of a lifetime. Someone called to her that Nelson was down at the end, jolting her out of her reverie, and then she saw him, his face beaming with his dear and welcoming smile.

Every visit to Robben Island was taxing and emotionally draining. More often than not, relatives were given less than twenty-four hours' notice that a visit had been approved, and it was never clear whether this was due to bureaucratic inefficiency or a deliberate attempt to make life as difficult as possible for the families of political prisoners. Often, however, the short notice made it impossible for visits to take place, as loved ones could not make the long journey to the Cape in time. Winnie always dressed with great care when she visited Mandela, and no matter how much strain she was under, tried to hide her feelings from him. With two warders standing directly behind her, and three behind Nelson, their thirty-minute conversations were anything but private, and precious minutes were sometimes wasted when the warders insisted on knowing their relationship to some of the people they mentioned. Despite this vigilance, they had a secret code that allowed Winnie to pass on snippets of crucial information about political developments, but most of the time they talked about the children and other family members.

The visits flew by, and it seemed like seconds before a warder barked 'Time up!' With six months to wait until they could next see one another, they were not even given time for a proper goodbye, barely managing to place their hands on either side of the thick glass separating them before Nelson was hustled from his chair and out of the tiny cubicle. At the end of her first visit, Winnie walked back to the ferry and crossed the grey sea to Cape Town in a daze, turning the words she and Nelson had exchanged over and over in her mind, almost sobbing when she remembered something she had meant to tell him, but had not. Her despondency was not helped at all by the fact that when she arrived home, she found the police had raided and ransacked her house – again. It was just as well that she had no inkling, at that moment, that it would be two years before the authorities allowed her to visit Nelson again.

The security police stepped up their campaign against Winnie almost immediately. She was spared the physical violence meted out to many other people only because she had become so well known that the authorities realised any evidence of assault would evoke an international outcry, but, even so, her arm was broken by two policemen who didn't know who she was.

Adelaide Joseph's husband, Paul, was being detained at the Mondeor Police Station, and because Winnie's house was closer than Adelaide's, she took food to him every other day. One day, when it was Adelaide's turn, the policemen on duty asked her whether the black woman who sometimes brought the food was their servant. Adelaide did not reply, and when Winnie arrived at the police station the next day, the policemen asked her why a 'kaffir girl' was taking food to a 'coolie'. The insults turned to pushing and shoving, and in the ensuing altercation, Winnie's arm was broken. She did not identify herself to her tormenters, but immediately afterwards, in great discomfort, insisted on seeing the station commander. He was horrified when he saw that the woman two of his policemen had injured, was Winnie Mandela. She told him she wanted to lay charges, and he had no choice but to register a charge of assault against the two policemen. However, Winnie was later notified that the Attorney-General had decided not to prosecute.

10

The noose tightens

'THE FIRST WEEKS and months after Nelson was gone,' Winnie reflected later, 'that was utter hell. Solitude, loneliness, is worse than fear – the most wretchedly painful illness the body and mind could be subjected to. When you suddenly realise that you are stripped of a man of such formidable stature, of whom you were just a shadow, you find yourself absolutely naked. He was a pillar of strength to me. I fumbled along and tried to adjust.'[1]

Winnie had little choice but to carry on with her life as best she could. She worked, she helped others, and she made every effort to spare Zeni and Zindzi from suffering any more than they already had as a result of their father's imprisonment. She was determined that their lives would be as normal as possible, and that they would not be deprived of any advantages they would have enjoyed if Nelson had been around, like a good education. It had been ingrained in Winnie since childhood that education was the key to a better life, and she was determined that her daughters would not have to settle for less.

As Zeni's sixth birthday approached, Winnie decided to enrol her in a Roman Catholic nursery school in Kliptown. She was just settling in and starting to make friends when, after four days, the nuns sent Winnie a letter, informing her that Nelson Mandela's child could not stay at the school. Since they had known who Zeni was when she was registered, Winnie recognised the hand of the security police in the sudden decision. She had no illusions about the extent to which the authorities would go to make her own life difficult, and would suffer any measures stoically, but the realisation that her children, too, were going to be victimised brought her close to breaking point.

Paul and Adelaide Joseph saved the day, and with their help Zeni was placed in a privately run Indian kindergarten that accepted black children. But the simple act of enrolling her daughters in school would be a recurring problem for Winnie. As soon as the authorities found out what school they attended, pressure would be applied and the girls would promptly be expelled. Prohibited by her banning order from entering any educational premises, Winnie had to rely on friends and family members to help her sort out the problem time and again.

When Zindzi, too, was old enough to go to school, Winnie sent both children to City and Suburban, a school for coloureds close to her office. One of Nelson's relatives, Judith Mtirara, was light-skinned enough to pass for a 'coloured', and had sent her children there. She agreed to enrol Zeni and Zindzi under the name of Mtirara – a subterfuge, but in keeping with the extended family system the children were entitled to use the name, along with other Madiba clan names such as Matanzima and Dalindyebo. In the afternoons, the two little girls were looked after by Amah Naidoo, a member of the family who had been prominent in the Indian Congress since Mohandas Gandhi had been politically active in South Africa, and the mother of Indris and Shanti Naidoo, who were both in detention.

Inevitably, the security police became aware of the arrangement, and made much of the fact that by attending a school reserved for coloureds the Mandela children were breaking the law. After dropping them off one morning, Judith was arrested by the security police and, under interrogation, admitted that she had arranged for Zeni, eight, and Zindzi, seven, to go to the school. The principal was detained, and the girls were expelled. Winnie didn't know which way to turn, and became severely depressed.

It was her father who, unintentionally, lifted her from her despair. Her family at home had heard that she was struggling, and her brother Msuthu – the son born shortly before their mother Gertrude died, and also known as Thanduxolo – decided to go and stay with her in Johannesburg. He had matriculated the previous year and found a job in market research, and Winnie revelled in the presence of another adult in the house. But as soon as the security police realised that Msuthu was living under her roof, they raided the house and demanded to see his permit to work in Johannesburg, which he didn't have. He was arrested and charged with being in an urban area illegally – a victim, like millions of others, of the government's influx control laws. But because both his father and sister were prominent political figures, the newspapers reported his arrest, and headlines screamed that the Transkei Minister of Agriculture's son had been detained.

The incident gave rise to the first and only serious quarrel Winnie ever had with her father. Columbus accused her of using Msuthu for political propaganda. Winnie, in turn, railed at her father that his decision to toe the line as a member of Matanzima's puppet regime did not oblige his children to follow suit in selling out the birthright of their people. She was so angry that she sent him a telegram repeating what she had already said over the telephone. Hilda later told Winnie that Columbus was so distressed by the row with his daughter that he took ill and stayed in bed for a week.

However, Winnie's anger had the effect of shaking her out of her melancholy, and she attacked both her work at the Child Welfare Society and in politics with renewed vigour. But she still struggled with loneliness at night. A sympathiser had provided the fees for Winnie to take a degree by correspondence course, and her studies helped to fill the hours. Friends telephoned as often as possible, but knowing that Winnie's line was almost certainly being tapped, conversation was confined to small talk.

As both the wife of the man they most feared and hated, and a banned person in her own right who had shown that she would not shy away from the fight against apartheid, Winnie remained the target of constant security police surveillance and harassment. The state did everything in its power to weaken her resolve, including repeatedly refusing permission for her to visit Mandela. Far from accepting such treatment, Winnie confronted it head on, soliciting the support of the media at every opportunity. She hated having everything she did or said automatically interpreted as a directive from her husband, and tried hard to reconcile her own views with what she knew or thought Mandela would expect. But her trusting naivety ensnared her in the quagmire of dirty tricks and double-dealing. She was often reminded of Nelson's warnings about betrayal and traps – but usually too late. She would know great pain before learning that the underhand measures employed by the authorities were far harder to deal with than the overt harassment, and that the ANC had been effectively infiltrated by numerous spies posing as dedicated activists.

Throughout her political career, Winnie courted a fatal flaw: no one's credentials were ever questioned, everyone's bona fides were taken for granted.

Tongues were ever ready to wag, and it didn't take much to start a whispering campaign. The security police were only too aware of this, and knew how easily Winnie's reputation could be sullied. In the interest of her welfare, Mandela had asked a number of his friends to watch over her. One of them was Brian Somana, a journalist who had been detained under the ninety-day law and had written several sympathetic reports about both Mandela and Winnie. His reputation as a supporter of the struggle seemed impeccable, and Winnie not only trusted him implicitly, but often turned to him for help, and Somana was always available when she had problems.

He made no secret of the fact that he harboured great bitterness towards Walter Sisulu, who, he claimed, had persuaded him to abandon a well-paid job in the insurance industry to join the *New Age* newspaper. Not only did he struggle to make a living as a reporter, but the paper was banned and shut down soon afterwards. However, his resentment seemed to be confined to Sisulu, and he was widely regarded as being a close friend of the Mandelas. During the Rivonia Trial, when Winnie was summoned to meet with the Mandela family elders, it was Somana who drove her and Mandela's sister to the Transkei. While there, he sat in on the frank family discussions that were also attended by one of Mandela's uncles, Jackson Nkosiyane. Soon after they returned to Johannesburg, Nkosiyane was arrested on what seemed to be fabricated evidence involving a plot to murder Kaiser Matanzima, and sentenced to six years in prison. Somana was also trusted enough to convey Mandela's sons, Thembi and Makgatho, to school in Swaziland, and helped the family in many other ways.

But Somana was a police spy, and although some ANC officials suspected him of having exposed the Lilliesleaf Farm operation, no one told Winnie that, for the second time, someone endorsed by Mandela might not be trustworthy. They were either extremely negligent, or she was being set up to fall by certain elements within the ANC.

Even when Somana bought himself a new car and Winnie noticed that he seemed to have access to an unlimited amount of money, she believed his prosperity was the result of a sweet distribution business he had set up. He gave one of her sisters a clerical job in the business, and Winnie often visited the office. One day, Winnie mentioned that she had a large number of files that she needed to move from her own office, and Somana offered to transport them for her. The time they agreed on was determined by Winnie mentioning that she was also expecting someone from the ANC to collect certain political documents from her. As it happened, the ANC official came much earlier than scheduled, but at the exact moment he was supposed to have arrived, the security police stormed in and went through every file in Winnie's office. They found nothing incriminating and left, and Winnie waited for Somana to keep their appointment. He never came, and eventually she went to his office to find out why. While she was telling her sister about the raid, a white man walked in and asked to see Somana. Her instincts honed by numerous encounters with security policemen, Winnie was convinced that the caller was one, and for the first time her suspicions about Somana were aroused. The man left an envelope for Somana, and as soon as he left, Winnie opened it. Inside were typed instructions for a meeting, with a cryptic reference to 'the same time and place'.

All ANC officials were instructed on how to handle situations involving possible informers. Under no circumstances were they to confront the suspect, and Winnie made a special effort to treat Somana normally. But something must have tipped him off, and he began coming to her house more frequently than usual, and seemed to be probing her for information. He became such a nuisance that she asked attorney Joel Joffe for assistance, and he sent Somana a letter threatening legal action unless he stopped pestering Winnie at home.

To her astonishment, Somana's wife suddenly sued for divorce, citing Winnie as co-respondent. She was aghast at the groundless accusations, and turned to the Supreme Court for leave to intervene, explaining that she, and various other people, had discovered that Somana was a security police informer and that his wife's allegations had no basis and were designed only to damage her reputation and, by extension, that of Mandela.

The divorce proceedings were halted almost immediately.

Winnie believed she had emerged with her reputation intact, until she noticed that some of her acquaintances were avoiding her. She mentioned this to a friend, who reminded Winnie that even Christ had been forsaken by his disciples. It was scant comfort, and Winnie sought solace in Nelson's few letters, reading and rereading them when she couldn't sleep at night.

Once again, it was Father Leo Rakale – her spiritual adviser during the months that Mandela was on the run – who proved her salvation. He spent hours with her at home and strongly encouraged her to go into retreat at the Rosettenville Priory. Winnie later said that he helped her to renew her faith, and they grew so close that Nelson appointed him as one of the children's guardians, along with Winnie's uncle and Dr Nthatho Motlana.

In 1965, a new and even more restrictive banning order was issued against her. The dusk-to-dawn house arrest was inconvenient, but it had not impinged on her work. Now, however, the security police barred her from movement in any area except Orlando West, where she lived. Winnie immediately understood that she would have to give up her work as a social worker. Mary Uys, director of the Child Welfare Society, burst into tears when she confirmed that Winnie would have to leave. The organisation had resisted all previous pressure to dismiss her, even though police raids regularly disrupted their work, but if Winnie could not travel to where her clients were, she could be of no use to them. She loved her job, and she and Janet Makiwane had by far the heaviest caseloads. But Winnie had never complained, and dedicated herself totally to helping those in need, even when this meant taking shortcuts to get around the ubiquitous red tape. She was never intimidated by senior officials and frequently clashed with the Commissioner of Child Welfare on matters of adoption, which were strictly regulated along ethnic lines.

With her career abruptly cut short, Winnie had to find some other means of support. After a long search, a furniture store gave her a job at a much lower salary than she had been used to, but just a few months later, in August 1965, she was dismissed without explanation. As with her children's schooling, this would become a familiar pattern. It took her three months to find her next job, as a clerk at a correspondence college for black journalists, and just a few weeks for her employer to tell her the police had been making enquiries about her, and that she would only be allowed to stay on if she agreed to divorce Nelson. At regular intervals after that, he would ask her when she was getting her divorce, and eventually she was notified by the chief magistrate of Johannesburg that she had to quit the job as it violated her banning order, which prohibited her from entering any educational premises.

The employment pool was shrinking, but Winnie next went to work for an Indian dry-cleaner, who paid her R20 a week – more than either the furniture store or the college. But, three weeks later, the police arrived and accused the owner of contravening the Factories Act by having one more shoe-repair machine on the premises than he was allowed. The police offered to overlook the offence, provided he sacked Winnie, so she left.

The hunt for a way to support herself continued, but most often she was told that even if she were perfectly capable of doing a job, her political views would not allow employers to take her on board. For a while she worked as an assistant to her own attorney, Joel Carlson, for R10 a week, but even he let her go when the police began paying undue attention to his practice. Another attorney, James Kantor, had been sent a sum of money to be shared by dependants of the Rivonia triallists, but when Winnie was called to his office to be paid what she was due, she refused to take it. Some of the other wives and families were utterly destitute, and she knew that however dire her own circumstances, she could still rely on help from friends and relatives. Her next job was in a shoe store, for the princely wage of R4 a week. She could no longer afford the cost of commercially baked bread, and drew on lessons learned from her mother in childhood until she could bake the perfect loaf at home, a forgotten skill that would stand her in good stead in later years as well.

But for the most part, Winnie had to rely on the charity of well-wishers to pay the rent and feed her daughters. For a while, she took comfort from the presence of her sister Nancy, whose husband, Sefton Vuthela, had worked at the University of the Witwatersrand until he became one of South Africa's many 'banned' persons. He had fled to Botswana rather than face imprisonment, and found a position as manager of the Botswana Book Centre. As soon as he was settled, he sent for Nancy and their two children to join him in exile. Winnie hated the thought of losing Nancy, but she gritted her teeth and asked an old friend, Elija Msibi, to help smuggle her sister and the children across the border.

Although illiterate, Elija was extremely wealthy, and one of the most successful shebeen tycoons in Soweto. Prohibited by law from buying any alcohol except 'kaffir beer', a brew made from maize meal, black people had turned to illegal establishments that opened all over the townships, where they could not only drink what they liked, but socialise with friends. The police generally turned a blind eye to the shebeens, which were also frequented by their own informers, and were a mine of information. When Winnie asked Elija to help Nancy, he readily obliged, but her departure left a huge void in Winnie's life.

Every aspect of Winnie's life, whether she was working or at home, alone or in company, was punctuated by anxiety. One evening, while bathing the children, she saw the outline of a man holding a firearm through the bathroom window. Her neighbours had been keeping an eye out for trouble, and one of them spotted the man as he climbed onto boxes next to the window. They shouted, scaring the intruder off. The police were called but no one was ever arrested.

Winnie had avoided sending her daughters to safety elsewhere, but now she realised she had to take steps to protect them. The problem was how to find a school for them, when she was not allowed to travel. Once again, she turned to shebeen owner Elija Msibi, who not only drove to Swaziland to find a suitable school for Zeni and Zindzi, but enrolled his own daughters at the same institution as support for the girls.

Sending her children away was one of the hardest things Winnie had ever had to do, but she knew she had no choice. The two little girls cried bitterly when they had to leave her, and Winnie felt as though her heart would break. She always believed it was the stress of parting with her daughters that caused the hypertension and heart condition she subsequently developed.

Zeni and Zindzi were desperately unhappy at the Convent of Our Lady of Sorrows, which was run on austere discipline that left no room for compassion. Winnie had become involved in a programme to organise correspondence courses for Nelson and the other Robben Island prisoners, backed by Sir Robert Birley, a former headmaster of Eton College, who was a visiting professor at the University of the Witwatersrand. His wife, Elinor, became friends with Winnie, and when she heard about the problems the children were having at school, Lady Birley arranged that they transfer to Waterford, an exclusive school in Swaziland with an excellent reputation. The fees were way beyond Winnie's means, but Lady Birley and Helen Joseph organised funds to pay them. Winnie treasured Elinor Birley's kindness and assistance, and their friendship continued long after the Birleys returned to England.

The cost of Winnie's dedication to the struggle was mounting, but she had embarked on a journey from which there was no return. She had not chosen the quest, it had chosen her. Having grown up with an awareness of injustice, encouraged by her father's fervour to bring about change and her own attempts to challenge the system ever since she became a social worker, it was impossible for her to turn away from the suffering and oppression of her people. Prevented from formally practising her profession, she improvised and helped those in need whenever and however she could.

Winnie's spirit was far from broken, but she was amazed that the authorities would waste endless time and financial resources contriving schemes and frivolous charges against her, which constantly failed. It took a long time for her to understand that every incident was a cog in a slow-moving wheel that was intended to ultimately pulverise her. Once, woken at four in the morning and told that she was being arrested, she closed her bedroom door while dressing. A white policeman,

Detective Sergeant Fourie, pushed open the door and grabbed Winnie by the shoulder. Incensed by the intrusion, and without stopping to think of the consequences, she grabbed him and threw him to the floor. As he fell, he pulled her dressing table down on top of himself. Six of his colleagues waiting outside carried her bodily to a police vehicle, wearing only one stocking and one shoe, and took her to prison. Fourie's neck was fractured, but he recovered. Winnie was charged with resisting arrest, and when the case was heard two months later, her advocate, George Bizos, cautioned her sternly that he wanted her to behave like a lady in front of the magistrate, not like an Amazon. Winnie was a calm and eloquent witness, and the magistrate acquitted her, ruling the police testimony contradictory.

For two years, Winnie had been prevented from visiting Nelson on Robben Island. In July 1966, she was finally given permission to go, but only on condition that she had a pass, or reference book. She had gone to prison in the mid-fifties rather than carry a pass, and she knew the condition was aimed at humiliating her and Mandela, who had burned his own pass in defiance. But she was desperate to see him, and capitulated for the sake of the greater good. People who saw her at the airport on her way to Robben Island, wearing a long, pale-blue dress and turban, proud and regal as a queen, could not guess at the hardships she was experiencing.

She hardly recognised the island as the place where she had visited Nelson two years earlier. As more and more political prisoners were incarcerated, facilities for visitors had been upgraded and telephones installed. But warders still monitored every word, and sessions were still limited to thirty minutes.

After the long separation, during which they could exchange only a handful of heavily censored letters, the atmosphere between Winnie and Madiba was almost strained. What, after all, could one say in half an hour after a two-year interval? He noticed that she looked thin and drawn. They touched briefly on the children's schooling, Nelson's mother, who was not well, and their finances. To overcome the ban on discussion of non-family matters, they used clan names and nicknames to deceive the warders. The ANC was 'the church', and mention of 'priests' and 'sermons' allowed Winnie to pass on valuable information about the struggle. All too soon, the painful moment of parting was upon them and the warder yelled 'Time up!' Winnie mouthed a quick goodbye, and then she was gone.

In truth, Madiba knew more about Winnie's life than anyone would have thought possible, taking into account the ban on newspapers, the almost total absence of information and carefully censored letters that were part of life on the island. He knew that she had been under constant harassment since her last visit, that her siblings were being persecuted by the security police, and that the authorities intimidated anyone who gave consideration to moving into the house with her. Curiously, any negative publicity about her was brought to his attention.

More than once, when he returned to his cell from the limestone quarry where the prisoners performed hard labour every day, he would find a selection of neatly cut newspaper clippings on his bed.

Winnie's infrequent visits to Robben Island were governed by petty and time-consuming rules. She was allowed to travel to and from Johannesburg only by air, and thus denied the option of cheaper transport. On arrival at Cape Town, she had to take the shortest and swiftest route to Caledon Square, the main police station, to sign various documents recording her visit. She was tailed by security police along each step of the journey, and on returning from the island, she had to go back to Caledon Square and sign more papers before going directly to the airport. After her second visit, she fell foul of the law once again. It was raining and bitterly cold, and she had to make the trip from the island on the deck of the ferry, as she was not allowed to mix with the other passengers. As she stepped ashore, still struggling with the emotions stirred by the unsatisfactory and all too brief time spent with Nelson, someone called to her, asking her name and address. She ignored him, thinking it might be a newspaper reporter, but it turned out to be a policeman, and she was duly charged with failing to identify herself or report her arrival in Cape Town. She was sentenced to one month's imprisonment on the charge of refusing to identify herself, and one year for not reporting her presence in Cape Town. All but four days of the sentence was suspended.

In Madiba's next letter, he reminded Winnie how much he cared for her, how unbreakable the bond between them was, and how courageous she was. It was both a love letter and a reaffirmation of the emotional support she so sorely needed.

In September 1966, HF Verwoerd, the arch-enemy of the oppressed, was assassinated in parliament by an apparently deranged messenger of mixed parentage. Hope that the political situation in South Africa might improve flared briefly after his death, but his successor, BJ Vorster, who had been interned on suspicion of sabotage against the government during World War II, soon snuffed the flame of optimism by giving the police even more extensive powers, and establishing the infamous Bureau of State Security (BOSS).

Winnie consoled herself with Mandela's credo that unjust laws were meant to be defied, and carried on with her political work in secret. The ANC was targeting the younger generation, establishing cells throughout the country, and organising study groups and lectures to teach them the organisation's doctrines. Almost another year would pass before she was again granted permission to visit Mandela in June 1967. By then, they both knew that they could not take visits every six months for granted. Warder James Gregory later wrote that Mandela was clearly very much in love with his strikingly beautiful wife, who was always elegantly dressed and dignified. Gregory also admitted being surprised when he saw tears rolling down Winnie's cheeks during their visits – something he had not expected from this woman whose pride was as fierce as that of a lioness.

In the spring of 1968, Mandela received his first – and only – visit from his mother, who was accompanied by his sister Mabel, his eldest daughter Maki and youngest son, Makgatho. Because they had travelled all the way from Transkei, the prison authorities agreed to allow them an extra fifteen minutes together. Mandela was concerned about his mother, who had lost weight and looked ill. With a sense of dread, he realised that he would probably not see her again, and he was right. She died of a heart attack a few weeks later. He sought permission to attend her funeral, but was refused.

Nosekeni Mandela was buried in October 1968, and her funeral, filled with pomp and ceremony, formed a stark contrast to her modest life. She had been a quiet and retiring person, but her death was exploited by those with political motives, and her funeral became an extension of South Africa's political battle-field. Because she had been a member of a royal house, senior representatives of the so-called Transkei government attended the funeral to honour her both as a kinswoman and the mother of a prominent political figure, albeit their rival. The police had never visited Mandela's mother in life at her home in Qunu, but they turned out in force around her grave, to spy on her daughter-in-law, friends of her son and other family members.

Winnie was given permission to attend the funeral, and at the graveside she wept bitterly, as much for the loss of her mother-in-law as for her husband, denied the opportunity to pay his last respects to the woman who had borne him. It was three months before Winnie could visit Madiba and give him details about his mother's illness and the funeral ceremony. It would be another two years before they spoke again – but mercifully, when they parted, neither had any idea that Winnie was about to face her worst ordeal yet.

11

A year in solitary confinement

JOHANNESBURG WAS A CESSPOOL of informers, and Winnie was surrounded by spies. The security police crackdowns had pushed all black political activity underground, but Winnie remained high on the list of suspects plotting the overthrow of the apartheid government. They saw her as both an intermediary between the ANC leadership on Robben Island and the grassroots supporters, and as an instrument that could be used to demoralise Mandela. They spent an inordinate amount of energy hatching plans to achieve their objectives: neutralising Winnie and breaking Mandela's power.

Winnie yearned for the man she loved, for his support and the normal life that was lost to her. 'I had been looking forward to leading a married life one day and having a home; it sustains you,' she said.[1] She knew her only hope of remaining sane was to focus her attention on helping others – particularly those with ANC links. While assisting the families of detainees, she heard about a large group of political prisoners at Nylstroom, most of them from Port Elizabeth, 1 120 kilometres away. Obviously, the distance prevented them from receiving many visitors, and Winnie heard that they also received little mail. Knowing that families were often deliberately not told where their loved ones were taken after being arrested, and how distressing it was for prisoners not to hear from their families, she set to work.

She managed to find out the names of the long-distance prisoners and enlisted the help of various women in Soweto, who wrote to them as 'family members' and visited when they could, taking basic necessities such as soap, toothpaste and toilet paper, just to make their incarceration a little more bearable. Through Helen Joseph and the Anglican Church, she also arranged that those who could not be visited were sent money by postal order, ostensibly from family members. Maude Katzenellenbogen volunteered to help, and Winnie's small efforts to provide humanitarian aid for those in distress were added to a growing list of transgressions that would soon be used against her. In due course, she would learn the truth about Katzenellenbogen, under truly horrific circumstances. Winnie also enlisted the aid of one of her friends, Mohale Mahanyele, who worked for the US Information Agency, to print and distribute pamphlets for the ANC. This, too, would backfire.

Wittingly or unwittingly, the security police recognised Winnie's strength and ability to lead, and they feared her influence. That was the impetus for their relentless efforts to crush her, and according to undercover agent Gordon Winter, General 'Lang Hendrik' van den Bergh, the head of BOSS, was hell-bent on stifling the political life of this troublesome woman.

On the night of 12 May 1969, Winnie woke to the familiar banging and shouting that signified a raid. She rose with pounding heart, and as she opened the door, policemen poured into the house, searching every corner.

There was unusual excitement when the raid yielded a copy of *Black Power and Liberation – A Communist View*, but even textbooks Mandela had used as a law student, his typewriter and the clothes he had worn during his trials were seized. Zeni and Zindzi were home for the school holidays, and the police lifted them, terrified, out of their beds and searched the mattresses and bed linen. After turning the entire house upside down, Major Johannes Viktor, the officer in charge, ordered Winnie to pack a bag, as she was being detained and would not be coming back 'for a long time'. Having been dragged off to prison at all hours of the day or night, Winnie had taken to keeping a small suitcase packed with necessities next to her front door, so that she could grab it on the way out when needed.

'Detention means that midnight knock when all about you is quiet,' she said later. 'It means those blinding torches shone simultaneously through every window of your house before the door is kicked open. It means the exclusive right the Security Branch have to read each and every letter in the house. It means paging through each and every book on your shelves, lifting carpets, looking under beds, lifting sleeping children from mattresses and looking under the sheets. It means tasting your sugar, your mealie-meal and every spice on your kitchen shelf. Unpacking all your clothing and going through each pocket. Ultimately, it means your seizure at dawn, dragged away from little children screaming and clinging to your skirt, imploring the white man dragging Mummy away to leave her alone.'[2]

Zeni and Zindzi began to cry, but the police would neither allow her to comfort them nor make arrangements for their care. Ignoring her heartfelt pleas that she could not leave the children there, unattended, they jostled Winnie to the door, where rough hands prised the screaming children from their mother's side and someone said they would drive them to the home of one of Winnie's sisters. Winnie was taken away, her daughters' terrified wailing still ringing in her ears. Zindzi and Zeni were nine and ten years old respectively, their father was in prison and they would not see their mother again for eighteen months. Winnie was not yet thirty-five and Mandela had been on Robben Island for five years.

When the police refused her permission to contact her lawyer, relatives, friends – or even her clergyman – Winnie began to steel herself for what she knew must come next. In terms of the Terrorism Act, No. 83 of 1967, the brainchild of Prime Minister John Vorster, the South African police could arrest anyone suspected of committing acts that endangered the maintenance of law and order, or of conspiring or inciting people to commit such acts. The legislation was structured in such a way that almost any opponent of the South African government – including children – could be arrested without a warrant, detained for an indefinite period of time, interrogated and kept in solitary confinement without access to a lawyer or relative.

To all intents and purposes, Winnie Mandela had ceased to exist. Only her small daughters knew that she had been taken away by the police. She was taken to Pretoria and placed in solitary confinement. Winnie didn't know that she was one of twenty-two people arrested in coordinated countrywide raids that night. They were the first detainees held under Section 6 of the Terrorism Act.

When the door of her cell clanged shut, Winnie strained her ears, but all she heard was an occasional faint cough and the distant sound of prison doors slamming open or shut.

News of her detention reached Mandela almost immediately, but it took attorney Joel Carlson the best part of a day to find out where Winnie was being held, and on what charges.

In his autobiography, *Long Walk to Freedom*, Mandela wrote: 'Prison is designed to break one's spirit and destroy one's resolve. To do this, the authorities attempt to exploit every weakness, demolish every initiative, negate all signs of individuality – all with the idea of stamping out that spark that makes each of us human and each of us who we are.'

The United Nations' definition of torture is 'aggravated and deliberate forms of cruel, inhuman or degrading treatment or punishment'. Torture may take the form of beatings, rape, sleep deprivation, electric shocks, burning, mutilation, extended solitary confinement, starvation, sham executions and more. In apartheid South Africa, it was primarily employed as a form of social control, subjugating entire communities through terror and intimidation by destroying the trust upon which nations are built.

For the next seventeen months, Winnie Mandela would be subjected to extreme emotional, psychological and physical torture. For most of this time, she was held in isolation in an icy cage: four cement walls, a cement floor and a cement ceiling, lit by a single naked light bulb. Her bed was a coir mat on the floor, and three filthy blankets suffused with the stench and stains of urine were her only protection against the biting chill of early winter. When she unfolded a blanket, bugs crawled over her arms and legs. She flung the blanket into a corner, but then realised she would have to use it. Gritting her teeth, she rolled up one blanket to use as a pillow and slept under the other two. The only other items in the cell were a plastic bottle of water, a mug and a sanitary bucket without a handle. Winnie, whose standards of cleanliness bordered on the pathological, was revolted by the conditions. In addition to using the bucket as a toilet, she had to wash over it, which she did by pouring a little water from her one-litre ration onto her hands and vigorously rubbing her hands and face, then pouring a little water onto her panties to sponge her body, because there was nothing else.

For the first 200 days, she had no normal contact with another human being. She heard no other voice, spoke to no other living soul. The first few days were the worst of her life. She had only her thoughts for company, and she was overwhelmed by excruciating uncertainty and insecurity, a sense of hopelessness, the feeling that this was the end.

It was deathly quiet, and the silence became another instrument of torture.

The light burned constantly and there was no way of knowing whether it was day or night.

Time had no beginning and no end. She was trapped in an infinite vacuum of nothingness.

Winnie had nothing to keep her hands or mind occupied, except troubling thoughts of Zeni and Zindzi. Their cries echoed over and over in her mind. She beat her head with her clenched fists to try to kill the mental images that came unbidden. Where were her children, what had happened to them? What if the police had not taken them to her sister, but thrown them out of the vehicle somewhere? If only she could know that they were safe. In helpless frustration she rolled her hands so tightly into fists that her nails bit into the flesh. From somewhere deep in her subconscious came Mandela's voice, telling her he was proud of her courage, and she realised she could not afford to lose control of her senses. She had to think clearly, try to remain lucid, no matter what. She sat on the mat, prayed aloud and talked to herself. She lay on her stomach, turned onto her back, rolled onto her side. She got up, sat down, got up again, sat down again. She tried to remain rational, to analyse the situation objectively and not give in to panic. The knowledge that she could be kept there indefinitely, denied any contact with anyone, could drive her over the edge. She had to find ways of driving off the utter despair hovering over her like vultures waiting to feed on carrion. She had to come to terms with her revulsion over the conditions in the cell that made her want to scream and bang her head against the wall. She started pacing up and down the tiny cell. Four steps from one end to the other, three steps from side to side. One, two, three, four. One, two, three. One, two, three, four. One, two, three.

She made a ninety-degree turn. One, two, three. One, two, three, four. One, two, three. One, two, three, four. Turn. One two three four. One two three. One two three four. One two three. Turn. One two three. One two three four. One two three. One two three four. Turn. Onetwothreefour. Onetwothree. Onetwothreefour. Onetwothree. Turn. Onetwothree. Onetwothreefour. Onetwothree. Onetwothreefour. Turn. Onetwothreefouronetwothree. Onetwothreefouronetwothreeturnonetwothreeonetwothreefouronetwoonetwooneoneoneone. She felt dizzy, she needed air, she needed to see whether the sky was blue and bathed in sunlight, or cold and dark and dotted with stars.

In the morning her body felt sore and bruised from a long night on the cold cement. She started doing the Canadian Air Force exercises for women, which she had always done at home. It helped to focus her mind on something other than her surroundings. But without decent food or proper rest, she tired quickly. Her obsession with hygiene was the most difficult obstacle to overcome. It was many days, perhaps weeks before she was given a small plastic bucket with water to wash herself. She was certain it, too, was a sanitary bucket, because it smelled dreadful. The entire cell stank. Her sanitary bucket was removed once a day for emptying, but was never properly cleaned. At mealtimes her plate of food was placed on top of the stinking bucket. She started dreading the sound of the cell door being unlocked, even though that was the only time she saw another person. The three locks had to be opened with three different sets of keys. After what felt like an eternity of meshing and grinding, a white wardress would kick open the door and a black prisoner would dash in, put the food on top of the sanitary bucket and dash out, not even glancing at Winnie. Then the locks were turned again, one after the other, mocking her, sealing her fate again and again.

Breakfast was porridge, often not properly cooked, and without sugar or milk. Lunch consisted of whole maize cobs, and supper was porridge again, sometimes with a small helping of spinach, slimy and unwashed. Winnie shuddered when grains of sand crunched under her teeth. On Sundays, a small piece of tough pork, with more fat than meat, was added to the porridge. The only drinks were black and bitter coffee, or a beverage made from maize and served in clay pots. The food was clearly not meant to sustain, but literally just to keep the prisoners alive. Even behind bars, apartheid reigned – coloured and Indian prisoners were also given bread, tea and sugar, but black detainees never saw such luxuries.

Winnie scratched the dates on her cell wall, but the complete isolation and utter silence made it difficult to keep track of time. The days could be measured only by the three meals she received, and sometimes she got confused, uncertain whether the food was for lunch or supper, so she started marking every day as soon as she got her plate of breakfast porridge.

Two weeks after she was arrested, the police began their interrogation. Ironically, she was relieved when they came to fetch her. At least she would be with other

141

people, hear their voices, escape from the endless hours alone in the claustrophobic cell. But her relief was short-lived. Her chief interrogator was Major Theunis Jacobus Swanepoel, described by many prisoners before Winnie as a skilled torturer, who had been implicated in Babla Saloojee's death in detention. Joel Carlson had described him as a man with an evil soul, and said Swanepoel made him shudder. Winnie knew that she would have to draw on all her resources, courage and resolve to survive whatever lay in store for her.

Swanepoel was flanked by other officers, all in uniforms with shiny buttons, and it seemed to Winnie that they took a sadistic pleasure in appearing before her neatly groomed, emphasising their superiority, while she was unkempt and confused after a fortnight in the most unhygienic conditions imaginable.

Clearly, the first two weeks had been a 'softening-up' period. At the end of this time, many prisoners were already mentally broken, and readily supplied the information the police wanted. Those who resisted usually obliged after application of a minimum amount of brutality. But Winnie was a special case, and the security police knew it. Apart from being Mandela's wife, she had become well known in her own right and they dared not subject her to the same physical torture they meted out to less prominent detainees. They would have to make use of other ways to break her spirit. Few people could withstand solitary confinement and prolonged sleep deprivation, and neither left any visible scars.

The questions centred on Winnie's ANC activities and the banned organisation's 'communist' contacts outside South Africa. Standing under a bright light, she was interrogated for hours about the assistance she had organised for the Nylstroom prisoners, and told that a number of other people were also in detention, and that her sister and Peter Magubane had been arrested. She had thought Zeni and Zindzi were with her sister, and was filled with fear for her children. The police said they had eighty witnesses against her, and named many of her close friends and confidantes, claiming that these people had already told them virtually everything they needed to know, and that all they required from Winnie herself was corroboration. A policeman was sitting at a typewriter, ready to take down her confession.

In the present age, when the world has become a global village, when communication across several continents and many oceans is instantaneous, when flesh and blood have been reduced to a series of DNA symbols and sequences on the human genome map, the human psyche remains the last true frontier of exploration. Science and technology can help us to understand how we function, even explain certain behaviour patterns, but nothing and no one has yet been able to dissect the soul, that unique and ephemeral core that not only makes us who we are, but governs the 'why' and 'how' of our actions.

In writing this book, I have constantly been confronted by the 'why' of Winnie

Mandela's choices. Some are easily explained by the circumstances that presented themselves at various stages of her life. Others, however, demand far deeper examination. In the absence of empirical evidence, I found it impossible not to wonder about, and imagine, her reflections and fears, and in particular those that might have been conjured up by her gruelling ordeal at the hands of her interrogators. I trust that readers will indulge my use of poetic licence to share the pictures that unwittingly came to mind as I tried to place myself in another woman's shoes. Some of the interpretations are mine alone, while others are based on pointers to Winnie's thoughts, observations and perceptions, as recorded in various publications and paraphrased here.

In classic manner, the interrogation switched between polite and gentle prodding and naked brutality. After a while, Swanepoel complained that she was being tiresome, boring and useless, and assured her, menacingly, that she *would* tell them everything they wanted to know. Then he told another man, Gert, to take over.

Gert was a large man with a red face and a malevolent manner. He didn't talk, he shouted, and Winnie constantly felt as though he was about to assault her. She tried to think of other things, to remain in control of her mind and not allow fear to take over. She tried to remember Nelson's voice, and how he recited the verse from his favourite poem, 'Invictus':

> It matters not how strait the gate,
> How charged with punishments the scroll,
> I am the master of my fate;
> I am the captain of my soul.

Winnie tried to imprint the words on her mind: *I am the captain of my soul ...* She knew what they were trying to do, she'd heard about it often enough: the good-cop, bad-cop technique. Determined not to let this well-known tactic, accompanied by much shouting, scare her, she tried to think of something else in order not to focus on the questions. She wasn't planning on telling them anything, anyway. Gert's red face turned a deeper shade of red as the shouting continued. Winnie quite feared for his blood pressure, and the thought momentarily amused her. She willed herself not to smile, knowing only too well that the police had no sense of humour. She concentrated on keeping her mind occupied: *I am the captain of my soul ...*

Gert shouted that all the others were cooperating; what made her think that she was so special? He wanted to know who she was protecting, shouting that they had taped information of Mandela's secret instructions to Winnie, of her telephone conversations with Tambo. In short, *everything* had been recorded! They were going to put her away in any case, so why didn't she just cooperate?

Winnie smiled inwardly at the thought of calling Tambo from her telephone at home. She could just picture herself telling him about Nelson's latest secret instructions and his suggestions for overthrowing the government. And, of course, about the sabotage they had in mind, and how they were going to spring Nelson from Robben Island, and then fly Tambo back to South Africa in triumph … and all the while knowing that the security police were listening to their every word. Winnie wondered what kind of fool Gert took her for. And wasn't it illegal listening in on other people's private telephone conversations?

Time dragged by. She had no idea how long she had been in that room. A day? More than a day? There was no way of telling whether it was day or night, because the room was constantly flooded in bright electric light that invaded every corner, every bit of space. In Soweto, Winnie thought bitterly, there were no street lights, and most people didn't have electricity in their homes. Here, they kept the lights on night and day.

She tried measuring time through the changing shifts of the interrogators. She calculated that each shift was four hours, but this calculation only worked for a while. As the interrogation wore on, the shifts – and time – blurred into one long torturous harangue. She didn't look at her questioners, identifying them by voice alone. She allowed the blinding light to blot out as much of the appalling surroundings as possible, trying to visualise the light as a barrier between her and her interrogators. One would bombard her with questions, another would shout and threaten. Swanepoel's speciality seemed to be personal insults, while one of his colleagues would feign compassion, offer to help her – if she would just cooperate and give them satisfactory answers. Food was brought in during the 'good cop' sessions, but although her stomach was burning with hunger pains, she couldn't eat, and just drank some water. When she needed to use the toilet, a woman warder went with her.

During one of Swanepoel's sessions, he asked if she wanted a cigarette. She said she didn't smoke. He offered her coffee and, without even waiting for a response, instructed one of the policemen, in Afrikaans, to get her some. Then, suddenly switching to English, he added that the policeman should get Mrs Mandela some toasted chicken sandwiches.

He then made a preposterous suggestion. If Winnie cooperated and made a radio broadcast calling upon ANC forces on the country's borders to lay down their arms and start talking to the government, she would be released. Moreover, she would be flown by helicopter to see Nelson on Robben Island, and he would be moved to the cottage where Robert Sobukwe had been held, so that he could hold secret talks with high-ranking police officers.

Winnie was appalled that Swanepoel could think, even for a moment, that she would betray Nelson's dream in order to save her own skin with the mediocre justification that he was suffering in more comfort. And after he had given the best

Nelson and Winnie Mandela on their wedding day on 14 June 1958

Winnie participated in the anti-pass demonstration in October 1958,
marching with hundreds of women to the Central Pass Office in Johannesburg

In the Sharpeville massacre on 21 March 1960, police killed 69 people,
most of them shot in the back, and wounded another 176

Walter and Albertina Sisulu

Winnie in happier days

With her daughters Zeni and Zindzi in 1975

Winnie arrives at the YMCA in Durban, accompanied by George Sithole,
a member of the Umlazi Residents' Association, 14 May 1976

Police and protestors clash in Soweto on 16 June 1976

Winnie and Reverend Buthelezi at the funeral of Hector Petersen,
the first victim in the Soweto uprising

Winnie was exiled to the small Free State town of Brandfort,
400 kilometres away from her home in Soweto

Zindzi, Winnie's younger daughter, accompanied her to Brandfort

At her home in Brandfort

Winnie and Zindzi

With Zindzi at the Brandfort post office

At an ANC Women's League rally in Cape Town

Addressing an Umkhonto we Sizwe rally in Stellenbosch in April 1983. Behind Winnie is Peter Mokaba

Winnie and others give the Black Power salute at a rally in 1985

Winnie and Zindzi talk to reporters after visiting Nelson Mandela
in Pollsmoor prison in July 1988

Winnie and Albertina Sisulu move through a guard of honour at Jan Smuts Airport
to meet Govan Mbeki, the first of the political prisoners to be released

Hand in hand with Winnie, Nelson Mandela walks to freedom
from Victor Verster prison on 11 February 1990

Nelson and Winnie at home in Soweto in 1990

Winnie, Nelson and Joe Slovo at an SACP rally in August 1990

The Mandelas and the Tambos, December 1990

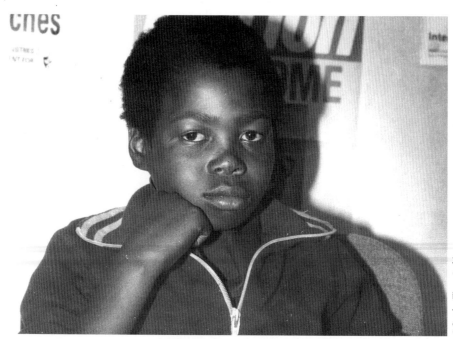

Stompie Seipei, who was murdered in January 1989

Jerry Richardson, one of the accused in the Mandela United Football Club killings

Appearing before the Truth and Reconciliation Commission

Winnie and TRC chairperson, Archbishop Desmond Tutu

Arriving late for a rally on 16 June 2001, Winnie greets President Thabo Mbeki, before he pushes her aside and knocks off her cap. The incident confirmed the sour relations between the two

Outside court after her trial for fraud and theft, on 25 April 2003

years of his life to the cause. Did they honestly think her and Nelson's principles were for sale?

When she refused, he became menacing again, threatening that she would be broken completely, and that she might as well accept that she was finished. People thought that Nelson was a great man, and that he was in prison because he was prepared to sacrifice himself for his people. But, said Swanepoel, he knew better. He knew that Nelson had run away from her – and who could blame him? If he, Swanepoel, had a wife like Winnie, he would have done exactly the same, seeking refuge from such a woman in prison.

A harsh voice called out her name. Bad cop was back.

Winnie wondered what kind of person Gert was. What kind of man becomes a torturer, makes a living out of tormenting others, and accepts money for it? She speculated, sardonically, on where he had been trained; was there a training college for torturers? In that case, Swanepoel must have passed the advanced course. Did they have practical assignments to do? Was *she* Gert's practical assignment?

Swanepoel again. He shouted that her innocent act wouldn't work with them! He threatened that if she didn't tell them what they wanted to know, they would tell her people a few things about her. That, Swanepoel said, would finish Winnie's ambitions of being a great ANC leader. Who, he asked, did she think she was anyway? All she deserved was a kick on the arse!

Then he lowered his voice and hissed that he knew she had all the secret plans written in code in invisible ink. She needn't think that they couldn't decipher them. Swanepoel said that they were giving her a chance to help herself. If she was smart and helped them, they would make life easier for her.

Winnie would not even contemplate the idea, and scoffed at his mention of the non-existent, coded letters. Even in her current dire straits, she could see through his absurd lies. She knew that Swanepoel would not be talking to her if he had what he needed – he'd be presenting her with the evidence in triumph, as befitted his over-sized ego. They mistakenly thought she was stupid, but that was not necessarily a bad thing – it might even help her.

She caught a glimpse of him and quickly looked away. His face was puce and he was looming over her. She thought he might pick her up and throw her on the floor, and almost wished he would, so that she would be knocked unconscious, maybe even die. That would put an end to the agony.

When 'good cop', Major Coetzee, took his next turn, she told him she was feeling faint and had severe palpitations. He promised to get her a doctor, then asked: 'Why go through this hardship?' She was young and beautiful, and she owed it to Zeni and Zindzi to live a normal life, he said.

Although Winnie's heart was shattered at the loss of her daughters, she vowed that they would not break her by reminding her of Zeni and Zindzi. They had to know that she was anxious about her daughters, and that she was in agony not knowing what had happened to them, but that cheap tactic would get them nowhere. She was exhausted and in pain, but they could forget it – she was getting out of there, even if only in her mind. She was going to go to Pondoland, to its soft green fields in summer, to the voices of the boys as they run and laugh and fight …

He could get her a job with the police, Swanepoel said. Someone like her could easily become one of them.

Suddenly, Winnie understood. This was the point where informers usually stumbled and fell. They would feel like she did now, or worse, because of the beatings and the pain inflicted on them, and they just wanted it to end. They would be convinced that they could take no more, and when they agreed, they would sell their birthright for a pot of apartheid soup. But not Winnie. They had just said exactly the wrong thing if they wanted her to cooperate. She would never become one of *them*. How could they think, even for a second, that she could become one of them?

In his soothing voice, good cop urged her to think about his proposal – then all her problems could soon be over.

Winnie willed herself to remember Madiba's voice, planning a holiday in Durban, images of the waltzing waves, the sun bouncing off the water, Zeni and Zindzi building sand castles on the beach …

Good cop woke her up abruptly, telling her she could not sleep. They had to finish so that she could get out of there. Winnie wondered where Gert was. But then she was back in Pondoland, walking in the fields with her Tata, picking mealies. It was a good crop, and Tata promised that with the money he made from the sale, Winnie would go to boarding school. Then Winnie's mind drifted from the Pondoland fields to Orlando, her home; Buthelezi and Mandela were standing in the doorway …

She tried to estimate how long she had been there, and thought it might be the morning of the third day. Her head was spinning. Coetzee asked whether she would like to take a shower, and someone led her to a cubicle further down the passage.

Winnie was in a daze, her body swaying with fatigue. She felt close to death, as if she was floating, and she wondered if she were dead. But she could still hear sounds, which came from far away. Longing to sleep, she knew they would not let her, yet exhaustion threatened to engulf her. Then she felt the water on her body, cold, clear water with which she could wash away the pain and the fear. She was shocked to see that how swollen and blue her body was.

Winnie felt stronger and fresher after her shower. The policeman said everyone was very concerned about her, they knew about her heart condition. And they all respected her. Winnie doubted that very much. She was sure they couldn't care less whether she lived or died. They saw her as a cheeky maid who had risen above her station in life, and had the gall to resist the white *baas*.

He asked about her meetings with various people, the addresses she had used to receive mail, the pamphlets she had printed at Maude Katzenellenbogen's house. That was when she realised that they knew too much – and that someone must have talked. Over and over he asked about her role, accusing her of inciting people to commit sabotage, claiming that other detainees had taken their instructions from her. He told her they had arrested a young mother named Charlotte, who had stayed briefly with Winnie, and said unless Winnie made a statement, Charlotte would be held indefinitely. Winnie wanted to weep. Charlotte was not involved with the ANC, but she knew her denials were useless. This had nothing to do with finding out the truth. This was about getting her, Winnie Mandela.

It was Swanepoel's turn again. He asked why she was resisting, told her they had already spread the message that she was cooperating fully with the police, had agreed to work for them in future. Her political career was over, she would have not a single friend in the ANC, he said, adding sarcastically that she should be grateful that they were keeping her company all night long, because they knew she suffered from insomnia. She felt herself floating into unconsciousness and thought she would die. Her eyelids drooped, her head slumped forward. Swanepoel thumped on the table and shouted: 'For God's sake, give us something! You can't die with all that information! Not before you have told us everything!'

By the fourth day, she started passing blood in her urine. Four days and nights without sleep were taking their toll. She knew she was close to breaking point. Her whole body shook, and there was a severe pain below her left breast. As a wave of blackness engulfed her, she thought: Who will take care of Zeni and Zindzi?

When she came to, Swanepoel was standing over her. He was the one she feared the most. As soon as she opened her eyes, he began shouting. She was nothing but a bitch! She did everything for money! She pretended to care for her people, but she took their money to buy clothes! Her husband was in prison! Who was she tarting herself up for? Did she think they didn't know? Poor Nelson must have been desperate to pay so much lobola for a woman like her!

Winnie flinched. Some of Swanepoel's words stung her to the quick. They made her sound like a cheap opportunist, but they were wrong. She had no money, and she was always struggling to keep head above water. She relied on other people for food, and for money to keep her children in school. The clothes were gifts from women who were also in the struggle. They wanted to imply that she was no good to her people because she liked to feel and look good, but they knew nothing about her. She needed to look good because it was important for her spirit, and it had nothing to do with anyone else. As a woman, it was important to feel good about oneself, and the worse matters got, the more dangers she faced, the more important it became to hang on to that.

Swanepoel's voice penetrated her thoughts and she drifted up, as if through water, then forced herself down again, blocking out the voice that fell on her like physical blows.

She was fainting more frequently, and knew it was nature's defence against the unendurable. But as soon as she came to, she was put on her feet and the interrogation continued, for five days and nights, without respite.

Winnie and Rita Ndzanga were the last of the twenty-two detainees rounded up on the same night to be interrogated. Because they were both banned, they were seen as more prominent activists, and the police had wanted to extract as much evidence as possible from the others first. Barred from attending meetings or gatherings, both women had made use of go-betweens to keep abreast of what was happening and to convey messages on their behalf. When Winnie failed to respond to the questions put by Swanepoel and his colleagues, they told her Rita had already talked, that they knew everything about meetings at Ndou's store-room, in Diepkloof, in Alexandra. They told her not to be a fool, that she would stand alone in the dock, since all the other detainees had already agreed to testify against her.

Rita Ndzanga, who had been forced to leave her four small children at home when she was arrested, and whose husband later died in detention, was severely tortured. She described the experience to Joel Carlson years later:

> A white security policeman began to hit me; I fell down; I then began to scream; they closed the windows; I continued screaming; they dragged me to another room hitting me with their open hands all the time … In the interrogation room the security police asked me what makes me not speak. They produced three bricks and told me to take off my shoes and stand on the bricks. I refused to stand on the bricks. One of the white security police climbed on top of a chair and pulled me up by my hair, dropped me on to the bricks, I fell down and hit a gas pipe. The same man pulled my hair again, jerked me and I again fell on to the metal gas pipe. They threw water on my face. The man who pulled my hair had his hands full of my hair. He washed his hands in the basin. I managed to stand up and they said, 'On to the bricks.' I stood on the bricks and they hit me again while I was on the bricks. I fell, they again poured water on me. I was very tired, I could not stand the assault any longer.[3]

Having done everything they could to force Winnie to confess, her interrogators played their trump card. She was drifting in and out of consciousness when she suddenly heard piercing, agonising, inhuman screams from the next room, again and again. Swanepoel told Winnie that the screams were from one of 'her brave men'. By the time they were through with him, Swanepoel said, he wouldn't be of much use to anyone. He knew the man would talk, and soon.

As the blood-curdling screams flooded the room once more, Winnie finally broke. What had they been doing to her sister and her friends? How could she carry on resisting if it was causing others so much suffering? She knew she was the one they really wanted, no one else.

Finally, she said the words they wanted to hear, that she was guilty of everything they had accused her of, and that she would confess. She begged them to let the others go. Swanepoel was so excited, he didn't care that she heard him tell his colleagues that their strategy had worked. They had her.

Winnie felt sick. It had been a ploy. Or had it? Were they torturing her comrades just to get to her? It no longer mattered; she couldn't carry on if there was the slightest possibility that her defiance was causing harm to others. All the interrogators and other policemen flooded into the room to celebrate her capitulation, and witness her humiliation. They began reading to her from piles of papers, asking for details and confirmation. All she said was, 'Yes, it was me, yes, it is true.' She admitted to calling meetings, writing and sending letters. Anything, anything not to hear those horrible screams again. They showed her a sheaf of correspondence. Letters sent to and from Maude's address. She wondered how they had got hold of them. She had to explain cryptic messages and decipher her own and others' handwriting. They drew conclusions, which they asked her to confirm. Like an automaton, she said 'yes' to everything. They seemed to know the name of every person to whom she had ever written. The interrogation went on for hours until, finally, Swanepoel said it was enough, they had what they needed, and Winnie was returned to her cell.

After being awake for five days and five nights, she could not go to sleep, and lay there for some time, muttering incoherently. When they brought her food, she said it was poisoned, and refused to eat. She had diarrhoea and was vomiting into the bucket. When she finally fell asleep, her rest was fitful and she awoke screaming from horrific nightmares.

It took days before Winnie regained some equilibrium. Severely traumatised, she had to start the slow process of reclaiming her life. She vaguely remembered the interrogation, and the fainting spells towards the end. She had no recollection of being brought back to her cell and thought it must have happened during one of her blackouts. In solitary confinement once more, she forced herself not to think about the horror of her interrogation. She tore one of the blankets to shreds, then wove the threads together as her grandmother had taught her to do when she was a child, making traditional mats with a grass called *uluzi*. For days she knitted the strands together, undid them, wove them together again. To keep her hands and mind occupied she unpicked the hem of her dress. When there was nothing else left to do, she scoured the cell inch by inch to see if she could find an insect. Once, she found two ants, and spent the whole day playing with them on her finger. The wardress noticed and switched off the light, plunging the cell into darkness.

As she slowly clawed her way back to normality, Winnie's innate defiance returned, and with it a white-hot anger. She had been in solitary confinement for weeks, and she knew her torturers hoped the isolation would drive her mad. In her newfound rage she thought of ways to register her protest at the horrific treatment meted out to her and other prisoners. She even thought of suicide, but she knew she could not do that to her children, and realised that she would also play right into the government's hands if she did take her own life.

One thing Winnie could no longer ignore was the fact that she had been betrayed by Maude Katzenellenbogen.

One morning, a security policeman opened Winnie's cell door, threw a Bible on the floor next to her and said, 'There, pray to your God to release you, but you better pray in Xhosa, not in English!' Afrikaners were extremely emotional about the language issue. Most blacks did not speak Afrikaans, unless they learned a little at their place of work, and after the apartheid government came to power, many refused on principle to use the 'language of the oppressor'. For Winnie, and many other black people who had been educated at mission schools, English was a natural choice after their mother tongue, but, conversely, many Afrikaners, especially in the public service, could not speak English well, sometimes not at all. She had seen Major Swanepoel raging like a mad animal at times when he could not understand her or express himself adequately in English, and she believed the language issue was at least partly responsible for the friction between black and white.

Having fought for the right to speak their own language under British domination, Afrikaners saw it as an integral facet of their identity, and blacks who refused to speak Afrikaans were seen as a challenge to their authority. Of equal importance to Afrikaners was their religion, and Winnie was shocked by the policeman's contemptuous disregard for the Bible, but not even the disrespectful way in which it was delivered to her could dampen her relief at having a way to pass the interminable hours alone. She had never thought it possible to do so, but she read the Bible from cover to cover during the long months in her cell. Sometimes it gave her a wonderful feeling of peace and tranquillity. At other times, depressed and dejected, she felt it was nothing but meaningless words. But on the bad days, too, she remembered the kind ministry of Father Leo Rakale, and often it was his words from the past that offered her comfort and inspiration.

In July, Swanepoel walked into Winnie's cell and asked who Thembi Mandela was. She said he was her stepson. 'Well, he is dead, he was killed in a car accident,' Swanepoel said callously, and walked out.

Winnie sank to the floor and, for the first time since she had been arrested, she wept, heart-rendingly and unashamedly. She thought of the nineteen-year-old boy whom Nelson loved so deeply, and remembered him asking anxiously, on her last visit to Robben Island, if she had news of Thembi. Nelson had told her once, while he was underground, that he found Thembi wearing an old jacket of his that was far too big, and when they said goodbye at the end of the visit, Thembi told his father not to worry, that he would look after the family. She wailed for Thembi, who had lost his father, for Nelson who had lost his son – and for herself, locked up, unable to be with her husband to console him at a time when his heart was being ripped out. And because the man who had brought her the terrible news showed not a morsel of compassion, as though neither she nor Thembi deserved any. She knew the security police were a special breed, with a disregard for human life that enabled them to torture people to death for any reason, or no reason at all. She knew that neither all whites nor all Afrikaners were like that, but it brought her little consolation; and she was disturbed by the bitterness she felt towards Swanepoel and his associates, fearing that it would turn to hatred and that she would end up being no better than them.

Prison inmates have their own inventive ways of communicating with one another, and when word of Thembi's death spread through the cells by way of this 'bush telegraph', Winnie received her first 'correspondence'. It provided her with indescribable comfort.

When her sanitary bucket was returned the day after she was told of Thembi's death, it had not been properly cleaned. That was nothing new, but when she later removed the plate of food from the top of the bucket, she noticed a piece of silver paper inside. She carefully removed the paper and opened it. To her surprise, it contained a note, expressing the sympathy of fellow prisoners on Thembi's death. The last sentence read: 'Mother of the Nation, we are with you.' Winnie was genuinely surprised that, young as she was, people loved and respected her as a symbolic mother. She had no pen or pencil but she had found a pin, and with this she laboriously stencilled a few words on the silver paper and placed it back in the bucket. A feeling of triumph surged through her as she realised there was a way of communicating with others after all.

The next message was wrapped in a banana skin, again at the bottom of the bucket, and warned Winnie that Joyce Sikakane had been broken, and that the police were arranging to transfer her to Nylstroom where she would testify against Winnie. Joyce was a young reporter at the *Rand Daily Mail*, and a granddaughter of one of the founder members of the ANC, the late Reverend AM Sikakane.

When brutality had not persuaded her to yield information about Winnie, the police had switched tack and plied her with special privileges. They knew this made other prisoners immediately suspect a detainee had agreed to turn informer. With her pin, Winnie scratched a message on the banana skin: 'Joyce, don't you dare.' Whether it was the message that did it, or a decision by Joyce herself, she refused to testify against Winnie.

Slowly, Winnie learned more about her fellow detainees. One day, after months of silence, she heard a woman singing in Xhosa from a nearby cell. She was sending a message, starting with, 'My name is Nondwe' and continuing to relate how she and others were detained. Through her song Winnie came to know that one of them, Michael Shivute, had died on the night of his detention, and another, Caleb Mayekiso, died nineteen days later.

More than five months after their arrest, the detainees were finally due to appear in court. Swanepoel had been informed that Mandela had arranged for Joel Carlson to represent Winnie. Carlson was an old friend but also a well-known human rights lawyer, and passionately opposed to apartheid. The police knew that if they did not have to contend with Carlson, it would strengthen their position, and they plotted to have him replaced with a lawyer of their choice, Mendil Levine. Arrangements were made for Winnie to see the other accused so that they could agree to the alternative, but the carefully constructed plan collapsed. Swanepoel had been confident that, with Levine representing the accused, the case would be over quickly. However, Carlson turned up in court and told the judge that Mandela had engaged him to defend Winnie, but that he had been denied access to her and the other accused, whose relatives had also engaged his services.

Several of the detainees, including Laurence and Rita Ndzanga and Elliot Shabangu, testified that the police had tried to coerce them into accepting Levine as their attorney after Swanepoel informed them that Carlson was not available. Those who had accepted Levine said they had done so under duress. The judge ordered that Carlson be given a chance to consult with all the accused, and they all returned to court, having fired Levine. Swanepoel was powerless to intervene, and Carlson included George Bizos and Arthur Chaskalson, who had defended Mandela during the Rivonia Trial, in the defence team as well.

Mandela's long-distance efforts to help Winnie had at last yielded results. Bizos immediately obtained a court order giving all the accused access to basic ablution facilities, and Winnie was finally able to take a proper shower after six months. But she was suffering from malnutrition: she had the characteristic pallid complexion, and her gums were bleeding. She developed fevers and continued to suffer blackouts. Finally, she was admitted to the prison hospital. Carlson was concerned about her. It seemed to him that she wavered between sanity and dementia, and he had no idea whether or not she could withstand months more of the conditions in prison.

The trial began in Pretoria's Old Synagogue, used as an extension of the Supreme Court, on 1 December 1969. The accused had been in detention for seven months, and were charged under the Suppression of Communism Act. The prosecution alleged that they had acted in concert and with a common purpose to re-establish and build up the ANC, knowing that its ultimate aim was the violent overthrow of the state. The ninety-nine counts specified that they had furthered the aims of an unlawful organisation – the ANC – by giving its salute, singing its songs, discussing or possessing its literature and 'polluting' the youth. The prosecution also alleged that they had revived the ANC during 1967 by recruiting members, distributing propaganda, establishing groups and committees, taking the ANC oath, arranging and holding meetings, arranging funerals of members, canvassing funds, visiting members in prison and organising support for their families, planning to assist guerrilla fighters in acts of sabotage, acquiring explosives and propagating communist doctrines. They had made contact with ANC members all over South Africa, including those imprisoned on Robben Island and in Nylstroom, and those exiled in London and Lusaka.

The evidence, however, was almost totally devoid of detail in support of the charges. Most of the eighty state witnesses were police officers or detainees who had been coerced into giving evidence against their comrades. The defence showed that many of them had been tortured and forced to make incriminating statements, or were promised indemnity if their evidence was satisfactory. Two witnesses, Nondwe Mankahla and Shanti Naidoo, were sentenced to two months' imprisonment when they refused to testify for the state. Shanti's brother, Indris, was also a prisoner on Robben Island, and Shanti had been held in solitary confinement for months and been forced to stand for days under interrogation. Winnie's sister, Nonyaniso, told the judge that she had been threatened with ten years in prison if she did not testify against Winnie, and said she had been so threatened and brainwashed during interrogation that she now found it difficult to distinguish between the truth and what the police had instructed her to say. Five other witnesses for the state admitted under cross-examination that they had been tortured prior to making incriminating statements.

Philip Golding, a British national, testified that he had been assaulted and made promises of release if he gave evidence in accordance with the statement he eventually made under duress. He admitted that he had taken messages to ANC contacts in Britain. Herbert Nhlapo said he had attended meetings where they discussed the need for an organisation to take up the grievances of black people.

To the shock of all in the Winnie camp, her friend Mohale Mahanyele was the state's key witness against the other accused. He said he had allowed Winnie the use of a duplicating machine at the US Information Agency where he worked, so that she could print leaflets urging opposition to the Urban Bantu Council elections and to publicise the ANC. He seemed to have an exceptionally good memory, recounting contact with the accused in the greatest detail, with total recall of exact times and dates. Eselina Klaas had served two-and-a-half years' imprisonment for furthering the aims of the ANC in 1964, and was too scared to admit, even in the safety of the courtroom, that she had been tortured into revealing her role in Winnie's scheme to aid prisoners at Nylstroom, although all she had done was distribute forms to their families to obtain personal details about them, and had one meeting in Johannesburg with Winnie and Rita Ndzanga about the plan.

Winnie was virtually the only detainee who showed no fear during the court proceedings. When asked to plead, she made a statement, saying that she had been held in detention for seven months in terms of a law she regarded as unjust and immoral, and which had claimed the life of one of her colleagues, Caleb Mayekiso, who had died in detention three weeks after the arrests. When the judge insisted that she enter a plea, she said she found it difficult to do so, as she felt that she had already been found guilty. As the case unfolded, it became clear that the state could prove only that Winnie's group had arranged relief for the families of political prisoners, and for the prisoners themselves. After twenty witnesses had been called, the case was adjourned.

Winnie had much to think about during the two-month wait: the past, the uncertain future, the terrible months in prison. And the shock of yet another betrayal by someone in whom she had placed her faith. The list was getting longer: Brian Somana, Maude Katzenellenbogen, now Mohale Mahanyele. She had trusted all of them implicitly, and it pained her deeply to admit that they had deliberately set out to destroy her.

Winnie felt sad and hurt rather than angry at their betrayal. She wondered what motivated people to callously exploit their fellow human beings for their own gain. And what did they gain, after all? What were they getting from the security police that made it worth their while to betray her and so many others? These were the people she had believed were her friends, with whom she had shared confidences. Now, she had to wonder how many others who pretended to be her friends were actually spies and traitors. But she wouldn't do that. The doubts would drive her insane. Without the support of her friends, she knew she would collapse. And the police knew that, too. They were trying to back her into a corner, where she trusted no one and was totally isolated, so that they could finish her off. She would not give them that satisfaction. If people she loved and trusted were going to betray her, and reward her friendship with torture and imprisonment, it would be on their heads. She was not going to change. She could not afford to.

Now categorised as awaiting-trial prisoners, the detainees were finally allowed to receive visitors, and have decent food brought in from outside. Winnie's first visitor was the faithful Father Leo Rakale. She also received visits from family members, who brought her clean clothes and toiletries, but the intimidation continued. On returning to her cell after consulting with her legal team one day, Winnie found all her clothes strewn on the floor, covered in hand and face cream, and trampled by muddy shoes. She had no way of washing or ironing her clothes.

When the trial resumed, the defence team intended calling Nelson Mandela as a witness – which they were perfectly entitled to do, since he was named in the indictment as a co-conspirator. Whether it was the prospect of having to transport Mandela from Robben Island to Pretoria and the massive publicity this would generate, or the way the media turned their spotlight on the revelations of torture that had been exposed so far, the state case died a sudden death. When the trial resumed on 16 February 1970, the Transvaal Attorney-General announced that he was dropping the case. All the charges were withdrawn and the accused were free to go. Counsel and prisoners alike were stunned.

But, within minutes, they found themselves surrounded by police. The public gallery was cleared, and all the accused were promptly rearrested under Section 6 of the Terrorism Act on the orders of General Hendrik van den Bergh. Instead of going home, they were taken back to prison, and placed in solitary confinement yet again. Nine months after their arrests, they were back where they had started.

The police action caused an outcry, but the government ignored all criticism. The relatives of fifteen detainees applied unsuccessfully for a court order restraining the police from torturing them, and widespread protests were staged. In June, formal charges were brought against the accused again. When the second trial began in October, Winnie was in hospital, running a high fever. The defence team drew the court's attention to the fact that all but 12 of the 540 charges in the indictment were identical to those withdrawn by the prosecution during the earlier trial, and began laboriously reading out the two indictments, word for word, to illustrate their argument. On the third day, the judge halted proceedings, acquitting the accused again, without a single witness being called. This time, they really were free to go home.

After being cut off from the world for more than 500 days, Winnie's ordeal was over. She had spent seventeen months behind bars, thirteen of them in solitary confinement, without a shred of proof being produced of her guilt. She walked out of the courtroom in a daze, with a single thought in her mind: she must send telegrams to Nelson on Robben Island and to her children in Swaziland to tell them she was free.

Winnie only discovered years later, in Gordon Winter's book, *Inside BOSS*, that he had intercepted her letters, and that the government had been so anxious to convict her that they had considered breaking his cover and bringing him from England to testify against her. However, neither he nor Maude Katzenellenbogen was called as witnesses.

Winnie found adjustment to normal life after the seventeen worst months of her life frightening. It took a considerable length of time for her to accept that she was safe, and that she was not only emotionally but also physically scarred by the experience. Her skin was blotched with the unmistakable signs of vitamin deficiency, and it was a long, slow process to regain her health and self-confidence. She knew that her detractors would make whatever political capital they could out of the fact that she had finally broken under interrogation, but she also remembered that Hilda Bernstein had said of Mandela's appearance during the Rivonia Trial that people were shocked at how he had deteriorated physically and appalled that the police had managed to reduce the proud and sophisticated man to a shadow of his former self. Winnie had been exposed to the terrible rigours of being a black political prisoner in apartheid South Africa. She understood so much that had not been clear to her before. She understood why people died in detention and she knew that the stronger one was, the harsher the treatment that would be meted out.

In an interview with the Institute of International Studies at the University of Berkeley, California, and as part of a study titled *Conversations with History*, the International Red Cross's medical coordinator for detention-related activities, Hernan Reyes, elucidated prisoners' reactions to, and assessment of, torture. Asked whether women were more vulnerable and less resilient than men, Reyes said female political prisoners were in many cases the stronger individuals. He recalled seeing how women political prisoners gave prison authorities 'a very rough time' with internal rebellion and resistance, despite severe intimidation and force. Women, he said, could be very tough.

Asked what the worst form of torture was, he said that political prisoners who had been severely beaten, tortured with electricity and endured other forms of torture had told him the worst form of torture was being in strict solitary confinement for months on end – six, eight, nine, twelve months.

Nelson Mandela, who had been imprisoned in harsh conditions and forced to perform years of hard labour, said he had found his own brief encounter with solitary confinement – three days – 'the most forbidding aspect of prison life'.

Winnie Mandela had been in solitary confinement for thirteen months.

12

Between the ANC and oblivion

I N THEIR EFFORTS to rid themselves of the Mandelas, the security police were not content with Nelson's incarceration on Robben Island and the concerted campaign of persecution against Winnie. In 1969, while she was in detention, and in the hope of killing the proverbial two birds with one stone, they grabbed an opportunity to get rid of Mandela – permanently.

Success depended on BOSS operative Gordon Winter, and the stage was set for a foolish escape plot hatched by a group of left-wing British sympathisers, who were more idealistic than competent. The plan was initiated by Gordon Bruce, a British left-winger who had become a friend of Mandela, and would be directed by Marianne Borman, a senior employee in the British Information Office.

According to one version of the conspiracy, a senior warder would be bribed to lace the coffee of the two guards on duty outside Mandela's cell with sedatives, then help South Africa's most famous prisoner to walk out of jail dressed in a warder's uniform and carrying a firearm. Bruce would be waiting offshore in a speedboat, and Mandela, after disguising himself in a diver's wetsuit, would be ferried to the mainland and quickly driven to an airstrip, where famous British aviatrix Sheila Scott would be warming up the engine of a light aircraft, ready to whisk him out of the country.

Bruce advertised in the London *Times* for a capable organiser who could take care of 'unusual work'. One of those who responded was Gordon Winter. His credentials as a 'dissident' South African were perfect for the task, and provided BOSS with the opportunity to infiltrate the plan without the British participants being any the wiser about Winter's true identity. While the British conspirators were planning to rescue Mandela, BOSS was intent on orchestrating his death. Winter would arrange that the gun given to Mandela was loaded with blanks, and he would be shot dead as he boarded Scott's aircraft. The South African authorities would claim every justification for killing Mandela after his armed escape from Robben Island.

Whether or not the plan could ever have succeeded became moot when the British secret service was tipped off by Sir Robert Birley, husband of Winnie's friend Lady Elinor, after Bruce had confided in him. The plan was aborted, apparently because Scott changed her mind, Marianne Borman became suspicious of Winter, and British intelligence threatened to blow the whistle on everyone to avoid the acute embarrassment the role of British nationals would have caused the government in Whitehall.

Winnie's banning order had expired while she was in prison, towards the end of 1970, and almost the first thing she did on being released was apply for permission to visit Mandela. She also travelled to the Transkei to see her father for the first time in several years. Both their lives had changed radically in the interim, and they were glad of the chance to heal the rift between them. Columbus was living in a government mansion in Umtata, but Winnie noticed immediately that he had aged visibly, and was not in good health. Columbus was equally concerned about Winnie's haggard appearance, but it was a happy reunion, nevertheless, and before long they were their old selves with one another.

During the visit, Columbus confessed that he was troubled and had developed grave doubts about the so-called independence of the Transkei. He had seen no benefits for their people, and, if anything, he told Winnie, the poverty, overcrowding and unemployment were worse than ever, with thousands of people having been uprooted from settled lives and jobs in the urban areas, only to be dumped in remote parts of the Transkei where there were no opportunities at all. He told her he had become bitterly disillusioned, and was heartbroken by the fact that the homelands were sustaining the migrant labour system. Columbus poured out his heart to Winnie, and admitted that he had been misled into believing that the homelands would redress the wrongs and injustices visited on black people by the apartheid government. As citizens of non-existent countries, people were deprived of their South African citizenship, and Columbus had belatedly understood that the entire homeland scheme was a ruse to prevent them from claiming political rights outside of their traditional tribal areas.

The pilgrimage to her roots and the reconciliation with her father restored Winnie's equilibrium. She returned to Soweto invigorated and determined not to be distracted from what she saw as her purpose in life: to keep Mandela's name alive and focus attention on the liberation struggle. But on reaching home, she realised almost immediately that the authorities had no intention of easing the relentless pressure on her. The house had been raided again in her absence, and while she was picking up the books flung carelessly on the floor, her Xhosa Bible fell open, exposing an expertly hollowed out recess in the pages, in the shape of a gun. She knew this could only be the work of the security police 'dirty tricks' squad and that it would serve no purpose to report it, but she did show it to some of her friends. Six years later, when she was banished to the Free State and the police packed up her belongings, the Bible disappeared.

Within days of her return from the Transkei, she was served a double blow: her application to visit Nelson had been turned down, and she was issued with a fresh and more stringent five-year banning order. She sat down and wept. It had been two years since she had seen Nelson, and her newfound resolve all but crumbled. She was forbidden from leaving her house from 6 pm to 6 am, and over weekends. That would be inconvenient, but she could live with it. Not being allowed to see Madiba, however, was almost more than she could bear. In the five years that he had been on Robben Island, Winnie had been arrested more often than she had been permitted to visit her husband in jail.

Many detainees were mentally shattered, some permanently, after months of detention, interrogation and torture, and Winnie's friends and family were anxious about the effect her terrifying experience might have had on her. But once she had recovered from the physical ravages of her imprisonment, she seemed to be her old self: cheerful, tenacious and more determined than ever to carry the struggle flag. If anything, she seemed stronger and more resilient than before, and those closest to her were in awe of her resolve. Winnie herself said prison had liberated her inner self and purified her soul. She understood why she had been imprisoned. All of South Africa, she said, was a prison for black people, and it was easier to comprehend the regulated suffering of formal incarceration than the endless hardships and injustices imposed on blacks in every aspect of their everyday lives.

Most people had no idea of the conditions under which Winnie and other activists were detained, since the Prisons Act prevented newspapers from publishing anything about life behind bars. However, when newspapers reported details of her two trials and acquittals, the new banning order that followed her release from prison, and especially the fact that she was refused permission to visit Mandela, there were stringent protests from religious leaders and the political opposition, and for once the authorities heeded the criticism. When Winnie again sought permission to go to Robben Island a month later, the Minister of Justice handled the matter personally, and her request was approved.

It was an emotionally charged meeting for both Winnie and Nelson. She had lost a great deal of weight in prison and still looked drained, and there was almost nothing Mandela could say except to assure her of his love and to remind her, yet again, that their cause was just. Winnie fervently believed that their sacrifice was not in vain, but she desperately needed his nearness and comfort. She couldn't even hold his hand, and could see him only from the waist up through the glass, the ever-present warders hovering over them, ears pricked for any breach of the conversation rules. In the background was the distinctive whirr of a tape-recorder, capturing their every word.

It was the first time since Thembi's death that Winnie had seen Nelson, and there was so much to talk about – and so little time. How do you encapsulate two years in thirty minutes? How do you console the man you love for the loss of his son? How do you make any decisions when there is no time to explore any one issue? How do you express longing for one another's physical presence with two hostile strangers listening to every word? They barely had time to even touch on the most important matters and reassure one another as best they could before the warder said 'Time's up' and Winnie had to leave.

She walked back to the ferry in a daze, struggling to keep her composure, trying to focus on getting to the airport and home. She felt weak and disorientated, and ineffably tired. She feared that she might collapse, and willed herself to reach the relative safety of her home, praying that it would not have been left in disarray by yet another raid.

She made it back to Orlando, probably as much through sheer determination as anything else, but once she shut the door behind her, the tidal wave of heartache and anxiety, frustration and trauma that had been welling up over the past few years, hit her. At the age of thirty-six, Winnie Mandela had a heart attack.

The illness compelled Winnie to rest and take care of herself. She emerged from a period of recuperation with restored vitality and energy – and she would need it. The security police were sorely frustrated that their attempts to silence her and keep her behind bars for as long as possible had failed. Until they had collected enough information to act against her again, they would have to be content with a renewed campaign of dirty tricks and harassment. During a raid on her home, they found her sister, brother-in-law and Peter Magubane (who was also banned), and charged Winnie with breaking her banning order. Her younger sister Nonyaniso was arrested for being in Johannesburg without a permit and given seventy-two hours to return to the Transkei. Sometimes, the police invaded Winnie's house four times in one day. Mandela lodged an appeal with the Minister of Justice for Winnie's ban to be lifted, but got no response. She might have been released from prison, but Winnie was living under siege.

During the early 1960s, the ANC was a vibrant and fast-growing organisation. Despite the apartheid government's repression and stifling legislation, it had been possible to organise national campaigns and conferences, stage the momentous Congress of the People, adopt the Freedom Charter, establish representation abroad, launch Umkhonto we Sizwe, and kindle international recognition and support. By 1970, however, the movement had been reduced to little more than a nuisance factor. At the end of 1969, a secret American intelligence report assessed the ANC's political influence as weak, and noted that the organisation had been widely infiltrated by government agents. American historian Thomas Karis wrote that the ANC had become little more than a shadowy presence, and when *Washington Post* correspondent Jim Hoagland visited South Africa in 1970, he found that Luthuli, Mandela and Sisulu were 'perceived dimly, as if they belonged to another time, long past and long lost'.

Mandela later acknowledged that during this period scant attention was paid to him or the ANC, and in November 1970 a draft ANC document conceded that the organisation was moribund. The leadership recognised that black people had become politically reticent, *tsotsis* were paid for information, and there were spies and informers everywhere. The Rivonia prisoners' worst fears were turning into reality. Ever since their imprisonment on Robben Island, they had been afraid that removal of the leadership from the political stage would see a parallel retreat from the ANC by supporters both in South Africa and internationally. As media reports about the liberation struggle slowed to a trickle, then stopped altogether, their concerns proved warranted.

Between the ANC and oblivion stood the lone and battered figure of Winnie Mandela.

In the political vacuum created by the virtual withdrawal of the ANC from the political arena, a new brand of black opposition evolved, and Winnie was one of the few members of the ANC's top echelon to embrace it. The next generation of young and angry blacks gravitated towards Black Consciousness, and Winnie, with her instinctive populist approach, had little difficulty identifying with the concept. She understood and empathised with the anger of the youth, and they, in turn, trusted and looked up to her, surreptitiously visiting her and seeking her counsel. From what she saw and heard, she realised that ways had to be found to accommodate the new mood and aspirations of young black activists under the banner of the ANC. It would not be easy, and Winnie was the only person who could act as the link between the Old Guard and the Young Turks. Since any political conversations were strictly prohibited, Winnie could not discuss the situation with Mandela, and had to be content with relaying her cryptic messages to him, then formulating his equally arcane responses into proposals that would be acceptable to the youth.

The government had long since ceased to regard Winnie merely as a branch of their vendetta against Mandela. Challenged initially by her refusal to capitulate, then by her growing political involvement, they recognised her strength and power and she became a target in her own right. Her avowed commitment to keeping both the struggle and Nelson Mandela's name alive was gaining momentum. Meanwhile, in seclusion on Robben Island and with no way of playing a direct role in politics, the ANC leaders increasingly focused their attention on survival of the spirit. Mandela, especially, concentrated all his efforts on preparing himself and the others for the day when they would be free men. He knew that some of them might not live long enough to see that day, but this did not deter him. He was single-minded

161

in his determination that the political prisoners would use the time in prison to further their studies, so that they would emerge as educated intellectuals.

Barely perceptible shifts in the attitude of the prison authorities made their lives somewhat more bearable. From 1970, the prisoners were allowed to have photographs of close family members. Winnie immediately made up an album and sent it to Nelson, and regularly updated the pictures of herself and the children, and later also their grandchildren. Mandela carefully pasted each new photograph into the album, which fellow prisoners often asked to borrow. Some of them seldom or never received visitors or letters, and the Mandela photo album became their only link with a lost family life, a 'window on the world', as Mandela called it. Eventually, the album had been paged through so often that it began to fall apart, and Mandela found that some of the photographs had been removed. Although this upset him, he forgave the photo thieves, reasoning that they were so desperate to have something personal in their cells that they could not resist the temptation.

The difference in the lives of the two Mandelas became ever more discernible. As Nelson retreated into a life of philosophy and academic zeal, Winnie was moving inexorably towards the front line of the battle against apartheid. In 1972, security policemen kicked down the door of her house, bricks were flung through a window, shots fired at the front door. She was watched more closely than any other banned person, and the campaign against her bore testimony to the fact that it had become a personal vendetta. The government was fully aware of the deadly blow it had dealt the struggle by jailing Mandela and other ANC leaders, and they did not want Winnie stepping into the breach. If anything, they wanted her out of the way and behind bars, and repeated efforts were made to get a criminal conviction against her, even though some of the charges bordered on the absurd.

After the police damaged her front door, three white sympathisers who had read newspaper reports about the attack called at her home and offered to lend her a guard dog for protection. The police, never far away, promptly arrested the callers and charged them with visiting a banned person. Winnie was charged with breaking her ban. When the dog was returned to its owners, a friend of Winnie's, Angela Cobbett, a prominent member of the Black Sash, gave Winnie a German shepherd dog. She, too, was arrested for visiting Winnie, and the dog, Sheba, was poisoned soon afterwards.

Next, a group of Winnie's friends employed and paid a nightwatchman to look after her, but he was powerless against the security police. On one occasion, three policemen entered the house while Winnie wasn't there, despite the watchman's attempts to prevent them. The next morning, he discovered that all the washing hanging on the line, including one of Winnie's dresses, had been slashed with a knife. By now, Winnie was convinced that the police were paying people to intimidate or even kill her.

Children were exempt from the ban on communication with Winnie, and for a while her ten-year-old niece lived with her. One night, Winnie was awakened by a sound in her bedroom. She switched on the bedside lamp and saw three men approaching her bed. One was holding a wire noose. It had been many years since Winnie had stood her ground in childhood fights with the boys who were her play-mates, but she was determined that if the intruders wanted to kill her, she would take at least one of them with her. As she sprang out of bed, charged with adrenalin and ready to do battle, her niece started screaming, and the three men fled.

Winnie telephoned her attorney and some friends, and on investigation they found that the burglar bars at one window had been sawed through, then carefully placed back in position. She had no doubt that this, too, was the work of the security police, but her friends insisted that she report the incident. The police took a statement from her, but, as she had known would happen, nothing ever came of it. Some time later, a bomb was thrown at the house and exploded against a side wall. Then the garage was burgled and the windows of her car were smashed. Finally, the car was stolen.

No one was ever apprehended for any of the numerous offences perpetrated against Winnie – all incidents of theft, housebreaking, assault, damage to property, bomb attacks and shots fired apparently baffled the usually efficient South African Police, who never solved a single case on behalf of the woman living at house No. 8115, Orlando West.

Zindzi, although she was only twelve, had witnessed enough to understand that the state was waging all-out war on her mother, and she appealed to the United Nations to protect Winnie. Both the UN secretary general and the International Committee of the Red Cross sought assurances from the South African government that Winnie would not be harmed. But her friends were not convinced, and decided that she needed more protection than the apartheid government's word.

Horst Kleinschmidt was a member of the Christian Institute and later executive director of the International Defence and Aid Fund. Father Cosmos Desmond was a Franciscan priest who had been banned and placed under house arrest after writing *The Discarded People*, which exposed the plight of victims of forced removals that underpinned the government's homeland resettlement scheme. Together, they directed construction of a wall around Winnie's corner property. Many years before, Mandela had planted an evergreen hedge along the boundaries, but while he and Winnie were in prison, it had died, and only a few brown stumps remained. Horst instructed the builders to follow the original hedgerow as their guideline for positioning the wall. It should have been a simple enough undertaking but, predictably, the project was beset with problems.

Construction was well under way when municipal officials pointed out that the demarcation line was skew, and that part of the wall had been built on the neighbouring plot. The builders knocked it down and started again, but, again at an advanced stage, the constructor went bankrupt and another had to be found. Meanwhile, Winnie had noted that the wall would be of little use as a security measure, as it was nowhere near high enough to keep intruders at bay. Despite the underlying seriousness of the project, it became a source of great amusement to all involved, and helped to distract Winnie, for a while, from her many other problems. Increasing the height of the wall was a major operation, and inevitably the 'wall committee' ran out of money. There was another delay while additional funds were raised. Finally, the wall was completed – but no one had made provision for the cost of gates, and for a while the gaping holes where they were eventually installed rendered the wall entirely useless as protection against unwelcome callers.

In 1974, Mandela, anxious about the series of attacks on Winnie, appealed to the government to restrain the police, and asked that she be allowed to own a firearm. The police refused, arguing that Winnie was too impulsive and quick-tempered to be considered a responsible gun owner. Having experienced their share of her angry response to intrusions, they obviously had no desire to encounter an enraged *and* armed Winnie Mandela.

One of Winnie's staunchest friends and supporters was Peter Magubane, the photographer for *Drum* magazine. His long association with Winnie had cost him dearly. Another one of those betrayed by Gordon Winter, he was detained for eighteen months, much of it in solitary confinement. But Magubane refused to be intimidated into turning his back on Winnie, and helped her in any way he could. In May 1973, he drove Zeni and Zindzi into Johannesburg to meet their mother during her lunch hour. While she and the girls were having a snack in Magubane's minibus on the corner of Troye and Jeppe streets, Winnie was arrested for being in the presence of another banned person. Magubane was arrested as well. The arresting officer, Sergeant Van Niekerk, gloated that Winnie was going to prison for a long time for the offence, and said that this time not even her 'friends in Bloemfontein' would be able to help her.

Frustrated at every turn in their quest to remove Winnie from public view, the security police were scathing in their criticism of and contempt for the courts that either dismissed charges against Winnie or gave her suspended sentences. The Appellate Division in Bloemfontein, which managed to maintain its independence and integrity despite heavy political pressure, was singled out for special malice.

Van Niekerk's prediction proved wrong. Winnie was sentenced to twelve months in prison, but the sentence was halved on appeal. Her daughters were in court when the initial sentence was handed down, and Zindzi burst into tears. As they left the building, Cosmos Desmond having paid Winnie's bail, she reprimanded Zindzi sternly, telling her never again to show her distress in front of the white authorities, as it gave them the satisfaction of knowing they had succeeded in hurting one. Zindzi never forgot her mother's words, and moulded her future reaction to hardships on Winnie's philosophy.

It pained Winnie to know that Magubane was suffering as a result of his friendship with her and his unfailing willingness to help. She believed emphatically that the photographer was banned and periodically imprisoned simply because he offered support to Nelson Mandela's wife and children, and not because he himself presented any kind of security risk. The police had successfully isolated Winnie from many of her old friends by threatening and harassing them, but when Magubane refused to yield to that kind of pressure, a more insidious approach was needed.

The authorities knew that any action taken against friends and family members was an indirect form of punishment against Nelson and Winnie. Through their collaborators in the media, reports of an inappropriate relationship between Winnie and Magubane began to surface, and, knowing that the innuendo and rumour would wound Mandela deeply, the authorities ensured that such reports came to his attention, despite the fact that he was not permitted to read newspapers. As before, he would simply find cuttings of all negative publicity about Winnie on the bed in his cell at the end of the day.

In September 1973, Winnie received news that her father was dying. She was granted permission to travel to the Transkei to see him, and took Zeni and Zindzi with her. Columbus was so frail that he could hardly stand or walk, but he was determined that he would not receive his daughter from his sickbed. Even in the final days of his life, he commanded respect and admiration, and insisted that Hilda help him dress in his best suit, which hung loosely on his emaciated body. Hilda also had to help him stand when he greeted his beloved daughter and her children, and despite the enormous effort it took, he told Winnie and the girls that this was how he wanted them to remember him – standing erect. Winnie, who had inherited his indomitable spirit, understood that he meant far more than the actual physical act. When she said goodbye to her father, Winnie kissed him, for the first and only time in her life.

Winnie began serving her six-month sentence in the Magubane case on 14 October 1974. This time, she was better prepared than when she was dragged off to prison in May 1969. She arranged for her daughters, who were home from boarding school, to stay in the Orlando West house under the watchful eye of family members. Dr Motlana, one of their guardians, and other friends were close at hand, and Horst Kleinschmidt would take care of their financial needs. The terrible memories of the two little girls clinging to her, screaming, when the police took her away five years earlier, still haunted Winnie and her daughters, but this time they were better equipped to deal with the parting stoically.

For the first month Winnie was held at the Fort in Johannesburg. After that she was transferred in the dead of night – presumably to forestall any attempted escape or demonstrations by supporters – to the women's prison at Kroonstad in the Free State. Unlike her previous sojourn in a penal institution, there was no solitary confinement, the food was decent, and Zeni and Zindzi were allowed to visit. She also had companionship. One of her fellow prisoners was a legend of the struggle, Dorothy Nyembe, who had been one of Mandela's close friends. She was one of South Africa's longest-serving female political prisoners, sentenced in 1968 to fifteen years for harbouring Umkhonto we Sizwe fighters.

Dorothy was a devout Christian and courageous to the core, and when Winnie arrived at Kroonstad she was already over fifty and had served almost six years of her sentence. Incarceration had taken its toll, and Winnie detected clear outward signs of suffering and sacrifice, but Dorothy's spirit was strong, and she was as committed to the cause as ever. She was also a pillar of strength for her fellow prisoners. Winnie greatly admired Dorothy, who had significantly influenced her own political growth, and was especially struck by her lack of bitterness. Dorothy would recount how Mangosuthu Buthelezi had testified against her, but rather than being angry or vengeful, she was remarkably conciliatory towards the Zulu leader.

Winnie and Dorothy's intimate circle was completed by Amina Desai, who was serving a five-year sentence. Amina had lent her car to Ahmed Timol, a thirty-year-old Indian schoolteacher, who was arrested while in possession of political pamphlets and who, according to the police, had dived from a window on the tenth floor of John Vorster Square, as police headquarters in Johannesburg had been renamed, while he was being interrogated. Years later, Gordon Winter set the record straight in his book about BOSS, and disclosed that two security policemen had dangled Timol out of the window while holding him by his feet, threatening to drop him unless he gave them the information they wanted. One of them lost his grip, and Timol plunged to his death.

Although conditions at Kroonstad were infinitely better than those under which Winnie had previously been held, she still suffered from periodic claustrophobia and depression. Along with Dorothy and Amina, she was held in a special self-contained section of the prison, and they had no contact with any of the non-political inmates. Each woman had a tiny cell, and they shared the luxury of a bathroom and a tiny exercise yard that was enclosed by a high wall that blocked out everything but the sky. They were allowed to sew and read, but the books selected for them by the warders were third-rate novels, and Winnie yearned for something more substantial to engage her mind. The young white wardresses who watched over them were poorly educated and could barely speak English, though the head of the prison, Erika van Zyl, who had a degree in penology, treated them with respect. She realised that they were accustomed to a decent standard of living, and ensured that they all had new blankets and prison uniforms.

Mandela agonised over the fact that Winnie was in jail again, and tried to help her in the only way he could, by giving her advice based on his own experience. He encouraged her to meditate before going to sleep at night, and shared his philosophy that a prison cell was conducive to self-discovery and exploration of one's mind and feelings.

Winnie was released on 13 April 1975. Dorothy Nyembe served her full fifteen-year sentence and stayed in prison until 20 March 1984. Amina Desai's friendship with Winnie endured, and when Winnie was prevented by her banning orders from earning a living, Amina showed her support by sending gifts of shoes and clothing.

Back in Johannesburg, Winnie found the first well-paying job she had secured since having to leave the Child Welfare Society. She went to work for Frank & Hirsch, a company specialising in consumer electronics, for R250 a month. Her employer, Helmut Hirsch, refused to be intimidated, and ignored pertinent suggestions by the police that she should be dismissed. He told them unequivocally that his company's policy was to employ people who were capable and efficient, irrespective of race or political affiliation, and that Mrs Mandela was a valued employee.

Winnie's fortitude had not gone unnoticed internationally, and British women nominated her Woman of the Year for 1974. For the first time in many years, she had cause for gratitude. She had a good job that offered the bonus of support and security from an employer who was undaunted by the official attention she drew, and her daughters were happily settled at Waterford, though they lived with the daily dread of what might happen to their mother. Zindzi was showing exceptional creative talent. She learned to play both the piano and the guitar, and found an outlet for her emotions and fears by composing songs and writing poems, which revealed something of her inner anguish, as this example shows:

> I need a neighbour who will live
> A teardrop away
> Who will open up when I knock late at night
> I need a child who will play
> A smile away
> Who will always whisper I love you
> To be my mummy.

When Winnie's banning order expired in September 1975, the police informed her that it would not be renewed. At first she refused to believe them, wondering what tricks they had in store. But after a few weeks, she accepted, albeit cautiously at first, that she really *was* free, for the first time in thirteen years. She could associate with other people, go wherever she wanted, entertain visitors at home, even address meetings – though she said she would never consider herself truly free while her people remained in bondage to the apartheid system.

After more than a decade of isolation, it was as though Winnie had been brought back from the dead. Invitations began arriving for her to speak at meetings and appear at rallies. The first was a reception arranged by Fatima Meer, a sociologist at the University of Natal who had been subjected to lengthy periods as a banned person due to her anti-apartheid leadership in Natal. She and Winnie had been instrumental in establishing the Black Women's Federation, which was also later banned. Winnie was to be the keynote speaker at the Durban meeting, and when she arrived on Sunday 12 October, she was met by hundreds of supporters and well-wishers who carried her shoulder-high through the airport terminal. Outside, a group of traditional Zulu dancers performed a welcoming ceremony, and as Winnie's motorcade drove through Umlazi, cheering residents lined the streets to catch a glimpse of the 'other' famous Mandela.

At the crowded YMCA hall, more than 1 000 people of all races roared a welcome for Winnie, who was regal in a Xhosa tribal dress. It was a daunting experience for her to appear in front of a crowd and make a speech again after having been gagged for so many years, but she quickly recovered her confidence, and her address was a triumph.

Winnie was back in the land of the living.

When Fatima took Winnie to the airport the next day, someone pointed out the Minister of Justice, Jimmy Kruger, pulling up in his official car. Fatima deliberately steered Winnie towards the vehicle and, while the minister was gathering his luggage, audaciously introduced herself and presented Winnie to him. The minister beamed at the two women and said he was pleased to meet them, as though nothing was more normal than sworn adversaries making small talk. Winnie seized the moment and asked Kruger when he was going to release Mandela. His reply stunned her. Wagging a finger of reproach at her, he said: 'That's up to you.' What, Winnie asked, did she have to do with her husband being freed?

'You must behave yourself,' said Kruger as he walked off.

In her next letter to Madiba, Winnie told him everything about her exciting time in Durban, even the encounter with the minister, though she had no idea how much would be censored. Nelson, in turn, wrote that he wanted to see Zindzi, who was almost fifteen. Prison regulations prohibited visits by children between the ages of two and sixteen, and Madiba had not seen any of his children for years after being sent to Robben Island. This was a source of great sorrow to him, but with the exception of Thembi, who had been killed, each of the children had reappeared in his life as soon as they turned sixteen. Zindzi was the youngest; she had been a toddler when he last saw her at the end of the Rivonia Trial, and he was impatient to see the young woman she was becoming.

In their letters to one another, with the help of codes and hints and their lawyers acting as intermediaries, a plan emerged. Winnie would alter Zindzi's birth certificate to show her age as sixteen, so that she could see her father. It proved relatively easy for Winnie to doctor the document, and she duly applied for permission to visit Mandela. But the whole subterfuge was almost scuppered by Winnie's stepmother Hilda, who went to visit Mandela a few weeks earlier, and was bemused when he told her excitedly that he would be seeing Zindzi soon. Surely, said Hilda, that could not be so, Zindzi was not yet sixteen. Mandela realised that no one had told her about the ruse and tried to gloss over it, but Hilda stubbornly would not let it go, and in her best schoolteacher's manner, lectured Mandela about his miscalculation. Eventually, he could do nothing but widen and roll his eyes to signal a warning to her. She seemed to get the message, and changed the subject.

Winnie, Zeni and Zindzi visited Robben Island together in December. A full year had passed since Nelson had last seen Winnie, and this was their first meeting after her imprisonment at Kroonstad. It was also the first time since he had gone underground in 1961 that the four of them had been together as a family, but the joy of reunion was marred by the awkwardness of the long separation. Nelson was enchanted by Zindzi, and amazed at how closely she resembled her mother. But the visit stirred an acute sense of loss in all of them, and Nelson, in particular, was wracked by guilt at not having been there for his wife and children and deeply conscious of how much he had missed. He wondered whether Zindzi harboured anger and resentment over the fact that he had chosen the cause of his people over his own family, and went out of his way to make her feel special and at ease. He asked about her life, school and friends, and told her his memories and recollections of her as a little girl. When he mentioned that she had rarely cried, he noticed that she was struggling to hold back her tears.

Mandela continued to rely on Winnie as the mainstay of his life, both as his wife and political partner. He poured out his love and longing for her in deeply romantic and touching letters, often hinting at physical intimacy, baring emotions he had always kept carefully hidden from others. His many friends and relatives did their best to boost his spirits, but Winnie remained his primary source of strength – and political information. She never failed to convey news in their special coded language, and not only Mandela but all the other prisoners looked forward to her visits eagerly, knowing she would share insights and information that they otherwise might not receive.

The authorities had given Winnie a reprieve in so far as the banning orders and house arrests went, but that did not mean they had stopped persecuting her. In January 1976, Winnie sent Mandela a message that her application for a visit had been turned down, on the grounds that he did not wish to see her. Mandela was aghast and immediately made an appointment to see Lieutenant Prins, head of the Robben Island prison. He lodged a strong protest against the lie, but Prins, clearly disinterested, responded that he thought Winnie was just seeking publicity. Then he made a derogatory and very offensive remark about Winnie, and for the first time in twelve years on the island, Mandela lost his temper. He was on the verge of physically assaulting Prins when he regained control of himself and unleashed a verbal barrage on the warder instead, calling him both dishonourable and contemptible. The next day, Prins charged him with insulting and threatening the head of the prison, but on the day the case was due to be heard, the authorities withdrew the charges.

If Winnie had proved only one thing during her solo crusade, it was that she was no shrinking violet. She refused to be intimidated by the threat that her banning order could be reinstated at any time, and used every opportunity to speak out against the regime and the mainstream media. At the meeting in Durban in April 1976, she commented on the discriminatory reaction of the media to the banning of blacks and whites, a subject on which she could speak with some authority. While media outrage had shaken the rafters when eight white student leaders were banned, the same newspapers had offered no more than a muffled tut-tut when an equal number of black student leaders were banned.

Winnie made no pretence of respecting anyone in authority following her harrowing experience in prison, and some of her friends thought she had actually become slightly unhinged. Far from crushing her, the apartheid government had created a truly formidable adversary, who remained unflinching in her opposition. 'You cannot intimidate people like me any more,' she said emphatically.

To the annoyance and alarm of her opponents, far from having been bludgeoned into submission, Winnie was emerging as a major player on the political stage, a protagonist in her own right and with her own support base. To the downtrodden masses, she had become a heroine, an African Joan of Arc: a leader to be reckoned with. And despite anything her detractors said, she was keeping the Mandela name alive, both inside South Africa and beyond. It was Peter Magubane who would later voice what many black South Africans had long believed: without Winnie, Mandela could not have remained what he was. When journalists could not write about him, Winnie saw to it that they were kept up to date about his problems and his progress. Winnie, said Magubane, was the only person who had stood by both Mandela and the ANC without wavering, the only one who had dared the authorities to try to stop her. There was never any doubt, he said, that if she had to, Winnie Mandela was prepared to die for the liberation struggle.

13

'They are shooting
our children!'

IN 1975, PORTUGAL'S WITHDRAWAL as the colonial power in both Mozambique and Angola ushered in a significant period of political change and upheaval in southern Africa. With only South Africa, South West Africa and Rhodesia still under white minority rule, blacks at the southern tip of the continent were filled with hope, and there was a sudden surge of militant expectation, especially among the youth.

On a visit to Mandela early in 1976, Winnie managed to tell him in her coded language about the rising discontent and emergence of a new generation of young black rebels. They were both militant and Africanist, and regarded the older struggle leaders as moderates. Winnie warned Mandela that they were changing the nature of the struggle, and that the ANC should take them seriously.

The Black Consciousness movement had been established in 1969 by Steve Biko, a young medical student at the University of Natal, who was vehemently opposed to what he termed the paternalism of white liberals in the leadership tier of the National Union of South African Students (NUSAS). This led him to form the all-black South African Students' Organisation (SASO), which soon attracted a significant following on black university campuses and also inspired teenagers still at school. In 1973 the government banned eight SASO leaders, including Biko. The ANC leadership was not enthused by Biko's initiative, but Winnie found both him and his ideals inspiring. She said Biko stepped into the political hiatus created by the ANC being banned and its leaders jailed, and she embraced the new pride in being black that had begun to surface. She became both a friend and supporter of Biko, and when he was in Johannesburg he always made a point of seeing Winnie, who was steadily shifting into a new political role.

Mandela found it intensely frustrating to be marginalised from politics and life in general at this crucial point in South Africa's history. He fluctuated between a desperate longing to get out of jail and resignation that he would spend the rest of his life there. His name had been carved on his cell door – to remind him, said Winnie, of eternity, that this would be the end of his life. His emotions see-sawed between guilt over not being able to protect and provide for his family – and continue the political struggle – and dreams of freedom. With other prisoners like Mac Maharaj and Eddie Daniels he considered daring escape plans, and occasionally these went further than mere hypothesis. When one of the warders left a key lying around, Jeff Masemola made a soap imprint and fashioned a duplicate key, which would have given them access to sections of the prison not normally open to them, but they never used it. In 1974, Mandela, Maharaj and Wilton Mkwayi planned to escape during a trip to the dentist in Cape Town, but abandoned the idea at the last minute when they suspected that they were being led into a trap set by the police. The most ambitious plan was a proposal made by Eddie Daniels to the ANC leaders in Lusaka that a helicopter, painted in the livery of the South African Defence Force, should pick Mandela up on the island and drop him on the roof of a sympathetic foreign embassy in Cape Town, from where he could apply for asylum. They never received a reply from Lusaka.

If Winnie found it a burden to be the emotional keystone of South Africa's liberator-in-chief, she never said as much, and never complained. She was the one person with whom Madiba shared his inner fears and feelings, and his letters to her were the only record of his deep anxieties and longing, his every dream and aspiration. He had told her in 1964 that he would rely on her support to sustain him in prison, and more than a decade later, that still held true. In February 1976 he wrote that he thought of her as sister, mother, friend and mentor, and pictured in his mind everything that made her the person she was, physically and spiritually. He recalled that she had lovingly accepted the numerous difficulties of life with him, which would have defeated another woman; told her he carefully dusted her photograph every morning, for it gave him the feeling that he was caressing her as he had in the old days; reminded her of their special intimate habit of rubbing their noses together, and said he touched his nose to hers on the photograph to 'recapture the electric current' that used to flush through his blood. 'I wonder,' he wrote, 'what it'll be like when I return.'

While their leaders were reminiscing about their lost lives and hankering for freedom, foremost in the minds of angry young blacks were their grievances against the Bantu Education Act, which, two decades after its introduction, was still a bone of contention. The system was widely despised and condemned, especially by young urban blacks whose parents had known the benefit of a superior education and had escaped what was indisputably schooling for servitude. Conversely, the youth had greater access to the media than their mothers and fathers had enjoyed, recognised the limitations of the education system imposed on them and became ever more determined to change it. Practically all Soweto's children seemed aware of the statement by the late Dr Verwoerd that except as labourers, there was no place for blacks in the white community. While white children were being taught mathematics and science, biology, German and Latin, black children were forced to learn arithmetic, agriculture (to prepare them for working on white farms),

Bible study, African languages (which would not equip them for university study) and Afrikaans. Their anger was fuelled by the introduction of a regulation that made it compulsory for certain subjects to be taught in Afrikaans rather than English. Apart from the fact that this would further limit their development, Afrikaans was deeply resented as the language of the oppressor.

As always, there were a number of children living at Winnie's home, and she was aware of the growing anger. After her ban expired in 1975, she warned in public speeches and media interviews that the rage felt by young blacks could lead to disaster, and appealed to the authorities to heed the protests of the children. Other prominent Sowetans also sounded the alert that a dangerous and potentially explosive situation was brewing. Desmond Tutu, then Anglican Dean of Johannesburg, wrote to Prime Minister John Vorster that he feared bloodshed and violence were almost inevitable. But the repeated caveats and appeals to drop Afrikaans as a language of tuition in black schools were ignored.

Frustration turned to action, and in dozens of schools, children as young as eight began boycotting classes in protest. Anxious parents, who felt that an inferior education was better than no education at all, were seen by their children as having capitulated, and large numbers of them, not knowing how to deal with the animosity of the young, turned to Winnie for advice.

Problems with the education authorities also brought parents to Winnie's door in search of help. When a group of children on a school trip to Swaziland died in a bus accident, the authorities refused to offer any financial help or compensation, even though the pupils had been in their care at the time. The parents struggled to raise the money to bring their children's bodies home, but several days after handing the funds over, they were told that the money had disappeared, and they could still not bury their offspring. After exhausting every other avenue, they turned to Winnie.

Over this period, she was inundated with requests and appeals for assistance, and realised that an organisation was needed to assist parents with their numerous and varied complaints, and look after the children's interests. She approached several of her influential friends, and in May 1976 the Soweto Parents' Association was launched. The chairman was Dr Aaron Mathlare, a former ANC activist, and both Winnie and Dr Nthatho Motlana served on the executive. The authorities clearly disapproved of the organisation, and whenever Winnie addressed a parents' meeting, the security police were conspicuously present and taking notes.

The spark that lit the 1976 student uprising was an incident at Naledi High School. During school hours, two security policemen arrived to arrest one of the student leaders, Enos Ngutshana. The headmaster asked the policemen to leave the premises and wait until the end of the school day to detain him, but they refused. When they tried to carry out the arrest, however, enraged pupils set the police car alight and beat up the two officers. Soon afterwards, under the banner of the Soweto Students' Representative Council (SSRC), the students organised a mass demonstration against the use of Afrikaans in the classrooms. The organisers emphasised that this was to be a peaceful protest, and those taking part were instructed to wear their school uniforms and gather at their schools. The children threw themselves into preparations with an efficiency that would stun the entire country. They made placards with slogans that slammed education in Afrikaans, and worked out precise routes for pupils to follow from each school to the mass protest venue. Conscious that police might intervene, the student leaders asked the principals of primary schools to declare a holiday for younger pupils. However, the smaller children had no intention of being sidelined, and arrived in force, albeit uninvited, to join the march.

On the morning of 16 June, thousands of children took to the streets of Soweto carrying banners, singing freedom songs and clenching their fists in the familiar black power salute. No one, least of all the organisers, could have foreseen that what started out as a youthful protest against being forced to learn in what amounted to a foreign language would set first Soweto, then the whole of South Africa alight, and launch a revolution that would change the face of the country forever.

Like most adults in Soweto, Winnie knew about the planned march, but had no reason to doubt the students' assurances that it would be peaceful. She later made the point that if parents had had the slightest idea that there might be any trouble, they would not have gone to work that day.

When she herself left for the office that morning, she hardly spared a thought for the student march, and was following her normal routine when she received a telephone call from a mother in Soweto, who screamed hysterically: 'Please come, the police are shooting our children!'

Winnie drove back to Orlando West as fast as she could. Word of the situation spread even faster, and thousands of black adults left their workplaces all over Johannesburg and rushed home, using whatever form of transport they could find. Railway stations, taxi ranks and bus stops were swamped with commuters, and people with cars stopped and picked up as many passengers as they could. It seemed as though all roads led to Soweto.

Dr Motlana was one of the few adult eyewitnesses to the early events on that fateful day. Between 7 am and 8 am, he noticed a constant parade of schoolchildren passing his house in Dube, and followed them. At the Orlando West school the police tried to stop them from going any further, but the children kept on marching. Suddenly, the police opened fire – but instead of achieving the desired, tried and tested result of halting the march and dispersing the protestors, the shots ignited bedlam. What followed was a crazed anger and trail of violence and destruction that took everyone, including the police, by surprise. In the blink of an eye, Soweto became a bloody battlefield, with children trying to shield themselves from police bullets with dustbin lids, and police using live ammunition in preference to more common anti-riot measures such as dogs, tear gas and baton charges.

For Winnie, the images of 16 June could never be erased. As she drove through Orlando, a sea of young black faces met her. Hector Petersen, the thirteen-year-old boy who was the first to die, had just been killed. She was in agony at the sight of dying children whose bodies were torn apart by bullets.

Dr Motlana saw police on the back of a truck shooting at a group of children, all around six years of age, playing by the roadside. He rushed to the police station and demanded to see the commanding officer, asking what the hell the police thought they were doing, shooting at small children. The brigadier's reply was both crude and abusive.

Motlana worked tirelessly all day, removing bullets and shrapnel from wounded children, cleaning and suturing gaping wounds. The victims were too scared to call for ambulances or go to Baragwanath Hospital lest they be arrested, so their parents and friends carried them to Motlana's surgery. The scenes played out there were duplicated in doctors' rooms all over Soweto.

Winnie's heart was in her throat as she saw the crowd of children move to the main road, and she watched, aghast and helpless, while they unleashed their pent-up rage on the police and anyone else who crossed their path. Some estimates put the number of children involved in the 16 June protest at 30 000, but whatever their number, nothing and no one could stop the rampage.

Stones rained down in showers, like giant-sized hail. Cars were smashed and property was set on fire. Children as young as eleven hijacked buses, teenagers dragged drivers out of government cars. They smashed and burned everything in sight. The noise was deafening, and no one could get close enough to even try to reason with the crowd. An elderly man in a van tried to drive past to deliver his goods, but was ordered to stop and get out of the vehicle. Seeing children in school uniforms, and clearly unaware of how grave the situation was, he ignored them. Winnie watched in helpless horror as the children started throwing bricks through his windscreen. One of the bricks hit him on the head and he flung himself out of the van. As he fell on his back in the road, he lifted his arm and shouted 'Amandla!' before he was pelted with stones, and died. In years to come, whenever Winnie recalled the terror of 16 June, it was the face of that man she remembered, and it always brought tears to her eyes.

The situation rapidly spiralled out of control. Winnie was horrified when she saw the police pulling a white body from a dustbin while children looked on and sang freedom songs. The volcano of blind anger and hatred that exploded in Soweto in 1976 was no different from that of the French or Russian revolution, Tiananmen Square, the Mau Mau uprising in Kenya and countless other violent confrontations.

Nothing could stop the red-hot spewing lava until the anger was vented. The children of Soweto had planned a demonstration, not a street war, but the ill-considered response by the police was all that was needed to turn the protest into a powder keg.

Before 16 June, black parents were inclined to oppose any action that interfered with their children's schooling. After that date, although the pupils' militant reaction filled them with apprehension, parents were united in their condemnation of police brutality. In a single day, control had passed into the hands of the children, and parents found themselves powerless to stop the madness. The children called for boycotts against certain stores, and if adults were found with shopping bags from those shops, the contents were confiscated and destroyed. The children called for strike action, and the adults had to comply or face merciless reprisals. The parents became the pawns with which the children challenged apartheid. If the adults did not go to work, or stopped buying from stores owned by whites, the economy would suffer. It was a powerful weapon, and the children were wielding it.

Only a small section of Soweto had electricity, and at night the sprawling township was usually plunged into darkness. But in the weeks following the riots, the flames of youthful rage lit up the sky. Dozens of government buildings, many of them schools, were burned to the ground. Shops, post offices, houses and hundreds of vehicles were set on fire. Beerhalls and bottle stores were razed to punish those who lured fathers into squandering their wages on liquor and prevent the proceeds from financing the hated Bantu Administration Board. Shebeens, too, were targeted, and rivers of alcohol flowed down Soweto's streets and alleyways. Winnie's old friend, shebeen king Elija Msibi, found himself in an unusual situation. Thinking that a man of his wealth would automatically oppose the revolution, or at least the wanton destruction of property and livelihood, the police asked him to become an informer. But Elija's sympathy lay with the youth, and he consulted the ANC leadership on how he should proceed. They told him to play along, using his illiteracy and inability to speak English as excuses if the police grew impatient with the quality of information he fed them. The ploy succeeded, and Elija was able to pick up a great deal of useful information, which he passed on to Winnie, not the police. Thanks to him, many of the young militants escaped arrest, and sometimes he hid them in his own house until the danger passed. The entire body of student leaders was on the run, and so were thousands of schoolchildren. Tsietsi Mashinini, the president of the SSRC, was among those who fled the country. He had become known as 'the little Mandela', and one newspaper even published a report suggesting that he bore such a close physical resemblance to Mandela that he might well be his illegitimate son.

During the weeks that Soweto was a war zone, Winnie and other prominent residents had their hands full. She went from one police station to another demanding the bodies of children who had been killed, spent hours comforting bereaved parents, arranged more funerals than any individual should ever have to, and coordinated the help that poured in, including donations of coffins. Taxi drivers ferried people to the burials free of charge. The violence had quickly spread to other townships, and it seemed as though the killing would never end.

The police blamed Winnie and Dr Motlana for inciting the students, and claimed they had been responsible for setting South Africa aflame. Winnie reacted by stating she could only wish she had so much influence, and Motlana lashed out at the Minister of Justice, Jimmy Kruger, describing him as a 'particularly stupid' man whose actions had aggravated the situation. A more perceptive politician, said Motlana, would have demanded that the police show more restraint. Winnie and other black leaders knew only too well that the uprising was a manifestation of deep-seated anger, fuelled by youthful indignation and reckless disregard for the traditional structure of a society that had short-changed its young.

The government put the number of dead in Soweto at 600, but Winnie estimated the fatalities at more than 1 000, mostly children, some younger than twelve. More than 4 000 people were injured, and thousands of youngsters fled into exile in neighbouring states. An untold number vanished into detention, and hundreds of parents never found out what had happened to their sons and daughters.

South Africa was at war with itself. Smoke from the fire started in Soweto drifted across the entire country and formed a large black cloud over the future of white South Africa. As Winnie and others had predicted, the anger was contagious, and by the end of 1976, few black townships had not been touched by violence, school and consumer boycotts, and the death of youthful militants. Winnie urged the Soweto Parents' Association to join forces with other organisations to form a national Black Parents' Association that could liaise with the children. She insisted that the onus was on the older generation to fight for their rights rather than leave it to the youth, and she remained steadfast in her opposition to the system that had bred the state of anarchy, declaring publicly: 'We shall fight to the bitter end for justice.'

The Black Parents' Association (BPA) was formed under chairmanship of Bishop Manas Buthelezi, a cousin but political opponent of Chief Mangosuthu Buthelezi. Winnie, Dr Motlana and Dr Mathlare served on the executive, and the organisation agreed to convey the students' grievances to the authorities. They sought a meeting with the Minister of Justice, but he refused to see them. While one of the BPA's main tasks was to muster medical, legal and financial assistance for the students and their families, it also aimed to bridge the divide between the ANC, the PAC and the Black Consciousness movement. Winnie was a pivotal figure in forging unity, because the youth related to her, trusted her, and never questioned her leadership. Dr Motlana said she, the only woman on the executive, was 'more than a man:

powerful, faithful and honest'. Above all, she was brave. It frightened some of her colleagues that she would stand in front of police armed with machine guns and speak her mind, showing no fear. When they threatened to lock her up, she merely shrugged. Motlana was struck by her *savoir-faire* and her ability to switch between angry defiance and the aloof dismissiveness of 'an Englishman with a stiff upper lip'.

In his book, *Goodbye Bafana*, Warrant Officer James Gregory recounts how Winnie once arrived to visit Mandela, only to be told that the boat trip to Robben Island had been cancelled due to bad weather. A brisk north-westerly wind was howling and whipping up dangerous breakers, but Winnie insisted that they put to sea. When Gus Basson, captain of the ferry, the *Diaz*, told her it was impossible to make the trip that day, Winnie, beautifully dressed as always, smiled and said she had not travelled all the way from Johannesburg only to be stymied by a bit of wind and high seas. She called a senior official in Pretoria, who ordered Basson to take her to the island. Perhaps he was secretly hoping that the boat would capsize and that Winnie would be a problem no more, but the upshot was that the trip would be made.

Basson was livid, and insisted that he would take only a minimum crew so as not to endanger any more lives than necessary. Once the *Diaz* entered the main Benguela stream, it began rolling and twisting violently, tossing around like a matchbox in the ferocious seas. All that could be heard above the roar of the wind and the crashing of the waves were the thumping of the water against the hull as the boat lurched into a trough and the scream of the engine as it was reversed. In the cabin below deck, Gregory and Winnie had to hang on for dear life, and Gregory couldn't believe his eyes when he looked at Winnie and she tossed her head back and laughed. They reached the island, and while Winnie saw Madiba, Gregory went to arrange that she could spend the night at the guest house. But as soon as the visit was over, Winnie announced that she wanted to go back to Cape Town. The captain was speechless, Gregory incredulous. But Winnie insisted, and they had no choice but to repeat the nightmare trip across the choppy seas.

Raw courage was exactly what the BPA needed. The organisation drew hostile and fierce resistance from the government-sponsored Urban Bantu Councils (UBC), which translated into personal attacks on BPA members. The situation became so serious that Winnie and Dr Motlana had to obtain an urgent court order restraining the Soweto UBC from taking any action against members of the BPA, their children or their homes. Evidence was presented that one of the UBC councillors, Lucas Shabanga, had suggested attacks on the homes of both Winnie and Dr Motlana, and had proposed the killing of children who prevented their parents from going to work. The disclosures discredited the UBC to such an extent that all the executive members and councillors had to go into hiding.

The government appointed a one-man judicial inquiry to determine the causes of the Soweto uprising, but long before his findings were released, a scapegoat had to be found. Winnie fitted the bill, and on 12 August, two months after the uprising, she and various other Sowetans, including Dr Motlana and his wife, Sally, as well as Dr Mathlare, were detained.

Once again Winnie was held at the Fort, under the Internal Security Act. Conditions had not improved at all since 1969, but she did escape the earlier brutality and, because it was simply not in her nature to do otherwise, she challenged the warders head-on when she saw a wrong, and made it right. When she discovered that non-political female inmates who were responsible for cleaning the prison were not allowed to wear underwear and were not issued with shoes, Winnie confronted the female officer in charge and told her that even if these women were criminals, they deserved to be treated with a modicum of dignity. Within a week, the cleaners had both underwear and shoes.

Sally Motlana had complained several times to the warders about a broken window in her cell, but nothing had been done. One night, she dragged her sleeping mat and blankets into the corridor and told the warder she refused to sleep in her cell, which was freezing cold. While Sally and the warder argued, Winnie rounded up all the other prisoners in the section and informed the warder that none of them would go back into their cells until the window was repaired. A senior officer was summoned, an undertaking given that the window would be attended to, and early the next morning workmen arrived to replace the broken glass.

Zeni and Zindzi came home from boarding school to find that their mother had been detained – again. When they visited her, Winnie was struck by the irony that this was the same prison in which she had come close to a miscarriage when she was pregnant with Zeni in 1958. Almost two decades later, she was in the same place, still pursuing the same ideals, and South Africa was no closer to becoming a normal society than it had been when Winnie and 2 000 other women were jailed for opposing the pass laws. In fact, Winnie felt that in some respects, black people were actually worse off than they had been in the 1950s.

In December, after five months in jail and without any charges being brought against her, she was released. Dr Motlana was also freed, and one of their first tasks was to set up a committee of prominent residents to take control of Soweto. Motlana was elected chairman of the Committee of Ten, which stepped into the gap left by the discredited UBC and would become the most influential body in the township.

The security police increased their surveillance of Winnie, and after knowing freedom of movement, speech and association for more than a year, she was served with a new five-year banning order in January 1977. She continued to work at

Frank & Hirsch by day, and, to fill the long hours between 6 pm and 6 am, enrolled with the University of South Africa for a degree in social work by correspondence course. In a sense she was back in solitary confinement, and her life was becoming increasingly difficult.

By contrast, Mandela's hardship was abating. It was almost as though the authorities had decided to focus their efforts on Winnie, knowing it would be punishment enough for Mandela to be aware of her suffering but impotent to do anything about it. He had entered a pensive stage of his life, conscious that the years were slipping by, and started contemplating old age. In December 1976 he had written to Winnie that he was not used to seeing his skin loose and sagging as if he were sixty-two (he was in fact fifty-eight), but as she well knew, he joked, he was really only forty-five, and once he could resume his regular exercise programme no one would challenge his 'youth'. The letter was written in lighter vein, but between the lines there was a sad and earnest attempt to assure Winnie that he was still worthy of her love. Their relationship occupied much of his reflection at this time.

Shortly after arriving on Robben Island, Mandela had requested permission to start a garden in the courtyard. For years this was not allowed, but finally the prison authorities agreed, and he and the other prisoners were allowed to plant their garden. For most of them this was little more than a hobby, a way to while away the hours, but Madiba threw himself into gardening heart and soul. Every spare moment was spent working there, or reading and studying ways to improve the 'crops'. For Mandela, the tiny patch represented far more than the growth of plants. He saw it as a parable for the country's people, so sorely in need of nurture and care. He wrote to Winnie about a particularly beautiful tomato plant he had tended from a tiny seedling to a magnificent plant, producing healthy fruit. But when it began to wither, nothing he did could restore it to its former strength, and when it finally died he dug up the roots, washed them and buried them in a corner of the garden, thinking of 'the life that might have been'. He hoped that Winnie would read between the lines and understand his longing to nurture the people who mattered in his life, and know how he feared that lack of care – his inability through circumstance to cultivate the single most important relationship – would see their marriage share the fate of the tomato plant.

Winnie understood all of it, and as a mother, still grieving for the many children who had died in and since the Soweto uprising, she could extend the allegory to South Africa's young black people, whose parents gave them life and looked after them, only to see them mowed down on the streets.

That letter marked an important point in the lives of both Nelson and Winnie. As he seemed to be moving into the autumn of his political career, she was about to enter the summer of her own. Despite fifteen years of being banned, Winnie was more popular than ever, and her power was about to bloom. The future of black

South Africa and the continuation of the struggle had never been more important to her, and the government realised with alarm that none of the measures they had previously applied had done anything to diminish her influence. Having tried to clip her wings and failed, but still determined to isolate and silence her, the authorities devised a new form of punishment for Winnie.

They exiled her to the heartland of Afrikaner patriotism and segregationist fervour.

14

Banished to Brandfort

A S SHE HAD DONE for months, Winnie spent the night of Sunday 15 May 1977 studying until well after midnight for her degree. Zindzi, now seventeen, was home for the school holidays, but had gone to bed early.

At four o'clock in the morning, Winnie was woken by a clamour far worse than the customary banging on the front door that announced a police raid. Being arrested in the middle of the night was nothing new, but since Winnie had no intention of disappearing without trace, as had happened to so many other people in the hands of the security police, she always tried to alert someone when it happened. That night, she telephoned Horst Kleinschmidt's wife, Ilona.

After dressing and giving Zindzi a few quick instructions, Winnie picked up the suitcase next to the front door, but the police told her to leave it, that she wouldn't need it.

As she stepped outside into the bright lights trained on her house, she noticed that there were several trucks and a number of policemen in camouflage uniforms. Winnie was driven to the Protea Police Station in Soweto where, like everything else about this particular raid, the procedure differed from previous experiences.

She was neither charged with any offence nor directed to a cell. The officers on duty kept making snide remarks about what awaited her, but none approached her, and she was left to sit on a hard bench in the charge office for the rest of the night. She was shivering, both from the cold and her anxiety over what lay in store, worrying about Zindzi, who had yet again witnessed her mother being dragged off to prison. But, as always, Winnie hid her concerns behind a poker face.

When daylight came, Zindzi was escorted into the police station, carrying the house keys. Only then did the station commander, Colonel Jan Visser, present Winnie with a document authorising her banishment to Brandfort in the Free State – on the direct instructions of the Minister of Justice, Jimmy Kruger. She had been neither accused nor convicted of a crime, but as in the case of detention without trial, would have no legal recourse against the order.

Winnie had no idea what was going on. At first, she thought she was to be imprisoned in the Free State, but the police kept saying she was being banished. Then she remembered the trucks parked outside her house, and slowly it dawned on her that she was being sent into exile, forcibly removed, lock, stock and barrel. In her own country.

It had happened to other political figures, including Chief Luthuli, but they had usually been confined to their so-called homelands. Winnie had never even heard of Brandfort, and had no idea where it was. Her mind racing, she tried to ignore the shock and fear clutching at the pit of her stomach, the uncertainty of what came next, mentally running through what she had to do before she left, who to call, what instructions to give. She had no idea that she would not be allowed to pack her things, take leave of her family and close friends, nor even be able to lock her own front door one last time.

Visser told Winnie that the minister had allocated an amount of R100 a month for her expenses, from which rental for a house in Brandfort would be deducted. Coldly, she told him that they could keep their money, that she had nothing left but her pride, and nothing on earth would persuade her to accept a penny from her oppressors.

She and Zindzi were ushered to one of the military trucks outside, piled high with Winnie's possessions, bundled into the back of one with some heavily armed men, and driven away from the police station.

On the way to Brandfort, Zindzi told Winnie how the police had moved through the house, carried the furniture outside, haphazardly emptied cupboards and wardrobes, and tied the contents up in sheets and blankets pulled from the beds. By the time the journey ended, most of Winnie's crockery was in pieces.

When the house stood empty, Zindzi said, a policeman asked if she wanted to stay there, or go with Winnie. She chose to go with her mother.

Winnie realised Zindzi had not grasped the magnitude of the sacrifice she was making, and that her teenage daughter had acted instinctively out of support for her. Her mind was in turmoil and she was filled with dread as she watched the city disappear behind them. How long would she be away? Would she ever be allowed to return to her beloved Soweto? It was so much more than just a township to her. She loved the people, their indomitable humour and spontaneity, the courage and community spirit that lit up their drab, often hopeless lives. She had worked among them, she relished the bustle of the crowds. What was it like where she was being taken? She felt as though she had been pushed over the edge of a cliff and could do nothing except wait and see where she would land, and whether she would survive.

As the trucks trundled on, the landscape did nothing to improve her frame of mind. The flat, pale veld was empty except for the occasional farmhouse nestled in a clump of trees at the side of the road. There were no signs of life anywhere.

Winnie tried her best to ignore the nagging despair, reminding herself that this was exactly what the government wanted, and if she succumbed they would emerge victorious – not only over her, but over Madiba, the ANC and all the black people of South Africa. She could not give in. She had to scrape the barrel and find enough courage to live through this enormous challenge – alone, without the support of friends, family or political comrades, with only Zindzi for comfort.

The short, bespectacled cabinet minister who had wagged a finger at Winnie at the Durban airport and cautioned her about her conduct had shown that, in 1977, he approved of her behaviour even less than he had two years before. Sending Winnie to the Free State, the most racist of the four provinces, was a far harsher step than the forced relocation of two million black South Africans who had been driven from their homes to the apartheid government's Bantustans. At least those victims usually had some tribal or traditional connection to the places they were going, and in many cases they had family as support when they arrived. She and Zindzi would be alone in a place that was as alien as a foreign country, which, of course, was just what the government intended. Neither mother nor daughter could speak or understand the local language. Blacks in the Free State spoke Sotho or Tswana and some Afrikaans, whereas Winnie's mother tongue was Xhosa, and she spoke fluent English, but no Afrikaans. The authorities had clearly calculated that the language barrier would make it impossible for her to communicate with any of her new neighbours, and thus influence them politically.

In almost twenty years of dealing with Winnie Mandela, the South African government and the security police had learned nothing about her.

It was a four-hour drive to Brandfort, which lies some 400 kilometres south-west of Johannesburg and 50 kilometres north of Bloemfontein, the Free State capital. The town was a shock – a drab and dusty rural hamlet with unimaginative houses, an old-fashioned two-storey hotel, small shops lining the main street and a pervading atmosphere of lethargy and inactivity. Winnie and Zindzi were taken to the police station and formally handed over to the Free State security police. She was tired, and asked where she could refresh herself. She and Zindzi were taken to the hotel, but, since they were 'non-white', they were not allowed to use the facilities, which were strictly reserved for whites only. They were shown to the laundry – a ramshackle outbuilding – instead. From there, they were accompanied to the township superintendent's office to register Winnie as a new resident.

The forlorn township had no official name, but the black residents had baptised it *Phatakahle*, meaning 'handle with care'. Winnie's heart sank as she took in the desolation that was almost palpable. When the police stopped in front of what was to be her home, she had to fight back the tears. It was one half of a tiny, semi-detached square house with a flat roof. There was no fence, and not a sprig

185

of green. As far as the eye could see, there was nothing but the beige Free State dust. Winnie's little box was No. 802, an address that would become as well known as No. 8115 in Soweto. A gang of prisoners was moving a mound of earth from the interior – and Winnie reeled as one shock followed another. The only entrance was a narrow door that opened directly into the kitchen, and there were just two other rooms, neither of them big enough in which to swing the proverbial cat.

The toilet, a pit latrine, was in the backyard. There was no running water, electricity or water-borne sewage system. And worse, there were no floors. The bare earth outside merely extended into the house.

Winnie and Zindzi watched, numb and speechless, as their furniture and belongings were offloaded. When the prisoners tried to move the furniture inside, they discovered that the kitchen door was not wide enough. Despite themselves, Winnie and Zindzi started to giggle as they watched the efforts to squeeze the furniture through the door, turning it from side to side and upside down. But no matter how hard the men tried, they could not move a single piece of Winnie's good and solid furniture into the house – not the lounge suite, dining table, refrigerator, stove or even the beds. They finally gave up, and the police loaded everything but the bundles of bedding back onto the trucks, and carted it off to the police station, where it was stored for the next year. Winnie's refrigerator was plugged in at the police station so that she could make use of it, though it meant she had to walk there each time she needed something.

The first night in Brandfort was a harrowing end to a day of trauma and distress. There was one communal tap serving about eighty township houses, and Winnie and Zindzi had to queue with a long line of strangely uncommunicative residents to fetch water. During the previous week, the residents of Phatakahle had been informed by the Bantu Authority that a woman – a dangerous terrorist – would be moving there, and they were warned to avoid her at all cost. True to form, they did as they had been told, hence the fact that Winnie found them curt and aloof. Having had a proper bathroom and running water in Soweto, she didn't even have a basin in which to wash, and there was no way to heat any water. She and Zindzi bought potato chips for supper, but they were too tired to eat, and huddled together on bundles of clothing and linen dumped on the dirt floor in an empty house. It took a long time before Winnie slept that night.

Early the next morning, she and Zindzi were awakened by voices from the adjoining half of the semi-detached house. In the light, Winnie saw that the dividing wall stopped well short of the ceiling, with the result that one could hear perfectly well what was going on in the house next door. As soon as she was dressed, Winnie walked to the police station and insisted that the gap be closed. She was told her neighbour was a security policeman assigned to watch her, but she made it clear that even if his orders were to monitor her every word and move, she had no interest in his. Her neighbour on the other side was also a security policeman, but at least he lived in a separate house.

Winnie realised that for the time being, at least, she was stranded in the godforsaken town, and had to find a way of letting her family and friends know what had happened, but there was not a single telephone in the entire township. Fortunately, thanks to Ilona Kleinschmidt, the press soon learned that she had been whisked off to Brandfort, and reporters and photographers raced to the Free State to get the story.

After assessing the situation, Winnie decided she would have to make the best of her dilemma, redirect her bitterness into action, and turn the blow the authorities had dealt her into a challenge. She and Zindzi walked to the town to buy some basic provisions, blissfully unprepared for the caustic small-town racism they had not encountered in Johannesburg. At the first shop, they were told blacks were not allowed inside, but had to queue at a side window for service. Winnie pointedly ignored the rule and walked into the shop, straight past the flabbergasted attendant. Other blacks who watched her stride into the store, and expected to see her thrown out, were amazed when instead all the whites who had been in the shop walked out, outraged by Winnie's audacity. In the face of her imperious conduct, and totally intimidated by the presence of journalists, the shop assistant meekly served her. Suddenly, Brandfort had a celebrity, albeit a 'dangerous terrorist'. While the authorities had taken the precaution of alerting the black community to Winnie's arrival, white residents had been told nothing, probably because the police assumed they did not need to be cautioned against associating with her. The mayor arrived and said although he had not been given prior notice, Winnie was welcome in the town. The deputy mayor remarked, prophetically, that she had put their small town on the map.

Winnie descended on Brandfort like a thundering tidal wave, assaulting racial prejudice, narrow-mindedness, intolerance, bigotry and injustice with her usual unhesitating boldness. The police had the dividing wall in her house built up to the ceiling and provided her with a small coal stove to replace her electric one, which could not fit through the door. Trudging to the police station whenever she needed something from the refrigerator was inconvenient, but she decided to live with it for the time being. The authorities in Brandfort had never encountered any black person daring enough to make demands, and Winnie was convinced they had given in to her requests more out of surprise than a desire to be helpful.

The next obstacle was the black community. Winnie knew instinctively that the police were behind their unsociable behaviour, and decided not to force the issue. She understood that the police had thought the language barrier would isolate her from the local residents, and she made it a priority to learn their languages so that she could first communicate with them, and then convince them to do something about their servile existence. After years of watching her every move, intercepting her letters and telephone calls, brutal interrogation and more than a year of solitary confinement, the security police had still not fathomed the depth of Winnie's courage, her strength of character and will, her determination and extraordinary tenacity. They clearly did not understand that her spirit was far from broken, and that she would confront every obstacle they put in her way. If they did recognise her strength, they apparently believed that exile in Brandfort would cower her and force her to admit defeat.

To Winnie's joy her employer, Helmut Hirsch, forwarded her salary for May, even though she had worked for only half the month and had not given notice. With the money, Winnie bought two single beds, narrow enough to fit through the kitchen door, and paraffin lamps to replace the candles she had used since her arrival. Slowly her spirit was lifting, and she was preparing for battle.

Within days, Winnie was receiving visitors who came from all over the country. Whites were not allowed to enter black townships without permits, but despite this, many of her friends – and a large number of people she hadn't known before – travelled vast distances to see her, bringing food and other gifts. She was deeply touched that people she had never heard of would go to such lengths to show their support.

Among her first visitors was Ilona Kleinschmidt, who came all the way from Johannesburg. She was shocked at the conditions in which Winnie was expected to live, and when she returned home she contacted various other friends and spread the word of Winnie's predicament. Another early visitor was Bunty Biggs, who made the trip from Pietermaritzburg in Natal with food for Winnie and Zindzi. The steady stream of visitors gave Winnie new heart.

Over the years, friends had helped and supported her in different ways. Ray Carter, a devout Christian she had met through Helen Joseph, had called her every night while she was in Johannesburg, and they prayed together on the telephone. Winnie, knowing her telephone was tapped, told Ray it didn't matter who was listening, the prayers could only help them. With no telephone in Brandfort, she and Ray could not maintain this ritual, but they agreed to pray for each other every night at the same time. In a letter to Ray, Winnie said she would always regard her as an angel, sent by God to sustain her spiritually while she was in Brandfort.

When she ventured out into her new neighbourhood, Winnie was appalled. As a social worker, she had dealt with abject poverty in Soweto and in the Transkei, but there was a depth of impoverishment and hopelessness in Phatakahle that she had never seen before. There were 725 houses in the township, all similar to hers, and the total population was 5 000. Winnie discovered that there was a high rate of infant mortality as a result of malnutrition, and a disturbing level of alcohol abuse. Phatakahle was a sad, desolate place. The government had exiled Winnie to

Brandfort to destroy her very spirit, but, ironically, far from being crestfallen, she had a liberating influence on Phatakahle's residents. Her professional training and caring heart allowed her to devise plans to help the destitute blacks and infuse them with hope and inspiration. She firmly resolved to prove to the authorities that she would continue to work for her people, and serve them wherever she was.

Winnie's presence turned the sleepy hollow of Brandfort upside down. Following her early victory over where she could shop, a sprinkling of other blacks nervously followed suit, and when they were not thrown out, as had previously been the case, a steady trickle stopped queuing at the serving hatches and shopped inside. A prohibition that had been in place for years without question, died a quiet death, but white residents were bitterly unhappy at this turn of events. When Winnie or other blacks entered the shops, white customers promptly left. Winnie was not beyond exploiting the situation, and when this happened she took her time, browsing and looking over the merchandise for as long as she liked, while the irate whites fumed outside. In newspaper interviews they attacked the government's decision to place Winnie in their midst, and demanded that she be moved elsewhere. They said that she was rude, resorted to outbursts and temper tantrums if they tried to put her in her place, and was corrupting black residents and giving them dangerous ideas. The government knew that wherever they sent Winnie, the reaction would be the same, so she stayed.

Even complaints by the former minister of justice and state president, Blackie Swart (in Afrikaans the word 'swart' means black), had no effect. He owned a farm in the district and insisted on being accompanied by an armed guard when he visited Brandfort, in case he was confronted by the dangerous terrorist. This provoked ironic smiles among even the town's staunchest Afrikaner residents. Swart was one of a handful of non-executive state presidents appointed over a period of less than two decades after South Africa became a republic. His successor, Dr Nico Diederichs, was a former minister of finance, whose tenure as state president was plagued by rumours that he had hoarded millions – plundered from South African taxpayers – in secret Swiss bank accounts. The last office bearer before the post was abolished was former prime minister BJ Vorster, who was forced to resign in disgrace when he was implicated in the infamous Information Scandal amid more rumours of millions being spirited out of the country and allegedly stashed in Paraguay.

The black population of Phatakahle had expected Winnie to retreat into docile servility like the rest of them, especially after the briefing they had received from the Bantu Authority officials, and the way she had been dumped on them by the police. They were astonished at the impact she made on the town within weeks. For the first time in their lives, they saw a black person with the temerity to interact with whites as an equal – even to argue with them. It was all the more astonishing that she got away with it. In no time, wherever Winnie and Zindzi went, they were followed by curious onlookers, who watched and learned. Blacks in Brandfort had always had to buy clothes without first trying them on, and could not return purchases if they were the wrong size. Winnie's growing entourage was astonished when she insisted on trying on a dress in a well-known fashion chain store. The shop assistant refused, and a furious argument erupted. Winnie refused to budge, the assistant called the police, and the altercation turned to farce.

The police called the Security Branch in Bloemfontein, thus suggesting that Winnie's desire to try on a dress posed a threat to state security. A large group of onlookers formed outside the shop, but the assistant stuck to her guns, and Winnie never did try on that particular dress. For the first time, however, the rigid petty apartheid policy backfired on the white community. Blacks boycotted the store for months – something that had never happened before – and white residents complained even more loudly about the effect of Winnie's presence on 'their' blacks. Left with no choice, shop owners eventually capitulated, and black clients were allowed to try on clothes before buying.

Winnie persisted in her efforts to learn Sotho and Tswana. She began by exchanging a few words with children walking past her house, and progressed to brief conversations with their mothers. Before long, she was talking to her neighbours with ease, and as township residents came to realise that she was not the dangerous criminal they had been warned against, more and more women stopped to speak to her.

Winnie had her work cut out for her. Black mothers could not afford milk for their infants, and fed them a thin porridge of flour and water instead. Many died of malnutrition. Each weekend, Winnie said, was marked by 'another pathetic walk to the cemetery' for a township baby's funeral. But it was not just the children who were malnourished. A decent meal three times a day was a mere dream for most of Phatakahle's residents. Blacks working in Brandfort, and women employed as domestic servants by whites, earned meagre wages. The women were usually given a midday meal of maize porridge with gravy, or sometimes just a dab of dripping. Many of the women did not eat the unsubstantial meal, but took it home to share with their families at night.

It enraged Winnie that, while there was no clinic for blacks, no doctor or social assistance, the township authority had built a municipal beerhall, where already destitute blacks spent their money on alcohol. At the end of the month, over weekends, even on the day that pensions were paid, the Brandfort prison was filled to capacity with people locked up for drunkenness and public disturbance. This severely irked Winnie, and she set in motion projects that would help uplift the downtrodden community.

Her own life, meanwhile, remained mired in practical problems. One of the worst hardships was the absence of running water, a crucial component of her strict regimen of personal hygiene. Without even a sink or washbasin in the house, when Winnie wanted to take a bath, she had to join other residents in the laborious walk to the single tap in the street, collect several buckets of water, one at a time, and heat it on the coal stove before pouring it into a zinc tub on the bedroom floor. She was grateful that as a girl she had learned the art of carrying a pail of water on her head, which made the chore less tortuous, but the fact that she had to fetch her own water led to a constant battle with the police. Forbidden by her banning order from leaving her house after 6 pm, Winnie simply ignored the restriction, and went to fetch water in the evening. The police threatened her with action, but she paid no attention. If she needed water, she said, which she did every night, she would fetch it. With her bucket on her head, she strode past them defiantly.

The security police kept her under constant surveillance and the raids on her home continued, just as they had in Soweto, sometimes several times a day. Sergeant Gert Prinsloo had been drafted from Bloemfontein to watch Winnie during the day, her two neighbours being deemed sufficient of a 'night watch' after dark when she was confined to her house and forbidden to have visitors. Initially, Prinsloo stood outside her house all day long, backed up by a police van that patrolled the dusty road at fifteen-minute intervals. When Winnie's lawyer complained, Prinsloo took up position on a hill opposite her house, from where he scanned the premises through binoculars. The authorities never relaxed their vigil, day or night, seven days a week. Zindzi complained that the police never left her mother alone. Letters to and from Winnie simply disappeared. The delegate-general of the International Committee of the Red Cross for Africa, Jacques Moreillon, discovered that a malicious prison warder was censoring Winnie and Mandela's letters to one another, intentionally distorting their words. Winnie's only means of talking to her family and friends was the public telephone at the Brandfort post office. She arranged with people to call her there at 11 am and 4 pm, and twice a day, every day, she walked the considerable distance to the post office and waited for a call. Often, none came, and she returned home dejected and disappointed.

Soon after being taken from Orlando West, Winnie learned from friends in Johannesburg that a security policeman and his family had moved into house No. 8115 – the home she and Nelson had shared. She was livid. The Johannesburg municipality had leased the house to Nelson for as long as he lived, and as far as Winnie was concerned, no one had the right to occupy it without his permission. She instructed her lawyer to evict the illegal occupants, but it took a year before this was finally accomplished, at which point the police removed all Winnie's furniture from storage and returned it to Orlando West.

As always, anyone who befriended or supported Winnie became a target of the relentless security police campaign to isolate and harass her. A neighbour, Albertina Dyas, learned early on that the most innocent encounter with Brandfort's 'terrorist' could have frightening consequences.

While passing the Dyas home, Winnie had stopped to ask Albertina where she might buy coal for her stove. As they chatted, a third person joined them, offering a chicken for sale. Sergeant Prinsloo immediately decided this constituted an illegal gathering, and swooped down on the trio. He questioned a terrified Mrs Dyas harshly, demanding to know what they had been talking about. Winnie was charged with violating her banning order, and when she appeared in court, the prosecutor asked why she was dressed in the colours of the banned ANC. Drawing herself up to her full height, she replied haughtily that although she had almost no rights in South Africa, she was still entitled to choose her wardrobe.

When some of Zindzi's friends came to visit, Winnie was charged with contravening her banning order, found guilty and given a six-month suspended sentence. Disregarding an earlier court ruling that if a second person was staying in her house it could not be assumed that visitors had come to see Winnie, the magistrate declared that she should not be allowed to circumvent her banning order by claiming that callers were Zindzi's guests.

Winnie never pleaded for mitigation of any offence, regardless of how petty, unfair or untrue the charges. The ANC's philosophy was that to do so would undermine morale, since anyone accused of political crimes was innocent, having been indicted by a system that was inherently immoral and unjust. She knew from experience that the only hope of a reprieve lay with the higher courts on appeal, and that it was virtually impossible to win any case heard by a magistrate. The only time she had been acquitted by a lower court was when she assaulted Sergeant Fourie, who accosted her in her bedroom. Winnie was struck by the irony: that she was consistently found guilty of things she had not done, yet declared innocent of the one act that afforded her deep satisfaction, namely punching a policeman.

It hardly seemed possible, but the police harassment was even more intrusive in Brandfort than it had been in Soweto. With only Winnie to watch, Prinsloo was zealous in the extreme, searching her house at all hours for forbidden visitors who might be hiding under beds or in cupboards. Because whites were not allowed in the township, they had to meet Winnie on 'their' side of the road that separated the town from Phatakahle. When Helen Joseph and Barbara Waite visited on Winnie's birthday with a cake and other gifts, Prinsloo suddenly jumped out of the bushes at the road's edge, a caricature with a 'camouflage' crown of leaves and twigs around his head. All three women were placed under arrest, and when Joseph and Waite refused to testify against Winnie in the ensuing court case, they were sent to prison – Joseph, aged seventy-two, for two weeks and Waite for two months.

The same fate befell Ilona Kleinschmidt and Jackie Bosman, who received sentences of three and four months respectively. As soon as they were released, they went back to Brandfort. Winnie's friends knew that the police were trying both to scare them away and find any excuse for arresting her, but they showed their mettle by continuing to visit and refusing to provide any information that might be used to exacerbate her hardship.

In September, Mandela, upset that Zindzi was being intimidated by the police, brought an urgent application for an interdict against Prinsloo and Sergeant Ramathlwane, Winnie's neighbour, to stop them harassing his daughter. Zindzi and her friends had been threatened by the police, and some claimed they had been arrested and assaulted. At least one teenager had been asked by the security police to act as an informer. The judge ordered that Zindzi was to be allowed to receive visitors in peace, and that in future the police would have to supply evidence to support allegations of illegal visits to Winnie.

That same month, still reeling from the upheaval of being banished, Winnie received news that her friend Steve Biko had died in detention. While in solitary confinement, Biko was so severely beaten and tortured that he sustained a brain injury before his captors threw him – shackled and naked – into the back of a police van and drove him from the Eastern Cape to Pretoria. He died there twenty-four days after being arrested in Grahamstown under the Terrorism Act on 19 August. Paying tribute to Biko, Winnie said: 'You felt your blood rise as you stood up, and felt proud being black, and that is what Steve did to me.'

Though many of the black residents still treated Winnie with caution, some bypassing her house in order to avoid the experience suffered by Albertina Dyas, the attitude towards her changed perceptibly after a single incident of goodwill. When a child cut her foot on a broken bottle in the street in front of Winnie's house one day, she rushed out, carried the little girl inside, and cleaned and bandaged the wound. But many hurdles remained. In terms of her banning order, Winnie was not allowed to enter any educational institution, and since she was not permitted to be in the company of other people, she could go to church only if she made special application to do so. She refused to do this, saying she would seek no man's permission to worship God, and denouncing the authorities for appropriating the power to decide whether or not she could.

But she took spiritual support from the visits of Archdeacon John Rushton, who travelled to Brandfort from Bloemfontein every fortnight for six years to conduct a solo communion service for Winnie. Only once did she make an exception, seeking permission from the authorities to attend the christening of her grandchildren in

Bloemfontein Cathedral by Rushton and the Dean of Bloemfontein, Aidan Cross. The security police attended the ceremony as well, to ensure that Winnie did not talk to Helen Joseph, who was godmother to two of the children and, at the age of eighty, was as feisty as ever in her condemnation of apartheid.

In terms of her banning order, Winnie was confined to her house for twelve hours every night, and to the magisterial district of Brandfort by day. With scant chance of finding a job in Brandfort, she was condemned to live on the charity of others – a painful situation for a woman who had worked since completing her studies in social work, had a bright future in her profession, and had supported herself and her family. But while her situation forced Winnie to accept material help, she resolved not to surrender her fierce pride. She was endlessly grateful to Helmut Hirsch, who continued to pay her R250 a month for the first year of exile in Brandfort. The money covered certain basic necessities and day-to-day living expenses for Winnie and Zindzi.

With donations from her many sympathisers, she gradually bought items of furniture that could fit through the narrow door of her house, which slowly became more habitable, though Winnie continued to regard it as a prison and refused to pay rent or service charges. Discomfort became a way of life, and in the absence of her furniture, Winnie resorted to storing dry food in one of her cupboards at the police station. When she opened the cupboard one day, she found that rats had gnawed their way into a month's supply of groceries, damaging not only the cupboard but other furniture as well, and even some of Madiba's law books.

But although she was making the best of a dire situation and, as countless times before, focusing her energy and attention on the plight of others, Winnie's life was austere and devoid of real support. The gifts and donations, visits from her friends and sympathisers, even Zindzi's presence, could never compensate for the loss of her life in Soweto, where she had been rooted and happy. She hid her pain behind a bright smile and willingness to serve others, but the emptiness accosted her at night, when she was alone. Despite her determination to prove to the government that she would survive in exile, her resolve to challenge the appalling conditions and privations proved taxing in the extreme. She realised that the authorities had no intention of allowing her to return to Soweto any time soon, and was often overcome by an acute sense of despair when she imagined years of isolation in Brandfort. However hard she tried, she could not ignore the stark contrast between her stimulating and exciting life in Soweto, and the blandness of Phatakahle.

The only relief was Zeni's happiness. Having finished her schooling at Waterford, she had become engaged to Prince Thumbumuzi Dhlamini, the fifty-eighth son of Swaziland's King Sobhuza II. Though he was far from being a contender for the throne, the prince would be afforded a royal wedding, with all the pomp and ceremony this entailed. The authorities had turned down Winnie's application for permission to attend the festivities, and she had resigned herself to the fact that she would not be at her older daughter's wedding. Then, out of the blue, she was informed that the Swazi monarch had asked the South African government to allow her to attend. Recognising that it would be a diplomatic slight to refuse, they had agreed. As a member of the Tembu royal house, Mandela viewed the marriage as a historic joining of the royal houses of the Swazi and the Tembu, and so did King Sobhuza. Winnie was delighted.

In Swaziland, she was given a welcome fit for a queen. She had been refused a passport, but the Swazi officials allowed her to cross the border without any formalities. A fleet of twenty limousines awaited her, and as she crossed into Swaziland the drivers all hooted a resounding welcome. Her future son-in-law was the first Swazi prince who had chosen a royal bride, and a special state reception was held in Winnie's honour. She was overwhelmed by the red carpet treatment, pomp and splendour, and as the guest of honour, felt a little like Cinderella after the long years of deprivation.

Winnie knew that by marrying Muzi, a banker, Zeni would not only be well cared for, but would escape the vitriolic attention of the South African authorities. An added bonus was that as a member of King Sobhuza's family, she was accorded diplomatic status, which among other advantages allowed her the right to have contact visits with Mandela. When Zeni visited her father after the wedding, he was allowed to touch one of his family members for the first time in fourteen years.

Though Winnie felt restored on her return to Brandfort, the desolation of Phatakahle was all the more striking after the opulence of her retreat in Swaziland. Visitors came less often, and she felt increasingly besieged. She had befriended some of the township residents, but the differences in their interests and backgrounds were all but insurmountable. Winnie was desperate for the intellectual and political stimulation of Soweto, and fearing the degeneration that came of constant disappointment and frustration, she concentrated all her efforts on the township projects she had begun, and which had made giant advances in the face of the harassment and negative propaganda against her.

Accounts of the grim conditions in Phatakahle brought a steady stream of reporters and photographers to Brandfort. White residents were angered by the negative reports about their town, but their black counterparts were amazed and intrigued by the spotlight on Winnie and their own, previously ignored circumstances. People who had never heard of Brandfort before sent messages of support and sympathy to Winnie, along with gifts and donations. Having the Mandela name and the accompanying media attention spread to a part of the country that had never really known either, was certainly not what the security police had envisaged. Furthermore, it was clear that Winnie's presence was having an unwelcome effect on the people of Phatakahle. She was stirring dormant feelings of self-respect and dignity, reminding them with her conduct that they were human beings like any others, and that the spirit could be sustained even in the face of assaults on one's physical well-being. She showed the downtrodden that they could be black and proud, and persevere despite seemingly insurmountable odds, which was no mean feat, considering the extent of their resigned submission.

When the police saw township residents flocking to Winnie's house, wandering in and out to talk to her, they decided some action was needed to halt this communion. Their solution was the erection of a fence around Winnie's house, much to her delight. When a foreign newspaper reported on the stark contrast between Winnie's house and neighbouring structures, the municipality put up fences around all the houses in the immediate environment. The rest of the township was ignored, but the residents were counting their blessings. The fences were the first improvements in the township in decades, and esteem for Winnie continued to grow.

Ill-informed residents who neither knew nor understood that the government's agenda was to isolate Winnie admired her for managing to get things done. It was almost comical that the security police's stringent efforts to quarantine Winnie actually enhanced her stature. As their strategy escalated, it continued to boomerang. When they noted that there was much merriment and spirited conversation around the communal tap when Winnie went to fetch water, the mere possibility that she could be spreading ANC propaganda sparked a flurry of urgent planning to devise ways of keeping her indoors.

The answer, the police decided, lay in providing Winnie with her own water supply. Convinced that this would prevent her from mixing with – and corrupting – township residents, they sent workmen to extend the water pipes from the street to a tap outside Winnie's door. No other house in the township had a tap, and her neighbours were agog as they watched the unthinkable materialise before their very eyes. The security police's solution was yet another moral victory for Winnie, and an unintentional but welcome boost for her morale.

After a few months in Phatakahle, Winnie had identified countless opportunities for social assistance to her hopeless fellow residents. As soon as the tap was installed, she started turning the barren soil around her house into a garden, encouraging her neighbours to follow her example. Practising the thrift she had learned as a child, she saved every seed and pip, planting them in her garden and distributing seedlings to other residents. Even though her closest neighbours were security policemen, their initial animosity faded as their wives and children got to know, and like, Winnie. They, too, gratefully accepted her gifts of seedlings, and soon fruit trees were taking root on the plots around Winnie's house. She asked her visitors to bring seeds and planted vegetables, flowers and shrubs, and when curious passers-by stopped to watch, she gave them seeds and advice on how to grow them.

She also cultivated a lawn, digging up the grass growing around the street taps and planting it in her garden. It was excrutiating manual labour, but Winnie, pushing a wheelbarrow and spade down the dusty streets, kept at it.

The lush green lawn transformed Winnie's little plot. Her endeavours became known as the garden project, and with her own home as proof that it could be done, she persuaded a group of township women to join her in growing their own vegetables. This not only provided them with much-needed food, but also altered the appearance of the drab and dusty plots, with tufts of green soon sprouting everywhere. When the Council of Churches heard of her efforts, they donated seeds for the women to share, and while some people were too lethargic to bother with a garden, the efforts of those who responded encouraged more and more residents to become involved.

Winnie's banning order placed no restriction on communication with children, and they came from far and wide to come and play on the grass. The fact that she could talk and laugh with the children alleviated some of her loneliness and isolation, and when mothers walked their little ones to her home, she seized the chance to offer them counsel on nutrition and child care. Before long, one at a time, as dictated by her banning order, women were bringing their babies to Winnie for advice and treatment when they were ill.

White doctors in Brandfort had set aside consultation hours after 5 pm for black patients, but few could afford the cost of a visit, and when people began queuing to seek Winnie's help, she told her friends and supporters that she would like to start a clinic. Dr Motlana, Archdeacon Rushton and others provided her with basic medical supplies so she could treat minor problems like coughs, colds or upset stomachs, and administer basic first aid. She used some of the cash donations to buy baby food to try to reduce the high infant mortality rate. There was no room in her tiny house for the supplies, so she kept them on top of a cupboard in the lounge. As word spread, sick and injured people increasingly lined up at her door. The security police regularly took down their names, but this didn't scare them off. Police or no police, they needed help, and they got it from Winnie. Many of those who sought her aid were elderly, and with no jobs or income they were literally starving.

To her horror, Winnie discovered that the fathers of some of the starving children in Phatakahle were white men from Brandfort, who refused to acknowledge their existence and were wholly unconcerned about their fate. She set up a soup kitchen to feed pre-school children, the elderly and unemployed. For the first time in living memory, hot meals were available to Phatakahle's destitute, and soon they, too, formed a queue at Winnie's door for a daily bowl of soup. Then older children from farms in the district, who had to walk long distances to school and back, often on an empty stomach, heard about the soup kitchen, and joined the queue. Although she was struggling to feed an increasing number of people, Winnie refused to turn them away hungry. Some days she fed up to 200 people. When she ran out of soup powder and other ingredients, the queues would disappear, but as soon as donations of fresh supplies arrived, the people would return. When Winnie's visitors and sympathisers asked what she needed, she said soup powder, and when the Black Sash heard about her feeding scheme, they sent her large sacks of it.

In time, with the help of Operation Hunger, other organisations and individuals, the township's poor could always find a meal, but Winnie continued to introduce new projects to improve the living conditions of Brandfort's black population. While she was in town one day, she was shocked to see that blacks were buying single slices of bread, because that was all they could afford. She decided instantly to teach a group of women how to bake bread, which they sold to the people of Phatakahle at cost price. The bakery project was another popular and enduring success.

However, the gratitude and relief of black residents were not echoed by the white community, which had benefited from selling food and clothes to them. As her popularity rose on one side of the road, it declined on the other. When she realised that many women left their small children at home alone when they went to work, Winnie asked the Methodist minister for permission to use a room on one side of the church as a daycare centre. She recruited four women to run the centre, which opened with twenty children. Soon, Winnie's friends were donating toys and books, and more than seventy toddlers were able to play and learn under supervision, and receive balanced daily meals.

Her personal experiences had led Winnie to the conclusion that Afrikaners would never treat blacks as equals, since they regarded them not as human beings but as little more than cheap labour. She was convinced that Brandfort's Afrikaners were neither interested in, nor concerned about, the dire circumstances in the ghetto on their doorstep. Then she met the De Waals.

Ismail Ayob, Winnie's attorney in Johannesburg, had advised her to make contact with a lawyer in Brandfort, so that he would have someone on the spot with whom he could liaise in matters concerning her situation. There was only one attorney in Brandfort, Piet de Waal, and when Winnie went to his office to introduce herself, he was speechless – and she noticed that his hands were shaking. An old friend of the National Party member of parliament Kobie Coetsee – who had a farm near Brandfort and would later become Minister of Justice – De Waal was loath to accept Winnie as a client, but Ayob pointed out that he was compelled by legal ethics to represent her, since he was the only lawyer in Brandfort and she could not leave the town. De Waal apologetically explained his unfortunate and embarrassing position to Coetsee, to Jimmy Kruger and the police in Brandfort, but gradually his attitude began to change, and in time he and his wife, Adéle, were so struck by Winnie's intelligence and charm that they came to regard her as a friend. Adéle, in particular, identified with Winnie's loneliness in a strange place, offered her books to read and invited her to visit at any time, even to use her bathroom so that Winnie could take a hot bath.

Whereas many whites were deeply committed to apartheid, there were also a significant number who, as a result of the system's credo of divide and rule, never met or spoke to any black people except their maids and gardeners, and therefore were never challenged to question either the government or their own prejudice. Adéle de Waal, néé Retief, was a descendant of Piet Retief, the revered Voortrekker leader who had been murdered by the Zulu king, Dingane, when he and a delegation of Afrikaners attempted to buy large tracts of farmland in Natal. When she – like Bram Fischer, also a member of a prominent Afrikaner family – extended the hand of friendship to Winnie, a 'terrorist', other whites in Brandfort shunned her. Adéle took their rejection in her stride, and she and Winnie became good friends. But when Winnie met Adéle's parents, her elderly father told her, solemnly, that they bore her no grudge. Winnie was stunned by this rare glimpse into the hearts and minds of whites in general. If anything, it was she who might have offered forgiveness, not them. She graciously let the moment pass, and in later years said she had learned a lot from and through Adéle de Waal, things she would otherwise not have known or understood about Afrikaners.

While Winnie was making every effort to come to terms with life in Brandfort, Zindzi was showing signs of discontent and depression. Not even the fact that her boyfriend, Johannes (Oupa) Seakamela had moved in with them seemed to help. He was of great assistance to Winnie, and made many improvements to the house. He installed a kitchen sink and tap connected to the outside pipes, so that, at last, Winnie had running water inside the house. Oupa also helped her put up shelves, carpet the floor and stencil a pattern on the lounge wall so that it looked like wallpaper. Gradually, as money became available, Winnie added necessities such as a paraffin refrigerator and a gas stove. A ginger cat took up residence and a coop in the backyard housed a well-wisher's gift of chickens. Oupa also laid a path from the kitchen door to the gate, and Zindzi wrote their names in the wet cement, creating a permanent memorial of their stay.

But Zindzi could not settle in Brandfort. Before leaving Johannesburg she was being treated by a psychiatrist for depression, and the cessation of treatment, combined with the incessant attempts of the police to intimidate her, aggravated her condition. She had passed up an opportunity of going to Wits University, and she and Oupa had a daughter, Zoleka, but eventually the constant police harassment became too much for her. When her relationship with Oupa fell apart, she announced that she was returning to the house in Orlando. As much as she had been a comfort and company, Winnie realised it would be best for Zindzi to leave. Back in Soweto, she dedicated herself to her dream of becoming a writer, and made impressive progress for such a young person. Jim Bailey, the owner of *Drum* magazine, offered her a position as columnist for his new women's magazine *True Love*, and she continued to write poetry. In 1978, she published a volume of her poems, *Black as I Am*, which opened with this poem about her father:

A tree is chopped down
And the fruit was scattered
I cried …

The book won a prize of $1 000 in the US, and critical acclaim from promi-nent literary figures such as Alan Paton.

When Mandela turned sixty on 18 July 1978, the United Nations Special Committee on Apartheid called for the occasion to be celebrated internationally. Anti-apartheid activists in Britain collected and sent 10 000 birthday cards, but not one was delivered to him. Winnie had been refused permission to visit Mandela, and he was allowed only eight birthday messages from family and friends – one of them, interestingly enough, from Govan Mbeki's son Thabo, who would succeed Mandela as South Africa's president two decades later. In the absence of his family, Mandela's close friends and fellow detainees, Walter Sisulu and Ahmed Kathrada, made the relevant congratulatory speeches on Robben Island.

Reporting on the event, the London *Times* called Mandela 'the colossus of African nationalism'. It was a dramatic departure from the pervading view, eight years earlier, that the ANC had died, and the leadership with it. Winnie's determination to keep the struggle alive was paying off, but at staggering cost.

For Mandela, her support had become more important than his life's blood, and he often acknowledged this. He idealised Winnie, admired her tenacity and concern for others under the most difficult of circumstances, and frequently reminded her how much he depended on her. 'Had it not been for your visits, wonderful letters and your love, I would have fallen apart many years ago,' he wrote in one of his letters to her. 'Your love and devotion has created a debt which I will never attempt to pay back.'

Winnie had formed a friendship with another one of Brandfort's Afrikaners, a local doctor, Chris Hattingh. He provided her with some financial assistance, and in October 1978 offered her employment in his practice, but she struggled for months to get permission from the authorities to take the job. While she waited, Winnie was told by Hattingh that he was being followed by four men in a car. Winnie was convinced it was the security police. Finally, she was granted permission to start working for Hattingh on 1 March 1979.

But on his way to Winnie's house that morning, Hattingh had a fatal car accident.

Winnie was distraught. No other car had been involved in what appeared to be a freak accident, and for a long time after his death, rumours persisted that his friendship with Winnie had cost him his life. Three months later, she wrote to Mary Benson: 'They killed him and have got away with it – like the Steve Bikos, but this one is worse, as the world will never know. I haven't got over the shock yet, and I never knew I could grieve so much for someone other than my own kind. In a way, it's taught me a depth of love which might have been superficial and ideological, now it's real and honest for those who identify so completely with us.' Hattingh's sister had become friendly with Zindzi, but was scared away by the security police.

After Zindzi left, Winnie took a lodger, a young artist friend of Zeni and Zindzi by the name of Matthews Kganitsiwe Malefane, or MK. He had initially come to visit and stayed, taking on the role of major-domo, and assisting Winnie with the many projects in the township. He also painted when he could and his pictures brought in a little money. Since he did not have the necessary permit to live in Phatakahle, he was arrested and charged with being there illegally, but the court ruled that he was entitled to stay as a lodger and member of the household.

Winnie continued ceaselessly, almost frenetically, with her efforts to uplift the community. On the one hand, this was a natural extension of her role as a social worker, and stemmed from her commitment to improving the lot of her people in any way she could, but it was also a classic manifestation of long-term exposure to trauma. Research has shown that trauma survivors often have an overdeveloped sense of being able to cope, as though doing a good job would prove that hideous experiences had been overcome. At the same time, filling the present with activity helped to lessen anxiety about the chances of surviving similar trauma in the future.

Being confronted with death, as Winnie had been over the course of many years, and especially during the 1976 uprising, also leads people to re-evaluate the meaning and purpose of their own lives, to develop a new value structure and an enhanced appreciation of life itself. Winnie wrote to Mary Benson that she was regularly taking stock of herself. Zindzi's presence had served as a buffer against the pain and loneliness, but after she left, life in Winnie's 'little Siberia' was reduced to deadly solitude and long, empty days that dragged on, one much like another. But no one was allowed to glimpse her soul-destroying loneliness, and to the outside world she showed nothing but a stiff upper lip, her bright smile and courageous defiance.

Her next project was a sewing group, called *Lift Up Your Home*. Interested women gathered in the Methodist church hall, where they learned to sew, knit, crochet and embroider. In adherence to her banning order, Winnie sat in a room by herself, and taught the women one by one. A security policeman watched closely, to ensure that Winnie broke no rules of her detention. Some of her pupils developed excellent skills, and started thinking of an outlet for their crafts, which could provide them with a small income. Winnie's many friends were ever supportive, and Professor Harvey van der Merwe, a Quaker who lectured at the University of Cape Town, arranged for the donation of two new sewing machines. Winnie used cash donations to buy another four, second-hand machines, and Ismail Ayob sent her an enormous bale of black cloth, from which the women made school uniforms that were sold to parents who paid for the garments in two or three instalments. In appreciation of her support, the women made Winnie some beaded jewellery in the ANC's yellow, green and black, which was later confiscated by the police during a raid on her home.

While working in her garden one day, Winnie heard screams from the veld opposite her home. She rushed into the long grass, just in time to rescue an eleven-year-old girl from a rapist. When she found out that the child was an orphan, Winnie took her in and cared for her, thus setting the stage for a new project: the rescue and rehabilitation of orphans, strays and juvenile delinquents.

Not all of Winnie's endeavours were successful, and she was realistic enough to accept that they could not be. Some of the young offenders turned their backs on the opportunity to reform, but she refused to become disheartened. The child she had saved from a rapist started going to school, and stayed with Winnie for a number of years.

Throughout her time in exile, Winnie's friends were constantly amazed by her irrepressible optimism and perseverance. Dr Motlana once observed that while he and others who visited her became depressed by the conditions under which she was living, Winnie herself was always cheerful, and nothing seemed to get her down.

In stark contrast to what the government had set out to achieve, Winnie's banishment diminished her support not one iota. Opinion polls taken during her first two years in Brandfort showed that she was the second most important political figure in the country after Zulu chief Mangosuthu Buthelezi. It was Rita Ndzanga who voiced what many people felt: despite the fact that Winnie was in Brandfort, she remained firmly in people's hearts.

15

Death threats and murder

IN 1980, THE END of the bloody guerrilla war in Zimbabwe, followed by democratic elections that saw a landslide victory for Robert Mugabe, ushered in a new era of hope for black people in southern Africa. Whites, on the other hand, generally viewed the demise of yet another minority regime as a portent of doom for the subcontinent. The South African government had not only supported the illegitimate government of Ian Smith, but had poured millions of rands into the election campaign of Bishop Abel Muzorewa in the hope of ensuring a 'friendly' black government on its northern doorstep.

Deeply involved in an escalating war in Angola and the South West Africa operational area and facing ongoing unrest in black townships closer to home, the government now also had to contend with renewed grassroots demands for Nelson Mandela's release.

In March, Percy Qoboza's *Sunday Post* launched the 'Free Mandela' campaign, initiated by the ANC in exile from Lusaka. The United Nations Security Council joined the call for Mandela to be released after eighteen years in prison, and, before long, the cause was resonating around the world, despite the fact that many foreign supporters knew so little about the ANC leader that they thought 'Free' was his first name.

Surprisingly, the campaign found growing support among white South Africans who had begun to realise, as Zindzi told a rally at the University of the Witwatersrand, that a free Mandela was the only pragmatic alternative to a bloodbath. Former BOSS chief Hendrik van den Bergh, stripped of his power as the result of the Information Scandal (which, inter alia, exposed the fact that the government had been funding the daily newspaper, *The Citizen*), caused ructions in high circles when he told a Johannesburg newspaper that Mandela had never been a communist – and he, after all, should know.

The campaign was the first direct support that Winnie Mandela had received in almost two decades of tireless efforts to keep Mandela's name, and the struggle, alive. Suddenly, the ANC leaders in exile realised that she was a highly marketable commodity, a tailor-made symbol of the struggle, who had single-handedly secured donations of tens of thousands of dollars from international sources. Winnie had become an icon, the visible face of the liberation struggle at a time when the youth, in particular, had no idea what Mandela or the other jailed and exiled leaders even looked like. Winnie had sales value. She was a tragic heroine: a young and beautiful woman who had been jailed, tortured and banished; she was educated, eloquent and charismatic; she was loved and admired by the masses; and she was Nelson Mandela's wife.

In addition, by exiling her to Brandfort, the security police had inadvertently placed her in a position to directly influence the future of South Africa. Her friendship with lawyer Piet de Waal would play a major behind-the-scenes role in political events when *his* old friend, Kobie Coetsee, became Minister of Justice. De Waal appealed to him to lift Winnie's bans and to consider releasing Mandela, and Coetsee later acknowledged that it was De Waal's representations on behalf of the Mandelas that set the process of real change in motion, and ultimately led to the democratic elections in 1994. Sadly, Winnie was never accorded the credit she deserved in this regard.

The increased media attention generated by the 'Free Mandela' campaign did not deter the security police one iota from harassing Winnie. In her book, *The Lady*, British author Emma Gilbey wrote that persecution of Winnie was 'no more constructive than slowly pulling the wings off a fly'. Winnie had long since realised that she was not being targeted only as an individual, but also as the personification of black political aspiration.

In April 1980, a new round of school boycotts was launched in protest against Bantu Education. The government shut down hundreds of black and coloured educational institutions, including training colleges and universities. Major industrial action followed, with thousands of black workers going on strike, and the police reacted by sealing off affected areas and detaining hundreds of people. Many were also killed or injured when the police opened fire on protestors, and the situation deteriorated still further when black mineworkers – the backbone of the economy – joined the strike.

Isolated at Brandfort, Winnie was frustrated at having to watch the unfolding drama from a distance. Not only did she want to be in a position to know what was really going on, she desperately yearned to be where she was at her most effective – in the front line, with her people. But, since circumstances made that impossible, she concentrated on finding a job. She had introduced a number of community projects at Brandfort, but the terms of her banning order precluded any interaction with the various groups involved. She was heartened when the Bloemfontein Child Welfare Society offered her a position as a social worker, but, inevitably, the authorities refused to grant permission for her to travel from Brandfort to Bloemfontein every day to do the job. She had completed all the written requirements for her academic degree, and all that remained was a course of practical fieldwork. Yet again, because she was not allowed to communicate with any groups of people, she was stymied. Moreover, her lecturers at the University of South Africa did not agree with her assessment that Brandfort offered sufficient scope for the casework she had to do. Unable to complete her social science degree, Winnie enrolled for a new course, in politics and communication. By day, she still spent her energy on improving the lot of Phatakahle's people. With a sizeable donation from abroad she bought a second-hand minibus and put it to work as a mobile clinic, serving not only the township but also farm labourers in the district and blacks working in Brandfort itself. The vehicle did double duty as a soup kitchen on wheels.

In November 1980, Winnie's older sister, Nancy, died of leukaemia at the age of forty-seven. Although Nancy had been living in exile in Botswana for several years, she and Winnie had stayed in touch. Since childhood, they had been closer to one another than any of their other siblings, and her death came as a terrible blow to Winnie.

Six months later, she was hit by another crisis.

After twenty years, Winnie could hardly remember a time when she had not been warring with the state over control of her life, and had come to stoically accept whatever the authorities threw at her. But no matter how many times she was stabbed in the back by those she considered her friends, each fresh betrayal wounded her as deeply as the first.

In May 1981, newspapers reported that Dr Aaron Mathlare had told the one-man Cillié Commission investigating the cause of the 1976 Soweto uprising that Winnie and Dr Nthatho Motlana had instigated the student riots. Mathlare testified that he had heard Winnie and Motlana instructing students to attack government institutions and bottle stores. He also claimed that Winnie and Motlana were having an affair.

Winnie was livid, but for once she was in a position to hit back. She and Dr Motlana sued Mathlare for defamation, and the judge ordered him to pay each of them R3 000 in damages, make a public apology and withdraw the allegations. Soon afterwards, Mathlare and his wife moved to Botswana.

For Winnie, the outcome of the court action was not enough. Mathlare had worked closely with her and Dr Motlana in both the Black Parents' Association and the ANC, and during the 1976 uprising he had toiled side by side with them to treat injured children, and all three had been detained at the same time. She needed to find out why Mathlare had told such blatant and damaging lies about his old friends. Discreet enquiries revealed that Mathlare had been broken under torture, and had agreed to falsely implicate Winnie and Motlana in the uprising.[1] Having been subjected to the rigours of solitary confinement and torture herself,

Winnie had some sympathy for those who were unable to withstand the tactics employed by the security police.

Amid all the hardship and tragedy, Winnie's sense of humour was her saving grace. In the most trying circumstances, she could usually find something to laugh about. Even security policeman Gert Prinsloo, the bane of her existence, became a source of entertainment when he began drinking heavily, possibly to counter the effect of years of boredom induced by watching Winnie and having little or nothing to report. Winnie believed that Prinsloo's surveillance duty had become more of a punishment for him than for her, and for a time she was wryly amused by his antics when he would stagger into her house and search the tiny cupboards, even under the carpet, for illegal visitors. After a while, though, his absurd behaviour became an irritation, and Winnie complained. Prinsloo was duly transferred, but lest Winnie imagine she had scored any kind of victory over the security police, his superior officer made a special trip to Phatakahle to impress upon her that Prinsloo had merely been moved to another post, not demoted.

Winnie's life changed significantly when she became a grandmother. In the space of a few years, Zeni had three children and Zindzi two, and in keeping with tradition, they regularly stayed with their grandmother. The silence and solitude of her small home was invaded by laughter and chatter, and for Winnie, who had always adored children, they were an endless source of joy and comfort. In part, their presence made up for the many years of separation from her own daughters while they were growing up. Her grandchildren often stayed with her until they were old enough to go to nursery school, after which they visited during the holidays.

After years of hard work, Winnie also began to reap the rewards of the many projects she had initiated in Phatakahle. The trees she had planted during her first months in exile started bearing fruit, and she had the gratification of picking peaches in her own garden. In spring and summer, the trees framed the small, uninspiring house in soft, green foliage and it stood as an oasis in the monotony of the desolate landscape and drab, unvaried architecture of the township.

In March 1982, she was involved in a car accident, suffering a leg injury that appeared superficial at the time, but would later have life-threatening repercussions. Mandela was told by the prison authorities about the accident, but given no details. On 31 March, his attorney and friend, Dullah Omar, visited him and filled in the details. That night, without warning, Mandela, Walter Sisulu, Raymond Mhlaba and Andrew Mlangeni were told to pack their things, and were whisked to the mainland. Mandela's stay on Robben Island was over – he would spend the next six-and-a-half years at Pollsmoor Prison.

When Winnie visited him there for the first time, she saw the Cape in all its splendour. Her trips to Robben Island had followed a set route: airport–police headquarters–harbour, and she had seen nothing of the beauty for which the peninsula was known throughout the world. But the road to Pollsmoor, in Tokai, wound through the upmarket southern suburbs of Rondebosch and Constantia, along thoroughfares lined with sturdy oak trees planted by colonists 200 years before, and fringed with tracts of open veld covered, at certain times of the year, with the spectacular Cape flora, including the colourful proteas and gentle-hued heather. Winnie's heart ached when she compared the lush scenery to the dusty, overcrowded landscape of Soweto, Phatakahle and other townships.

Not only was it a far simpler journey to visit Nelson at Pollsmoor than on the island, but conditions for their visits were a great improvement. They could both see and hear one another more clearly, and the warders were less obtrusive. Warrant Officer James Gregory, who was more sophisticated and courteous than many of his colleagues and showed consideration to both Mandela and his wife, supervised most of Winnie's visits. Nevertheless, on her first visit, Nelson asked her to lodge a formal complaint with his lawyer about the conditions at Pollsmoor, which, he said, were worse than on Robben Island. He wanted the outside world to know that he believed the transfer had been designed to add to the hardship of the jailed ANC leaders. On the island they each had their own cell, and were allowed to exercise and mix with other prisoners in a communal area. Now, six of them were confined to a cell day and night, and there was no space in which to exercise. In addition, they were no longer allowed to send or receive telegrams. Since it took weeks, and often as long as two months, for a letter to be checked and passed by the censors, it had become imperative for telegrams to be used in the case of urgent matters, such as a death in the family.

Over the years, many of the concessions and privileges for political prisoners on Robben Island had been the result of Winnie's protests, and she passed Mandela's complaints on to his lawyer, as asked. She also wrote to her friend Mary Benson in London, who facilitated publication in some of the British newspapers of reports about the unfavourable prison conditions. Subsequently, conditions at Pollsmoor improved.

There was little that Winnie could do to improve her own lot, however. In May 1982, she received an anonymous letter, reminding her that two of her acquaintances, Petrus Nzima and his wife, had been killed by a car bomb in Swaziland – and warning that the same could happen to her. It was an ominous reminder that there were people who would like to see her dead, and that assassination had to be something the authorities had contemplated more than once. It did not escape her notice that this particular piece of mail, unlike all her other letters, had not been intercepted by the security police. Her life had often been threatened, however, and she did not pay undue attention to this latest attempt at intimidation. But a few days later, when she went to start her minibus, she saw a length of electrical wiring dangling from the battery. She called her neighbours, who told her they had seen suspicious-looking men at the vehicle late the night before, and that when they went to investigate the men quickly left. Some of Winnie's friends contacted the media, and reports of an apparent attempt to rig her vehicle with a car bomb were published both in South Africa and abroad. Just three months later, Winnie's acute awareness that mortal danger was never far away was reinforced when a parcel bomb killed Joe Slovo's wife, Ruth First, in her office in Maputo.

The 'Free Mandela' campaign brought foreign emissaries from various countries to Winnie's humble house in Brandfort. Never afraid of speaking her mind, she was harsh in her criticism of President Ronald Reagan's policy on South Africa when American diplomats visited her. The German ambassador was received more amicably, and after his visit, he regularly sent food parcels to the residents of Phatakahle. He also gave Winnie a battery-operated television set, and apart from providing her with an additional source of information and much needed entertainment, the appliance brought an element of magic to the township. Wide-eyed children, squealing with delight, came to watch their favourite programmes, transforming Winnie's house into a makeshift local cinema. When her neighbours crowded into the tiny lounge to watch TV, she, curbed by her banning order, stayed in the bedroom.

In October 1982, Piet de Waal, Winnie's friend and attorney, called at her house to deliver an urgent message. He found her virtually unconscious, delirious with pain and fever from an infection in the leg she had injured in the car accident six months earlier. He called the local doctor, who ordered that she be admitted to hospital immediately, as her life was in danger. After getting the necessary permission from the police, arrangements were made for her to be rushed to Universitas Hospital in Bloemfontein. But special permission would first have to be obtained, as the hospital was only for whites, and Winnie obstinately refused. She would rather die, she said, than apply for special privileges – and if she had to go to hospital, it would have to be in Johannesburg. Her doctor made it clear to the security police that unless she received the proper treatment, soon, there was a good chance that she might die. The security police, in turn, knew they could not afford the international outcry that would erupt if she *did* die as the result of being refused permission to travel when she needed urgent medical attention. Eventually, and reluctantly, they agreed that she could be flown to Johannesburg, where she was admitted to the Rosebank Clinic, a private hospital that accepted patients of all races.

Emergency surgery was carried out on Winnie's leg, and she spent seven weeks in hospital recovering. As always, the security police were close at hand, and monitored her every visitor. When she was discharged, five police cars were waiting outside the hospital to follow attorney Ismail Ayob's car to the airport.

However, the last flight to Bloemfontein that day was fully booked, so Ayob took Winnie to spend the night at his home.

During the course of the evening, he and his wife realised that Winnie was far too weak to take care of herself in Brandfort, and Ayob sought permission for her to return to her house in Orlando West until she was stronger. The security police refused, but Winnie, true to form, defiantly told Ayob to take her to house No. 8115, anyway.

Five years after being dragged from her home in the middle of the night, Winnie was back – and as soon as her presence became known, hundreds of people lined up outside to see her. Already in breach of her banning order, Ayob advised her not to irk the security police any more than necessary, and to receive only one person at a time. Winnie complied, but her initial excitement at being home was soon dampened. The soul of Soweto had changed. On the surface, the township was still the same – an overcrowded, noisy city with endless rows of identical houses, thousands of people queuing for trains and buses, impatient taxi drivers hooting and swerving around potholes in the roads – but the people, and the atmosphere, were different. British prime minister Harold Wilson had once observed that a week was a long time in politics – and she had been gone for more than five years. She had tried to stay in touch with individuals and follow political developments as closely as possible, but there was no substitute for personal involvement, and she was alarmed to find that Sowetans were embittered and far more resentful and polarised than they had been before the 1976 uprising. People made it clear that they had set their sights on total political change, and would settle for nothing less. Imprisoning their leaders and banning their political parties were seen as no more than temporary setbacks. The South African government had introduced crisis management measures, one of which was the accelerated creation of a black middle class as a buffer against the ANC, still seen as a communist organisation. Another was pressuring the so-called front-line states into refusing support for the ANC. But, by taking the temperature of Soweto, Winnie became more certain than ever that she would live to see change; that the day would come when Madiba and Oliver Tambo would be free to lead their people; that justice would ultimately prevail.

While she was in Johannesburg, Winnie had a meeting with the head of the Security Branch, Major General Johan Coetzee. He had been a young constable when Winnie was first banned twenty years before, and was now the man who held sway over her very life. Winnie asked him why they had banned her in 1962, since she had done nothing except be Nelson Mandela's wife. He quoted her an Afrikaans proverb, which amounted to presumption of guilt by association. Winnie was dumbfounded. As with so many tactical blunders committed by the security police against Winnie at Brandfort, hindsight would show that by embarking on their ill-founded and unconsidered crusade against her in the early 1960s, the authorities had created their own worst nightmare.

When Winnie returned to Brandfort after an absence of several months, she still had difficulty walking, and Mandela arranged with Ayob to use funds from an award made by the Austrian government to buy her a car. A shortfall in the price of the spanking new red Audi was made up by Dr Motlana, Yusuf Cachalia and Ayob himself.

Soon after going back to Phatakahle, the security police served Winnie with a summons for violating her banning order by staying in Orlando West during her recuperation, and raided her house. Helen Suzman, who happened to be visiting at the time, witnessed the three-hour search, during which the police confiscated books, documents and anything even remotely linked to the ANC, including a yellow, green and black crocheted blanket and the jewellery that had been made by the women in Winnie's sewing group. When news of the raid appeared in the international press, twenty-six leading American politicians sent her a quilt patterned on an old Pennsylvania Dutch design that was said to ward off evil spirits.

Notwithstanding the persistent harassment, Winnie's visitors found her as indomitable as ever. Sally Motlana waxed lyrical about her old friend, and predicted that no one would ever succeed in sidelining Winnie, whether they banished her to a homeland, desert or forest. 'This woman is so dynamic, she will make the birds sing and the trees rustle wherever she goes. You can be sure of that,' said Sally.[2] When her old friend Ellen Kuzwayo saw her in 1982, she was surprised and impressed by Winnie's composure. Her charm, dignity and singing laughter were still those of the woman she had come to know during the 1950s, said Ellen.

In his biography of Mandela, Anthony Sampson writes that, nevertheless, some of Winnie's friends thought the twin ordeals of jail and exile had, indeed, wrought unwelcome change in her. In Brandfort, there were rumours of reckless behaviour, violent outbursts and alcohol abuse. If that were true, nobody did anything to help or harness a woman who was almost certainly in the early stages of an emotional breakdown, not even when the signals became louder. In July 1983, a woman from Phatakahle laid a complaint against Winnie for allegedly assaulting her nine-year-old son. The boy said Winnie had hit him with a belt, and that the buckle had caught him on the head, causing a deep cut. Winnie said the boy, Andrew Pogisho, had stolen a tricycle from her house, and had fallen while running away from her. The magistrate found the evidence inconclusive, and Winnie was acquitted.

The government, desperate to counteract black political aspirations, had invented a 'tricameral' parliament, aimed at forging an alliance with coloureds and Indians. But the exclusion of blacks provoked a fresh wave of violent unrest and stayaways, and for the first time troops were deployed in the townships, where police were clearly losing the battle. White members of parliament from the Free State began agitating for Winnie's removal from Brandfort, blaming her for a new mood of defiance within the black labour force and community. Winnie ignored the furore and continued, unapologetically, to preach the gospel of black pride and political rights.

But the mood of white South Africans was changing, too, even in the most unexpected quarters. Winnie received a letter from a young Afrikaans policeman who had been involved in the 1976 Soweto uprising. He said he had been experiencing inner conflict over the political situation in the country, and that he had disobeyed orders to shoot at the 1976 rioters, firing over their heads instead, because, even then, he could not conceive of shooting children his own age simply because their skin was a different colour. He followed the letter with an unexpected visit to Winnie, but parked his car some distance from her house and told her his parents would 'kill him' if they knew how he felt. Students from the University of the Free State, one of the bastions of conservative Afrikaner youth, approached Winnie for information about Black Consciousness. They said they wanted to know what was going on in the hearts and minds of their black peers, and had started campus discussions on the burning political issues facing South Africa.

To the average black person, even those actively working for change, it might have seemed, for most of the 1980s, that there was little hope, but once in a while positive signs touched the lives of some, including the Mandela family. Since the sentence in the Rivonia Trial was handed down in June 1964, no family member except Zeni, thanks to her diplomatic status as a member of the Swazi royal house, had been allowed any physical contact with Nelson. But in May 1984, when Winnie and Zeni went to visit him, Warrant Officer Gregory informed both Mandela and Winnie, mere moments before they met, that they could see one another in the same room – and would be permitted to have physical contact.

It had been more than two decades since they touched one another, and the experience was so unexpected that they simply stood there, their arms around one another, without saying a word. For Winnie, this relaxation of the rules was the clearest sign yet that she should dare to hope Madiba *would* be freed. She still cherished the top tier of their wedding cake, and she vowed anew that on the day he walked out of prison, they would complete the tribal formalities of their marriage ceremony.

Back at Brandfort, another surprise awaited her. After seeing Winnie run a rudimentary clinic for years from her tiny house, the Methodist Church had decided to add two rooms and a bathroom to the back of the house, so that she would be able to run a proper facility. In addition to the basic assistance Winnie herself provided to those who were ill, she had arranged with two doctors, her own physician, Joe Veriava, and a friend of his, Dr Abu-Baker Asvat, to make regular visits to Phatakahle to treat patients in need of more specialised care. Asvat had his own mobile clinic, a caravan full of medical supplies, which he financed himself and used to visit squatter camps to help those in need. Now he would also have adequate facilities from which to work in Brandfort.

Winnie's surprise was complete when Fatima Meer told her she had arranged for electricity to be installed in the house. For the first time in almost eight years, Winnie would once again have some of the basic commodities she had left behind in Soweto, and new projects as outlets for her energy. The crèche she had started was still housed in the Methodist church hall, and was now attended by close on 100 toddlers, and suddenly the municipal authorities announced that they would make land available for the building of a youth centre, something Winnie was looking forward to. But, as usual, good news was quickly followed by bad. In June, Zindzi's boyfriend and the father of her second child, Zondwa, attacked her, stabbed her in the head and left her for dead in the veld. Winnie was given permission to travel to Johannesburg to be with her daughter, who spent several days in intensive care after a scan showed possible brain injury. Her family and friends tried to protect her privacy by saying she had been injured in a car accident, but the police, who knew the truth, leaked the details to the media.

Unlike her sister, Zindzi had no special credentials, and she became almost as much a victim of the Mandela name as her mother. Though she shared her parents' opposition to the pass system, she had hoped to continue her studies in Swaziland, but once she turned sixteen she needed a passport in order to do so. And she could not get a passport without a reference book.

But the government refused to issue one, offering one feeble excuse after another for several years, before finally telling her to apply for an identity document in her 'homeland' of Transkei. Zindzi refused to do that, as it would have meant forfeiting her South African citizenship, and when not even intervention by Helen Suzman was able to secure her a pass, she took matters into her own hands.

In June 1981, she managed to obtain a legitimate travel document, albeit via irregular channels. But the ruse was discovered and the document confiscated, and Zindzi abandoned her plans for further study in Swaziland. She went to work for the Institute of Race Relations instead. Later, she enrolled as a student at the University of Cape Town.

At intervals throughout the 1980s, Winnie received various international awards in recognition of her contribution to the struggle. Haverford Quaker College in Philadelphia gave her an honorary doctorate, and, unable to accept the award in person, she asked Zeni and her old friend, Adelaide Tambo, to do so on her behalf. The Caribbean state of Grenada invited her to the celebrations marking their first anniversary of independence, and she shared the Freedom Prize – awarded by two liberal Scandinavian newspapers, the Danish *Politiken* and the Swedish *Dagens Nyheter* – with Helen Suzman. In October 1984, Zeni and her husband travelled to Denmark to receive the award on Winnie's behalf, and played a tape recording of her acceptance speech to the audience.

By the end of 1984 the South African government, confronted by a struggling economy and violence that threatened to spiral out of control, was forced to rethink its policies. On 31 January 1985, President PW Botha made a dramatic and very public conditional offer of freedom to Mandela. He chose parliament as the platform for his gesture, but made it clear that Mandela would have to renounce violence and the armed struggle in order to unlock the prison gates. Mandela requested an urgent meeting with Winnie and Ismail Ayob to convey his response, and they visited him on Friday 8 February.

Two days later, at a rally organised by the United Democratic Front (UDF) in Soweto's Jabulani Stadium, Zindzi read the statement Mandela had prepared. It was the first time in more than twenty years that South Africans had heard any direct message from the ANC leader, and as Zindzi spoke the words, 'My father says …' the packed stadium shook with cheers. By the time she had finished, many of the people at the rally were in tears.

Mandela rejected the conditions imposed by Botha, but emphasised that negotiation was the only way forward for South Africa.

Momentous as the events of that week were from a political standpoint, they were overshadowed, for Winnie, by personal grief. Her sister Irene had died, and Zindzi had sent her father a telegram to tell him the news, but the letter of comfort he wrote to Winnie did not reach her until two weeks later. Though not as close to Irene as she had been to Nancy, Winnie had become more emotionally vulnerable with each passing year, and the timing of Irene's death had been unfortunate, coinciding as it did with the offer for Mandela's freedom. As always, politics had taken precedence over personal matters, but this time Winnie had been left feeling lost and spent. In a letter to Nelson on 20 February, she bared her soul:

> I returned in the early hours of today after almost three sad weeks of the most emotional storms in our life of separation. I however had one thing to look forward to, the letter from you which I knew would make my year. I knew it would reconstruct my shattered soul and restore it to my faith – the nation. Moments of such self-indulgence bring shame to me at such times when I think of those who have paid the supreme price for their ideological beliefs. Some of those fallen ones were dearer to me than my own life.
>
> The letter was there, dated 4.2.85. I'm rereading it for the umpteenth time. Contrary to your speculation at first, I do not think I would have had

the fibre to bear it all if you had been with me. You once said I should expect the inevitable fact that the struggle leaves debris behind; from that moment those many years ago, I swore to my infinitesimal ego that I would never allow myself to be part of that political quagmire.

If life is comprised of the things you enumerate and hold dear, I am lost for words, due to the fact that in my own small way life feels a little more monumental, material and demanding of one's innermost soul. That is why the love and warmth that exude from you behind those unkind concrete grey monotonous and cruel walls simply overwhelm me, especially when I think of those who in the name of the struggle have been deprived of that love.

You refer to moments when love and happiness, trust and hope have turned into pure agony, when conscience and sense of guilt have ravaged every part of your being. It is true, darling, I've lost so much of what is dearest to me in the years of our separation. When you have lived alone as I've done as a young bride and never known what married life is all about you cling to minute consolations, the sparing of one from the indignities that ravage us. In our case, with all those we have lost, the dignity of death has been respected ...

I was so proud of your message to us. I've often wondered how I would have reacted if I had met you, Uncle Walter and others on the Pollsmoor steps and was told to take you home ...[3]

Five months after Mandela's rejection of Botha's offer, black South Africans had made it abundantly clear that they were not about to sit around and wait for change. They heeded Oliver Tambo's call to render the country ungovernable in droves, and by July, law and order had effectively broken down, and many townships were close to anarchy. On 20 July, the government declared a state of emergency, which gave the police sweeping powers to detain and interrogate people. Television coverage nightly depicted major battles in the townships between ANC supporters and the police, and public confidence in the government's ability to maintain stability began to wane. Oliver Tambo said the state of emergency was preparing the ground for a serious eruption of violent conflict, and in August an opinion poll showed that 70 per cent of blacks and 30 per cent of whites expected civil war in South Africa. As if the violence wasn't bad enough, the economy was on the brink of destruction due to the withdrawal of capital by international investors and the introduction of sanctions.

It was only a matter of time before the wave of violence washed over the tiny community of Brandfort. On 5 August, pupils from Phatakahle boycotted classes and staged demonstrations. The police reacted with a baton charge and fired tear gas and rubber bullets, and a number of children sought shelter in Winnie's house, pursued by the police. In the melee, doors and windows were broken. The next day, Winnie had to travel to Johannesburg for a medical check-up, but her sister stayed at the house with Zindzi's son, Zondwa, or Gadaffi as the family called him. The pupils of Phatakahle came out in protest again, and once again some fled into Winnie's home ahead of the police. This time, the damage was far worse. Petrol bombs were thrown into the house and the clinic burned to the ground. In the chaos, Gadaffi disappeared. Ismail Ayob received news that he was missing while Winnie was in his office, and immediately drove her back to Brandfort. She could hardly believe her eyes. Her house was in ruins, with debris and shattered furniture everywhere. There was blood on the walls and a blood-stained cloth was draped over a bust of John F Kennedy that had been a gift from American sympathisers. Fortunately Winnie's neighbour, the security policeman's wife, turned up with Gadaffi, who was unscathed. He had run into her house when the fracas broke out and she had kept him there.

Since her house was in ruins, Winnie decided to return to Johannesburg, but the police refused to give her permission to go back to the house in Orlando West. She had to stay in a hotel while they decided where she could live.

In the midst of this period of intense personal and political developments, a routine examination determined that Mandela had an enlarged prostate, and needed surgery. The government knew very well, given the political climate, that there would be a bloody revolution if Mandela died, and he was provided with the best medical care the country could offer. Surgery was scheduled for November. Winnie flew to Cape Town to see him the day before his operation, and, coincidentally, the Minister of Justice, Kobie Coetsee, was on the same flight. Winnie seized the moment, and spent most of the two-hour flight talking to Coetsee. In John Carlin's television documentary for the BBC, *Frontline*, Coetsee later said: 'All of a sudden, I became aware of the presence of this very interesting and imposing woman. I recognised her of course, immediately. And there she was standing, and she didn't speak a word. She just indicated with her head that I was to move the briefcase. She wanted to sit next to me. I did so, and she sat next to me for the remainder of the flight.'

Mandela had earlier requested a meeting with Coetsee, but had received no reply from him. Now Coetsee decided to visit him in hospital. Winnie – whose friendship with and influence on Piet de Waal had initially been responsible for a shift in Coetsee's thinking about Mandela – cemented the change on that fateful flight. Coetsee arrived at the hospital unannounced to visit Mandela, inquired about his health and the surgery, but did not talk politics. Mandela took advantage of the visit to raise the question of Winnie's situation. He asked Coetsee to allow her to remain in Johannesburg, and Coetsee said he would look into the matter but could make no promises.

After the visit, however, Coetsee summoned Winnie to his official residence and told her she could return to Johannesburg, provided she did not cause any problems. It was Winnie's turn to make no promises, and soon after arriving home, she flouted the terms of her banning order and addressed a funeral at Mamelodi, outside Pretoria, for twelve people – including a baby – who had been killed when the police opened fire on them.

A few days before Christmas, Winnie was notified that the Minister of Law and Order, Louis le Grange, had relaxed her banning order. She need not return to Brandfort, and would no longer be required to report to the police every day. She could attend social events, but was still prohibited from attending political meetings or making political speeches. It sounded marvellous – but there was the inevitable sting in the tail. She could go anywhere in South Africa, except into the magisterial districts of Johannesburg and Roodepoort. Quite simply, that meant that Winnie could go nowhere near Soweto. She could not go home.

She defied the restriction, and returned to house No. 8115 in Orlando West. The police arrived, negotiated with her to leave, and she agreed, but returned at the first opportunity. The police returned, dragged her out of the house, arrested her and detained her overnight. There was an international outcry, and when Winnie appeared in court on 23 December, she was released on bail. She went to Cape Town to spend Christmas with Mandela, but as soon as she returned to Johannesburg she was arrested again. When she appeared in court in January 1986, the case was postponed. In March, Le Grange announced that the case had been postponed indefinitely.

After more than eight years in exile, Winnie Mandela went home to Soweto.

16

'With our boxes of matches ...'

AFTER WORLD WAR II, and especially following the Vietnam War, post-traumatic stress disorder (PTSD) became a buzzword. The psychological, psychiatric and medical fraternities, military and security services, employers, educators, parents and spouses the world over became sensitised to the causes and symptoms of the syndrome, initially identified in soldiers returning from combat zones, but gradually extended to include civilian victims as well as survivors of serious car accidents, natural disasters, assaults, hijackings, domestic violence, sexual abuse and torture.

Towards the end of the 1990s, clinicians and researchers found that the accepted diagnosis of PTSD did not cover the severe and far-reaching psychological effects of protracted, repeated trauma over periods of months or years. They determined that continuing trauma causes a multitude of serious and complex symptoms, including changes in emotional behaviour, often manifested by delayed and lasting mental illness. Long-term effects suggest a close association between escalating levels of trauma and psychosocial dysfunction. The risk of mental illness is four times greater in people who have been exposed to more than three traumatic experiences, and reactions related to post-traumatic stress often persist for substantial periods of time – and can be latent for up to ten or more years after the trauma itself. To distinguish the typical symptoms of continuing trauma and persistent victimisation from those of common trauma, researchers defined it as 'complex PTSD'.

A disturbing finding of the research was that people who have suffered trauma, victimisation or violence and suffer from post-traumatic stress are, ironically, at high risk of becoming perpetrators of violence, including torture and rape – and even murder or massacres. Experts believe that for some people, the pain of being a victim becomes unbearable, and they attempt to 'shift' their own pain onto someone else. And thus they become perpetrators, and create other victims.

The extent to which violence disturbs the intricate and fragile balance of society is alarming. Even people who don't experience violence at first hand are affected. The more one empathises with a victim, the more one becomes a co-victim, even suffering the same symptoms of helplessness, anxiety and despair. In situations where an entire society is victimised and traumatised, virtually every member of the community becomes a potential perpetrator of violence.

By the mid-1980s, South Africa's black population had suffered three decades of gradually escalating government-sponsored victimisation and violence at the hands of the police, and, after 1976, the military. Townships had been turned into war zones, where security forces committed acts of brutality with impunity and total disregard for human life or acceptable norms of behaviour. New laws gave them sweeping powers and they were not held accountable for their actions. In the larger townships, displaced and orphaned children roamed the streets, and delinquency and behavioural problems were at an all-time high. The ANC in exile contributed to the mayhem with the call – from the safety of other countries – for black South Africans to render the country ungovernable. For criminal elements, it was a licence to commit crime unchecked. For young blacks, many severely disturbed by years of fear and violence, it offered justification to vent their anger and need for revenge on virtually anyone. The smallest incident could provoke a brutal attack, even cost a life.

Complex PTSD is a common result of organised violence, including the politically motivated victimisation of large numbers of people or entire sections of a population. There were tens of thousands of troops and police in the townships. The Defence Force had ostensibly been deployed to curb the unrest, but there was widespread evidence of excessive security force violence, often aimed at the youth. The effects of the intensifying brutality on the black youth were far-reaching. Township children grew up in war zones, their childhoods essentially no different to those of children in Beirut or Bosnia. They witnessed violence against their families, and large numbers saw their parents and other relatives arrested and imprisoned for years at a time, even killed. What made the situation in South Africa worse was that children as young as twelve or less were imprisoned. Gangs of aimless youths started copying the terrifying tactics of the security forces, beating and abducting people, interrogating and sometimes killing them: the unbridled and angry barbarism of the victim turned perpetrator.

Young, uprooted blacks saw themselves as soldiers of the liberation struggle, and by the mid-1980s, thousands of them had formed groups and gangs, many acting as vigilantes in their neighbourhoods. The police took full advantage of the situation, playing them off against each other through informers who infiltrated the gangs, provoking suspicion, betrayal and fierce reprisals. More than a decade later, during hearings of the Truth and Reconciliation Commission (TRC), numerous black South Africans testified to the demise of normal life in their communities and the deep suffering this had caused.

As so often happens during war, women were brutalised by both the enemy and their own comrades, and they were far more willing than men to publicly record their suffering, especially emotional and psychological distress. The TRC heard chilling evidence of the depravity that surfaced during the 1970s and 1980s, and how it influenced black communities. The testimony of Sheila Masote, daughter of former PAC president Zeph Mathopeng, was a painful precis of the devastating consequences of apartheid.

Sheila came from a privileged background. The Mathopengs lived in Orlando West, the Soweto suburb that was home to the black elite, including the Mandelas, the Sisulus and the Motlanas. Her parents were both teachers, cultured and intellectual individuals. Her father was the first chairman of the Johannesburg Bantu Music Festival. But her supportive family and healthy society were systematically eroded by apartheid. As a result of her father's political activities, both her parents lost their teaching jobs and were imprisoned, her father frequently. Hundreds of relatives, friends and acquaintances were either jailed or fled the country. Denied the right to earn their living as teachers, her parents became impoverished, and her mother, traumatised, lonely and frustrated, started beating her.

Sheila married a classical musician, the only black in Africa with a licentiate in violin tuition, but, as the political mayhem grew, both he and Sheila were detained. One of her brothers went into exile, the other became an abusive alcoholic.

At the TRC, Sheila Masote exposed her deepest anguish to the world when she testified that she had abused her son, as she herself had been abused by her mother. She whipped him so badly that neighbours had to intervene. When he was six, he tried to hang himself.

The Masotes were but one example of the anguish and confusion that infiltrated the lives of millions of ordinary black South Africans.

During the latter half of the 1980s, certain elements of the security forces embarked on a campaign of unmitigated torture and murder against so-called enemies of the apartheid state, their heinous crimes cloaked in 'top secret' classifications or covered up by burning or blowing up the bodies of victims with explosives. Detainees were drugged, poisoned or shot, their remains dumped in unmarked graves or thrown into the sea. Those who survived the brutal interrogations and lengthy incarcerations returned to their communities bearing permanent emotional scars and psychological lacerations.

During prolonged periods of isolation, many detainees contemplate suicide. Ruth First tried to kill herself while she was in solitary confinement. Winnie Mandela considered it.

The Soweto to which she returned in 1986 was a changed and dangerous place, but, as always, Winnie's primary concern was for those who needed help. Evidence of the ravages of a decade of violence was everywhere, and as soon as she could,

Winnie set up an informal welfare office, aimed specifically at the troubled youth. She gave shelter under her own roof to many of the homeless teenagers and young adults who roamed the township streets, fed them, clothed them and sent them back to school, paying their tuition fees herself. House No. 8115 became a refuge for children on the run from the police, and for those with nowhere else to go. Towards the end of the year, Winnie became involved in the resolution of internal conflict in the Orlando West branch of the Soweto Youth Congress (SOYCO), and subsequently a number of the youths she had come to know in the process moved into the outbuildings at her home. There was already a Sisulu Football Club, and boys and young men living with Winnie formed the Mandela United Football Club (MUFC). The girls called themselves the Mandela Sisters. Winnie provided accommodation, food and education for them, and helped them when they needed money. They had come from all over the country, and many of the boys were Zulus from the rural areas of Natal.

Winnie never went into the outside rooms where the young people lived, and they, in turn, did not frequent the main house, where Zindzi and her children were also living. There was only one unbreakable rule: all the young people living on Winnie's property had to sign a book showing when they were at home, or not. Youths were often picked up by the police and disappeared without a trace, and the register made it possible to see if anyone did not come home, so that enquiries could be made.

Winnie was busy. She went to her welfare office every day and spent long hours dealing with the many social problems that beset the community. She attended funerals, comforted bereaved families, organised help for the needy and the elderly, and enrolled at the University of the Witwatersrand for part-time studies in social anthropology and politics.

Rumours begun while she was in Brandfort, that she had lost perspective on her role in the struggle, and specifically as Mandela's representative, followed Winnie to Soweto, where they were fuelled by some of her own actions. She seemed more defiant than ever, often wearing a khaki military-style outfit, and making statements that evoked strong criticism. In his biography of Mandela, Anthony Sampson observes that Winnie 'appeared to sail into dangerous storms like a ship in full sail, towering over both her acolytes and her adversaries'. In April, at Munsieville near Johannesburg, Winnie made a highly inflammatory statement that evoked widespread reaction: 'Together, hand in hand, with our boxes of matches and our necklaces, we shall liberate this country.'

The media outcry was unmitigated. Winnie was called irresponsible and accused of inciting violence against whites. The ANC refused to publicly condemn either Winnie's words or the abhorrent practice of 'necklacing', which her statement appeared to endorse. At a summit of non-aligned nations in Harare, Oliver Tambo said whereas the ANC was not happy about necklacing, the organisation would not condemn people who had been driven to such extremes by the situation in South Africa. Privately, however, he contacted Dr Motlana and told him to gag Winnie.

Like Tambo, Mandela was shocked that Winnie seemed to support necklacing, but he, too, refrained from public condemnation. Winnie's reaction was that she had been quoted out of context, and that her intention had not been to approve necklacing, but to illustrate what measures people had been driven to by apartheid.

However controversial her public utterances, Winnie had a clear understanding of, and insight into, the political situation. Anthony Sampson writes that she showed 'clear-sighted judgment' about the unfolding crisis. During her banishment to Brandfort, the United Democratic Front had been formed to create a surrogate ANC pressure group by bringing various political interest groups together under a single umbrella. Gossip and her critics alleged that Winnie did not support the new movement, but she went on record as saying the UDF embodied the South Africa of the future, a broad-based organisation that embraced both the workers and the intelligentsia, with room even for those who supported different ideologies. She favoured the ANC's vision of a multiracial South Africa in which wealth was shared, but not as a democracy. Winnie advocated a socialist state as the only way to solve the problems of poverty and starvation, and remedy the disparity between population groups, with equality for all and universal franchise. Notwithstanding her relationship with Helen Suzman, she was unequivocally critical of the Progressive Federal Party's preoccupation with white minority rights, accusing the PFP of being supportive of the government. She was equally scathing in her condemnation of what she called the politics of exclusivity advocated by the Azanian People's Organisation (AZAPO), which was the other extreme.

From 1986, the juxtaposition of Winnie's world, and that of Mandela, became increasingly one of contrast. She was the overt revolutionary, angry, defiant and controversial; he was the statesman-in-the-making, steadily garnering respect and rising in international stature. There was mounting pressure on the South African government to release Mandela and bring about political change. The response to the ANC's call to render the country ungovernable saw the townships in a permanent state of siege, despite an extension of the state of emergency. Political upheaval took on a predictable pattern: black resistance rose in direct relation to the level of fresh repression, and the government response became positively Stalinist. Thousands of UDF leaders and supporters were detained and tens of thousands went into hiding. But for every leader removed from the public stage, there was another waiting in the wings. The names and faces changed, but the tactics that had begun to foil government reaction stayed the same: enforced consumer boycotts of shops, non-payment of rental and township service fees, mass protests and rallies, toyi-toying demonstrations and stirring political orations at the open graves of fallen comrades. And there were funerals almost every weekend in the troubled townships around every major city. Church leaders became more vociferous, and one of the loudest voices belonged to Desmond Tutu, the newly elected first black Archbishop of Cape Town. Morale was further boosted by the growing success of guerrilla fighters, who had launched a campaign of successful attacks throughout South Africa. Trade unions, too, had entered the fray, creating an additional political platform, and when the Congress of South African Trade Unions (COSATU) joined the struggle, strike action became a powerful weapon in the struggle arsenal.

After being all but ignored by the international community during the late 1960s and early 1970s, Mandela was now *the* name on lips all over the world. A flurry of publicity and diplomatic activity had turned him into a celebrity – the most famous prisoner on earth. South Africa's Minister of Justice, Kobie Coetsee, had dared suggest to PW Botha that Mandela should be freed on humanitarian grounds after his prostate surgery in November 1985, but Botha would not hear of it. Two years later, with the government's back firmly against the wall, Coetsee was finally given permission to open a secret dialogue with Mandela. When Mandela's fellow prisoner Govan Mbeki, father of future president Thabo Mbeki, was unconditionally released at the end of 1987, there could no longer be any doubt that South Africa was slowly being steered onto a new course. It was not a moment too soon. The anti-apartheid movement was gaining momentum on all fronts, and June 1988 brought a sobering indication of the ANC's potential to unleash widespread chaos when a powerful car bomb exploded outside the Ellis Park rugby stadium in Johannesburg, killing two whites and injuring thirty-five. After more than a decade of mounting violence, a sprinkling of white South Africans tentatively took up the call for Mandela's release.

As his seventieth birthday in July 1988 approached, the call became a clamour. A massive rock concert was staged at London's Wembley Stadium on 11 June under the banner 'Freedom at 70', with world-famous performers like Harry Belafonte, Stevie Wonder and Whitney Houston taking part. The concert was televised by the BBC, and millions of viewers heard a message from Mandela that had been smuggled out of prison. The South African government was incensed, and threatened to expel the BBC's correspondents. It made no difference – international support had outstripped the besieged apartheid government's influence, and its voice was steadily diminishing.

But events on the ground in South Africa's townships were grimmer than ever. Anarchy ruled, and because of her continued involvement with the youth, Winnie was directly affected. Whether as the result of police instigation or not, the Mandela United Football Club had become embroiled in a confrontation with the football team from Daliwonga High School in Dube. For months there was intermittent fighting between members of the two teams, but the conflict esca-lated when the Daliwonga players arrived at Winnie's house and fired shots at members of the MUFC. Then one of the Mandela Sisters was gang-raped by Daliwonga pupils. She pointed out her attackers, and the MUFC rounded them up, took them to the rooms behind Winnie's house and beat them up. A few days later, on 28 July, a mob of Daliwonga pupils retaliated by scaling the perimeter wall and setting Winnie's house on fire. Neither she nor the MUFC members was at home. Someone called the fire brigade, but their water tanks were empty, and house No. 8115, the home of Nelson and Winnie Mandela, went up in flames.

Apart from the loss of Winnie's furniture and personal effects, the fire claimed an irreplaceable treasure – family photographs, letters, and the layer from her wedding cake that Winnie had preserved for half a lifetime. She was devastated. For two days, she said not one word, shed not a single tear. The only home she had shared with Nelson was destroyed – not by their oppressors, but by the very people for whom it had stood as a symbol of resistance and courage.

Mandela was equally shocked by the news, but he was adamant that no charges should be laid against the arsonists, and that the matter should be resolved by the people of Soweto. The Reverend Frank Chikane, who had witnessed the fire, was concerned that there might be further violence, and approached several influential figures, including Cyril Ramaphosa, Sydney Mufamadi, Sister Bernard Ncube and the Reverend Beyers Naudé, to manage the situation. They formed what became known as the Mandela Crisis Committee, and vowed to disband the MUFC.

Being back in Soweto had not brought Winnie the contentment and fulfilment she had longed for while in Brandfort. More than ever, she was a target of the security police's covert dirty tricks and spies, and her life had become mired in controversy and alarming rumour. After the fire, she moved into a luxurious mansion in Diepkloof, said to have been built and furnished with funds raised by an American entrepreneur, Robert Brown, who had close links with Boston University, where Zeni and her husband had studied thanks to scholarships, which Brown evidently arranged for them. Far from disbanding, the Mandela United Football Club moved with Winnie. The members were said to have assumed responsibility for her safety, and became known as her bodyguards, but township residents were making serious allegations against them, charging that they had become a vigilante gang and were out of control. The club coach, Jerry Richardson, had served some time in prison and was rumoured to be a police informer. Residents claimed that boys who refused to join the MUFC were intimidated, and some said they feared for their lives. Some accused the MUFC of operating like the mafia, which no member was allowed to quit. By far the most disquieting rumour was that Winnie was not only aware of the MUFC's reign of terror, but might even be involved.

When Nelson was apprised of the club's unsavoury reputation, he told Winnie he wanted it disbanded, but, in a rare display of defiance against his wishes, she ignored him and made no attempt to curb the behaviour of its members. Winnie's own behaviour was becoming ever more reckless and erratic. She wore her khaki outfit at every opportunity, and it was common knowledge that she had begun to harbour MK fighters in her home. Her alliance with the MUFC was about to immerse the ANC in a grave political crisis, and for the authorities, rumours of the difference of opinion between Nelson and Winnie and the prospect of a rift between Winnie and the ANC, were a gift.

Meanwhile, Mandela was slowly being prepared to rejoin the world beyond the prison gates. He was allowed more visits, given unlimited access to newspapers and permitted to watch films, which he loved. James Gregory started taking him on secret excursions in and around Cape Town, always accompanied by armed guards. Mandela understood that these trips were either meant to reacquaint him with the country prior to release, or to dangle the prospect of freedom as bait and lure him into making rash concessions to the government. The population at large knew nothing of the activities taking place behind the scenes, and the political turmoil continued unabated under a permanent state of emergency. South Africa reinforced its reputation as a police state as the numbers and activities of the SAP were expanded, and soldiers were permanently deployed in the townships.

At the beginning of August, Mandela fell ill. Following his prostate surgery, he had not returned to the top-floor cells at Pollsmoor that he had shared with his comrades, but was housed instead on the ground floor, where he had a 'suite' of three large cells all to himself. However, the accommodation was damp and dark, and for the first time in twenty-five years, he was alone. No one noticed that he had become listless and developed a nagging cough, but when he started vomiting on 4 August, he was taken to Tygerberg Hospital, where tuberculosis was diagnosed. Winnie was furious, and blamed the prison authorities for neglecting him. The government was alarmed. Kobie Coetsee personally monitored the situation, and a Swiss specialist was summoned to treat Mandela. On 21 August, the London *Sunday Times* aptly summed up PW Botha's dilemma by reporting that for the South African government, 'the only thing worse than a free Mandela, is a dead Mandela'.

After being treated at Tygerberg Hospital, Mandela was transferred to the Constantiaberg Clinic, a private hospital, for a period of convalescence. When he was discharged on 9 December, he was not taken back to Pollsmoor, but to the Victor Verster Prison at Paarl, twenty-two kilometres from Cape Town. The government was no longer taking any chances with his welfare, and instead of being placed in a cell, Mandela was installed in one of the largest and most comfortably furnished houses normally occupied by senior officials who lived on the sprawling prison farm in the heart of the picturesque Cape winelands. Every possible convenience was at his disposal – a well-tended garden, swimming pool, television, *en suite* bathroom, even a personal chef, Warrant Officer Jack Swart, who prepared all his meals. The man who had spent more than a quarter-century in cold, dank prison cells was suddenly living in luxury – but he was still a prisoner, and all contact with his comrades had been cut off.

As for Winnie, the curtain was about to go up on a drama that would shake her life to the core, and reverberate around the world.

Two schools of thought developed around the crisis that enveloped Winnie as 1988 drew to a close. One held that she had either become mentally unhinged as the result of a relentless twenty-five-year campaign against her, or had always been fundamentally evil, but had managed to hide this, and was, in fact, guilty of everything she was accused of – and more.

The other theory was that Winnie posed a serious threat to those in the ANC whose philosophy differed from hers, and that the only way of neutralising her considerable power was to pile up enough damning allegations against her to ensure that she could never become president of South Africa. This would involve a complex – but not impossible – web of lies and intrigue. Winnie's naivety and trusting nature were well known, and she was therefore vulnerable. It would be easy to trap her in a situation where she was surrounded by spies and criminals who would lie at the behest of the highest bidder and implicate her in deeds that would shock not only the nation, but the world.

Winnie steadfastly denied all the accusations against her, and on occasion said she was satisfied that the truth would one day be known, hinting that the full story had not yet emerged. She never felt the need to exonerate or explain herself, and eschewed invitations to talk about the upheavals of her recent past. Against that background, the official record of events was largely assembled from allegations and testimony against her.

One of the young ANC activists, Lolo Sono, was closely involved in providing assistance to MK guerrillas who needed temporary shelter. When one of them was killed in a shoot-out with police, Lolo was accused of being a spy. On Sunday 13 November 1988, Winnie went to his father's home in her minibus. Lolo was in the vehicle and had obviously been physically assaulted. She told his father, Nicodemus, that Lolo was being taken away. Nicodemus pleaded with her to leave the injured youth with him, but he later testified that she seemed particularly aggressive, not at all like the Winnie he knew, and she refused. She left, and Lolo Sono was never seen again. Five days later, Nomsa Tshabalala – one of the Sono neighbours – discovered that her son Sibuniso, a friend of Lolo's, had been taken away by young men who had come looking for him. He, too, disappeared.

225

The list of Mandela United victims was getting longer, and some of them reported their assaults to the police. Peter and Philip Makhanda were taken to Winnie's house, and after being beaten up, the letter 'M' was carved into Philip's chest and the words 'Viva ANC' into one of his thighs, as well as on Peter's back. Then battery acid was poured on the open wounds. They escaped, and both boys told the police that not only was Winnie present, but that Zindzi had also taken part in the assault.

Sibusiso Chili and Lerotodi Ikaneng had refused to join the Mandela Football Club. When members of the club attacked Sibusiso, his brothers went to his rescue, and during the ensuing fight they killed a football club member, Maxwell Modondo. Ikaneng arrived on the scene when the fight was over, but was nevertheless seized and branded by the MUFC. Later, club members attempted to murder Ikaneng, and attacked the Chili home with firebombs, killing a family member.

Xola Mokhaula and Mlando Ngubeni were shot in cold blood by Oupa Seheri, another Mandela United member, who made Xola's mother and sister watch while he killed the boy.

The turning point was the abduction of Kenneth Kgase, Thabisa Mono, Pelo Mekgwe and Stompie Seipei.

The Methodist Mission House in Orlando, known as the manse, was run by Father Paul Verryn, and offered sanctuary to teenage boys and young men, much as Winnie's house did. In mid-December, Stompie Seipei, aged fourteen, arrived at the manse after staying for a while with prominent human rights lawyer Arthur Chaskalson's son Matthew, who worked for Priscilla Jana, another well-known attorney, who had acted for the Mandela family on several occasions.

Verryn's unofficial housekeeper was Xoliswa Falati, one of Winnie's acquaintances and a regular visitor to her house. Falati told Winnie that Verryn was a homosexual and was sexually abusing boys living at the manse. She also alleged that Stompie was a police spy.

On 28 December, Stompie, Kgase, Mono and Mekgwe were taken to Winnie's house by members of Mandela United, severely beaten and held captive. The following evening, Stompie was beaten again, while Jerry Richardson took Kenneth, Thabisa and Pelo, along with Lerotodi Ikaneng, to a deserted stretch of veld and ordered Stompie's three friends to kill Ikaneng. They slit his throat and left him for dead, but, miraculously, he survived.

After repeated attacks on Stompie, Katiza Cebekhulu, one of the club members who took part in the assaults, had an anxiety attack, and Winnie took him to the surgery of her old friend Dr Abu-Baker Asvat, whose nurse was Walter Sisulu's wife, Albertina. By New Year's Day Stompie Seipei was vomiting and couldn't eat, and Dr Asvat was called to the house to examine him. He found that Stompie had sustained permanent brain damage.

When Stompie and his friends had not returned to the Methodist manse after being abducted, other youths reported the matter to the Mandela Crisis Committee. On 4 January, Aubrey Mokoena, a member of the committee, went to Winnie's house to enquire about the boys, but she denied that they were there. Two days later, Dr Nthatho Motlana went to see Winnie and she admitted that the boys *were* there, but refused to let him see them.

Later that day, a woman came across the body of a teenage boy on the outskirts of Soweto. He had three stab wounds in the neck. It would be more than a month before the body was identified as that of Stompie Seipei.

In the early hours of 7 January, Kenneth Kgase escaped from Winnie's house and contacted Paul Verryn, who took him first to a doctor and then to his friend Geoff Budlender, a lawyer. Kgase made a statement about the abductions and assaults carried out by the Mandela United Football Club, but no one contacted the police. Those who were opposed to apartheid saw the police as the enemy and were, as were people in the townships, generally loath to contact them.

On 11 January, members of the Mandela Crisis Committee and the Methodist bishop, Peter Storey, went to Winnie's house. She said that the boys who had gone missing from the manse were there, but that they had come of their own free will and that she was protecting them against further abuse by Verryn. When committee members asked to see them, she told them to come back the next day.

Instead of going to the police, the influential and respected community leaders simply left, and sent a report to Oliver Tambo in Lusaka, outlining the situation and complaining that Winnie was being obstinate. When they returned the following day, Winnie wasn't home, and Zindzi told them that one of the boys had 'escaped'. When they saw Mono, Mekgwe and Katiza Cebekhulu, they noticed that Mono and Mekgwe had fresh wounds. They spoke briefly to the boys, then left again, and still took no further action. On 14 January, Frank Chikane wrote to Mandela and begged him to intervene.

The Methodist Church sought legal advice and was told they could get an interdict against Winnie to prevent further violence against the youths. However, the members of the Crisis Committee, concerned about the effect of negative publicity on the ANC, were not prepared to testify against her. Finally, on Monday 16 January, the boys were released, and that evening a meeting was convened in Dobsonville, where some 150 community leaders and the Crisis Committee discussed the situation. Katiza Cebekhulu had been brought to the meeting, and he told them Stompie was dead. Lerotodi Ikaneng told them of the attempt to kill him, and the fresh scar across his throat spoke louder than any words.

On Friday 27 January, Dr Asvat was murdered in his surgery by two young men posing as patients. Albertina Sisulu heard a gunshot, heard Asvat scream and saw two youths run out of the consulting room. Cyril Mbatha and Nicholas Dlamini were subsequently convicted of the murder.

Earlier that morning, the *Weekly Mail* had carried a report about the meeting in Dobsonville, and the name of Stompie Seipei was first brought to South Africa's attention. Combined with Asvat's murder, the media realised there was a major story in the making, and began tracking down the rumours that had been running rife in Soweto for months. On 12 February, the *Sunday Star* reported that Winnie had been linked to Stompie's beating. Two days later, his body was identified, and the police opened a murder investigation. Statements by Mono, Kgase and Mekgwe implicated Winnie, Jerry Richardson and Jabu Sithole, and the two men were arrested, along with Xoliswa Falati, her daughter Nomphumelelo and Winnie's driver, John Morgan.

On 16 February, Murphy Morobe, publicity secretary of the Mass Democratic Movement (which had replaced the UDF) called a media conference and read a statement expressing outrage at Winnie's complicity in the abduction and assault of Stompie Seipei who, he said, would have been alive if he and the three other boys had not been abducted by the Mandela United Football Club. The MDM was not prepared to remain silent to protect people who violated human rights in the name of the struggle against apartheid, said Morobe. Oliver Tambo also issued a statement from exile in which he chastised Winnie, though his criticism was more restrained. He expressed sadness at having to voice his reservations about her judgement regarding the football club.

Winnie's supporters in Soweto sprang to her defence, declaring her the victim of a vicious smear campaign, most likely orchestrated by her perpetual enemies, the security police.

By April, with Stompie's murder still under investigation, Winnie was bumped off the front pages by speculation that her husband's release was imminent. But there was a major stumbling block: the government insisted that the ANC would first have to renounce the armed struggle, sever ties with the South African Communist Party and abandon the principle of majority rule. Mandela refused, making it clear that only an unconditional release would be accepted.

Oliver Tambo had declared 1989 the 'Year of Mass Action for People's Power', and political protest became more vigorous, even as PW Botha was losing his grip on the National Party's forty-year domination of South Africa. To all intents, Mandela's position had already become that of a man under house arrest, albeit within the confines of a state prison. He was allowed to receive scores of visitors, and on his seventy-first birthday in July, almost every member of his family was present, along with some of his oldest comrades, who were brought from Pollsmoor for the celebrations. Behind the scenes, Oliver Tambo was shuttling between Lusaka, Europe and America to muster international support for the ANC, and working tirelessly to convince the organisation that it should endorse Mandela's private talks with the apartheid government.

In one of his last notable acts as head of state, PW Botha finally held a secret meeting with Mandela. Barely a month later, he was forced to resign by his own cabinet, and was succeeded by the more moderate FW de Klerk. On 10 October, the new president announced that Walter Sisulu, Raymond Mhlaba, Ahmed Kathrada, Andrew Mlangeni, Elias Motsoaledi, Jeff Masemola, Wilton Mkwayi and Oscar Mpetha were to be unconditionally released. Five days later, the only senior ANC leader still behind bars was Nelson Mandela.

On 13 December 1989, the world's most famous prisoner was driven to Tuynhuys, official Cape Town residence of South Africa's president, to meet De Klerk. Within six weeks, Africa's last white tribe would sound the death knell of apartheid.

17

Comrade Nomzamo

AS 1990 DAWNED, excitement about Mandela's release reached fever pitch. After visiting him on 8 January, Winnie told the media: 'I don't think we are talking about months … this is the real thing.' At the end of the month, she indicated that there were still problems to be solved regarding the unbanning of the ANC, so it was hardly surprising that South Africans on all sides of the political playing field were stunned when FW de Klerk used the opening of parliament on 2 February to demolish forty-two years of apartheid in less than an hour.

In the time it took for the president to deliver his historic speech, the old South Africa became the new South Africa. The ANC and thirty-one other organisations were unbanned. Political prisoners who had not committed violent crimes would be freed. The execution of prisoners on Death Row was suspended.

And Nelson Mandela was to be unconditionally released.

Overnight, symbols, sentiments and individuals that had been hidden in deep shadow for decades became visible everywhere. The ANC flag was hoisted by jubilant supporters, along with the Communist Party's distinctive red flag bearing the hammer and sickle that had personified white South Africa's greatest fears and had been used to justify sending tens of thousands of its young men to war. In townships and streets all over the country, those who had toyi-toyied in anger the week before now danced in celebration.

But as South Africans of all population groups tried to digest the full meaning of the government's bold move, the world held its breath for an expected backlash against whites. Conservative Namibians who had been preparing to trek across the border and escape life under SWAPO, the former enemy and newly elected government of the neighbouring state, unpacked their bags and took down the 'For Sale' signs outside their houses. Former Rhodesians, who had moved south when majority rule came to Zimbabwe, dusted off their passports and began readying themselves to follow the sun to Australia.

A week after the dramatic announcement, De Klerk summoned Mandela to his office, and told him he would be released in Johannesburg the next day. Mandela stubbornly refused, and said he wanted time for the ANC to prepare his reception, as chaos would erupt if he simply walked out of prison unannounced. He also wanted to be released at Victor Verster, and Winnie had to be present. It was precisely because the government did not want to give the ANC time to organise mass demonstrations and rallies that it had decided to give Mandela so little advance warning of his release date, and there was a tense stand-off between the incumbent and future presidents of South Africa. Eventually, they reached a compromise: Mandela would walk out of the main gates at Victor Verster Prison in Paarl, with Winnie at his side, at 3 pm the next day.

In anticipation of this momentous event, the ANC had already appointed a national reception committee, but in the end they had less than fifteen hours to arrange Nelson Mandela's first public appearance as a free man after more than twenty-seven years.

While Mandela, his lawyers and political advisers worked on his speech, arrangements were hastily made for a top-level ANC delegation, headed by Winnie and Walter Sisulu, to fly to Cape Town on the Sunday morning. The flight was delayed – in Warrant Officer James Gregory's opinion, deliberately, to give the ANC a little more time to put adequate security for Mandela in place – and by the time Winnie arrived at the prison gate, hundreds of thousands of people had gathered outside and along the route they would take to Cape Town.

In the mid-1980s, Winnie had said of her marriage to Nelson: 'I had so little time to love him, and that love has survived all these years of separation.'[1] Now, just minutes away from reclaiming her position at his side while the whole world watched, her excitement knew no bounds. She jumped from her car and ran ahead of the others to the house where Madiba was waiting.

At 4 pm on 11 February 1990, Nelson and Winnie Mandela walked hand in hand into the future. He was genuinely astonished at the scene that awaited them. He had expected a few warders and some journalists, not thousands of well-wishers and hundreds of newspaper, radio and television reporters from every corner of the globe. It was an overwhelming introduction to the media circus that would henceforth follow his every step, and he was momentarily taken aback by all the fuss. But he recovered quickly, and when he raised his right arm in the Black Power salute, the roar of the crowd was deafening.

Winnie was radiant, triumphant, and the cheers were as much for her as for Madiba.

In the heart of Cape Town, hundreds of thousands of people had gathered at the Grand Parade opposite the City Hall, from which Mandela would make his first public address. The sun was setting as he appeared on the balcony overlooking the historic market square, raised his fist and shouted '*Amandla!*' The city bowl reverberated to the mass response, '*Ngawethu!*' Then Mandela shouted '*iAfrika!*'

and the crowd roared back: '*Mayibuye!*' When he removed the pages of his speech from his jacket pocket, he realised that he had left his reading glasses at the prison, and had to borrow Winnie's. It was a small incident, but rich with symbolism: he would read his first words as a free man through both their eyes.

But, although he paid tribute by name to a long list of friends and colleagues for their support and contribution to the struggle over the years, he did not single Winnie out. In fact, his only reference to her was an oblique one, when he expressed 'deep appreciation for the strength given to me during my long and lonely years in prison by my beloved wife and family', and added: 'I am convinced that your pain and suffering was far greater than my own.'

Two days later, after addressing 120 000 people at the First National Bank Stadium in Soweto, Mandela went home to house No. 8115, Orlando West, for the first time in thirty years. The house had been restored after the fire, and an ANC flag was flying proudly outside. The first weeks after his release passed in a blur of visitors, meetings and interviews, and there was no question of Nelson and Winnie taking time off to put their personal life back together. He was reluctant to move to the Diepkloof mansion, saying it was an inappropriate abode for a leader of the people, and that he wanted to live not just among his people, but like them. In all likelihood, he was sincere, but the remark was nevertheless construed as a thinly veiled rebuke for Winnie's chosen lifestyle. However, with the black cloud of Stompie Seipei's murder and events surrounding the Mandela United Football Club still hovering, he staunchly defended Winnie against all negative criticism. According to his closest friends, he could never allow himself to forget that Winnie had kept the struggle alive through even the darkest days, and had borne the brunt of the government's attacks in his absence. Some said he knew she had made serious mistakes, and even suspected she was guilty of some of the allegations against her, while others said he never questioned her innocence. Either way, he remained loyal to her, and expected his friends to do the same – at least until she was convicted.

In March, the Mandelas went on a tour of Africa, including Zambia, seat of the ANC in exile, Zimbabwe and Namibia, where they attended the independence celebrations on 21 March. Everywhere they went, they were met by large and joyful crowds. In Dar es Salaam, an estimated 500 000 people gathered to welcome Mandela.

Next, they went to Europe, travelling to Stockholm to visit Oliver Tambo, who was recovering after suffering a stroke, and to London to attend a concert in Mandela's honour at Wembley Stadium. In June, Winnie and Nelson went to Paris, Switzerland, Italy, the Netherlands and England, then on to America.

Winnie was still a beautiful woman, and thanks to the media, was more recognisable in some countries than Mandela himself – and perhaps as much of a drawcard for the crowds. For the first time in its history, New York had a black

233

mayor, David N Dinkins, and when the Mandelas came to town, the Big Apple went wild. One million people lined the streets as the Mandelas were accorded New York's ultimate honour, a ticker-tape parade, a tradition dating back to 1927 when aviator Charles Lindbergh was the first recipient. During their three days in the city they visited Harlem, which Winnie described as the Soweto of America; Brooklyn, where a high school student, Kalil Davis-Manigaulte, had taught 5 000 people to toyi-toyi in their honour; and Yankee Stadium, where 45 000 frenzied fans turned out for a rally and concert.

The main purpose of the visit was for Mandela to address the UN General Assembly. I was working in New York at the time and, as a South African, was allocated one of the much sought after broadcasting booths, and had the honour of doing a direct radio broadcast from the UN to South Africa and Namibia. At 11.03 am on 22 June, Mandela walked into the massive General Assembly hall to a standing ovation that lasted several minutes. The public gallery was packed, and in his introduction, Secretary General Xavier Perez de Cuellar said Nelson Mandela symbolised the unconquerable spirit of the people of South Africa in their struggle against apartheid. In Mandela's address, he said it would forever remain a challenge to all men and women of conscience to explain why it took so long to say 'enough is enough'. Future generations would ask how apartheid could have happened in the aftermath of the Nuremberg Trials, and the world's determination never again to allow a racist system to exist.

In the midst of this historic event, I was struck by the level of adulation for Winnie among Americans, notwithstanding months of negative publicity about the Stompie Seipei case. Her long years of harassment and banishment had been well documented by the media, and Americans wanted to honour and show their support for the woman who was widely credited with keeping the liberation struggle alive at enormous personal cost. People told me they had nothing but the highest admiration for her, that she was a courageous fighter for human rights and women's rights, charismatic and elegant, loved by the downtrodden and oppressed.

Having eschewed the fashion capitals of Paris and London in favour of shopping in Manhattan for the clothes she needed for the various formal functions, including a purple satin ballgown with beaded bodice for dinner at the White House, Winnie also endeared herself to the American fashion industry. The owner of the elegant Victoria Royal showroom was so dazzled by her charm that he insisted Winnie accept the expensive outfits she chose as a gift.

Home again, Winnie managed to convince Mandela to move to the Diepkloof house, which she proudly said she had built specially for him. Before long, however, the rumours started again: she was out alone until the early hours of the morning, often returning having had too much to drink. Little more than a week after Mandela's release, *The Star* had posed the question: How long can Winnie's demure image last? Now the media became relentless in its criticism, casting suspicion on her every word and deed.

The ANC was anxious to find solutions to the problems surrounding Winnie, because they realised that when it came time for all South Africans to go to the polls, they would need her strong and particular appeal to those on the fringes of society. Mandela was burdened with both the multitude of problems facing the country and a simmering marital crisis, but most people appeared oblivious to the tension building between him and Winnie. Friends said he clearly still loved her and saw her as the adoring, supportive wife he had left behind thirty years before. But circumstances had forced Winnie to become independent, to make her own way, and she found it difficult to revert to the pattern of their early years together. Mandela continued to practise the habits of a lifetime, rising before dawn and going to bed early. Winnie, on the other hand, had grown accustomed to staying up late, and, after years of battling insomnia, her routine included a great deal of after-dark activity. Mandela tried to woo her away from what he viewed as undesirable associations, but with little success. It was Fatima Meer who pinpointed the underlying problem. Ironically, during the long years of separation, they had been able to maintain a togetherness, but once they were reunited, both Nelson and Winnie discovered how different – and distant from one another – they had become.

The weight on Mandela's shoulders was about to increase, both on the domestic and the political front. On 2 May, the ANC had entered into preliminary talks with the government at Groote Schuur, FW de Klerk's official Cape Town residence. After three days of intense talks, the government agreed to create a climate conducive to negotiations by lifting the state of emergency, releasing political prisoners and revoking repressive laws. In May, as well, Mandela United Football Club coach Jerry Richardson went on trial for the murder of Stompie Seipei, the attempted murder of Lerotodi Ikaneng, four counts of kidnapping and four counts of assault with intent to do grievous bodily harm. Kenneth Kgase, Thabiso Mono and Pelo Mekgwe testified to Richardson's role in their abduction, and their attempt to kill Ikaneng on the coach's orders.

Winnie was repeatedly implicated in the assaults by the youthful witnesses, but Richardson denied under oath that she had been present or involved. She had not even been at home when Stompie was beaten, he said, having left for Brandfort on 29 December and returning only on 2 January. He insisted that Mono, Kgase and Mekgwe were lying when they said Winnie had assaulted them. Richardson claimed Xoliswa Falati had gone with him to fetch the boys from the manse, that they had gone with them voluntarily, and that on the way to Winnie's house they were singing and chatting. He admitted punching and slapping all four

235

boys but denied harming them in any other way. He also claimed that he had stabbed Ikaneng in the neck and tried to kill him, and denied telling Mono, Kgase and Mekgwe to cut his throat. He denied killing Stompie, but the evidence suggested otherwise.

On 24 May, Richardson was found guilty of Stompie's murder, four counts of kidnapping, four counts of assault with intent to do grievous bodily harm, and one count of attempted murder. Significantly, the judge found that Winnie *had* been at home for at least part of the day on 29 December, the day after Stompie was taken to her house and first beaten. On 8 August, Richardson was sentenced to death for the murder of Stompie Seipei. He was also sentenced to five years' imprisonment for the four kidnappings and three for the assaults, with an additional two years for the aggravated assault on Stompie and eight years for the attempted murder of Ikaneng. In mitigation, his defence counsel claimed that he had been influenced by Winnie.

Later that month, another former member of the Mandela Football Club, Charles Zwane, was found guilty on nine counts of murder, eight of attempted murder and one count of arson, and in September he was given nine death sentences. His defence, too, was that he had acted under Winnie's influence.

For months, Witwatersrand Attorney-General Klaus von Lieres had been under pressure to charge Winnie with the kidnapping of the four boys from the Methodist manse, and for Stompie's death. He had stalled, but the day after Zwane was sentenced, he announced that Winnie would be charged along with seven co-accused: Xoliswa Falati and her daughter Nomphumelelo, John Morgan, Jabu Sithole, Brian Mabuza, Mpho Mabelane and Katiza Cebekhulu. Because Richardson had already been convicted of Stompie's murder, the others would be tried only for kidnapping and assault.

Mandela had to weather a major political crisis after the security police uncovered a top secret ANC operation, code-named Vula: a sophisticated plan directed by Mac Maharaj and Siphiwe Nyanda to deploy MK operatives and hide arms caches throughout the country, so that in the event of negotiations breaking down, the armed struggle could be resumed and power seized by force. Maharaj had returned to South Africa under deep cover to run the operation while he was ostensibly in Moscow, receiving medical treatment. His wife, Zarina, even travelled to Russia to bolster the cover story, and it was by pure chance that the operation was exposed when police arrested two Vula operatives on an unrelated matter. Maharaj and other operatives were arrested on 25 July and charged with plotting to overthrow the government. Mandela, who denied knowing anything about the secret plot, was placed in an extremely difficult position, and De Klerk exploited the government's advantage to the full, denouncing the ANC as perfidious revolutionaries in cahoots with the communists. On the advice of Joe Slovo,

Mandela offered De Klerk an immediate cessation of the armed struggle. De Klerk, in turn, undertook to release all remaining political prisoners and offer blanket indemnity to exiles so that they could return home.

The crisis was defused, but between Vula and the court cases involving members of the MUFC, the media had a field day – and there was more to come.

In September, Mandela announced that Winnie had been appointed the ANC's head of social welfare. It was a controversial decision, vehemently opposed by one faction within the organisation on the grounds that she had become irresponsible and a burden to the ANC. But there was no denying that Winnie had built up a powerful support base among the youth, in particular, most of whom would be eligible to vote in the 'new' South Africa's first election, and ways had to be found of accommodating her.

With her trial set for 4 February, Mandela publicly offered his full support, slating the prosecution as part of a government campaign to discredit Winnie. On the other hand, there were rumours that De Klerk was urging Von Lieres to drop the case, in light of Mandela's pivotal role in the all-important political negotiations. On the first day of the trial, ANC supporters turned out in force to support Winnie, led by Mandela, Slovo, Alfred Nzo, Chris Hani and Fatima Meer. Oliver and Adelaide Tambo sent a message from London assuring her of their love and confidence.

As if the presence of this array of ANC luminaries in a court where the country's potential next First Lady was facing charges of abducting and beating children was not sensational enough, the day was filled with drama. First, the judge was told that four of the accused had fled the country since being charged, and only Winnie, the two Falati women and John Morgan were in the dock. Then the prosecutor announced that Pelo Mekgwe, a key witness as one of the boys who had been kidnapped from the manse, had been abducted again. Whether this was true or whether Mekgwe had changed his mind about testifying, he had disappeared, and the trial had to be postponed while the police tried to find him.

When the court reconvened on 6 March 1991, neither Mekgwe nor the missing defendants had been found, but the state announced that it would introduce evidence of assaults on two other boys and the disappearance of Lolo Sono to support its case.

In February 1989, Winnie's driver – and co-accused – John Morgan had made a statement claiming that Winnie had, in fact, been at home when Stompie was assaulted, and had slapped the boy after accusing him of having sex with Paul Verryn. During the trial, he retracted this statement, saying he had made it only because he was tortured by the police. Xoliswa Falati testified that she had taken the four youths to Winnie's house because they were being sexually molested by Verryn; and that after taking Katiza Cebekhulu to Dr Asvat's surgery, Winnie had left for Brandfort. Thabo Motau, one of Winnie's neighbours, testified that he had driven her to the Free State on 29 December, and Norah Moahloli, a schoolteacher and old friend of Winnie's from Brandfort, testified that Winnie stayed with her that night and over the next two days, visited the elderly, attended township meetings and held discussions on some of the projects she had launched while living in Phatakahle.

As they had done at Richardson's trial, Kenneth Kgase and Thabisa Mono testified that Winnie had taken part in the assault on them and Stompie.

Winnie spent five gruelling days on the witness stand, but never wavered from her alibi: she had been in Brandfort and knew nothing of the beatings.

The judge found her guilty on the charges of kidnapping, and as an accessory to assault. She was, he said, a 'calm, composed, deliberate and unblushing liar' who had undoubtedly authorised the abductions, but he accepted that she was not at home when the assaults were carried out. However, by continuing to hold the boys captive, she had associated herself with the crime. Winnie was sentenced to five years in prison on the four counts of kidnapping, and one year as an accessory to assault. Xoliswa Falati was found guilty on all charges and sentenced to six years in prison. Morgan was found guilty of kidnapping and sentenced to one year's imprisonment, suspended for five years.

Winnie was granted leave to appeal and her bail was extended. Mandela told the media of the world that, verdict or no verdict, as far as he was concerned, her innocence was never in doubt. But despite his very public show of support, their marriage was clearly in trouble, although Fatima Meer believed this was more because of the power struggle within the ANC than serious personal issues. Winnie was increasingly critical of Mandela's political outlook, and had been shocked when he described De Klerk as a man of integrity. She argued with Mandela over his view, denouncing De Klerk as no less a murderer than PW Botha. And Mandela's call on ANC supporters in Natal to disarm enraged her.

Independent political journalist Max du Preez's *Vrye Weekblad* had exposed a so-called Third Force, made up of elements of the police and military and working in close collaboration with Mangosuthu Buthelezi's Inkatha Freedom Party against ANC supporters in Natal. Unlike Mandela and other ANC leaders, Winnie was by no means ready to renounce the armed struggle. She continued to wear her khaki uniform in public and made several statements about fighting for freedom. But the unsavoury nature of her trial had cost Winnie some of her political following. At the ANC's Durban conference, she was elected to the national executive, but lost her bid to become president of the Women's League. Soon afterwards, her powers as head of welfare were curtailed amid whisperings of financial irregularities involving the use of welfare funds to pay for trips, buy clothes and luxury gifts for Dali Mpofu, a young articled clerk she had met through the Mandela Football Club's lawyer, Kathy Satchwell. Mpofu quit his job with the law firm and was appointed Winnie's deputy in the welfare department, giving rise to fresh rumours that they were having an affair.

In the whirlwind of events following Mandela's release from prison and the start of negotiations designed to ensure a peaceful transition rather than a bloodbath in South Africa, the focus was constantly on him: what he had missed, how he had changed, his expectations of the future, his remarkably conciliatory attitude towards his white oppressors, his hopes and dreams. No one bothered to find out what Winnie needed and wanted, how her life had changed or what her aspirations might be. She had received almost no public credit or acclaim for the personal suffering she had endured, or the damage it had caused, or her phenomenal courage, and from the moment she was implicated in the serious crimes involving the football club, it was as though her entire past had been erased from the public mind.

A chance meeting and short conversation with popular satirist Pieter-Dirk Uys in the early 1990s offered a brief glimpse into Winnie's soul and state of mind. They were both on their way to Cape Town, and while waiting for the flight at Johannesburg International Airport, she recognised Uys. They had never met, but she introduced herself and gave him a warm hug. He was struck by the fact that she was smaller in real life than in photographs. They chatted amicably, and he told her he was on his way to a performance in his signature role of the fictional ambassador to the imaginary homeland of Bapetikosweti.

Uys has a self-confessed passion for shopping bags, and had collected a fine selection from elegant stores in London, Paris, Toronto and New York, in which he always carries his hand luggage. While they were talking, Winnie asked him what was in the bag he was toting on that particular occasion. 'Evita Bezuidenhout,' he said, explaining that the bag contained the costume, wig and cosmetics he needed to transform himself into the imperious female character.

'Do you know what is in my bag?' Winnie then asked. Uys said no, and she answered: 'Mrs Mandela. My husband has been awarded an honorary degree and I have to perform the supportive wife.'

She said it with such melancholy that Uys asked if that was difficult for her.

Winnie replied, 'I'm out of practice.'

He said she seemed lost and overwhelmed, and he felt real sympathy for her. However, from the moment she stepped off the aircraft in Cape Town and was surrounded by bodyguards and a welcoming, admiring crowd, she was 'transformed into a kugel, and one almost lost all empathy with her'.[2]

On 21 December 1991, the political negotiations that would shape South Africa's future began in earnest. International observers monitored the process, named CODESA, with great interest. While there was bloody war in Yugoslavia and continued violence in Northern Ireland and the Middle East, the world watched with bated breath as South Africans moulded a peaceful transfer of power from the ashes of apartheid. But Mandela's attention would again have to be divided between the crucial political developments and the high drama of his personal life. Xoliswa Falati, who had been living under the Mandela roof for some time, suddenly raised Winnie's ire, and was kicked out. She took revenge by contacting the media and retracting every shred of evidence she had given in support of Winnie at their trial. She now alleged that Winnie had not only been involved in the torture of Stompie, but had ordered the murder of various other people, including Dr Abu-Baker Asvat.

The media exploded in a frenzy of reports and speculation about both Falati's sensational claims and the future of the Mandela marriage. Falati's defection had opened a veritable Pandora's box. Mandela was accused of cover-ups and interfering with the media to prevent publication of certain stories. The ANC announced that Winnie had been ousted as head of welfare. Mandela demanded that she be reinstated. Winnie continued to be seen in public with Dali Mpofu, and when she travelled to America against Mandela's wishes, taking Mpofu with her, Mandela moved out of the Diepkloof house. To add insult to injury, Winnie's driver, John Morgan, also retracted the evidence he had given, and told the *Sunday Times* that Winnie had *not* been in Brandfort as she claimed, but had, in fact, led the assault on Stompie Seipei.

On 13 April 1992, Mandela called a media conference, and flanked by his oldest friends, Oliver Tambo and Walter Sisulu, announced that he was separating from Winnie. In a prepared statement, he paid tribute to her contribution to the struggle, but said that because of their differences they had agreed that a separation would be best for both of them. He said he was not parting from Winnie with recriminations, but embraced her with all the love and affection he had felt for her since the first moment they met. Tellingly, he referred to her throughout as Comrade Nomzamo, as though she was someone he hadn't known very well, or perhaps signalling that he had already distanced himself from her.

The storm had finally broken over Winnie's head. She became increasingly estranged from the ANC leadership, which was baying for her resignation after Mandela ordered an investigation into the alleged misappropriation of funds in the welfare department. But the coup de grâce came via one of Dali Mpofu's former lovers, who had somehow got hold of a letter Winnie had written to him, and gave copies to both the *Sunday Times* and the *Sunday Star*. The *Sunday Times* published it, unedited, on 6 September 1992. In the letter, Winnie angrily berated Mpofu for sleeping with another woman, referred to a deteriorating situation at home and the fact that she had not spoken to Mandela for months, and, most damning of all, mentioned ANC welfare department cheques that had been cashed for Mpofu.

Four days later, Winnie resigned all her positions in the ANC, saying it was in the best interests of her dear husband and beloved family to do so, but ascribing the situation to a malicious campaign against her. A month later, Zindzi married Zweli Hlongwane, and Winnie organised a wedding reception for hundreds of guests in the posh Carlton Hotel in Johannesburg. Mandela attended the function but looked strained, and ignored Winnie. When he made his speech, he pointed out that all freedom fighters paid a costly price for their beliefs, since their private lives and those of their families were totally destabilised. One wondered, he mused wistfully, whether it was worth it.

On the political stage, however, Mandela was the star act, although his decisions often infuriated one or other faction within the ANC. When he proposed abandoning nationalisation, he was accused of betraying the Freedom Charter, but his carefully considered pragmatism scored valuable political concessions, and by December 1992 FW de Klerk was all but ready to concede to the demand for simple majority rule.

But for every step forward, there seemed to be at least one more major obstacle to overcome. On 10 April 1993, Chris Hani was assassinated by a right-wing Polish immigrant, Janusz Waluz, in a plot that included Conservative Party politician Clive Derby-Lewis. The senseless killing brought South Africa to the very brink of civil war. It was the Easter weekend, and Mandela rushed back to Johannesburg from the Transkei to intervene in the most potentially explosive situation since the 1976 student uprising. Hani had been the second most popular ANC leader in the country, and, in the aftermath of his death, violence did break out and dozens of people died, but it was Mandela, not De Klerk, who went on national television and appealed for calm. The people listened – and the world knew that South Africa had found its first black president.

On 2 June 1993, the Appeal Court upheld Winnie's conviction for kidnapping, but ruled that she had not been an accessory to the assaults. After 'careful and anxious' deliberation, the court reduced her sentence to two years' imprisonment, which was suspended, and a fine of R15 000.

It was all she needed to stage a political comeback, and by the end of 1993 the ANC Women's League had elected her their president. Her detractors were exasperated, her supporters jubilant. Winnie was back, and not a moment too soon, from the ANC's point of view. Campaigning for the first democratic elections began on 12 February 1994. The Inkatha Freedom Party, with a predominantly Zulu power base, and the Afrikaner Volksfront, which represented right-wing Afrikaners, announced they would boycott the election, along with the regimes still running the so-called independent homelands of Bophuthatswana and Ciskei.

The Volksfront, led by former South African Defence Force chief General Constand Viljoen, formed a brief alliance with Bophuthatswana leader Lucas

Mangope when ANC cadres launched a final push to make Bophuthatswana un-governable. Mangope asked Viljoen to mobilise his commando of farmers and former SADF troops to put down the uprising in Mmabatho, but specifically told Viljoen not to include any members of Eugene Terre'Blanche's ultra right-wing resistance movement, the Afrikaner Weerstandsbeweging (AWB). The AWB, however, gatecrashed what they saw as a chance to make a last stand against the hated ANC, and by their bumbling intervention put paid to any credibility the white right might have had. In the process, three AWB members who became separated from the rest were shot in cold blood by a black policeman while the world's TV cameramen and news photographers captured the murders on film. It was the end of Mangope, of the Volksfront's tenuous alliance with the AWB and the right-wing boycott of the election.

In Natal, however, the bloody conflict between Inkatha and the ANC continued, with thousands of people killed and tens of thousands displaced. On 28 March, Inkatha supporters bearing traditional weapons, including spears and *knobkieries*, marched on the ANC's Johannesburg headquarters, Shell House. ANC security personnel, fearing an attack, opened fire on the marchers, killing eight. Yet again, the transition to a multiparty democracy and government of national unity teetered on the brink of civil war, but, against all odds, Buthelezi decided at the last minute to take part in the elections that ran over three days in the last week of April.

On 10 May 1994, Nelson Rolihlahla Mandela was inaugurated as president of South Africa in the amphitheatre at the Union Buildings in Pretoria, seat of the apartheid government since 1948. At his side was his daughter Zeni. His estranged wife was not even seated among the most important guests from both South Africa and abroad. Jessie Duarte, who ran the Office of the President with Barbara Masekela, said her heart went out to Winnie. She had waited and laboured her entire adult life for this day, and, when it came, she was reduced to no more than a spectator, snubbed in the most public manner imaginable by her husband at his moment of supreme triumph. Duarte said attempts had been made to somehow include Winnie in the main party, but Mandela would not hear of it. In his inaugural address, Mandela said he had never regretted his commitment to the struggle, and was always prepared to face the personal hardships. But, he said, his family had paid a terrible price, perhaps too dear a price, for his commitment.

Winnie would never be First Lady of South Africa, but she was still beloved and admired by millions of black South Africans. In December 1994, she was once again elected to the ANC's national executive, even though Mandela had struck both her name and that of her friend Peter Mokaba off the list of nominees. Delegates insisted on nominating them both, and enough votes were cast to place them among the top five of the sixty-strong committee.

Winnie was also one of the 400 members of democratic South Africa's first parliament, and perhaps hoping she had learned her lesson, Mandela appointed her Deputy Minister of Arts and Culture. But, as with the welfare department, rumours quickly surfaced of financial irregularities. Winnie's reaction was to lash out at the ANC government, accusing them of bending over backwards to placate the whites. Mandela was furious, and demanded an apology. Winnie complied, but made it clear that she was doing so under pressure, and levelled a new accusation at the government, namely that it was undermining free speech. When she vowed after being released from prison in 1969 that she would never again have respect for authority, she clearly did not have only the apartheid government in mind.

After their very public spat, she left on a trip for West Africa, against Mandela's express instructions, and while she was away the police raided her home, as they had so many times during the apartheid years, and confiscated a number of documents.

In August 1995, Mandela instituted divorce proceedings against Winnie. He had put his life with her behind him, and within months began courting Graça Machel, widow of Mozambican president Samora Machel, who had died in an aircraft accident fifteen years before. In March 1996, after living apart for four years, the divorce was finalised in the Rand Supreme Court. After a marriage that had endured for thirty-eight years, and survived twenty-seven years of separation, during the darkest days of apartheid and tragedy, what had ranked as one of the world's great love stories was over.

PART III

Winnie
Madikizela-Mandela

'He who allows oppression, shares the crime.'
– Erasmus Darwin, grandfather
of Charles Darwin

18

'Things went horribly wrong'

FROM THE MOMENT of her birth, the reality of Winnie's life acted as a foil to expectation. She was the daughter who should have been a son; the highly visible activist who should have been a demure and dutiful spouse; the tragic heroine who should have been an ingénue; the ex-wife who should have been First Lady.

She had long since shed the cocoon of Winnie Madikizela from Bizana, the unassuming, statuesque beauty who arrived in eGoli with her luggage balanced on her head, and emerged from four decades in the chrysalis of Winnie Mandela, consort to a god-man, as an icon in her own right, melding all the stages of her development into the person who would henceforth be known as Winnie Madikizela-Mandela.

If the ANC, or Nelson Mandela's advisers, had hoped that divorce would put an end to her uncanny knack for stealing the headlines, they would learn, soon enough, that cutting her adrift was no more the way to confront 'the Winnie factor' than the security police's relentless campaign of harassment had been. Still, Winnie was officially on her own now at a time when she was sorely in need of support.

Exhaustive studies by the World Health Organisation emphasise that victims of trauma and injustice cannot heal until justice is seen to be done. Mandela understood that it was crucial to deal with the loss and anguish of those who suffered most under apartheid, and that the horror of South Africa's recent past could not simply be dismissed as bygones. Ideally, the ANC government had to find ways of dispensing justice to those responsible for torture, persecution and death that would not paralyse the court system for decades, or undermine the fragile peace and stability of post-1994 South Africa.

The result was the Truth and Reconciliation Commission (TRC), launched in February 1996. The principle of a qualified amnesty had been agreed during multi-party negotiations leading up to the first democratic elections, and the TRC was a compromise between the National Party's proposed blanket amnesty for all members of the apartheid government and its security forces, and the ANC's determination to expose the full horror of the past. It would offer a quasi-judicial forum where victims could expose their suffering and perpetrators could seek amnesty from prosecution, provided they could persuade a panel of judges that their actions – including murder – had been politically motivated, and on condition that they disclosed the full, unvarnished facts, no matter who else might be implicated.

The mechanisms of the TRC were controversial on both sides of the political spectrum. Many black people considered the process far too lenient in relation to the misery and loss they had suffered, while most whites, and especially serving and former members of the military, saw it as a witch-hunt. In the end, self-confessed killers *did* go free, but there were also remarkable instances of genuine reconciliation between former enemies, and although the final report fell far short of being a complete chronicle of apartheid's history and legacy, it did fill in many of the gaps previously shielded from public scrutiny by legislation, cover-ups and lies.

Mandela appointed Archbishop Desmond Tutu as chairman of the TRC, underlining the intention of forgiveness rather than revenge. Misgivings about and harsh criticism of what was seen as the vociferous anti-apartheid churchman's inherent bias in favour of the government were largely allayed by his threat to resign unless former members of the liberation struggle also availed themselves of the opportunity to disclose acts committed in the name of their 'just' war, especially those that took the lives of civilians or their own comrades.

By 1997, Mandela started looking at who would succeed him. He had made it clear that he intended serving only one term as president, and Thabo Mbeki had long been groomed to lead both the ANC and the country from 1999. As deputy president, Mandela favoured Bantu Holomisa, who had overthrown the Matanzima government in the Transkei in a military coup. The ANC leadership was thus thrown into disarray when it became clear that Winnie was positioning herself for election to the crucial No. 2 post on the ANC's national executive. Had it not been for recurring allegations during TRC hearings of her involvement in the murders of Stompie Seipei, Dr Abu-Baker Asvat and others, she might well have mustered enough popular support to fulfil her ambition.

But in September 1997, the BBC screened a sensational television documentary, subsequently also shown in South Africa, called *Katiza's Journey*. After disappearing in 1991 when he jumped bail while awaiting trial in the Stompie Seipei case, Katiza Cebekhulu made a spectacular reappearance through the TV programme and in a book by British journalist Fred Bridgland. For the first time, Cebekhulu was uncloaked as a police informer, who had provided an eyewitness account of Winnie stabbing Stompie with a sharp object. It was also claimed that Nelson Mandela had personally arranged for Katiza to be deported to the Zambian capital Lusaka, where his British benefactor, Lady Emma Nicholson, discovered him in jail.

The TRC could not ignore the numerous accusations against Winnie, and she was subpoenaed to appear at an *in camera* hearing of the Human Rights Violations Committee. She demanded a public hearing in order to clear her name before the ANC's national conference in December, where the future office bearers would be elected. The TRC had no way of knowing what Winnie might reveal or claim in her bid to present herself as a suitable candidate for a senior ANC position, and decided to go ahead with *in camera* sessions on 26 September and 13 October, followed by a public hearing on 24 November, at which she would be afforded the opportunity to respond to the accusations against her.

The cases that drew the most attention were those involving the disappearance of Lolo Sono and the deaths of Stompie and Dr Asvat. Officially called to investigate the activities of the Mandela United Football Club, the hearings were quickly dubbed 'the Winnie hearings', and dealt for the most part with her involvement in human rights abuses. For nine days, a recreation centre in the lower-middle-class Johannesburg suburb of Mayfair became the focus of international media attention as forty-three witnesses – including victims, former MUFC members, religious and community leaders, police and members of the Mandela Crisis Committee – testified both for and against Winnie. More than 200 print and electronic journalists from all over the world were on hand to record and rehash the bloody violence that reigned in Soweto in the mid-1980s. But the focal point of all the interest was the woman who personified the struggle against apartheid and injustice more vividly than any other individual, the Mother of the Nation who stood accused of killing one child and abusing several others.

In her best-selling book, *Country of My Skull*, author and poet Antjie Krog described Winnie's dichotomous domain as 'the house of the liberation movement's most revered political lineage and the house of lowly informers. The house of famous, regal personalities and the house of a particular kind of gangster personality.' From the patchwork of testimony it heard, the TRC faced the conundrum of stitching together the most likely picture of what had happened in that house, and deciding what to do with their findings. The following are concise summaries of the information the commissioners had at their disposal, and their conclusions.

Xola Mokhaula and Mlando Ngubeni
Xola Mokhaula was executed in front of his family on the evening of 24 January 1987, apparently after he had confiscated a firearm from MK operative Oupa Alex Seheri. In attempting to retrieve the firearm, Seheri shot Mokhaula in cold blood and fatally wounded Mlando Ngubeni. Police found one of the guns used in the attack in Zindzi Mandela's bedroom in Winnie's house. An Audi used in the incident belonged to Winnie. Oupa Seheri, S'thembiso Buthelezi and Charles Bongani Zwane (also known as Bobo) were convicted of the murders, and Seheri

later sought amnesty from the TRC. Buthelezi admitted in testimony at the trial that he had driven the Audi during the operation and had hidden the recovered Scorpion machine pistol at the Mandela house.

Winnie denied all knowledge of the events.

The TRC found there was no evidence that either Winnie or Zindzi had any direct involvement in the incident.

Peter and Phillip Makhanda

On 26 May 1987, the Makhanda brothers were taken by force to the back rooms of Winnie's home. They were assaulted, had ANC slogans carved into their bodies and battery acid rubbed into their wounds. Two MUFC members, Absolom Madonsela and Isaac Mokgoro, and Winnie's driver John Morgan, were charged in the case, but acquitted owing to insufficient and contradictory evidence. However, the testimony of former MUFC member Gift Ntombeni and from other witnesses confirmed that the incident had taken place. Although the Makhanda brothers had implicated Winnie in the incident, she was never questioned by the police, and denied any knowledge or involvement.

The TRC found that the assaults and mutilation of Peter and Phillip Makhanda did take place in the back rooms of Winnie's home, and that members of the MUFC participated in the assault and mutilation of the youths.

Sicelo Dhlomo

Sicelo Dhlomo had been abducted, and was found dead in Soweto on 25 January 1988. The security forces were assumed to be responsible. However, according to an amnesty application, Sicelo Dhlomo was killed by members of an MK unit led by John Itumeleng Dube, allegedly because he was suspected of being a police informer. Xoliswa Falati alleged that Winnie had been involved in this incident, but Winnie denied any knowledge of Dhlomo's death and the TRC found no evidence of her involvement.

Phumlile Dlamini

Phumlile was the sister of Kenneth Thole Dlamini, one of the original members of the MUFC. He was later killed by Sizwe Sithole. She testified that she had been assaulted by Winnie and members of the MUFC in August and September 1988, while pregnant with the child of Johannes 'Shakes' Tau, who sometimes acted as Winnie's driver. Tau had told Phumlile he was also having a relationship with Winnie. When she was first taken to Winnie's home, Phumlile was assaulted by Winnie. Tau apparently disappeared, and a week later Phumlile was again picked up by Winnie and members of the football club, and again assaulted by Winnie. Later, she was repeatedly assaulted by the men for a period of five hours, until

Lindzi intervened. Phumlile wanted to report the matter to the police, but her brother begged her not to, as he feared what Winnie and the MUFC might do. Winnie denied any knowledge of the incident, or involvement in the assaults.

The TRC found that Phumlile Dlamini was a credible witness, and that Winnie as well as members of the MUFC had assaulted her.

Thole Dlamini

Kenneth Thole Dlamini, Phumlile's brother, was shot dead after attending a night vigil on 16 October 1988. He had fallen out with prominent members of the MUFC after testifying against a member, Absolom Madonsela. The testimony led to Madonsela's conviction. Winnie denied any involvement in Dlamini's killing.

The TRC found that, although Dlamini had probably been shot dead by Clayton Sizwe Sithole, and Winnie was not in Soweto at the time of the incident, she knew about it and attempted to cover it up by assisting potential witnesses to go into hiding, and helping Sithole to evade prosecution.

Tebogo Maluleke, Sipho Mbenenge and Sergeant Stephanus Pretorius

Frans Tebogo Maluleke (also known as Peter) and Sipho Mbenenge were MK cadres who were staying temporarily at MUFC coach Jerry Richardson's house. On 9 November 1988, following a tip-off from Richardson, the police attempted to capture the two. In the ensuing gun battle they were both killed, as was Security Branch Sergeant Stephanus Pretorius – Richardson's police handler. This incident led directly to the subsequent disappearance of Lolo Sono and Sibuniso Tshabalala.

The TRC found that Winnie had placed the two MK cadres in Jerry Richardson's care, and Richardson admitted that they were killed after he had informed the police that they were at his house. He was released from police custody two weeks after the incident. Winnie refused to answer questions during the *in camera* hearing on whether she had had any suspicions following Richardson's quick release, considering the serious circumstances in which he had been arrested. The TRC found that she had been negligent and that her misplaced trust in Jerry Richardson was the direct cause of their deaths.

Lolo Sono and Anthony Sibuniso Tshabalala

Tebogo Maluleke was a relative of the Sono family. On Wednesday 9 November 1988, Winnie arranged for both Lolo and Sibuniso to go and see Tebogo. Lolo's father, Nicodemus Sono, testified that Lolo had told him when he got there that a police helicopter was flying around Richardson's house. Tebogo was nervous and told them to leave. They hid at a nearby shop, from where they witnessed the attack by the police, during which Tebogo was killed.

Nicodemus Sono testified that on Sunday 13 November, Winnie visited his house in the company of a number of other people. Her driver, Michael Siyakamela, called him outside and he spoke to Winnie, who was in the front seat of the minibus. His son, Lolo, was sitting in the back. His face was swollen and bruised, and he was shaking and crying. Nicodemus begged Winnie to leave Lolo with him, but she said the movement would deal with 'this dog'. Lolo was never seen again.

Winnie denied any knowledge of an assault on Lolo Sono, or his disappearance.

The TRC had obtained a statement from Michael Siyakamela that verified Nicodemus Sono's testimony, and found that Lolo was abducted by members of the MUFC on 13 November 1988 and taken to Winnie's home where, with her knowledge, he was severely assaulted. Winnie and members of the MUFC then took Lolo to his parents' home in Meadowlands, where she refused to hand Lolo over to his father, and told Nicodemus Sono that his son would be sent away so that the movement could deal with him. The TRC found that Lolo was killed by Jerry Richardson.

Sibuniso Tshabalala's mother, Nomsa, testified that members of the MUFC came to her house in search of Sibuniso on the evening of 13 November, but he was not at home. When he returned, his family told him what had happened to Lolo Sono. He refused to go into hiding and went out on the morning of 15 November. Later that day, Sibuniso called his mother and said only that he was with Lolo. He was never seen again.

Lolo and Sibuniso's distraught parents reported the incident to Captain Potgieter at the Protea Police Station, who told them to report it to the Meadowlands police.

During rigorous questioning, Richardson admitted he had been an informer. Earlier in the hearing, police commissioner George Fivaz admitted under cross-examination that Richardson had been paid R10 000 in 1995 for 'past services' and to 'oil his hand' for cooperation in a fresh inquiry into the disappearance of Lolo Sono and Siboniso Tshabalala.

Richardson testified that Winnie had ordered him to kill Lolo and Sibusisu because they were informers. He also admitted killing Koekie Zwane, a young woman accused of being a police informer, in December 1988.

The TRC found that Sibuniso Tshabalala had been assaulted at Winnie's home, and was subsequently murdered by Richardson. Both Lolo and Sibuniso had been falsely accused of being informers, and of being responsible for the death of Tebogo Maluleke and Sipho Mbenenge at the house of Richardson, who had admitted to being the police informer.

The TRC also found that Winnie was involved in Lolo Sono's abduction and knew that he was held on her premises, and that she had to accept responsibility for the disappearance of Lolo and Sibuniso.

Pelo Mekgwe, Thabiso Mono, Kenny Kgase and Stompie Seipei

A commissioner asked the Reverend Frank Chikane whether the Mandela Crisis Committee had demanded to see the boys when they visited Winnie's home.

'No.'

'Why not?'

'That was not part of our brief.'

Bishop Peter Storey rationalised that on the one hand they had attempted to find out the truth of Stompie's whereabouts and possibly save his life, and on the other hand there had been a political agenda, as the committee was involved in 'damage control'. He said there had been a hostage situation at Winnie's home, and that she alone decided how and under what conditions the youths were to be released. She was aware of everything that happened in her house, he said.

Sydney Mufamadi, one of the members of the Mandela Crisis Committee, said that if the committee had forcefully removed the youths from Winnie's home, they could have been charged with kidnapping. He didn't explain who would have charged prominent clerics and community leaders with 'kidnapping' injured children from a place where they were so obviously under threat.

In *Country of My Skull*, Antjie Krog said it became clear during the TRC hearings that the men who hadn't had the courage to stand up to Winnie in the past lacked it still.

Winnie denied any involvement in the abduction, assault and torture of the four youths, and said she had been unaware that they were being held against their will, having been told by Jerry Richardson and Xoliswa Falati that they were at her home voluntarily.

However, the TRC found that Jerry Richardson, John Morgan, Katiza Cebekhulu and Xoliswa Falati had abducted the four from the Methodist manse on Winnie's instructions. The TRC also found that Winnie was at home, and not in Brandfort as she had claimed during her trial, and had not only been present, but had initiated and taken part in the assaults. Furthermore, she had actively resisted repeated efforts by the Mandela Crisis Committee and other community leaders to secure the release of the youths held at her house.

Stompie Seipei

Winnie denied any knowledge of, or involvement in, the killing of Stompie on 1 January 1989. The TRC had to weigh three versions of the teenage activist's murder. Jerry Richardson claimed that he killed Stompie on Winnie's instructions. Former security policeman Paul Erasmus suggested that Richardson killed Stompie because he had found out that Richardson was an informer. Katiza Cebekhulu said he had seen Winnie stabbing Stompie. This was supported by John Morgan, who testified that he found Stompie in a pool of blood flowing from his neck, and had been instructed to dump Stompie's body. According to an unsigned, typed statement allegedly made in police custody, Johannes 'Themba' Mabotha – a Vlakplaas askari who had apparently defected and was frequently seen at Winnie's home – said he had been present at a meeting when Richardson told Winnie he had killed Stompie. He claimed Winnie had been shocked, and that she afterwards attempted to spread disinformation that Stompie was alive in a refugee camp in Botswana.

Richardson was brought from prison to testify at the TRC hearings. Following the abolition of the death penalty by the ANC government, his sentence had been commuted to life imprisonment and he had applied for amnesty for four murders, including Stompie's. He described graphically how Stompie was beaten, and then killed. The things they did as the Mandela United Football Club were horrible and barbaric, Richardson said, and they tortured youths in the same way that the police used to torture freedom fighters. While they were interrogating Stompie, they found a wristwatch in his pocket, and in the absence of a satisfactory explanation, this was taken as proof that he was an informer. He was thrown into the air and allowed to fall to the ground, and punched and kicked. Richardson said Winnie was watching them. The assault went on for about two hours and Winnie joined in, with her fists and a whip. Eventually, Stompie admitted to having supplied information about four guerrillas to the police in Parys, his hometown in the Free State, and pleaded for mercy. Richardson said he had been tortured so severely that it became apparent he would die. The next morning, Richardson reported to Winnie that Stompie was in very bad shape, and as he would die anyway, his opinion was that the youth should be finished off. However, they left him lying in the outside room, and that evening two members of the football club, Guybon Khubeka and one Sonwabo, again assaulted Stompie. The decision to kill Stompie was taken the next day but not carried out immediately, because members of the Mandela Crisis Committee arrived at the house. That evening, Richardson and Skhumbozo Mtshali dragged Stompie to Noordgesig, and stabbed him to death with a pair of garden shears.

'Mami did not kill Stompie,' Richardson said. 'I killed Stompie in accordance with Mami's instructions. She never killed anyone, but instructed us to kill people.'

Xoliswa Falati testified that she had gone to prison for Winnie. She said Winnie became aggressive when she drank 'hard' liquor. Asked why she had protected Winnie and gave false evidence in court about the killing of Stompie, Falati said it was part of their culture to protect their leaders. And, she said, she was scared, having seen how people were brutally beaten.

In the light of the corroborating testimony that placed Winnie on the scene and implicated her in the assault, the TRC found that she was probably aware of Stompie's condition and had failed to take responsibility for arranging medical treatment for him, compounding her own complicity. Her public statements about Stompie and the rumours that he was in Botswana were an attempt to divert attention from herself. She had been negligent in failing to take the necessary action to avert Stompie's death, the TRC found.

Lerotodi Ikaneng
Lerotodi Ikaneng and Gift Ntombeni, former members of the MUFC, testified that Winnie had assaulted them and accused them of being informers approximately six weeks before the attempt on Ikaneng's life on 3 January 1989. Ikaneng had made a statement to the police regarding the involvement of Sizwe Sithole, Zindzi's boyfriend, in the killing of Thole Dlamini, which made him a target for the MUFC. It was therefore 'most probable' that Ikaneng's life was at risk from the MUFC and, in this particular case, from the MUFC's patrons, Winnie and Zindzi. Ikaneng alleged that Zindzi had accused him of being an informer, probably because she was upset that he had implicated her boyfriend. According to Ikaneng, Zindzi had accused him and several other MUFC members of being 'sell-outs' when he was still a member of the club. Jerry Richardson confirmed that he had led the attack on Ikaneng, accompanied by other MUFC members and the three abducted youths Mono, Mekgwe and Kgase, and claimed that Winnie had congratulated him when he told her he had killed Ikaneng.

The TRC found that there was no apparent motive for Ikaneng to falsely implicate Winnie in the attempts on his life. Although Winnie denied any knowledge of the attack on Ikaneng, the TRC found that she was both involved in, and responsible for, the attempt to kill him.

Dr Abu-Baker Asvat
Albertina Sisulu testified that she knew nothing about a visit to Dr Asvat by Katiza Cebekhulu on 30 December 1988, the day Stompie Seipei was assaulted. However, Cebekhulu's patient card showed that he did visit the surgery on that day, and in a BBC documentary on Asvat's death, made at the beginning of 1997, Albertina confirmed that the entry on the card was in her handwriting. In testimony before the TRC, she denied that it was her handwriting, and it was subsequently proved that it was not, in fact, her handwriting. She said she did not believe that Winnie was guilty of involvement in Asvat's murder, and denied previous evidence that Winnie had a heated argument with Asvat just hours before he was killed.

A former member of the MUFC, Thulani Nicholas Dlamini, claimed that he murdered Asvat on Winnie's instructions. His accomplice, Zakhele Cyril Mbatha, who, like Dlamini, was convicted of the murder and sentenced to life imprisonment, also testified that he had shot Asvat on Winnie's instructions. He said she had offered him and Dlamini R20 000 to kill Dr Asvat.

Neither Dlamini nor Mbatha, who actually shot Asvat, provided the TRC with credible testimony or coherent reasons for the contradictions in their various versions of events, and as a result the TRC could not reach a conclusion regarding Winnie's alleged involvement in Asvat's murder.

Themba Mabotha

Following his arrest by members of the Soweto Security Branch, Mabotha was detained for a period of eight months, from April to October 1988. According to Captain Jan Potgieter, Mabotha was to have been produced as a state witness against Winnie in a pending treason trial for which Potgieter had been conducting investigations for more than two years. He testified that the failure of the Witwatersrand Attorney-General to make a decision regarding this prosecution had left him in a dilemma, as he was unable to extend Mabotha's detention. He wanted him to be available should a subsequent decision be made to prosecute Winnie, and requested Colonel Eugene de Kock to keep him at Vlakplaas, claiming that, at the time, he had no idea that Vlakplaas was the home of the police hit squads. De Kock testified that Potgieter had implied Mabotha was to be killed. He said he and Potgieter had worked together in the police counter-insurgency unit, Koevoet, in South West Africa and 'understood each other well'. Although he did not receive a direct order to kill Mabotha, Potgieter's intentions were clear, and therefore Mabotha was executed, said De Kock.

Katiza Cebekhulu

Katiza had been a member of the Mandela United Football Club and had been charged, with Winnie and six other people, for the kidnapping of Kgase, Mono and Mekgwe, and the murder of Stompie Seipei, but had disappeared before the trial, saying afterwards that he had been whisked out of the country by the ANC.

Katiza claimed he had seen Winnie twice stabbing a body lying next to the jacuzzi, which he believed was Stompie. He also testified that he had seen her savagely whipping Lolo Sono with a sjambok in her garage before he disappeared. He confirmed evidence given by Lolo's father, Nicodemus, that Winnie had arrived at their house with a badly beaten Lolo, claiming he was a police spy. Katiza said he was in the vehicle and heard Nicodemus pleading with Winnie to leave Lolo with him, and that she had said the movement would deal with him. They returned to Winnie's house, Katiza got out of the minibus and Winnie and the others drove away, Lolo Sono never to be seen again.

Katiza admitted taking part in the assault on Stompie, and said he saw Winnie stabbing the boy. He went to his bedroom, and when he enquired about Stompie the next day, he was told that Jerry Richardson had taken Stompie away the previous night. He never saw Stompie again.

Katiza said in 1991, during the trial, that Winnie had threatened that unless he went into exile in Swaziland, she would do with him as she pleased. He said she promised that if he went to Swaziland, she would help him further his education and give him money. He agreed because he was scared, and the ANC took him to Mozambique and Angola and then to Zambia, where he was jailed for two years and eight months. Baroness Emma Nicholson heard about his plight and secured his release through the United Nations High Commissioner for Refugees.

Winnie denied any knowledge of Katiza's flight from South Africa.

The TRC found that Katiza had been taken out of the country and placed illegally in a Zambian prison for almost three years at the request of the ANC and with the connivance of the Zambian authorities. Former Zambian president Kenneth Kaunda admitted that the ANC had requested his assistance with Cebekhulu. The TRC said it was likely that this had been done to protect Winnie from disclosures Katiza might make, and avoid embarrassment for the ANC. The ANC never admitted responsibility for its actions in the matter. Winnie's claim that she had not been directly involved was contradicted by the testimony of both John Morgan and Cebekhulu, and her argument that she had nothing to gain from Cebekhulu's incarceration was not credible, as her interests would appear to be the reason he was taken out of the country.

On the last day of the hearings, Winnie testified. The media had repeatedly high-lighted the fact that, since she was not applying for amnesty, it was not incumbent on her to tell the truth. However, her refusal to seek amnesty also meant that the Attorney-General was free to review her testimony and, irrespective of the TRC's findings, bring criminal charges against her, if there were sufficient grounds for such action.

Winnie told the TRC that as a member of the ANC's military wing, she had assisted MK cadres who infiltrated South Africa from neighbouring states. She dismissed all allegations that she had been involved in kidnapping, assault or murder as ludicrous, and said she was astounded by the many fabrications. When the TRC's deputy chairman, Alex Boraine, suggested that the football club had been a good idea that had gone very badly wrong, Winnie agreed, and conceded that, with hindsight, she would have acted differently. But she insisted that she knew nothing of the assaults on Stompie and the other youths, and said she had seen no signs of injury on any of them. Jerry Richardson's claim that she had ordered him to kill Stompie was 'the worst lunacy', and as far as she was concerned, Katiza Cebekhulu was 'a mental case', as shown by his allegations that he saw her stabbing Stompie and that she had taken part in the vicious assaults, when Richardson had already admitted to killing Stompie.

The logic of Nicodemus Sono's testimony defied her. Why, she asked, would she assault a boy, take him to his father and then kill him? She admitted she had been in the minibus with Lolo, but said she was taking him on a mission, and that he had never been assaulted. She had not known Sibuniso Tshababala and denied ever meeting either Dlamini or Mbatha. Her relationship with Dr Asvat had been close, and she was shocked and deeply saddened by his death.

Commissioner Yasmin Sooka observed that if Winnie's version of events was true, everyone else who had testified must have been lying. Winnie agreed, and said only the witnesses themselves would know why they had lied. She expressed sadness for the loss of life, and for the ordeal some of the boys had suffered, but said she had no regrets at all about sheltering and protecting them from the vicious system of the day.

When her testimony finished, Archbishop Tutu made an impassioned plea to Winnie. She had been a stalwart and iconic member of the struggle, who had overcome every effort to break her spirit. She was loved and admired by many, but, said an emotional Tutu, something had gone wrong, and he begged her to admit this and apologise for her part in the consequences.

As he spoke, it was as though Tutu had become oblivious to his surroundings, to the audience, the media and the world. Almost imperceptibly, the cold and impersonal chamber became a shrine, and Tutu implored Winnie to lay a sacrificial offering on the altar of truth. With utmost humility, he entreated: 'I beg you, I beg you, I beg you please ... You are a great person. And you don't know how your greatness would be enhanced if you were to say, I'm sorry ... things went wrong. Forgive me. I beg you.'

For endless moments, the packed auditorium was as silent as a chapel. Then Winnie switched on her microphone and spoke into the expectant hush. She thanked Tutu for his wonderful, wise words, saying he was still the father she knew. And then she said: 'I am saying it is true, things went horribly wrong. I fully agree with that. And for that part of those painful years, when things went horribly wrong – and we were aware of the fact that there were factors that led to that – for that, I am deeply sorry.'

Her words lingered, like incense, in the serene space created by Tutu's forgiveness. She apologised to the families of Stompie Seipei and Dr Abu-Baker Asvat.

The hearings were over. Somewhere in the tangled web of accusations, allegations, retractions and denial lay the truth.

South Africa's bloodstained past is littered with accounts of unbearable hardship and suffering, and thousands of dead: men, women and children, killed by vengeful hands, neglect and hunger. Many who survived made extraordinary sacrifices. One of them was Winnie Madkizela-Mandela, who had left behind a large part of her life in an unmarked grave on apartheid's abstract battlefield.

In the wake of the dramatic TRC hearings, the ANC convened in Mafikeng, capital of the former homeland of Bophuthatswana, for its hallmark fiftieth annual conference. There were 3 500 delegates in the hall, and the entire national executive was seated on stage as Mandela handed over the reins of leadership to Thabo Mbeki. But the eyes of the world were fixed on who would serve as his deputy. The Women's League nominated Winnie for the post – but the TRC hearings had damaged her more than her supporters had realised, and she polled only 127 votes out of 3 500. She was re-elected as a member of the national executive, but dropped from fifth to fifteenth in the ranking order. Her friend Peter Mokaba boldly predicted that she would regain her former status, but few believed him.

During the TRC hearings, suspicion had been cast on Winnie's relationship with the police. Azhar Cachalia had testified that although it was fairly common knowledge in the late 1980s that Winnie was hiding both guerrillas and arms in her house, the police never arrested nor even questioned her about such matters. This had led some members of the community to believe that she had sold out, and was working with the police.

In January 1998, the TRC held a special hearing into the activities of the Soweto security police. Apart from Winnie, it emerged that there were several common threads running through investigations into the disappearance of Lolo Sono and the deaths of Stompie Seipei and Dr Asvat. Henk Heslinga, Fred Dempsey and HT Moodley, members of the murder and robbery squad at the Protea Police Station at the time, had probed all three cases. In all three cases, documents had disappeared and the investigations had been botched, especially in regard to Winnie's alleged involvement.

In Lolo Sono's case, the driver of the minibus, Michael Siyakamela, had made a statement confirming that the severely assaulted youth was sitting in the vehicle with Winnie when she talked to his father. The statement was lost.

When Dr Asvat's alleged killers were arrested, they stated that they had stolen money from his surgery. The Asvat family was adamant that not a cent was missing, and the killers subsequently claimed they had been tortured into claiming that robbery was the motive for the murder.

In the case of Stompie, a police informer had made a statement that Winnie was involved in the assault. The security police removed the statement, and Vlakplaas commander Eugene de Kock killed the informer. Heslinga had served in Koevoet with De Kock.

The case of Themba Mabotha amplified the suggestion that Winnie had become a police agent. He had been an askari at Vlakplaas, and after he escaped he made his way to Winnie's home. Since Mabotha had compelling information about the activities of the hit squads operating from Vlakplaas long before they were exposed in November 1989 by the Afrikaans newspaper *Vrye Weekblad*, the question had to be asked: Why was he not smuggled out of South Africa for debriefing by the ANC's intelligence department?

De Kock made it clear that Winnie's high profile had made her a priority for attention by the security forces. Her attitude and courage infuriated the authorities, he said, and she was regarded as a thorn in their flesh.

Senior Superintendent André Kritzinger, formerly a captain in the Soweto Security Branch, said he had compiled a dossier of some thirty crimes implicating Winnie in the late 1980s, and believed he had enough evidence to charge her with high treason, harbouring terrorists and unlawful possession of firearms. However, Witwatersrand Attorney-General Klaus von Lieres had declined to prosecute her.

While the likelihood was raised that Winnie escaped prosecution due to an official directive from an unidentified source because she had secretly begun collaborating with the police, there was easily as much evidence that the authorities had simply decided to surround her with a phalanx of informers, and leave her be to exploit the increasing possibility of a split in ANC ranks between her supporters and critics.

The police had manipulated Winnie's image for decades. Gordon Winter disclosed in his book *Inside Boss* that the security police began spreading rumours that she was a BOSS spy in the early 1960s. Former security policeman Paul Erasmus told the TRC that there was an ongoing smear campaign against Winnie serious enough to destroy her marriage, and that as late as 1994, disinformation was spread in an attempt to prevent her election as a senior ANC office bearer. A number of British politicians, including Tory members of parliament, had helped disseminate the rumours, said Erasmus.

In January 1998, the *Weekend Argus* published an interview with Winnie in which she spoke candidly about a number of personal issues, and reiterated her deep commitment to the liberation struggle. She said the most difficult time in her life had been when she was in jail, but she had always believed it was her responsibility to maintain Nelson Mandela's name and legacy, and to that end she had sacrificed her youth and her freedom. Asked whether it had ever crossed her mind to get a divorce from Mandela, she said no, even though twenty-seven years was a lifetime for a young woman. She had been offered jobs abroad, by the United Nations, among others, and could have fled South Africa many times. But, she said, she had a deep conviction that her main purpose was to remain in the country, for the sake of both Mandela and the cause for which they fought. Her biggest regret was not being able to give their children a normal life. It haunted her, day and night, that she hadn't been there for her daughters.

Throughout the years of political persecution, Winnie often lamented the deprivations her children had to suffer. Thus, it was not surprising that she went to battle in February 1998 to preserve their heritage – not for the sake of politics, but as a family legacy. A dispute had arisen over ownership of house No. 8115 in

Vilakazi Street, Orlando West. The unassuming township street was the only street in the world to boast the homes of two living Nobel Peace Prize laureates, namely Mandela and Archbishop Desmond Tutu. However, neither of them lived there any longer. Winnie had turned the Mandela house into a museum, which she opened in December 1997 and which drew up to 1 000 visitors a day. Mandela's daughters, Zeni and Zindzi, were directors of the museum, but the problem was that the house did not belong to Winnie. A year earlier, Mandela – who had originally moved into the house on a ninety-nine-year lease – had donated the property to the Soweto Heritage Trust, along with approval for Winnie's eviction as, he said, he had given the house to the people of South Africa.

For Winnie, however, this was the house to which she had gone as a young bride, where she had brought her newborn daughters, and where she endured years of victimisation, first as Mandela's wife, then as an advocate of political change in South Africa. From here she was sent into exile in Brandfort, and this was the house to which she had dreamed of returning for eight long years.

After fruitless negotiations with Dr Nthato Motlana, Winnie's old friend and chairman of the Trust, she took legal action to prevent her children from being deprived of what she believed was rightfully theirs.

In the upper echelons of the new South Africa, as in the old, there was little empathy for Winnie's wishes and feelings. Yet again, she and her children would have to make a personal sacrifice in order that the nation be served.

19

A quiet exit

POLITICAL PUNDITS INTERPRETED the Truth and Reconciliation Commission's damning indictment of Winnie as a sign that her public life had finally expired. Like both the apartheid authorities and the ANC leadership after them, the commentators misjudged her resilience and popular appeal, though the TRC's findings unquestionably cast a shadow over her credibility and future conduct as head of the ANC Women's League and a member of parliament.

Over the years, Winnie received many tributes for her unflinching support of Mandela and the struggle. In the mid-1980s, Lutheran bishop Manas Buthelezi, then president of the South African Council of Churches, said she had suffered and been punished because her life symbolised the striving of black South Africans for justice and liberation, and suggested that Winnie ought to be counted among the heroes who had martyred themselves for their beliefs.

Two days before the twentieth century drew to a close, the Xhosa king, Xolilizwe Sigcawu, presented her with the Hintsa Bravery Award in recognition of her role in keeping the struggle fire burning while other leaders were jailed or in exile.

Winnie's millennium message was that she would continue to fight against poverty and unemployment, and for the upliftment of women and children. As the lone voice of criticism from within the ranks of the ANC she injected a powerful element of reality into the ruling party's politics, and as a parliamentarian she showed that it was possible to support, even represent, a political party and government without being a slave to obedience and loyalty. She was, in fact, unrelenting and unapologetic in her criticism of the government, and never let an opportunity pass to castigate them.

In June 2000, she attended the funeral of two pupils who had been shot and killed by police during a protest against evictions in the township of Alexandra, north of Johannesburg. She said it felt as though she was burying Hector Petersen all over again, and that her presence was an act of repentance on behalf of the government she represented. Shortly afterwards, she annoyed and embarrassed the government and angered white South Africans by travelling to Zimbabwe and publicly voicing sympathy and support for the so-called war veterans who were invading and seizing white-owned commercial farms. President Mbeki had been under considerable pressure to intervene in the crisis in Zimbabwe, or at the very least level public criticism at Robert Mugabe's ZANU-PF government, but had studiously avoided doing so in favour of 'quiet diplomacy' behind the scenes. Winnie was fully aware that her actions infuriated the government and the ANC, but as always the sound of her own drum dictated the route she followed.

In July, she arrived at an international AIDS conference in Durban wearing a T-shirt emblazoned with the words 'HIV-positive', and joined demands for the government to supply free anti-retroviral medication to the millions of South Africans infected with the deadly virus. Mbeki and his health minister, Manto Tshabalala-Msimang, had been at war with AIDS activists ever since the president publicly espoused the views of dissidents who claim that poverty, not the virus, causes AIDS, and that the anti-retrovirals are toxic. While Mbeki offered a stunned international community intellectual rather than scientifically based arguments to justify his stance, Winnie addressed some 3 000 people at a rally on the urgent need for people with HIV and AIDS to have access to the life-giving drugs. In a hard-hitting speech, she compared the battle for AIDS treatment to the struggle against apartheid, roundly condemned the health department for failing to provide access to affordable medication, and said that while the government wasted its time with rebel scientists, South Africa was facing a social holocaust.

In accordance with the habits of a lifetime, Winnie was invariably to be found where there was suffering or injustice, regardless of time or distance. Women's issues remained a priority, and as president of the Women's League she visited farm workers employed under appalling conditions in Limpopo Province, attended the funeral of Edith Erens, a young girl who had been murdered in Johannesburg, and on 9 August – National Women's Day – led a dramatised event to commemorate the historic anti-pass march on the Union Buildings in 1956. Far from waning, Winnie's star continued to glitter over the political landscape, as a member of parliament, head of the women's movement and member of the ANC's national executive and national working committee. But controversy was never far from hand, and with little love lost between Winnie and Mbeki, it could be only a matter of time before their differences spilled over into the public domain.

In January 2001, the *Sunday Times* acquired and published a letter she had written to Deputy President Jacob Zuma in 1999, asking him to intervene after President Mbeki attacked her from the podium at an ANC meeting in Durban and accused her of gossiping about his private life. She told Zuma that she had been hurt and shocked by the president's barbs, and yet again the media trumpeted the end of Winnie's political career.

Considering that she had charged in the letter that the ANC was plagued by intrigue, infighting and backstabbing, that the party leaders were systematically persecuting her and that she had been 'grievously maligned' by Mbeki, predictions that she had finally gone too far were not without foundation. But yet again, Winnie confounded the critics. A few weeks after the letter was leaked to the media, she was honoured with other famous Sowetans as a Soweto legend.

But as the year progressed, it became clear that Winnie's travails were far from over. Her financial affairs came increasingly under the spotlight, and by mid-1992 she was enmeshed in various probes into alleged irregularities and misconduct.

The government had announced in 1998 that it was considering taking action against Winnie to recover R170 000 for the unauthorised use of an official vehicle that had been damaged, and another R100 000 for an unauthorised trip she had made to Ghana. At about the same time, Absa Bank obtained a judgment against her for defaulting on a R500 000 loan she had taken, using the Diepkloof house as security. In May 2001, the *Sunday Times* reported that Winnie was at the centre of a R1-million scandal involving the ANC Women's League. She went to court to seek an injunction against publication of the report, but acting judge Geoff Budlender – who had taken Kenneth Kgase's statement after he escaped from Winnie's home in 1989 – ruled that the article was not defamatory. The newspaper revealed that the police were investigating loans made by the beleagured Saambou Bank to non-existent employees of the Women's League, on the basis of recommendations sent to the bank on Women's League letterheads. One of the loans had evidently been made to Winnie's daughter Zindzi.

Shortly after the report was published, Winnie was admitted to hospital suffering from high blood pressure, and, in her absence, police raided her home, ostensibly in search of documents related to the loan investigation. But the alleged fraud was knocked off the front pages by an extraordinary encounter, captured on camera by television news crews, during a Youth Day rally at Orlando Stadium on 16 June to mark the twenty-fifth anniversary of the Soweto student uprising.

Winnie arrived an hour late, and as she stepped from her car, the crowd began chanting her name. Mbeki, the guest of honour, was not amused by the outpouring of support, which disrupted a speech by the chairman of the National Youth Commission, Jabu Mbalula. The president was visibly infuriated by what happened next.

Making her way to her seat on the stage, Winnie stopped behind Mbeki's chair and bent down to greet him with a kiss. The usually urbane Mbeki roughly pushed her aside, knocking off her baseball cap in the process, then snapped angrily at her. Home affairs minister Mangosuthu Buthelezi left his seat on the stage, picked up Winnie's cap and placed it gently back on her head.

That night, and for days afterwards, television viewers throughout the world froze as the scene was replayed over and over. If there had been any lingering doubts that relations between Winnie and Mbeki were strained, this unsavoury public demonstration made it quite clear that all was not well with South Africa's head of state and his predecessor's former wife. The media fuelled the fire by reporting that a senior police officer believed Winnie had grounds to lay a charge of assault against the president, or possibly a case for *crimen injuria*, since her dignity had been impaired by an incident in full view of a large crowd of spectators and the international media. Women's rights campaigners and organisations accused Mbeki of doing immense harm to their work and the progress they had taken years to make by undermining the message that physical domination of women was not acceptable.

But the sympathy and support Winnie enjoyed was a temporary reprieve. It seemed there were fires to be put out wherever she turned. She was in hot water with the South African Revenue Service about her income tax, and First National Bank confiscated about R1 million from her because she had failed to repay a loan. Winnie filed an urgent high court application to prevent the bank from attaching funds in investment accounts belonging to her and her company, the Heroes Acre Foundation. The application was dismissed, and the bank threatened further legal action to recover an additional R100 000 which she owed. In September, the media reported that Winnie allegedly owed more than R50 000 to the Johannesburg municipality for electricity, and had to make arrangements for payment through her attorney. In October, she was arrested by the specialised commercial crime unit on charges of fraud and theft relating to the Women's League loans.

Meanwhile, parliament's ethics committee had launched an investigation into Winnie's failure to declare all her business interests. As accusations of impropriety mounted, Winnie's fate and future became one of the hottest topics in South Africa.

In December, the murder of another former president's ex-wife, Marike de Klerk, briefly moved Winnie off the front pages. Though poles apart in their lifestyles and political convictions, the two women had shared a unique bond, having supported their husbands to the pinnacle of public life, then losing them to divorce and marriage to other women. Unfortunate scheduling saw a memorial service for Marike coincide with the state funeral for erstwhile defence minister Joe Modise, and Winnie chose to attend the De Klerk service in what could have been perceived as a snub to the ANC. As if to underline her apparent chagrin, she told the media that Marike de Klerk's murder was an indictment against crime-ridden South Africa, and perhaps God's way of awakening the country to the reality of daily life.

In February 2002, Winnie lost her two-year legal battle over occupancy of the house in Orlando West, and was ordered to vacate the premises. Within a week, another judgment against her was granted, this time for repossession of her luxury Mercedes Benz, for which the instalments were in arrears. Her lawyers seemed to be in court almost every week, and it was hard to imagine that any silver lining lurked behind the gathering dark clouds. In June, personal tragedy struck with the death of her friend and political ally, Peter Mokaba. The ANC said the firebrand youth leader had died of acute pneumonia linked to a respiratory problem, but there was widespread speculation that he had died of AIDS. Mokaba had survived rumours of being a police informer and controversy as the chief proponent of the inflammatory youth rally war cry, *Kill the Boer, Kill the Farmer* – officially declared hate speech in mid-2003 – before taking his seat in parliament and on the ANC's national executive. Winnie, who had been one of his most loyal supporters, was sidelined at his funeral and prevented from speaking, apparently on the orders of Mbeki.

By the middle of 2002, Winnie's life was no longer merely punctuated with accusations of misconduct and financial infractions, but had become a seemingly endless battle against them. In July, the other accused in the fraudulent loan case, Addy Moolman, went on trial. Witnesses testified that they had signed blank application forms and had never been employed by the ANC Women's League, although their loan applications stated that they were. Other information on the forms also turned out to be false. The police established that only five of the seventy beneficiaries of the loans had, in fact, worked for the Women's League. A forensic expert confirmed that the signature on letters supporting the loan applications was, indeed, that of Winnie Madikizela-Mandela. The charges of theft against her arose from the fact that applicants were obliged to take out and pay the premiums on non-existent funeral policies.

In November, on the eve of the Diepkloof house being auctioned to cover the R1 million she owed Absa, Winnie's lawyers managed to come to an agreement with the bank, and her home was saved. A month later, despite the litany of charges and accusations levelled at her, Winnie was again among the nominees for election to the ANC's national executive.

But 2003 would be a watershed year for this apparently indestructible woman. After being bombarded for months by the media with salacious details of the case, few were surprised when a Pretoria magistrate found Winnie guilty as charged on forty-three counts of fraud and twenty-five counts of theft. On 25 April she was sentenced to five years in prison, with one year suspended, but seasoned regional court magistrate Peet Johnson ruled that she would serve an effective eight months of the sentence in prison, followed by community service. As so often in the past, public opinion on the outcome of the case was deeply divided, with whites generally favouring a spell in prison, and blacks vehemently opposed.

Adding to the controversy was the fact that the magistrate found no evidence that Winnie had personally benefited from the fraudulent loan scheme. In fact, he underlined the fact that she had acted like a modern-day Robin Hood to help the poor. Winnie has made no secret of her disdain for legislation based on the indifferent principles of a free-market economy that allow little grace for those who lack assets. Not for the first time, she had taken the law into her own hands to help those marginalised by endemic poverty. Her enormous debts, too, had been run up on behalf of the legions of needy who rely on her for assistance.

Those who have never understood the workings of Winnie's mind or heart gasped when court proceedings revealed that she needed R72 000 a month to meet her household expenses – including more than R10 000 for groceries, R6 000 for telephone calls, R5 000 for electricity, and a mortgage bond payment of R12 000. What her detractors fail (or refuse) to take into account is that Winnie's home, wherever she has made it, has always served as a haven for the homeless, the hungry and the hopeless. Throughout her life, black people have turned to her for help, and she has never, as far as is known, turned away anyone in genuine need. The massive bills for food and utilities are run up on behalf of those who knock on her door at all hours and in all seasons. Those who condemn her are incapable of grasping the African concept of *ubuntu*, the spirit of fellowship which she lives each day to the full. Her perceived inability to set boundaries, to turn away the drifters and the destitute, is not a weakness, but a duty. Among the urban masses, Winnie is regarded as a chief, and in times of need, chiefs are expected to provide for their people. It has ever been so in Africa, and centuries of Westernisation have done little to erode this culture of caring and compassion. Thus Winnie, during the apartheid years, often exposed herself to real danger by hiding MK fighters in the townships and tending to the wounded herself until they had recovered.

But for her, compassion is colour blind. Despite the fact that her demonisers have been predominantly white – the vast majority of them never even having met her – her innate kindness and generosity of spirit have extended to many from that population group.

When she was appointed Deputy Minister of Arts and Culture, Fanie Janse van Rensburg was a junior public servant in the department. Winnie learned that his parents had both been murdered and that he was deeply distressed and obsessed with anger towards the murderer. She took him under her wing, encouraged him to talk about his fears and feelings, counselled him and, in time, arranged a face-to-face meeting for him with the black man who had been imprisoned for the crime. She also had Fanie transferred to the ministry, and he became one of her most loyal supporters.

A similar example was Afrikaans journalist Herman Joubert's intensely personal encounter with Winnie, which is all the more remarkable because, although he was a total stranger, she helped him through one of the darkest nights of his life.

On 7 March 1995, Joubert wrote in the newspaper *Beeld* about his 3 am encounter with Winnie. It had happened, he said, many years before Nelson was released from prison and long before the Stompie Seipei case hit the headlines. Joubert was living in a flat in Hillbrow, Johannesburg, and one night he was overcome by ineffable loneliness. By 1 am he was still wide awake. His children were 'far, far away', his marriage was in tatters and he was 'on the edge of the precipice'.

As befits any 'good' journalist, he wrote, he had a beer and began paging through his contact book. There was no one he could call. Finally, he came to a page on which there was a telephone number, but no name. He had no idea who it belonged to, or how long ago he had written it there. 'To hell with it,' he thought, 'tonight I'm phoning a number with no name.'

A young woman answered politely and said cryptically: 'She's not here, she'll call you back later. It sounds as though you need help.' Joubert left his name and number, threw himself down on his bed and fell into a fitful sleep filled with grotesque nightmares.

'Around 3 am that morning, the phone rang,' wrote Joubert. 'I had forgotten all about my daring call, and I was damn annoyed when I picked up the phone. A voice said: "Hello, did you call earlier?"'

'At that moment, I lost my temper completely and slammed the phone down. How dare a *meid* (yes, to my shame, many of us still thought in those terms in the years before 1990) phone me at three o'clock in the morning?'

A little later, wrote Joubert, his telephone rang again. Still angry, he picked up the receiver and heard the same woman, in an extremely calm voice, ask: 'Are you Herman?'

Startled, he said yes, and the caller said she was Winnie Mandela, and she wanted to help him.

'Why would you want to help me? I don't need your help. Leave me alone,' Joubert answered.

Unperturbed, Winnie asked him why he was so lonely. 'Tell me. What is going on? Do you have children?'

What he told her was too personal to share with his readers, Joubert wrote, but, he said, 'for the first time in months, someone showed genuine concern, and listened to what I had to say'.

Towards the end of the conversation, Winnie said she wanted to give him some good advice. 'Go and make yourself a sandwich, get something into your tummy. Then drink a glass of warm milk, and go back to bed. Remember, you need to look after yourself. You are not alone in this world. There are people who care about you. We care.'

She made him promise that he would warm up some milk, and suggested he take an aspirin as well, wished him good night and gently replaced the receiver.

Joubert followed her advice, and for the first time in months, he got a good night's sleep. 'I felt,' he wrote, 'as though the angels themselves were watching over me.'

After that night, his situation began to improve, and he never called Winnie again, though he sometimes wondered if he should. The lesson he learned from 'Mrs Mandela', he said, was that very often there was a simple and practical solution to problems that seemed insurmountable.

He ended his account by wishing Winnie well with the problems she faced, and by paraphrasing the closing line from one of dramatist Henrik Ibsen's plays: It's not only the bad things you do that rebound. Any good you do comes back as well.

Both Winnie and Addy Moolman were granted leave to appeal against their convictions and sentences, and at the time of writing, Winnie's case was scheduled to come before the Appeal Court at the end of September 2003 – around the time of her sixty-ninth birthday. While the judges in Bloemfontein can base their decision only on legal grounds rather than merit, and while senior citizenship is no deterrent to imprisonment in South Africa, there have been indications that the state would not be crushed if, indeed, Winnie was to serve no jail time. Following her conviction, prosecutor Jan Ferreira consulted the National Director of Public Prosecutions, Bulelani Ngcuka, before recommending an appropriate sentence. According to NDPP spokesman Sipho Ngwema, Ngcuka made it clear that he did not believe Winnie should go to prison, and a suspended sentence was proposed. But in the end, it was the magistrate's prerogative to decide on a sentence he believed the crime warranted.

In July, Ngcuka confirmed publicly that, in his opinion, Winnie did not deserve to go to prison, adding that a 'caring' society did not send its grandmothers to jail. Furthermore, this particular granny had already 'suffered more than most', he said.

In a country that prides itself on the independence of its judiciary, Ngcuka's comments were quite extraordinary, particularly since they coincided with a demand by South Africa's 241 high court judges for more, rather than less, autonomy. Any action favouring Winnie that might be perceived as an attempt by government to interfere with the judicial process would almost certainly evoke a storm of criticism from the media and the legal fraternity – but 2004 is an election year, and the ANC is certainly aware that she still commands significant support among certain sectors of the voting population.

Immediately after her conviction, President Mbeki made it plain that the government would not interfere with the legal process, but, ultimately, he could be Winnie's only hope of staying out of jail, should he choose to offer her a presidential pardon. But Mbeki finds himself in an invidious position in this regard. He has publicly humiliated her in the past, and she has accused his government of colluding to have her imprisoned. It is an open secret that they dislike – if not despise – one another, and any move by Mbeki to circumvent an adverse decision by the Appeal Court would inevitably be seen as an election ploy.

On the other hand, should he do nothing and allow the law to take its course, the ANC could pay the price at the polls.

There is another factor that Mbeki would have to weigh, namely whether Winnie would even accept a presidential pardon if one were offered. On 20 May, Daniel Silke, an independent political analyst, wrote in the *Argus* that Winnie's battles with the ANC were essentially over the authoritarian tendencies within the party, and Mbeki's leadership. She has gone to prison before rather than compromise her principles, and the first decade of democracy has not broken the chains of poverty that tether the majority of South Africa's black population to lives of misery and want. For Winnie, political freedom is meaningless unless it goes hand in hand with economic upliftment, and she believes that the government's policies are perpetuating rather than relieving the lot of the downtrodden. Furthermore, her relationship with Mbeki is so damaged, and she is so stubborn, that she is quite capable of rejecting a pardon.

In the immediate aftermath of her trial, Winnie resigned as a member of parliament and vacated her seat on the ANC's national executive committee. She also relinquished her post as president of the Women's League. In May, the rift between Winnie and the ANC leadership was accentuated by the death of struggle stalwart Walter Sisulu, one of Nelson's closest friends.

At his state funeral on 18 May, the chief mourners represented those with whom Sisulu had shared the front line during the struggle: his widow Albertina, Nelson Mandela, Epainette Mbeki (widow of Govan and mother of Thabo), Oliver Tambo's widow Adelaide. Notably absent was Winnie, who had sacrificed and contributed as much as any of them, if not more.

But there have been signs that at least some of the ANC leaders are ready to welcome Winnie back into the fold, and she has been seen at various functions and events at their invitation. No longer a threat to those in power, she might well find herself being courted avidly in the run-up to the 2004 elections – provided she is not sent to jail.

Free for the first time in more than forty years of any formal political obligations, Winnie returned to her first and abiding love, welfare work, and was finally able to devote more time to her family. Those close to her say she has seldom seemed so well and so happy. But she is not yet ready to retire completely from public life and service to others. In the middle of August, she accepted an appointment to the jury of the South Asian Court of Women, sitting in Bangladesh. The court addresses the problems of violence against women, human trafficking in women and the issue of HIV-AIDS, and is convened by the Asian Women's Human Rights Council in conjunction with the United Nations Development Programme.

Winnie Madikizela-Mandela's life has come full circle, and while her political career has been marked by as many troughs as peaks, she has more than fulfilled her father's expectations as a caring and committed social worker and advocate of her people. For Winnie, providing food for the hungry and shelter for the homeless, consoling the bereaved and arranging funerals, helping one child tend a parent dying of AIDS and rescuing another from an abusive home, are all in a day's work – except on Sundays, when she goes to church.

In a radio interview broadcast by SAfm on 11 February 2003, Winnie said her community involvement was not an extension of her role as a politician, but a result of the fact that she still saw herself primarily as a social worker and a mother.

'It would be very sad if whatever I do is defined in terms of my ideological beliefs. I am a mother, a grandmother, and a great-grandmother, and I am all those before I am a member of the ANC. It is not the other way around,' she said. 'My family is my life. I don't think I could have been who I am had I not defined myself in terms of being a parent, and whatever is around me is for my family, my children. My daughters are like sisters to me. I have been with them through the most difficult of times. And at the worst times they are my friends, they are my sisters, they are my everything. And then of course I have an army of grandchildren and I now have great-grandchildren. I am blessed in that sense. There is nothing better than that in life, to live for your family.'

During the 1980s, Winnie told journalist Hennie Serfontein that she had never revealed to anyone what really happened to her during her thirteen months of solitary confinement from May 1969, and did not think she ever would. 'It was clear to see she still suffered a deep-seated distress from that experience,' Serfontein said. 'Knowing what the security police were like in those days, one can only guess at the scenario, imagine what might have happened when they were in control and a black woman was alone and isolated and totally at their mercy.'[1]

While the Truth Commission hearings were taking place in 1998, Deborah Matshoba, who had once been in prison with Winnie, said: 'When I look around, I marvel at how we battle to be normal – and no one knows how shattered we are inside …'[2] Marinus Wiechers, political analyst and former professor of constitutional law at the University of South Africa, said that for years Winnie always added the same postscript when she sent him a Christmas card: Pray for me.[3]

As she moves into the final phase of her momentous life, Winnie Madikizela-Mandela could ask for no more than the prayers of the nation she has served – perhaps not always wisely, but indubitably well.

'I am the product of the masses of my country and the product of my enemy.'
– Winnie Madikizela-Mandela

References

I N WRITING THIS BOOK I have had to draw from a small volume of published works about, or touching on, the life of Winnie Mandela. In the interests of uninterrupted reading I have kept the material as clear as possible of references and notes. The primary sources of information are listed in the bibliography, and I gratefully acknowledge the following specific references:

Prologue
1. Noël Mostert, *Frontiers*, p. 604

Introduction
1. EA Ritter, *Shaka Zulu*, p. 351
2. Fatima Meer, *Higher Than Hope*, p. 81
3. Noël Mostert, *Frontiers*, p. 268

Chapter 1
1. Fatima Meer, *Higher Than Hope*, p. 85
2. Fatima Meer, *Higher Than Hope*, p. 89
3. Winnie Mandela, *Part of My Soul Went with Him*, pp. 29, 30

Chapter 2
1. Winnie Mandela, *Part of My Soul Went with Him*, p. 32

Chapter 5
1. Nancy Harrison, *Winnie Mandela: Mother of a Nation*, p. 63

Chapter 10
1. Winnie Mandela, *Part of My Soul Went with Him*, p. 75

Chapter 11
1. Winnie Mandela, *Part of My Soul Went with Him*, p. 75
2. Winnie Mandela, *Part of My Soul Went with Him*, p. 91
3. Emma Gilbey, *The Lady*, p. 79

Chapter 15
1. Nancy Harrison, *Winnie Mandela: Mother of a Nation*, p. 162
2. Winnie Mandela, *Part of My Soul Went with Him*, pp. xviii, xix
3. Winnie Mandela, *Part of My Soul Went with Him*, p. 153

Chapter 17
1. Winnie Mandela, *Part of My Soul Went with Him*, p. 59
2. Conversation with the author, September 2002

Chapter 19
1. Conversation with the author, July 2003
2. Truth and Reconciliation Commission, *Special Report on Gender Hearings*
3. Conversation with the author, July 2002

Bibliography

Akhmatova, Anna. *Poems.* New York and London: WW Norton & Co, 1983.

Benson, Mary. 'The Struggle in South Africa Has United All Races'. *Notes and Documents*, No. 7/84, August 1984.

Bezdrob, Anné Mariè du Preez. *In Spring the Dead Come Closer and Closer – War Memoir of a Peacekeeper.* (Unpublished).

Breytenbach, Breyten. *The True Confessions of an Albino Terrorist.* Johannesburg: Taurus, 1984.

Buchanan-Gould, Vera. *Not Without Honour: The Life and Writings of Olive Schreiner.* Cape Town: Standard Press, 1949.

Callaghan, Karen. 'Movement Psychotherapy with Adult Survivors of Political Torture and Organised Violence', *The Arts in Psychotherapy*, 20: 1993. pp. 411–21.

Cameron, Trewhella. *Nuwe Geskiedenis van Suid-Afrika in Woord en Beeld.* Cape Town: Human & Rousseau, 1986.

Cataldi, Anna. *Letters from Sarajevo.* Longmead: Element Books Ltd, 1994.

De Kock, Eugene. *A Long Night's Damage* (as told to Jeremy Gordin). Johannesburg: Centra, 1998.

Frederikse, Julie. *None But Ourselves.* Johannesburg: Ravan Press, 1982.

Gilbey, Emma. *The Lady: The Life and Times of Winnie Mandela.* London: Vintage, 1994.

Goldenberg, Myrna. 'Testimony, Narrative, and Nightmare. The Experiences of Jewish Women in the Holocaust', in Maurice Sacks (ed.), *Active Voices: Women in Jewish Culture.* Urbana: University of Illinois Press, 1995.

Gregory, James, with Bob Graham. *Goodbye Bafana.* London: Headline, 1995.

Harrison, Nancy. *Winnie Mandela: Mother of a Nation.* London: Victor Gollancz, 1985.

Joseph, Helen. *If This Be Treason.* Johannesburg: Contra Press, 1998.

Karis, Thomas, and Gail M Gerhart. 'Toward Robben Island: The Rivonia Trial', in *From Protest to Challenge: A Documentary History of South African Politics in South Africa, 1882–1964, Volume 3: Challenge and Violence, 1953–1964.* Hoover Institution Press, 1977. pp. 673–684.

Katjavivi, Peter. *A History of Resistance in Namibia.* Paris, London and Addis Ababa: UNESCO, James Currey, OAU, 1989.

Khuzwayo, Ellen. *Call Me Woman*. Johannesburg: Ravan Press, 1985.

Krog, Antjie. *Country of My Skull*. Johannesburg: Random House, 1998.

Lasarus, BB. *'n Seisoen in die Paradys*. Johannesburg: Perskor, 1976.

Maass, Peter. *Love Thy Neighbour: A Story of War*. London: Papermac, 1996.

Mandela, Nelson. *Long Walk to Freedom: The Autobiography of Nelson Mandela*. Randburg: MacDonald Purnell, 1994.

Mandela, Nelson. *No Easy Walk to Freedom*. Oxford: Heinemann Educational Books, 1965.

Mandela, Nelson. *The Illustrated Long Walk to Freedom*. London: Little, Brown and Company, 1996.

Mandela, Winnie. *Part of My Soul Went with Him*. New York and London: WW Norton & Co., 1985.

Matshikiza, Todd. *Chocolates for My Wife*. Cape Town: David Philip, 1982.

Maxwell, Margaret. *Narodniki Women: Russian Women Who Sacrificed Themselves for the Dream of Freedom*. New York: Pergamon Press, 1990.

Meer, Fatima. *Higher than Hope*. Johannesburg: Skotaville, 1988.

Mitford-Barberton, Ivan. *Commandant Holden Bowker*. Cape Town: Human & Rousseau, 1971.

Morris, Donald R. *The Washing of the Spears*. Johannesburg: Jonathan Ball in association with Sphere Books, 1968.

Mostert, Noël. *Frontiers – The Epic of South Africa's Creation and the Tragedy of the Xhosa People*. London: Jonathan Cape, 1992.

Radzinsky, Edvard. *Stalin*. London: Hodder & Stoughton, 1996.

Reed, John. *Ten Days that Shook the World*. London: Penguin Books, 1977.

Report of the Truth and Reconciliation Commission, Volume Two, Chapter 6: Special Investigation into the Mandela United Football Club.

Report of the Truth and Reconciliation Commission, Volume Three, Chapter 1: Introduction to Regional Profiles.

Report of the Truth and Reconciliation Commission, Volume Three, Chapter 6: Regional Profile Transvaal 1960–1975.

Report of the Truth and Reconciliation Commission, Special Hearing on Women.

Reyes, Hernan. 'Negotiating Prisoners' Rights'. Interview in *Conversations with History*. Institute of International Studies, University of California, Berkeley, 1999.

Ritter, EA. *Shaka Zulu*. Harmondsworth: Penguin Books, 1978.

Sampson, Anthony. *Mandela – The Authorised Biography*. Johannesburg and London: Jonathan Ball and HarperCollins, 1999.

Schoeman, BM. *Vorster se 1000 Dae*. Cape Town: Human & Rousseau, 1974.

Selimovic, Mesa. *Death and the Dervish*. Chicago: Northwestern University Press, 1998.

Shevardnadze, Eduard. *Foreign Policy and Perestroika*. Moscow: Novosti Press Agency Publishing House, 1989.

Silber, Laura, and Allan Little. *The Death of Yugoslavia*. London: Penguin Books and BBC Books, 1995.

Silove, Derek. 'Specialist Mental Health Services Required for Refugees Exposed to Extreme Trauma'. Study by Psychiatry Research and Teaching Unit, Liverpool Hospital, University of New South Wales, 2002.

Slyomovics, Susan. Review of *The Groom: Candide in the country of torture*, by Salah El Ouadie. *Boston Review of Books*, December 2001/January 2002.

Solzhenitsyn, Alexander. *Letter to Soviet Leaders*. London: Index on Censorship, 1974.

Swift, Jon. *Alexandra I Love You*. Johannesburg: Future Marketing, 1983.

Theal, George McCall . *History of South Africa 1795–1828*. London: Swan Sonnenschein & Co., 1903.

'The Mandela Visit'. *New York Times*, 20 June 1990.

United Nations. *Everyone's United Nations: A Handbook on the Work of the United Nations*. New York: United Nations Department of Public Information, 1986.

United Nations. *The Blue Helmets: A Review of United Nations Peacekeeping*. New York: United Nations Department of Public Information, 1990.

Van Jaarsveld, FA. *Van Van Riebeeck tot Verwoerd: 1965–1966*. Johannesburg: Voortrekkerpers, 1971.

Van Vuuren DJ, NE Wiehahn, NJ Rhoodie and M Wiechers. *South Africa: The Challenge of Reform*. Pinetown: Owen Burgess Publishers, 1988.

Ward, Catherine L. 'Mental Health Effects of Exposure to Trauma: Prevention is better than cure'. Centre for the Study of Violence and Mental Health, University of Cape Town.

West, Rebecca. *Black Lamb and Grey Falcon: A Journey Through Yugoslavia*. Edinburgh: Canongate Classics, 1995.

Whealin, Julia M. 'Complex PTSD'. A National Center for PTSD Fact Sheet.

Abbreviations

ANC:	African National Congress
AZAPO:	Azanian People's Organisation
BOSS:	Bureau of State Security
BPA:	Black Parents' Association
COSATU:	Congress of South African Trade Unions
MCC:	Mandela Crisis Committee
MDM:	Mass Democratic Movement
MK:	Umkhonto we Sizwe, armed wing of the ANC
MUFC:	Mandela United Football Club
NDPP:	National Directorate of Public Prosecutions
NEUM:	Non-European Unity Movement
NUSAS:	National Union of South African Students
PAC:	Pan Africanist Congress
PFP:	Progressive Federal Party
PTSD:	post-traumatic stress disorder
SACP:	South African Communist Party
SADF:	South African Defence Force
SAP:	South African Police
SASO:	South African Students' Organisation
SOYCO:	Soweto Youth Congress
SSRC:	Soweto Students' Representative Council
TRC:	Truth and Reconciliation Commission
UBC:	Urban Bantu Council
UDF:	United Democratic Front

Glossary

Amandla!: power
assegai: spear
baas: boss
iHlambo: royal mourning ritual, requiring Zulu warriors to 'wash' their spears in enemy blood
impi: regiment of Zulu warriors
inqubebe: traditional soap made from herbs
inyanga: witch doctor
isidwebe: traditional cowhide skirt worn by Xhosa maidens
iziduko: tribes or clans
kaffir: derogatory term for blacks, now outlawed in South Africa as hate speech
karos: blanket made from animal skins
kraal: rural settlement or cattle pen
lobola: bride price, traditionally paid by potential bridegroom to bride's father in cattle
Mayibuye!: it must return (political slogan as in *Mayibuye iAfrika!* – Africa must return)
meid: derogatory term for a black woman
mfecane: literally 'the crushing', used to describe bloody conquests of Zulu king, Shaka
mlungu: white person
muntu: black person
muti: medicine or potion made up by witch doctor
Ngawethu!: to the people (traditional response to ANC slogan *Amandla!*)
rondavel: traditional round dwelling with clay walls and thatched roof
shebeen: illicit township beer house
tsotsis: street thugs
ubuntu: spirit of mutual support, caring for the well-being of others
uluzi: indigenous grass used to weave traditional sleeping mats
umphokoqo: traditional Xhosa dish of sour milk and coarse maize meal porridge
veld: open country or grassland

Index